THE SELF-DETERMINATION OF MINORITIES
IN INTERNATIONAL POLITICS

THE
SELF-DETERMINATION
OF MINORITIES IN
INTERNATIONAL
POLITICS

Alexis Heraclides

FRANK CASS

First published 1991 in Great Britain by
FRANK CASS AND COMPANY LIMITED
Gainsborough House, 11 Gainsborough Road,
London, E11 1RS, England

and in the United States of America by
FRANK CASS c/o International Specialized Book Services, Inc.
5602 N.E. Hassalo Street, Portland, Oregon 97213

British Library Cataloguing in Publication Data

Heraclides, Alexis
The self-determination of minorities in international
politics.
1. Separatist movements
I. Title
322.4'2
ISBN 0–7146–3384–4

Library of Congress Cataloging-in-Publication Data

Heraclides, Alexis.
The self-determination of minorities in international politics/Alexis
Heraclides.
    p. cm.
Includes bibliographical references.
ISBN 0-7146-3384-4 (hardback)
ISBN 0-7146-4082-4 (paperback)
1. Self-determination, National. I. Title.
JX4054.H46 1990
320.1'5'—dc20

Typeset by Selectmove Ltd, London
Printed and bound in Great Britain by
BPCC Wheatons Ltd, Exeter

To Zina 'A.Z.'

(and to five years of inter-species affinity)

'Sensitive rowing between the bays . . .'

O. Elytis

CONTENTS

MAPS

ACKNOWLEDGEMENTS FOR MAPS

Map 1 is reproduced from *Tumbled House: The Congo at Independence* by
Ian Scott (Oxford University Press, 1969); maps 2 and 3 from *The
Nigerian Civil War* by John de St. Jorre (Hodder & Stoughton, 1972);
maps 4 and 8 from *Eritrea and the Southern Sudan*, Report No. 5, Minority
Rights Group, May 1976 (out of print); map 5 from *The Kurds*, Report No.
23, Minority Rights Group, March 1977 (out of print); map 6 from *Can
Pakistan Survive? The Death of a State* by Tariq Ali (Penguin Books, 1983);
map 7 from Keesing's *Record of World Events*, Jan. 1987 (Longman).

ACKNOWLEDGEMENTS

A scholar's first book is often based on his doctoral dissertation and this is the case with this study. Thus my first and foremost debt is to Professor A.J.R. Groom, my thesis supervisor, who influenced my thinking in writing the original much more detailed version of this study. Professor Groom's invaluable comments and suggestions deepened my understanding of the subject matter and enabled me to put together diverse viewpoints. Without his constant and indeed very moving support and guidance the thesis and then the book would probably not have been written. I am also grateful to Professor J.E. Spence, my external examiner who, together with Professor Groom, urged me to shorten my thesis and publish it as a book.

I would also like to thank among others Professor John W. Burton, one of the fathers of what is known today as the pluralist paradigm in International Relations, who first initiated me into I.R. and conflict resolution at University College London (an 'aha experience' never to be forgotten), Professors Dennis Sandole, C.R. Mitchell and Rosalyn Higgins as well as Keith Webb for their very sound advice at the very early stages of my study. From the several people who provided me with valuable insight as to the case studies, I am particularly indebted to Peter Kilner.

At a totally different level, special thanks are due to two outstanding individuals who set me on course as a youngster to become a social scientist. They are my parents, Ambassador Dimitris Heraclides and the late Zina Heraclides, to whom the Ph.D. thesis was dedicated.

I also express my gratitude to several other individuals who assisted me during the difficult thesis years (difficult and distressing in more ways than one). They would include the indomitable Dr J. Kinnas, Dr Ch. Lyrintzis, Dr Y. Valinakis, Dr Y. Vardaxoglou, Admiral Th. Deyiannis, Antigoni and Kostas Ficardos as well as Nicos Mataras and my sister Corinna. I should also thank the British Council for a much needed fifteen-month scholarship.

Furthermore, I am grateful to my colleagues and seniors at my work in Athens and in inter-governmental meetings who accepted my priorities and enabled me to conveniently 'disappear' in order to write this book. I will not mention them by name for they are indeed too many and, who knows, they may even be reprimanded for their open-mindedness. Two, however, should be mentioned by name, retired Ambassadors Constantine Tsamados and Andreas Metaxas.

Finally, I would like to express my gratitude to a few other individuals who sustained my enthusiasm in writing this book (and incidentally put up with my various moods). They include Pericles Alkidis and Seriphos, Nicholas Karalis, Athina Syriatou, Niki Maroniti and last, but certainly not least, Zina Assimakopoulou.

A.H.
Athens

ABBREVIATIONS

AACC	All Africa Council of Churches
ALF	Azania Liberation Front
	Afar Liberation Front
ARG	Anyidi Revolutionary Government
ASALA	Armenian Secret Army for the Liberation of Armenia
ASEAN	Association of South Eastern Asian Nations
Balubakat	Association des Baluba du Katanga
CENTO	Central Treaty Organization
CIA	Central Intelligence Service
Conakat	Confédération des associations tribales du Katanga
ETA	Euzkadi Ta Askatasuna (Basque Nation and Freedom)
ELF	Eritrean Liberation Front
ELF-GC	Eritrean Liberation Front–General Command
ELF-GS	Eritrean Liberation Front–General Secretariat
ELF-PLF	Eritrean Liberation Front–Popular Liberation Forces
ELF-PLF-RC	Eritrean Liberation Front–Popular Liberation Forces–Revolutionary Council
ELF-RC	Eritrean Liberation Front–Revolutionary Council
EPLF	Eritrean People's Liberation Front
Fedeka	Fédération Kasaienne
FLNC	Front de Libération Nationale Congolais
FMG	Federal Military Government (of Nigeria)
ICRC	International Committee of the Red Cross
IGO	international governmental organization
INGO	international nongovernmental organization
INALWA	International Airlift West Africa
JCA	Joint Church Aid
KDP	Kurdistan Democratic Party
MIM	Muslim Independence Movement
Mistebel	Mission technique belge
MNC	Mouvement national congolais

xiii

MNLF	Moro National Liberation Front
NATO	North Atlantic Treaty Organization
NCNC	National Council of Nigeria and the Cameroons National Council of Nigerian Citizens
NGO	nongovernmental organization
NPC	Northern People's Congress (Nigeria)
NPG	Nile Provisional Government
NUP	National Unionist Party (Sudan)
OAU	Organization of African Unity
OIC	Organization of the Islamic Conference
OLF	Oromo Liberation Front
ONUC	Organisation des Nations Unies au Congo
OPEC	Organization of Petroleum Exporting Countries
PDRY	People's Democratic Republic of Yemen
PFLP	Popular Front for the Liberation of Palestine
PLF	People's Liberation Front (Eritrea)
PLO	Palestine Liberation Organization
PMAC	Provisional Military Administrative Council (Ethiopia)
PUK	Patriotic Union of Kurdistan
SACDNU	Sudan African Closed Districts National Union
SALF	Sudan African Liberation Front Sudan African National Union
SPLA	Sudan People's Liberation Army
SSA	Southern Sudan Association
SSLM	Southern Sudan Liberation Movement
SSPG	Southern Sudan Provisional Government
TULF	Tamil United Liberation Front
Ucol	Union pour la colonisation
UMHK	Union Minière du Haut-Katanga
USALF	United Sudan African Liberation Movement
WCC	World Council of Churches
WSLF	Western Somali Liberation Front

PREFACE

At the time of writing, not a day passes without some report of action by secessionists, be they Sikhs, Basques, Tamils, Kurds, the Baltic peoples – or any of a host of others.

Separatism, or secession, is an anathema to independent states and to the existing inter-state system. As a result it has been only partially studied. Indeed, any comprehensive study of secession and secessionist movements, made with a view to understanding the phenomenon rather than condemning or condoning it, can be seen even today as an affront, a retrogression, an undue preoccupation with unfortunate exotic events. Until recently, secession and separatism were obscured by other problems regarded as far more urgent: the East–West confrontation, the North–South gap, various inter-state conflicts, revolutions and anti-colonial liberation movements. The division of labour within political science itself works against secession, leaving it suspended between comparative politics and international relations, and at the crossroads of other social science disciplines, as well as law (international and constitutional law). But whether we like it or not, trapped as we are by value-laden concepts, images and paradigms, separatism abounds and is likely to multiply, even though it may still remain shrouded in a veil of mystery.

The last fifteen years or so have seen several noteworthy attempts to penetrate this veil and come to grips with separatism and secession as a modern phenomenon. In comparative politics success has been far greater than in international relations, but the issue has still not been inserted into the mainstream of scholarly research. It is clear, however, that the question is far more pervasive, complex and intriguing than it was thought to be, and that it calls for a reassessment of several longstanding approaches to integration and conflict. It has considerable implications for conventional wisdom and challenges powerful vested interests.

The aim of this study is to trace the reasons for separatism and secession and to single out the salient characteristics of secessionist movements in international politics today: namely, the international normative framework; the international activity of secessionist movements; third-party involvement; and the world reaction at large. The book is divided into two parts, a theoretical section and a section of seven case studies: Katanga, Biafra, Southern Sudan, Iraqi Kurdistan, Bangladesh, the Moro region in the southern Philippines and Eritrea.

A.H.

INTRODUCTION

THE FRAMEWORK OF ANALYSIS

The insurmountable complexity of living in one world – our village earth – which is at the same time an infinite number of worlds, some compatible, others locked in chronic conflict, has inevitably given rise to conceptions not only of coming together, but also of moving apart, of integration as well as disintegration.

Disintegration and its kindred concepts of separatism and secession have a negative connotation suggesting schism, decomposition, the destruction of unity and integrity, the tearing apart of society's fabric or the shattering of the natural order. Furthermore, they tend to assume the pre-existence of integration.

Disintegration or separatism is the antithesis of integration. It is the final stage or process whereby territorial units of a political entity assert themselves politically, challenging the scope of the particular authority. It may involve the bifurcation or fragmentation of a state or the coming apart – the dissolution – of the constituent units of a confederal or supranational entity.

Secession is a special kind of territorial separatism involving states. It is an abrupt unilateral move to independence on the part of a region that is a metropolitan territory of a sovereign independent state. Secession is opposed by the 'Centre',[1] the central government of the state. In secession there is a formal act of declaration of independence on the part of the region in question. Secession thus defined can be called secession *stricto sensu* or secession *simpliciter*. Secession in the wider sense can be regarded as including what can be called 'incremental secession', that is, political activity of a violent or non-violent nature which is aimed at independence or some form of self-rule short of independence from autonomy to a loose binational or multi-state federal system. In incremental secessions there is no formal declaration of independence: secession is a process. Needless to say, the post-Second World War period has seen more incremental secessions than *stricto sensu* ones.

We will speak in terms of a 'secessionist movement' when secession, whether *stricto sensu* or incremental, poses a credible threat to the Centre

1

and when not only the goal but also the means are legitimized by the majority of the people it claims to represent.

Otherwise, if support with regard to either the goal or the means is lacking, or if the secessionist group does not appear to pose a credible and direct threat to the Centre, then the group concerned will be regarded as a secessionist front, not as a movement as such.[2]

Secessionist fronts and movements should be distinguished from other types of independence and revolutionary movements.[3] Nearest to secessionist movements are secessionist-irredentist movements and secessionist-merger movements. The former have historical claims, but no firm territorial base (a distinct territory in which they form the clear majority), as in the case of the Jews in the inter-war period and the Armenians today with regard to eastern Turkey. The second category – secessionist-merger movements – regard independence as a mere stepping-stone to eventual union with an already independent state.[4] They tend to count on the support of their ethnic brothers across the border. The secessionist movements that we will be examining – 'pure' secessionist movements – rarely have such a prospect. As a result they are more likely to present a more complex and unpredictable international profile. They are so to speak the 'orphans of the universe', as one secessionist leader (Barzani of the Kurds) called his people. It is precisely with such cases that we will be concerned: with secessions *stricto sensu* such as Katanga, Biafra or Bangladesh and with incremental secessions such as the Eritreans, the Kurds, the Southern Sudanese or the Moros.

1

THE ETIOLOGY OF SECESSION

PARADIGMS OF STATE INTEGRATION

The nationalist principle, according to which all states should correspond to a nation and all nations should become states, fell into disrepute in the aftermath of the Second World War. It was vehemently denounced as *passé* and harmful to the new world society recovering from the war. It was invariably regarded as a manifestation of man's darker side, as the hallmark of prejudice and ethnocentrism that breeds intolerance and aggression. The new panacea pervading the literature of the 1950s and 1960s was none other than integration – integration within and between states – an idea incidentally that had also surfaced, though with less confidence, in the aftermath of the First World War (mainly among the so-called idealists). By the late 1950s it was assumed that there was a dynamic towards assimilation, an incessant trend heralding a new era of progress and prosperity across the world.

This world – which though perhaps not 'brave' was certainly in many respects 'new' as it emerged from the ruins of the Second World War – did not conform to the nationalist ideal: that states and nations should be congruent. By far the overwhelming majority among them were in fact multi-ethnic states, 'state-nations'.[1] And it was precisely these very states that were regarded as capable of attaining political, perhaps even national integration. Indeed, it was regarded as more or less axiomatic that nations could be 'built' from above. Thus 'nation-building' made its entry into the jargon, an incongruent concept which in fact implied 'empire-building'[2] and at best 'state-building' by way of 'nation-destroying'.[3]

Karl Deutsch has provided the best-known paradigm of national integration in political science, with his two master concepts: mobilization and assimilation. The basic thrust of his argument is that modernization within states leads to the mobilization of large segments of the rural population. Urbanization and greater communication in turn give rise to assimilation in a far shorter time span than had previously been regarded as possible. The outcome is 'complementarity of social communication', the very stuff of nationhood.[4]

The nation-building approach was a catalyst in the value-consensus tradition of social science. For Marxism, eminent among the conflict

3

theories, nationalism was a product of the development of capitalism. The creation of a nation needed an integrated home market and emerged when the bourgeoisie installed itself in power. With the erosion of the capitalist mode of production and the rise of proletariat solidarity, nationalism (and subnationalism) were bound to subside. For the working class national consciousness was a 'false consciousness', a 'transformed class consciousness', that obstructed the real engine of history, which was none other than the class struggle.[5]

Thus both Western nation-building theory and Marxism agreed that non-state nationalism was anachronistic, in conflict with the real goals of society and certainly supplantable, and not a perennial and independent force.

But the real world was not as compliant. Beneath the veneer of symbols of unity and 'we-feeling' that greeted the first years of the anti-colonial struggle, lurked rival loyalties and disintegrative tendencies. Yet, the nation-building edifice held its ground and there was no paradigm shift or competing alternative paradigms.[6] A simple modification, provided by Clifford Geertz and a few others, gave nation-building a new lease of life. Geertz argued that the main problem was 'primordialism', a pathological situation, characteristic of the developing world, whereby undue importance is attached to ascriptive ties, something which in effect denies the secular essence of modern politics. Developing states are urged to domesticate these disruptive primordial ties, thus divesting them of their legitimizing power and reconciling them with the unfolding modern civic order.[7]

Marxist and neo-Marxist scholars, on their part, broadened their original concept of nationalism to include nationalism outside the strict 'bourgeois capitalist' framework. According to two of the seminal contributions, those of Nicos Poulantzas and Samir Amin, there exists a dialectical relationship between state and nation in the modern world: a state emerges to coincide with an already existing nation (or the other way round) on the basis of two matrices, the spatial matrix of territory and geography and the matrix of shared historical and cultural traditions.[8] But Marxism, in general, continued to be preoccupied with state nationalism and not with sub-state (regional) nationalism, which was seen as relatively unimportant.

But reality continued to defy and baffle theoreticians. In the Third World, 'detribalization' as it was often called, proved evanescent, giving way to 'retribalization', even among the elites who were taken to be the natural 'nation-builders'. In the socialist states of Eastern Europe subnationalism persisted unabated, though certainly at a somewhat lower ebb than predicted by eager Western commentators. But most dramatically, there was a flare of ethnic resurgence in the very archetype of nation-states, the states of the developed Western World.

In the meantime, research emanating from a nearby social science field, social anthropology, began to gain in relevance. It was found that societies which are 'culturally plural' could be stable and survive for long periods without showing signs of disintegration. This suggested an alternative paradigm of state integration, or perhaps more accurately, of state cohesion. Soon two distinct approaches could be discerned: consociationalism and control or domination.[9]

According to consociationalism, introduced first by Arend Lijphard and Eric Nordlinger, states can remain stable without attempts at integration (which in any case is bound to be futile), provided a basis of cooperation is reached by the elites of the various cultural segments. The system may be fairly static and elitist and based on disproportional representation (minorities having more power than their numbers would entitle them to on the basis of the majority principle), but it is the most realistic way to deal with societies deeply divided on cultural grounds where strict majority rule is inappropriate and could easily amount to no less than a 'tyranny of the majority'.[10]

The alternative model of state cohesion, which was somewhat older, was set forth by social anthropologists and primarily by M.G. Smith. It presents the 'internal domination' and 'corporate control' of the institutionally and culturally distinct groups by one group.[11]

Today even these two broader models of state cohesion have increasingly been put into question. State systems along such lines have had their upheavals, as in the cases of Belgium and Canada. Some have broken down as seen with Cyprus and Lebanon. Control systems by way of domination have also run their course as seen with Ethiopia, after the fall of Selassie, and in revolutionary Iran. And the classic model of control, the *Herrenvolk* democracy of South Africa, is apparently nearing the edge of the precipice.

PRE-THEORIES OF STATE DISINTEGRATION

A theory of disintegration, which would also be relevant to the study of international conflict, should be able to provide answers to such questions as when and why separate groups persist, and collective identities, in defiance of class or state, emerge, persist or resurge, becoming politically salient? What are the conditions which facilitate a process of disintegration? When is autonomy or federalism the aim of the separatists, and when does the more extreme option, unilateral independence (secession), come to the fore as the goal? What is the role of the international system in an emerging or continuing quest for independence or other less extreme forms of separatism?

Disintegration or separatism is still regarded as undesirable, as a breakdown in modernization and state-building and as a major crisis, rather than as a legitimate alternative option that could be sought if others fail, as an option that could resolve deep-seated and seemingly intractable conflicts of interests between groups. In spite of this, the last dozen years have seen a number of theories of disintegration. Approaches concerned primarily with other questions are also of relevance to a theory of disintegration. Such approaches can be classified as (a) negative theories of integration; (b) negative theories of cohesion; and (c) indirect theories of disintegration or separatism.[12]

Among the negative theories of integration are the explanations provided by Karl Deutsch and others to take account of the disruption of the integration process (when mobilization outpaces assimilation). Geertz, Coleman and many others blame primordialism.[13] Neofunctionalist theories of integration between states also provide us with possible reasons for disintegration, for example 'high politics', the reversibility of elite interests, the unreliability of the 'functional imperative' which is inexorably tied up with economic output, instead of with an ever-rising sense of social–psychological community.[14]

Negative theories of cohesion are provided by consociationalism and to a lesser extent by theories of control. It is argued that cohesion is by definition precarious since it is based on institutionalized rewards and delicate inter-elite consensus. Counter-elites may emerge which cannot be incorporated into the system, or the balance of power between groups may alter. As for the various forms of domination by institutionalized control, they are today fraught with difficulties as established authority is no longer taken for granted.

Indirect theories of disintegration include the various interpretations of revolution, inter-group conflict and aggression, all of which contain clues which can lead to a general theory of disintegration. Most useful for our concerns among the various theories of revolution[15] are the social–psychological explanations which present the concept of relative deprivation, the sudden rise in aspirations that are frustrated, and, more generally, the discrepancy between expectations and attainments or capabilities. Equally helpful are the political approaches that highlight competition between interest groups, mobilization, resource scarcity, the inflexibility of institutions, revolutionary organizations and leadership. Finally, the most recent vintage of historical–holistic approaches are also helpful.[16]

From the vast field of inter-group conflict the following pertinent propositions are worth discerning for use in secessionist conflict: external threat leads to ingroup–outgroup boundary formation, it rigidifies existing ingroup–outgroup boundaries and strengthens group cohesion; conflict results from the need for change and the reaction to change; a clear top-dog/under-dog situation will invariably lead, under present circumstances, to militant assertions on the part of the subordinate group calling for structural change; conflict emanates from scarcity or assumed scarcity of values and is perceived as fixed-sum, win–lose, by the parties concerned; conflict attitudes, misperception, ethnocentrism, 'tunnel vision' and the like, are endemic in situations where conflict is rife and contribute to the perception of a conflict as intractable; ethnocentrism and latent ingroup hostility towards outgroups can manifest itself, regardless of the existence of a real overt conflict of interest.[17]

At an even higher level of abstraction, theories of aggression are also of use. In order to avoid the intricate details of the still lively debate on the origins of aggression, we will confine ourselves only to two of the fundamental rationales of aggression which have obvious implications for the main parties engaged in a separatist conflict: (1) aggression, regardless of its origins – be it inborn or learned, a reaction to frustration, or induced by the situation – is seen as an effective strategy to achieve a goal; (2) aggression can appear justified to the aggressor on a number of grounds – moral or legal, cultural, reasons of justice, *raisons d'état* and self-preservation – and is seen by third parties as well as a normal *modus operandi*.[18]

DIRECT THEORIES OF DISINTEGRATION

Two approaches of the last decade can be regarded as direct theories of disintegration: internal colonialism and ethnicity or primordialism. A third, somewhat older approach, concerned mainly with communal conflict in underdeveloped states, could be designated as a third paradigm which could perhaps be dubbed communalism. Some recent reviews lump what we call communalism with internal colonialism applying to both the term instrumentalism as distinct from primordialism. However, as will be seen below, there are obvious differences which warrant the distinction.[19]

The problem of internal colonialism was originally alluded to by theorists such as Lenin and Gramsci, and has more recently been taken up by students of Latin America, of the black ghettos of the United States and of the Palestinians of Israel.[20] It has been more thoroughly developed by Michael Hechter, who argues that states that are

7

not integrated tend to split into two cultural groups: the core, that is the dominant cultural group, and the periphery, those territories largely occupied by the subordinate or peripheral cultural groups. When the division of labour is cultural and when there are economic inequalities between the cultural core and the periphery, the deprived cultural group resists integration and tilts towards separatism.[21] Krippendorff, along the same lines, argues that the essence of all forms of separatism is social discrimination and class stratification, which are the outcome of existing social distances.[22] Similarly, Galtung claims that separatism emerges in a relation of dominance directed against a group or groups, when this dominance is linked with a specific territory within a state and with a distinct people living in that territory.[23]

The theory of internal colonialism is put to severe test by the separatist tendencies on the part of rich territories and privileged groups. While it can be claimed that separatism is due to external factors (the international division of labour or external sponsors), to past neglect or perhaps more ingenuously, that its basis remains economic, and that it essentially amounts to a question of injustice, it is still very doubtful whether the theory can predict and explain all, or even the majority of active secessionist movements.

The proponents of ethnicity or primordialists are a larger and more disparate group. They include early critics of the nation-building paradigm such as Walker Connor, Cynthia Enloe, Nathan Glazer and Daniel Moynihan, Donald L. Horowitz, Harold Isaacs and others, theoreticians of nationalism (nationalism being the intellectual forebear of theories of disintegration), such as Anthony D. Smith, and the proponents of consociationalism and control, in particular Lijphardt, Leo Kuper and van den Berghe.[24]

The fundamental tenet of this approach is that ethnicity – ethnic identity or ethnic consciousness – is the essential independent variable that leads to political assertiveness and militant separatism, regardless of the existence of inequality or dominance. Social and economic discrepancies *per se* create discontent and may incite revolution, but only discontent founded on ethnic symbols, such as language, religion, culture, origin or race can lead to separatism.[25] Distinct communities prefer to be governed poorly by their ethnic brethren instead of wisely by aliens. The latter is worse than oppressive, it is degrading.[26]

The ethnicity or primordialist approach has difficulty accounting for separatist struggles on the part of groups that can hardly be characterized as ethnic groups. And clearly many movements have their militant separatism grounded on an extreme level of inequality. Thus, at the end it could be said that primordialism and internal colonialism are

8

the two polar opposite models of disintegration within which separatism movements oscillate.

Communalism is a more general approach which acts as a useful bridge between these two opposed theories of disintegration. The main focus of the various communalist approaches is modernization, the rise of aspirations, scarcity, the distribution of rewards, elite interests and the compartmentalization of institutions on communal grounds. Communal politics is regarded as a modern phenomenon, above all a useful strategy within a constantly shrinking civic arena. The roots of separatism are to be found in elite disputes over the direction of change and grievances linked with the scarcity of resources. Separatism develops when previously acquired privileges are threatened or alternatively when underprivileged groups realize that the moment has come to redress inequality. Modern states, and in particular states in middle levels of economic development cannot cope with social mobilization and are unable to satisfy the aspirations they generate. Thus communal violence ensues. The main proponents of such theories are Immanuel Wallerstein, Samuel Huntington, Milton Esman, Rabushka and Shepsle, Orlando Patterson, Melson/Wolpe and Michael Banton.[27]

Theories of communalism tend to overemphasize the element of greedy elites and manipulative, power-seeking regional leaders who take advantage of the communal spirit for their own ends.[28] Thus they tend to play down the element of inequality and communal identity as well as the degree of ingroup legitimization for separatism. Undoubtedly, many a militant separatist leader and members of elites are motivated by the search for power, privilege and economic gain. But for a separatist front to gain mass support and become a true 'movement' it should be able to capitalize on a situation of disadvantage and rising group awareness. It must be able to tap a reservoir of group frustration and group pride. Naked self-interest cannot thrive on its own without the normative symbols of unity. But these very symbols of unity enchain the prospective manipulators, who either conform with the new requirements made upon them or are rendered redundant, being substituted by more genuine nationalist leaders.[29]

FROM STATE-NATION TO SEPARATISM

The origins and formations of state-nations (states with cultural pluralism) are varied. Several are the end result of older conquests that led to the formation of empire-states, such as in the cases of Ethiopia, India, Iran and Thailand. Others are the outcome of mutual agreements at the time of merger. Many are the products of the arbitrary boundaries of colonization

9

and their unqualified acceptance on independence. Whatever the origins may be, differences are usually accentuated by the policies and general attitudes of the Centre.

A plausible theory of how communal groups can emerge has appeared in the literature of social psychology. According to Henri Tajfel the incubation process commences with 'social categorization' which then leads to social comparison and concludes with 'psychological group distinctiveness'. The end result is a positive or a negative definition of one's identity as a member of a particular group. A negative social definition creates acute intra-psychic conflict, for man wants to have a positive self-definition of himself and of his community. However, changing a negative self-definition is no simple matter. There are several techniques whereby the tension can be suppressed, in which case there is no drive to attain a 'positive group distinctiveness'.[30] Such techniques range from the 'happy slave' situation,[31] to various elaborate rationalizations that render the negative definition to appear the natural order of things and therefore justifiable. (Into this category falls the example of Jewish self-hatred.) But in the world of today it has become increasingly difficult to satisfy one's self with psychological alchemy of this kind. The demonstration effect of other, at times successful, minority struggles for justice and participation plays its role and is too compelling to be conveniently swept under the carpet as irrelevant and unattainable.

The negative self-definition can become positive by way of a number of strategies. These include individual 'passing' into another group, presumably to the group with a positive definition; 'group self-effacement', that is merger with the topdog group; developing a positive definition by rejecting or arriving at the rejection of the validity of the comparison altogether; enhancing the position of the group as a whole. The first and second strategies may in fact not be available, due either to the policy of the outgroup or to racial and other physical characteristics that are immediately discernible. But even without such obstacles these two variants of assimilation are inadequate so long as a sizable portion of ingroup members choose to remain outside this one-sided integration process. The third strategy, rejection of the comparison, amounts to the development of group pride and ethnocentrism of the type 'we are what we are because they are not what we are'. Thus a Thai or a Malay rejects the salience of his lower social–economic position when compared with the Thai Chinese or Malaysian Chinese, for he believes in his cultural superiority and refinement, his not being involved in what he considers demeaning activities such as trade.[32]

The fourth strategy, enhancing the position of the ingroup as a whole, involves a process of mobilization and politicization. At this stage, integration, in the sense of two-way integration (the creation of a nation), can be sought, or several arrangements proposed whereby the group's distinctiveness and identity is secured. Goals within this latter option include the following: proportional representation, disproportional representation (the consociational model), dominance reversal (role reversal), non-territorial autonomy, territorial autonomy, multiple or dual federation, confederation, various as yet unrealized forms of semi-independence and independence.[33] The means to achieve these goals vary from essentially peaceful strategies (such as those used by Akali Dal, the Sikh party, the Parti Québécois and the Tamil United Liberation Front in Sri Lanka until 1983) to various kinds of violent confrontations from sporadic terrorist attacks (such as by Basque ETA, the Armenian ASALA or the Front de Libération de Bretagne), to extended guerrilla warfare and civil war such as with the Southern Sudanese, the Eritreans, the Karens and the Kurds. A group frustrated by one strategy or goal may move to a more radical goal, or revert to an older more limited one.

The type of policy chosen by the Centre in order to resolve the conflict is of cardinal importance for the road to secession and violent separatism. The various strategies that have been used by states can be placed under two headings: policies of 'denial' of the separatist group as a people and as an *interlocuteur valable*, and policies of 'acceptance'.[34]

Under the heading of denial one could include strategies such as removal or elimination (extermination, population transfers, expulsions), coercion (subjugation, state terrorism), domination within a framework of institutionalized cultural divisions, assimilation as well as individualization of the problem by way of non-discrimination and human rights (when in fact the least the separatist group want is their assertion *qua* group).

Acceptance includes the following strategies: integration in the sense of equal and joint contribution by both groups involved into a new superordinate nation and culture; minority protection and safeguards; consociational democracy in a unitary system; federalism or extended autonomy; very loose federation akin to confederation; redrawing of boundaries with a neighbouring country (in cases of irredentism); accepting the country's partition.

The whole process towards separatism can thus be seen as a path from a quest for meaning and group identity through disadvantage or inequality to a group demand for respect as a group and ultimately for political effectiveness and control.[35]

MODELS OF THE ETIOLOGY OF SECESSION

There exist today at least a dozen explanatory models and theories of separatism and independence; almost all are the product of the last fifteen years. Some follow the tenets of the theory of internal colonialism. Others are by and large within the confines of primordialism, and still others fall within communalism. The most useful models and hypotheses that have appeared include those of Ivo Duchasek, A.D. Smith, Crawford Young and D.L. Horowitz as well as Joseph Rothschild, Anthony Birch, Johan Galtung, John Trent, Anthony Mughan and Nafziger and Richter.[36] We will refer only to the four theoreticians.

Ivo D. Duchasek's contribution is noteworthy, among other reasons, because it brings into sharper focus the territorial aspect, thereby accounting also for those elusive cases where the separatists are hardly bound by ethnic, religious or communal links. This last group is called 'territorial–ideological', where 'territorial alienation' from the Centre leads to the emergence of a separatist ideology. According to Duchasek, the decision to secede is a result of action on the part of a separatist organization which regards independence as a feasible alternative. The roots of separatism include oppression and injustice, but also less poignant factors, such as benign neglect or a growing divergence of interests between the territorial group and the Centre. When separatism is under way, both ethnic and territorial–ideological movements are imbued with the emotional ingredients of nationalism.[37]

Anthony D. Smith offers an elaborate model of the socio-historical process which comprises three stages. The first is the introduction of a centralized bureaucracy, which can gradually give rise to discontent and a return to the ethnic community. The second stage is that of the 'ethnic revival', an outcome of international economic forces, growing state regulation and inefficient distribution of resources. The third and final stage is determined by the government's reaction to the demands of the ethnic movement.[38]

Crawford Young makes a useful distinction between primary factors (or resources) of separatism and catalysts. Primary factors include ethnicity, religion, territorial contiguity, injustice, neglect and some others. All or some of these factors may give rise to separatism only so long as a series of events takes place which function as 'catalysts' and if a future independent state is seen as viable.[39]

Donald L. Horowitz, one of the original proponents of the primordialist school, makes a very useful distinction between four types of potential separatist groups: backward groups in a backward region; advanced groups in a backward region; advanced groups in an advanced region; and backward groups in an advanced region. The first group secedes early on, irrespective of the economic costs; the second group secedes belatedly and only if the economic costs of secession are low; the third group (advanced groups in advanced regions) rarely secedes, and only if the economic costs are low; backward groups in advanced regions rarely secede, but, if they do, they secede irrespective of the economic cost.

According to Horowitz, the precipitants for separatism for each group are as follows: for the first group they are denial of proportionality in the civil service and symbolic issues such as language or religion; for the third and fourth group they are severe discrimination, violence and ensuing migrations; while for backward groups in advanced regions, separatism is linked with denial of proportionality and political claims made by immigrant strangers in the region.[40]

ESSENTIALS OF A MODEL OF SECESSION

At this stage of the literature it would be useful to attempt to harmonize and conceptually integrate the various views on separatism by way of a fairly simple and straightforward model of separatism and secession that could apply to all cases of separatist movements imbued with a noteworthy degree of ingroup support. The main questions to be addressed by such a model are why, when, by whom and under what circumstances does armed separatism and secession arise.

Three elements can be regarded as the fundamental and independent variables without which secession and any other form of territorial separatism is inconceivable, indeed nonsensical. One is territory and a territorial base for a collectivity; another is the existence of a sizable human grouping, a collectivity that defines itself as distinct; and third is the type of relationship existing between the Centre and this collectivity. All three variables interact with each other, and all three in conjunction make separatism at one historical point meaningful to the ingroup and a credible threat to the Centre. The main questions are, what territory and link with territory is more conducive to separatism? Is one type of collectivity more prone to separatism than another, and which one is it? What kind of relationship between the ingroup (the potential separatists) and the outgroup (the Centre) is more likely to give rise to separatism, including armed separatism, and secession?

Groups which are able to create a fully-fledged separatist movement, seriously challenging the Centre, are those with a strong territorial base, that is, groups which constitute a clear majority by living fairly compactly in a distinct and integral territory within a state. Independence can be sought even by groups with a weak or almost non-existent territorial base. But without extended ingroup habitation such irredentist claims remain unrealistic and cannot develop, at least not in the short run, into a secessionist movement. Sizable groups within a state, dispersed into various enclaves or city quarters, cannot realistically lay claim to independence, such as in the case of the black minority in the United States. Such aggrieved groups tend to seek other forms of change. However, habitation is far from fixed, and often in the course of acute conflict situations there are substantial population movements, or migrations within states, which may strengthen a territorial base (as in the case of the Tamils of Sri Lanka), or even create a territorial base for the first time (as with the Turkish Cypriots and increasingly with the rival communities in Lebanon). The archetypal example of this is the irredentist Jewish community in Palestine – the Yishuv – up until 1948, although it was of course not a secessionist movement.

Furthermore, a territory which is distinct from the Centre and distant from the centre of decision-making, the capital city of the country, can gradually inspire a sense of group identity formerly unbeknown to the group. Such a sense of group distinctiveness and common fate can cut across and obliterate ethnic and other valued ascriptive boundaries as seen historically in the independent movements of the New World and with the American Confederacy, and more recently in the cases of Eritrea, Katanga or the Southern Sudan. Note, however, that a territory inhabited by one group well known for its ethnic pride cannot readily develop a secessionist movement if the capital of the country is in its very midst, as seen for instance in the case of the Yoruba in Nigeria and the Flemish in Belgium.

A potential secessionist territory should appear to those concerned as having historical roots and as being viable as an independent state. Such considerations, together with legal and practical reasons, whereby it makes sense to seek independence as a whole province or federated unit, has led many secessionist movements to claim a larger territory than the one that could be considered as rightfully theirs on the basis of popular support and the majority principle. Finally, territories that have sought independence and posed a credible threat to the Centre are almost by definition those that have an international boundary or outlet to the sea.

Secessionist movements have developed from an array of collectivities: from groups with a distinct language or culture, such as the Kurds, to groups with the same language and culture as those of the group in control of the Centre, as in the case of the American Confederacy; from nations not based on a common language to multi-ethnic groups that are not nations. Is there a specific kind of grouping that may *eo ipso* be taken as being in a latent state of separatism, even if it has not manifested any separatist proclivity? The simplest answer is a tautological one: potential separatist groups are all those that have the ability to generate a secessionist movement, that is a legitimized secessionist organization that can engage the Centre in a secessionist conflict, be it armed or peaceful. Of course such answers beg the question. A variation of this approach is equally unhelpful. This is the 'heroic' argument, that if a group is willing to suffer in order to gain its coveted goal of independence then it is such a movement. In fact many secessionists are not willing to risk a violent confrontation. The armed conflict was simply not anticipated. For others, separatist activists, the arduous armed struggle from the bush or the mountains is a realistic choice, for the alternative is even worse: it is death or a fate worse than death, cultural assimilation and group extinction (what has sometimes been labelled 'cultural genocide').

Terms more commonly used to depict communal or separatist groups are tribe, race, minority, ethnic group, nation and their admixtures, as well as a host of recent compound terms proposed by various students of the phenomenon. The concept of race has run its course; it is discredited and in any event has very limited relevance to separatism. Tribe is derogatory and linked with Eurocentric social science. Minority has a far greater potential, but is overtaxed and too wide in connotation to apply. It is value-laden and means different things to different people, not least to sociologists and international lawyers who disagree as to the definition of the concept.[41] Though almost all secessionist movements spring from 'numerical' minorities (the legal definition), they do not necessarily arise from one minority, but from coalitions of minorities, or sections of one minority allied to other minorities. The separatist group may have no common ascriptive of cultural markers and need not be underprivileged as conjectured by both legal and sociological definitions of minority.

Nor does the more novel concept of ethnic group explain the emergence of separatist movements, in spite of the claims of the most extreme primordialists. Ethnic group in its restrictive sense is of limited value for it amounts to an ethnic category, that is, to an involuntary aggregate of people, who have discernible characteristics and are 'other-defined', though not necessarily 'self-defined'.[42] Broader definitions of ethnic group, on the other hand, tend to overlap with the concept of nation. They regard the objective attributes of ethnic groups as secondary – myths and symbols that can be invented, abrogated or reformulated.[43] But even if it were possible for the concept of ethnic group to be clearly distinguished from other relevant terms it would still represent only part of the picture. It would denote only one type of separatism, 'ethnic' separatism.

The concept of nation, one of the oldest terms, is more appropriate as a generic term, for it is more free of ascriptive criteria. However, it has been used loosely and has come to be unwarrantedly confused with

15

a concept of a different order, that of state.[44] But more importantly, not all secessionist movements claim to represent a nation, and several that do are not convincing.

At the end of this definitional journey stand two concepts which are less value-laden and certainly far less controversial than those discussed so far. They are community and society, and under them can be placed all the groups seeking some form of separatism from autonomy to independence, be they ethnic groups or ethno-nations, nations, groups based on religion, race or a common history and a separate administration, or on a separate ideology and distinct social system. A separate community can be regarded as any group within a state that can clearly define itself as distinct from other groups on the basis of ascriptive or cultural markers. A separate society is a society which though self-standing is not linked by such symbols of unity, but is founded on territory and perhaps history and ideology. A separate society is the one whose members are convinced that self-rule would result in far greater justice and equality for the various ethnic groups than the previous unified system or state.

Separate communities can be based on a sense of nationhood where a distinct language common to the ingroup is not the unifying external marker, as for instance in the case of the Nagas of India, the Karens, the Welsh or the Scots. It can be founded on an ethno-national identity, where language linked with history and culture is decisive, as in the case of the French Canadians, the Kurds (to a point), the Tamils, the Ibo or the Basques. It can also be founded on religious and historical identity and its cultural–societal repercussions, as for instance in the case of the Moros of the Philippines, the Muslims in Chad, the Sikhs of India or the Catholics of Northern Ireland. In somewhat fewer cases, separate identity can be fostered on the basis of race and a very broad definition of common culture, as with the Western Papuans of Indonesia, and the Southern Sudanese and Amerindians. A separate society can be an alliance of communities based on territory, as in the case of Eritrea and Katanga, or on one part of a community which defines itself as separate by virtue of a territory and distinct ideology, such as the independence movements of the Americas in previous centuries and the American Confederacy.

For a group to become a separate community or distinct society able to mobilize and politicize those concerned, it must be in the position to erect a psychological boundary, a 'communal' boundary between itself and outsiders. Such a boundary can even cut across religious, cultural, racial, historical or even linguistic ties and supersede other forms of identity, such as class, sex or ideology at a given historical juncture. It is a vertical barrier between ingroup and outgroups. There are no universal criteria for the boundary formation and the resultant dichotomy in the minds of men and women are subject to change, depending on the given social–historical factors of the situation.[45]

Finally, why is it, as Geertz has pointed out, that 'economic or class or intellectual disaffection threatens revolution, but disaffection based on race, language or culture threatens partition, irredentism or merger, a redrawing of the very limits of the state'?[46] It appears to be that only such identities, or such types of collectivities, have the potential to create an autonomous self-standing state with all its concomitant differences of sex, class or ideology.[47] Only there does the potential exist for the creation of 'total identities';[48] of a 'terminal community', which, as Rupert Emerson has put it, 'when the chips are down, effectively commands men's loyalties, overriding the claims both of the lesser communities within it and those which cut across it or potentially enfold it within a still greater society.'[49]

Once the distinguishing boundaries drawn by a separate and territorially distinct community or society are established, they are not as inflexible as they may seem. They can in fact be redrawn, but also rigidify, assuming new political significance. It is the concrete situation existing within a state that gives rise to the boundary in the first place, or renders salient an already existing divergence between the central government and the potential separatists. For separatism to be born there should exist some kind of disadvantage (inequality or a differential), past or present, actual or conjectured. Without such a relationship, which is perceived by the potential separatists as existing, no group will conceive of territorial separatism. Put bluntly, if a stark disadvantage does not exist in the first place it has to be invented. It is perhaps no coincidence that most secessionist movements make more of the fact that they are (or were) the victims of inequality and discrimination than they do of any claims that their group presents the vestiges of a nation.[50] Until today no absolute top-dog group, not even one in a numerical minority, has indicated a propensity to separate from the larger state.

For analytical purposes, inequality (or disadvantage) can be defined in two different ways. One is to differentiate the objective from the subjective aspect, that is the situation itself from the perception of the situation by the ingroup concerned. The other is to distinguish between absolute (and cumulative) disadvantage or inequality on the one hand, and relative disadvantage on the other; put differently the total underdog situation from the partial one, that of 'rank disequilibrium'.[51]

There is an abundance of generic terms for absolute disadvantage or inequality, terms such as intra-state imperialism, internal colonialism, dominance or domination or conversely, from the angle of vision of the aggrieved group, concepts such as injustice, direct and structural violence, discrimination and others.[52] However, the drawback with some of these terms is that they are value-laden. Equally, they are such forceful and pervasive terms, that when subdivided into various categories they tend to imply a cumulative effect or positive correlation among the various categories. They do not lend themselves to the recognition of more subtle forms of domination and exploitation by the Centre. And, most importantly, such terms leave no room for mixed situations, whereby the core ethnic group in the Centre is foremost in some areas, but not in others. In fact separatism has sprung also from such mixed situations of rank disequilibrium.

This problem can be settled in at least two different ways. One is a solution within the realm of the objective situation itself. Thus territorially-based communities need not suffer economically, socially, or even educationally, to become separatist, so long as there exists inequality in the political and cultural spheres. Equally, a dominant group politically and culturally, a group whose particular culture happens to be the state culture (such as the case of the Malays in Malaysia) does not contemplate seceding, even if it has been surpassed economically and educationally by other groups (in the Malaysian case by the Chinese). The Katangans and the Ibo of Nigeria on the other hand, though undoubtedly politically (and culturally) dominant in their respective regions, had limited political thrust in the central political apparatus (with the exception of the Ibo during the first part of 1966 under Ironsi). Furthermore, they were not culturally dominant in the whole country, nor was their culture of equal standing to the other major cultures of Zaïre and Nigeria respectively.

A second solution to this problem is by way of a subjective criterion, that is the ingroup's definition of the inequality which ostensibly gives rise to the grievance against the Centre. Perception is based in secessionist situations on two related standards of appraisal. One is to compare one's situation with a referent. The referent could be the outgroup (the Centre), other groups, or a more advantageous environment previously enjoyed by the group. The other is based on the ingroup's definition of its capability and on its view of distributive justice and advantages. Such appraisals vary greatly for they are based on the highly relative and subjective value-scales of a group within a particular historical setting. Thus, whereas one group would appear satisfied if it could secure a share of rewards commensurate with its percentage of the population, as in the case of the Iraqi Kurds, another could base its calculations on its contribution to the GNP and other such indicators, irrespective of its numerical strength in a country, as with Katanga in the early 1960s. Obviously, such considerations are congenial to rich centrifugal territories, or potentially rich ones, such as Katanga (today's Shaba), Eastern Nigeria, the Basque region of Spain, Croatia, the Punjab in India (the Sikhs), or even enclaves such as Cabinda in Angola, the Casamance province of Senegal or the island of Bourgainville in Papua New Guinea.

At this point we may put forward a tentative hypothesis. The more a group can be characterized as an ethnic group or nation, the more secondary is the role played by the factor of inequality or disadvantage in spurring active separatism (or, put differently, the lesser the degree of inequality necessary to spawn secession). Conversely, the more a group lacks the trappings of ethnic or national identity, the more decisive is the role of inequality, and the higher the degree of inequality required. Most, but not all, separatist movements conform to one or other of the two variants of this hypothesis.

Our three elements – a strong territorial base (territorial contiguity), a separate community or society, cognizant of its distinctiveness, and some form of disadvantage – can develop within various settings. They can be nurtured in developed, as well as underdeveloped societies, within artificial states, in 'empires', or even in states which have already gone through a successful phase of national integration. They may appear in the wake of independence or when the entity is still a colony. Separatism can be of recent vintage, or as old as the original revolutionary nationalist movements of the modern era (in the nineteenth century and early twentieth century). The historical experience and a series of related factors can be seen as independent variables which may enhance ingroup identity and the territorial base or inequality. They can be regarded as facilitating conditions, distinguished into political, social, economic, psychological and international facilitating conditions, or otherwise into structural and actor-oriented reasons. Among the considerable number of factors suggested by many a case study of communal conflict and separatism worth pointing out are background conditions such as colonialism and colonization, the rise of state intervention in social and economic affairs, modernization and communication, the alienation generated by the modern state, the fulfilment of non-material needs, the shrinking of the political arena, the lack of feasible alternative non-regional or non-communal forms of group action and the effects of the world system and the economic and political ties with third states.

A distinct community or society in disadvantageous relationship with the Centre and living apart in an integral territory, together with a combination of some of the above background conditions, can be defined as being in a situation of latent separatism. But politicization and then

19

separatism can only take place with the intensification of interaction with the Centre. Interaction can give rise to the need to set up a communally- or territorially-based political organization, or otherwise a discernible leadership which is vertical-sectarian in its scope. The various events prior to and, in particular, after territorial–communal politicization function as precipitants of separatism and secession. The precipitants consist of the actions and reactions of the Centre (or actions attributable to the central government) to the rising demands of the region. The Centre does not always realize that in the early stages it can nip separatism in the bud or accommodate it with the use of bold and far-reaching policies. Instead, it often reacts spasmodically, thereby unwittingly kindling separatism.

The decision to resort to an armed struggle for independence, or unilaterally to declare independence, could be based on considerations of feasibility and the prospects of future viability as an independent state. But in practice it has more often than not been the case that regional groups seeking autonomy through largely peaceful means are left with very little choice but to resort to armed violence. The final triggering event may be a measure taken by the Centre which functions as the last straw, or it can be an event which appears as an opportunity for declaring independence or resorting to a struggle for self-government.

Once a secessionist war ensues, and the issue is no more a peaceful process to autonomy or a federal framework, then an international dimension is inevitably injected into the conflict – some would say even before that, through ties with third parties and from the repercussions of the world economic system – even though the secessionist movement itself or the state concerned may be trying to avoid such an eventuality. It is with this international dimension that we will be concerned now, namely the international normative system with regard to secession and separatism in general and the international relations of secessionist movement, distinguished into international activity and then third-party involvement.

THE INTERNATIONAL
NORMATIVE FRAMEWORK

THE EXISTING NORMATIVE FRAMEWORK

It is abundantly clear that secession does not conform with the rules of international legitimacy, those fundamental legal and political principles that govern the present inter-state system and membership in that system. To begin with, secessionist movements are confronted by none other than the principle of self-determination, the very norm, ironically, that such movements invoke. Highly unfavourable also are two other groups of norms, both linked today with self-determination: the principles applicable to state formation and recognition, and non-intervention in the internal affairs of states.

The Principle of Self-Determination

The main legal bulwark against secession is the principle of self-determination which developed during the late 1950s and 1960s.

The 'self-determination of peoples' is mentioned twice, if 'somewhat cryptically'[1] in Article 1, par. 2 and Article 55 of the United Nations Charter. It has been elaborated since by a whole series of UN resolutions. The trail-blazer of the various UN resolutions is no doubt the momentous Declaration on the Granting of Independence to Colonial Countries and Peoples of 1960. It was followed among others by the first article of the two 1966 International Covenants on Human Rights, the advisory opinions of the International Court of Justice on Namibia and Western Sahara and by the 'Friendly Relations' Declaration of 1970. This 1970 UN declaration also rejects any right of secession from an independent state and condemns 'any action aimed at the partial or total disruption of the national unity and territorial integrity of any other state or country'.[2]

But who then are the beneficiaries of self-determination if 'national', that is secessionist self-determination, is excluded? The 'people' who benefit from such a right are exclusively the peoples under colonial rule. They can exercise this right once and for all and never again, without disrupting the territorial integrity of the colonial entity. And once a colony

21

has become independent, self-determination means non-interference and the exclusive right of a people to freely select their government.[3]

In its original conceptualization in the nineteenth and early twentieth centuries the principle of national self-determination was no doubt explosive.[4] It was in essence a form of self-assertion against any form of domination.[5] It was a threat to established authorities and a challenge to powerful vested interests. The international system as it emerged from the ruins of the Second World War appeared to have no other option than hasty retrenchment in order to control self-determination, that abominable creature which an earlier world system had mischievously spawned.[6]

The initial hard line was to strip the principle of any legal vestiges, mainly by portraying its absurdity and non-applicability: the alleged beneficiaries of such a right – the people – could not be defined; when defined they were defined arbitrarily without due regard to the real merits of each case; thus self-determination was inevitably destined to be the sport of international power politics. It was far from being an act of international justice designed to assist colonial and other oppressed peoples. And, in point of fact, only a fraction of the peoples of the world had ever exercised such a right; most were unlikely ever to exercise it.[7]

But the winds of change could not tarry with yesterday. The anti-colonial movement was on the agenda and would not permit such subtleties that smacked of classical colonial pettifogging. Thus by the late 1960s even fairly orthodox scholars of international law came to the 'inescapable conclusion' that self-determination had developed into an 'international legal right', though its scope and extent were still open to some debate.[8] United Nations' rapporteurs went even further stating that the principle had reached the status of *jus cogens* – a peremptory norm of international law (the equivalent of constitutional norms in internal law).[9] But the content of the principle for which the world settled in the second part of the twentieth century was different from the one advocated by the nationalists in earlier days down to Wilson and Lenin. It was not the right of a nation, but the right of a colony to independence or union with another state and the right of a majority within a colony or state. The basis was now territorial instead of ethnic or cultural. It applied to 'non-self-governing territories', not to metropolitan territories. It meant non-colonialism and in practice came to mean only independence from Western colonial rule. It concerned Western overseas empires, not non-Western empires. (The only other beneficiaries of such a right were territories under occupation and majorities subjected to institutionalized racism.) The new principle had, however, understandably, an 'anti-white' flavour.[10]

22

Thus self-determination, the hydra-like creature that had threatened to play havoc with the world system was firmly domesticated. The resultant household creature that governments and international governmental organizations (IGOs) have come to invoke with remarkable abandon may be theoretically shaky and superficial, but it has one basic merit. It is supported by the vast majority of states. Only very few states, most notably Somalia, have now and again indicated that they regard a right of secession as inherent in the right of self-determination.[11] More recently some Arab or Muslim states have appeared somewhat more lenient on the issue of self-determination, but only insofar as it presents a case of Muslim self-determination outside their territories.[12] India's recognition of secessionist Bangladesh on 6 December 1971, and the four African recognitions of Biafra in the spring of 1968, also imply that the adamant rule can be bent in some very exceptional circumstances.

The UN and the various regional political IGOs have been decidedly against secessionist self-determination, for it is obvious that they would be placing themselves in an almost untenable position if they were to interpret self-determination in such a way as to invite or justify attacks on the unity and integrity of their own member states.[13] Even the Organization of the Islamic Conference, which upholds Muslim solidarity, has been relatively restrained with Muslim secessionists outside the territories of its member states, refraining from openly endorsing their claims to secessionist self-determination.

Constitutional law operates in a way almost equally adverse to secession as international law. There has been an ongoing debate with regard to federal constitutions which has surfaced also in studies of European (EEC) integration,[14] but only three post-war constitutions have recognized a right of secession: those of Burma between 1947 and 1974, Yugoslavia and the Soviet Union. The Burmese constitution provided almost insurmountable rules of procedure and, not surprisingly, did not afford such a right to the two regional states most likely to seek independence, the Karen and the Kachin states.[15] The constitution of Yugoslavia stipulates that self-determination includes secession, but states unambiguously that territorial revisions are possible only with the consent of all six Republics and the autonomous provinces.[16] The constitution of the Soviet Union grants under its Article 72 'the right freely to secede' to each Union Republic. Needless to say this right has never been allowed to be taken up, and when invoked by Georgia and other Union Republics in the early days of the Russian Revolution, it was rejected.[17] The origins of this clause are no doubt due to Lenin's liberal approach to self-determination (in contrast with the more orthodox Marxist approach of Rosa Luxembourg, who condemned 'bourgeois

23

nationalism', including the nationalism of her native Poland). However, it is worth remembering that, on paper at least, one superpower regards secessionist self-determination as legitimate, while the other, again a federation, rejects it, and has fought a harsh and idealized 'war of national unity' (the American Civil War) to quell secession.

The established legal paradigm has only one anomaly, the secession of East Pakistan from Pakistan in 1971, which led to the creation of Bangladesh, following the Indian *fait accompli*. But Bangladesh, the only successful opposed secession after the Second World War, has not apparently created a precedent. In the first place, the East Pakistan case was far too unique and highly unlikely to be repeated.[18] Furthermore, this particular secession can be used to reinforce rather than to cast doubt on the existing principle of self-determination, for it happens to fit well with the very essence of the principle: that it applies only and exclusively to majorities. (The East Pakistanis were in fact conveniently a majority in Pakistan.) As Rosalyn Higgins concluded, a few years before the Bangladesh incident, 'self-determination refers to the right of a majority within a generally accepted political unit to the exercise of power ... there can be no such thing as self-determination for the Nagas.'[19]

State Formation and Recognition

New states can come into existence through the granting of independence, by the acknowledgement of already existing *de facto* independence, from the dissolution of an empire or federation, by the merger of two or more units (former colonies or parts of empires) or states, by partition (the formation of two or more states by mutual consent) and by the seizure of independence.[20]

Not any seizure of territory is creative of statehood. Above all, the entity declaring itself independent should be a 'self-determination unit', an integral self-determination unit, and not metropolitan territory of a state.[21] In practice the borderline between secession, which is unacceptable, and partition, which is acceptable, can often be blurred. Thus the cases of Syria's departure from the UAR (the union of Egypt and Syria between 1958 and 1961), Singapore's break with Malaysia, Norway's independence from Sweden and Senegal's abandonment of the Mali Federation have all been loosely called secessions. In fact, they can be better described as partitions. The acts of independence of Norway, Syria and Senegal were secessions to begin with, but soon developed into partitions, as the respective central governments gave, however reluctantly, their consent to the seceding territories' *faits accomplis*. Sweden and the UAR (Egypt), it is true, toyed for a while with the idea of dealing with the matter militarily, but conceded at the end. As for Singapore, it did not in effect secede – that is, unilaterally declare its independence – but was 'booted out' of the Malaysian Federation. (Note that ejection, like secession is not tolerated by international law.)[22]

Recognition of an entity by third states has always been an important issue in particular with regard to secessions *stricto sensu* (those with a declaration of independence). Today, contrary to the first part of the century, recognition as such is not a factor constitutive of statehood, but one of several indicators of statehood. Recognition is a political and not a legal act. According to the declaratory approach (which finally won over after several decades of debate with the constitutive approach) non-recognition does not imply lack of statehood.[23] However, even though recognition is an optional act, if an entity bears the usual marks of statehood, in particular if there is *de facto* control of a territory and its inhabitants by an organized government, other states put themselves at risk legally if they choose to ignore the basic obligations of state relations.[24]

An entity that bears the marks of statehood but is not a self-determined unit, such as Katanga and Biafra in the 1960s and the Republic of Northern Cyprus today, cannot be recognized by third states. Any such recognition defies the principle of self-determination of the majority in a state and is regarded at the very least as premature, hence an unwarrantable intervention in the internal affairs of another state.[25] On the other hand, if an entity is a self-determination unit, but does not meet the strict criteria of statehood, such as Algeria in the late 1950s, the former Portuguese colonies in Africa and more recently, and controversially, the Sahraoui Arab Democratic Republic, there is far greater leniency and third states may recognize such entities without being regarded as patently intervening in the internal affairs of another state.[26]

Traditional international law offered rebels another kind of recognition, a kind of half-way house recognition. This was insurgent status and belligerent status. The first was a 'catch-all designation', allowing third states to be free to determine the kind of legal relationships they intended to establish with the rebel party. For belligerency to be applicable, a number of criteria had to be met, the so-called 'factual test'.[27] The factual test was particularly strict as seen under present conditions of intra-state warfare. (Interestingly, even though a number of insurgents have met the test, none have been accorded such status during the present century.)[28] The present equivalent of belligerency is the status of 'legitimate combatant' or 'privileged combatant' afforded to 'freedom fighters', that is to those movements or peoples, such as anti-colonial movements, or the Palestinians, that are generally recognized as having the right to self-determination.[29] Such liberation movements have observer status in IGOs and in some cases even full membership. Needless to say secessionists have not attained such a status with the exception of a few cases such as in the Organization of the Islamic Conference.

The Non-Intervention Norm

The principle of non-intervention in the internal affairs of states is one of the cardinal principles of international law and can be seen as complementary to the non-use of force prohibition (respectively Article 2, par. 7 and Article 2, par. 4 of the UN Charter). Deviation from this fundamental norm can be justified in exceptional circumstances, and for such reasons as defence, peace and security (in which case there is collective intervention by an IGO or by its members following a specific resolution), and in rare cases for humanitarian considerations, in particular in flagrant instances of institutionalized racism and violence against a majority, and in classical colonialism. (There is also, in theory at least, the case of belligerency.)[30]

Secessionist movements are meticulously excluded from such a right – to seek and be given support – despite their claim that in substance their situation is not different from institutionalized domination and exploitation by aliens. At the same time, the secessionists cannot hope that non-intervention will at least work for both sides to the conflict. Traditionally, non-intervention means non-interference against a state and not non-intervention in its support. A sovereign independent state is entitled to request from any third state the aid that it deems necessary. At the same time, third states cannot assist secessionists, for they would in effect be using force against the territorial integrity of an independent state.[31]

The legal basis for refraining from supporting secessionists is the sovereign equality, independence and territorial integrity of states. From the point of view of international politics the basis is practical. It is 'designed to discourage states from becoming involved in unstable and ambiguous situations'.[32] In the context of normative political theory the basis of non-intervention (as non-support for insurgents) is that intervention is unlikely to serve the interests of a people. The people concerned should be left 'to work out their own salvation', for it is only then that they can develop the special virtues necessary for maintaining freedom and justice. Only freedom and justice that have been earned can ever hope to attain permanence.[33]

But to what extent does the non-intervention norm actually apply to everyday relations between states? This involves at least three empirical questions. First, is there a tendency in fact to avoid intervention in favour of either side in an internal war? Second, which type of internal war attracts greater external intervention, classical civil war or secessionist war? Third, which of the two parties in a secessionist war acquires greater external assistance?

Lewis Richardson, in his classical study of 'deadly quarrels' involving 129 internal wars within a span of 150 years, found that forty-five of them, that is 35 per cent, had experienced external intervention.[34] Richard Little in his study of intervention in the nineteenth and twentieth centuries found that the non-intervention norm is applied up to a point only, so long as there is no spill-over endangering the stability of the international system.[35] In the large-scale empirical studies undertaken by Istvan Kende for the period after the Second World War, which is of course our main interest here, it was found that 'tribal wars', that is, separatist or irredentist internal wars are far less likely to attract external support than classical civil wars.[36] This was also the conclusion of Robert O. Matthews with regard to Africa.[37] Kende's findings have a number of inaccuracies and they follow the traditional definition of intervention – support for the insurgents not for the incumbents – but they clearly indicate that separatists are less likely to receive external aid than other types of insurgents.

As to the third question – which of the two parties in a secessionist war is likely to receive more external aid – the clear indication of a detailed survey of various empirical studies is that the secessionists are likely to get less aid than the incumbents,[38] a state of affairs which very much confirms what has already been suggested by the lopsided legal framework favouring the Centre.

TOWARDS A NEW NORMATIVE FRAMEWORK

Qualified Secessionist Self-Determination

There are many important reasons why self-determination should henceforth remain for ever confined to colonial entities. If it is to return to its original sense as primarily a right to secession it could above all precipitate secessionist claims *ad absurdum*, which would leave hardly any existing state intact. The result could be chaotic.

The various specific arguments against secession which have been advanced through the years, have been summarized comprehensively by Lee C. Buchheit.[39] The strictly legal or legalistic arguments against secession include the following:

1. that the right of self-determination can only be exercised once on the basis of the maxim *pacta sunt servanda*;
2. international law is the law of states and not of peoples or individuals. States are the subjects of international law and peoples (majorities or minorities) are the objects of that law;
3. the so-called argument from mutuality; as states cannot oust one of their provinces, equally a province cannot secede.

In rebutting the first of the above arguments, another Latin maxim is of use: *rebus sic standibus* (provided the situation has not changed substantially). The second argument had been under heavy criticism in the earlier part of this century by certain eminent international lawyers, notably Nicolas Politis and Georges Scelle.[40] Today it is still the orthodox view, but has difficulty accommodating the international law of human rights and cases of international criminality. The third, social contract type of argument, has at least one stark exception in the real world, the ejection of Singapore from the Federation of Malaysia. There is also the possibility of population transfers or cedings of territory without a plebiscite, as with Eritrea and West New Guinea.

The non-legal arguments against secession, summarized by Buchheit, are far more substantial. They include:

1. the fear of Balkanization, the domino theory, or the spectre of the Pandora's Box;
2. the fear of indefinite divisibility, because very few states are ethnically homogeneous, and often neither are the secessionist territories themselves;
3. the fear of the effect such a right could have on the democratic system, by providing a minority with an opportunity for constant blackmail – threatening to secede if there is no conformity with its wishes;
4. the danger of giving birth to non-viable and particularly small entities which would rely on extensive international aid;
5. the fear of trapped minorities within the seceding state who presumably cannot themselves secede in their turn;
6. the fear of 'stranded majorities' in cases where the seceding territory is economically or strategically crucial to the original state.[41]

The case for a right of secession has hardly ever been presented as an unqualified right for anyone who claims it. It has rather been a call for the articulation of adequate criteria, or standards of legitimacy, whereby only legitimate claims to secession would fall within the scope of the self-determination principle.

Classical colonial self-determination will soon come to a halt, as there will be no more colonies and annexations will be finalized and accepted internationally. Self-determination will thus be a right with no subject other than in cases such as the Palestinians (initially irredentism), or South Africa's blacks (revolution). It would be totally 'denaturalized',[42] a synonym for non-intervention, external and internal sovereignty, and other such concepts already profusely provided by other legal norms. It would be a surrogate principle or a generic norm, and in essence no more than the empty defensive rhetoric of established authorities and 'barrack-room' legal experts, and despised ones at that. Of course there is nothing inherently wrong with the demise of a legal or political principle, even one which was regarded as of preordinate value as one of the cornerstones of the world system. The problem is that, come what may, separatism will persist unabated, but it will remain beyond a salutary filtering mechanism which could distinguish between good and bad cases of self-determination. And international law would be destined to play the ostrich game to what could be one of the most pernicious threats to peace. Furthermore, as one author has so aptly put it, can one seriously speak of national unity and territorial integrity, and by virtue of that, self-determination for an artificial colonial construct, while denying such a right to 'a manifestly distinguishable minority which happens to find itself, pursuant to a paragraph in some medieval territorial settlement or through a fiat of cartographers, annexed to an independent State'?[43] Indeed, can one possibly claim to be laying the foundations of a more just and equitable world society for the year 2000 and beyond on such morally suspect and intellectually unsound grounds?

Finally, if a territory is geographically fairly distinct and territorial integrity is in effect a 'mask' for 'alien domination and exploitation',[44] then these peoples are entitled to exercise the right of self-determination, or can at least make a case worthy of more than passing examination. There is after all the case of Bangladesh, as well as the partitions that began as secessions.

Proponents of a 'qualified' right of secessionist self-determination can be placed in a continuum, from those with very strict criteria to those with fairly permissive standards.

The strict approach holds that secession can be tolerated only as the ultimate remedy in a situation of marked oppression. This line of thought had appeared as early as the 1920s in the Aalands case, known then as *'carence de souveraineté'*, and applied to territories which were so 'badly misgoverned' that they became totally alienated from the metropolitan state.[45] The more recent proponents of the strict approach include Kamanu, Reisman, Nanda and Umozurike.[46] With only the case of Bangladesh at hand (with its implicit *ex post facto* acknowledgement of a right to self-determination), the strict approach leaves us with a lingering worry. As Buchheit has put it: 'One could paint a rather demonic picture of international opinion demanding sanguinary evidence of a people's suffering . . . before a claim to separation from their tormentors will be considered legitimate.'[47] And how many hundreds or thousands of deaths are enough?

Early proponents of the more lenient approach during the inter-war period included Scelle and Redslob who focused primarily on the concept of a people as well as on the position of the majority and the rump state.[48] More recently, Russell and McCall, Buchheit, as well as Beitz, among others, have set forth criteria for secessionist self-determination. Russell and McCall are concerned with democratic rights, racial and ethnic equality, the viability of the post-secession state, the effects of secession on other states and world order and the existing alternatives to secession.[49]

Buchheit's approach is based on the internal merits of the claim (the degree of distinctiveness of the secessionist group and its viability potential as an independent state) and the degree of world harmony resulting from secession as opposed to the disruptive consequences of the secession.[50]

Beitz argues that secessionist self-determination can be justified if the overwhelming majority of the inhabitants of a region favour it and if independent statehood is a necessary condition for the attainment of justice. Furthermore, in some cases it should be indicated that existing injustices are a fixed feature for the group seeking independence.[51]

To conclude on the issue of a qualified exceptional right to secessionist self-determination, there seems to be a good case for it and it need not be rejected out of hand when a separatist plea is particularly sound.

Qualified Intervention

It appears that, by and large, the whole regime of non-intervention is in urgent need of a new set of rules. In the first place, it is a lop-sided legal regime, favouring the established authority (the government) regardless of the nature of that authority. It suffices that it is the recognized government. Most importantly, third-party intervention is far from uncommon in internal wars, including secessionist wars, and is unlikely to diminish. There is a rising tendency towards covert intervention and other subtle forms of involvement in today's highly interdependent and inter-penetrable world. In addition, the traditional criterion of governmental invitation for involvement is highly inadequate and often misleading. The non-intervention norm is already riddled by exceptions such as the victims of colonialism, apartheid, self-defence, joint intervention for international peace and security and even the still controversial humanitarian intervention is increasingly condoned. Finally, it is unacceptable to leave a secessionist or other internal war in the realm of a gladiatorial struggle as if it were assured that 'right' could become 'might' and assert itself at the end.[52] Secessionist movements are more often than not the weaker party and can hardly ever win militarily. At best they can raise the costs and create a stalemate for a while.

In a nutshell, the cordon sanitaire approach, with its quarantine effect on both parties, is today neither practical nor, in many instances, desirable. It is thus high time, as one analyst has put it, to 'get our double standards right on intervention', so as to avoid 'unnecessary embarrassment'.[53]

Richard Falk was one of the first international lawyers to question the validity of the non-intervention norm in cases where the incumbent government was illegitimate by virtue of being based on racial supremacy or colonial subordination.[54] Equally, Tom Farer has set forth a number of criteria which could perhaps permit intervention under exceptional circumstances.[55]

Charles Beitz regards intervention in support of the insurgents as permissible, so long as the target is neither just nor likely to become just if left to its own devices, if intervention promotes justice and provided that the intervening party is not self-serving.[56]

John Burton, in his important contribution in the early 1970s, differentiates between 'constructive intervention' and aggression. Constructive intervention takes place if a legitimized authority intervenes upon invitation from a legitimized central authority, or when a legitimized third authority intervenes against the non-legitimized central authority. In practice these amount to humanitarian relief, invitation agreed by both parties in the civil war, and uninvited intervention by a legitimized third authority to 'offset the consequences of non-legitimized behaviour'.[57]

The concept of legitimate or legitimized authority, though very important, has its difficulties. It can be misused and is difficult to operationalize. Furthermore, it is 'relationships' that become legitimized or illegitimized, rather than authorities as such. In any event when authorities come to be legitimized it means that they are accepted by their ingroup because of their performance in the enactment of their role.

With regard to secessionist movements (defined here as 'legitimized' secessionist organizations) the Centre is by definition not legitimized by the secessionist group, though it may be legitimized by an important segment of the population or even by the majority. For both the Centre that resists autonomy or independence and the secessionist movement that seeks such drastic change, the position with regard to legitimization is far from static or secure. Any of the following permutations of events may occur. Majority legitimization may erode for the Centre which is at war with a secessionist movement as is the case with Addis Ababa's war with the Eritreans, or as was the case with Khartoum's fight against the Southern Sudanese in the early 1960s. Majority legitimization may in fact increase partly as a result of the common threat of secession, as with the Federal Military Government of Nigeria during the Biafran war. The secessionists themselves may lose the support they used to have among their ingroup. This is more often the case when a peace agreement is in sight and the original secessionist organization appears intransigent.

To conclude, it is obvious that the norms of interstate conduct are an important barrier against secession. The situation appears more restrictive than in the aftermath of the First World War, and in practice more hostile than even under the Concert of Europe (the Great Power system of the early nineteenth century). International law and the normative system in general are in need of change. Otherwise, the number of deviants from the anti-secessionist norm will simply continue to rise. Of course, a new normative framework is fraught with difficulties and will not immediately settle the problem. The problem of colonialism was not resolved because the colonial powers suddenly chose to relinquish their territories due to any solemn adherence to a nascent principle of international law. Cost was in fact the deciding issue. The cost of retaining the overseas colonies was found to be far greater than the possible ensuing benefits.

THE INTERNATIONAL·ACTIVITY
OF SECESSIONIST MOVEMENTS

For traditional international relations studies, which engage in the examination of inter-state relations along the 'billiard-ball' model,[1] secessionist movements and internal wars in general are not their subject matter, save in exceptional circumstances, when the issue has become one of international concern. The opposite is true for more modern approaches which follow a transactional, transnational or 'cobweb' model:[2] internal wars, and in particular secessionist conflicts, are by definition part of the broader study of conflict and peace research that embraces several system levels. In practice, however, the question remains: when can a secessionist conflict be regarded as internationalized? Some argue that the mere existence of a movement which questions the confines of a state internationalizes the issue.[3] Still others claim that the basis for internationalization could be none other than actual third state involvement in the armed conflict.[4]

So far as this study is concerned, the criteria of internationalization are a plea for international aid by the secessionists and discernible third-party involvement, albeit at a very low level.

Three levels of secessionist political activity can be singled out for analytical purposes: the internal ingroup level, the two-party conflict level and the international or transnational level. These three levels or settings are intricately interrelated. The first level concerns the activity of the leadership within the ingroup (its consolidation, recruitment, strategy and propaganda for internal use, etc.). The second is conflict politics, that is, direct conflict interaction with the adversary (the Centre) and with the adversary's constituency. The third level will concern us in the pages that follow.

DECISION-MAKERS AND DECISION-MAKING

Secessionist movements can be unified or split into two or more secessionist fronts. Unified movements are usually those that formally declare independence and have effective control over their territory. Most incremental secessions have no unified leadership, particularly if the armed conflict drags on for years. Covert polyarchy – a semblance of unity achieved by an overall umbrella organization – along the Palestinian Liberation Organization (PLO) lines has rarely appeared in secessionist situations. Perhaps the most notable exception is the case of the Moros of the Philippines from 1972 until 1977. More common is bifurcation, that is a split into two fronts, as has now and again been the case with the Iraqi Kurds, the Eritreans and others; or fragmentation, as seen again with the Eritreans, the Iraqi Kurds in the 1980s and the Southern Sudanese. Among the most widely-known sources of cleavage in the secessionist ranks are ethnic differences, the rivalry between the politicians and the military, personality clashes and personal ambitions, disagreements over goals and strategies and an important, though perhaps somewhat overrated reason for splits and permutations, namely ideological differences which are at times not unrelated to generational disparities (the older, more conservative leaders pitted against the radical new generation cadres). Another potent but elusive source of division, as well as a reason for unity, is sponsorship by a third party.

Ideology is one of the great unknowns of secessionist movements. It is generally accepted that whatever the professed ideology of a separatist front, separatist movements as a whole tend to be ideologically ambivalent.[5] This is partly due to the need to receive aid from anyone without imposing undue restraints, but it is also characteristic of separatism, particularly ethnic separatism, which is based primarily on the diffuse ideology of nationalism.

Most secessionist movements which have been able somehow to pierce the veil of silence that engulfs them, have had a charismatic or at least an able leader. An able leadership that commands respect and wields authority should ideally be the one that articulates the values and motivations, the aspirations and expectations of the ingroup and induces a course which is rewarding.[6] In secessionist situations the leadership can be based on traditional rather than charismatic or revolutionary authority.[7] The ultimate test of leadership in the long run is to attain or bring nearer the goal of self-determination without unduly endangering the survival of the ingroup. In the short run, the aim is to deliver the goods essential for the armed struggle – vital goods such as funds, arms, sanctuary and access. The fact that the secessionist situation is ambiguous, complex and unpredictable and role expectation not as precise as in other political settings, gives the secessionist leadership, for the most part, greater autonomy and 'idiosyncracy credit' than it gives the Centre's leadership, however centralized and authoritarian the latter may be.[8]

The ultimate aim of all secessionist movements, their *raison d'être*, is the 'durability'[9] of their respective communities or societies, that is, the survival, security, development and political effectiveness of their group *qua* group.

The various officially-stated goals of secessionist movements, goals such as independence, various forms of semi-independence such as a loose confederal framework, federal schemes and autonomy, or more vaguely self-determination, can be regarded as strategic aims. Such strategic aims, which are said to be the only guarantee for the survival and development of the separatist group are liable to change as the situation alters. This is particularly the case with incremental secessions. This inbuilt flexibility as to the goal is not shared by secessions *stricto sensu*, which by reason of their initial formal declaration of independence are seen by the Centre and third parties as far more inflexible and, try as they may, can rarely convince others of their willingness to settle for less than independence. Thus deprived of other realistic options they end up becoming wedded to independence till the very end.

Secessionist intransigence as to the stategic aim, which is more pronounced in 'declared' secessions, can lead to excesses which at times border on irrationality. Secessionists are known to continue with the armed stuggle and not to be prepared to reach a compromise, even when a good opportunity arises. Of course, there are several fairly obvious reasons for this attitude, above all a total distrust of the 'enemy' and a (however understandable) paranoid fear. This is no doubt reinforced by the known range of manifestations of conflict attitudes such as oversimplified bipolar images, tunnel vision, misperception and the like – all of which have a remarkable capacity for inducing inertia. This intransigence is not unrelated to another factor, well known in cognitive dynamics: the fact that, as Leon Festinger, a pioneer in the field has put it, 'rats and people come to love the things for which they have suffered'.[10] Independence has to be achieved; otherwise all the sacrifices, the thousands who met their death, were in vain.[11] Needless to say, the ultimate logic of such a course is the Thermopylae syndrome: to die to a man for the goal of self-determination. But despite some melodramatic gestures by some secessionists, the road to self-destruction or sacrifice to the last man (or woman) has yet to be taken by secessionist organizations. Separatists, when defeated or on the brink of disaster, often act wisely and abandon the armed struggle to fight perhaps another day, as with the Kurds of Iraq in the spring of 1975 and more recently in 1987 with the secessionist Tamils of Sri Lanka.

Other explanations for intransigent behaviour can be found in more self-conscious behaviour. Thus, if the real goal of a secessionist movement is complete independence, anything short of this goal can be unacceptable, as with the secessionist Biafrans and Moros. It could also be that the

Centre is not prepared to compromise, but simply insists on a return to the *status quo ante*, as did the Ethiopian government towards Eritrea and Tigray, and the Nigerian government towards Biafra. Being intransigent may also be functional for the assertion of leadership. Thus in the mid-1960s it was the uncompromising Southern Sudanese secessionist politicians who won the day over their more moderate colleagues in the struggle for leadership; and in late 1968 the Biafran leader's fearless attitude when the Nigerians were *ante portas* reinforced his authority and popularity. In this context it is also worth remembering an old premise: that politics in general, and secessionist politics are no exception, tend to attract forceful individuals who seek power (and, one could add, glory) for its own sake (the *homo politicus* model).[12] In several instances politicians and former military leaders engaged in secessionist politics have gained their fame largely due to their image of toughness. Obviously, they would have difficulty appearing to be inconsistent with their image (with what is expected of them).

At a somewhat higher level of sophistication, the nascent theory of so called 'role defence'[13] can equally provide useful cues for this tendency of secessionist leaderships to over-indulge in tightrope exercises which endanger their group. Leaders cling defensively to their roles and react aggressively when their role is under threat, particularly when, as in most secessionist situations, there is no alternative institutional framework for them to assume another acceptable role. For them the conflict of interest is zero-sum. There is 'issue rigidity', one either wins or loses, retains his much coveted role or is deprived of all worthwhile roles. Role defence can be seen as undergoing three distinct phases. The first could be called role exclusion, the second novel role attainment, and the third, role perpetuation and defence. When minority leaders are excluded from meaningful roles within the system, they invent new roles to which they cling. In some cases they cling for dear life, for military defeat and their arrest would mean physical death, as one of the Katangan secessionist leaders once told a commentator.

The last but most obvious reason for intransigence or, as the secessionists would say, a firm position, is the conviction that such a posture is the most appropriate one, given the circumstances; that if there is no 'give' they may win against all odds, even at the eleventh hour. This belief is strengthened by an apocalyptic mood often prevalent when almost everything seems lost. To conclude the question of undue intransigence, it is obvious that it is often self-defeating and foolish, but not irrational as such. Irrationality can be conjectured if an attitude is internally (cognitively) contradictory, as several authors have rightly pointed out. Otherwise, for all practical purposes, we can follow

Burton's postulate that 'parties to a conflict are responding to the situation in the ways that appear more beneficial to them in the light of knowledge they have of the motivations of others and the options open, irrational behaviour is behaviour not understood or not approved by others'.[14]

Activity at the international level aims at penetrating the international system by gaining external adherents, consolidating sympathizers; finding aid or otherwise securing the inflow of the fundamental goods of secession (funds, arms, sanctuary, access etc.); seeking mediators and neutralizing or limiting the extent of third party support for the Centre.

The wider strategic aims that guide the secessionist foreign policy are twofold: to achieve a peaceful settlement by way of negotiations and to continue with the armed struggle. The two can be pursued simultaneously. For the separatist movements which we will examine in more detail, the second predates the first, for it was regarded as more or less axiomatic that only by raising the stakes of the conflict could the Centre be persuaded to negotiate. Instrumental for both aims is third-party involvement. The secessionists, in this context, have to choose between limiting outside support and attracting it, which leads, in practice, to a variety of mixed strategies in order to evoke or regulate outside involvement.[15]

ATTRACTING THIRD PARTIES

It has been claimed that the weaker party in an internal war – which, in a secessionist war, is almost by definition the secessionist party – will inevitably seek to attract outside aid, in order to redress the military imbalance.[16] However, this is far from being a foregone conclusion.[17] By deliberate policy, or by force of circumstance, many secessionist movements have been known to follow a fairly self-reliant course.

The scope of secessionist appeals for third-party involvement is restricted by constraints imposed by the existing environment and resources, as well as by calculations of the costs involved in third-party intervention.[18] Secessionist movements are generally aware that third-party, in particular state involvement is costly, though they may not be fully aware of the full range of possible costs. According to C.R. Mitchell, one can conceive of a 'threshold of appeal' beyond which appeals take place, as the 'perceived losses of going it alone' outweigh the costs of extended involvement.[19]

The most obvious cost of external involvement is undue dependence on the donor. All secessionist movements which rely far too much on one donor can end up 'becoming mere pawns in a game played between and among states'[20] and being abandoned, with few qualms, by their former patrons.

Another obvious cost of external involvement is the tarnishing of the secessionists' image, should involvement be with a disreputable source or with a party which is regarded as incompatible with the secessionists' professed ideology. Appeals and involvement can also introduce a new dimension into the conflict, thereby limiting the pull of possible external supporters. Such a dimension can be chronic international antagonism or divide, such as the East–West conflict, the Arab–Israeli conflict; there may be a Muslim dimension, or possibly various traditional inter-state enmities, such as, say, the Sino-Indian antagonism. A somewhat lesser-known cost of an appeal is that it can result in recognition and world attention. Recognition and becoming a celebrated cause can in fact tie the hands of the separatists, who then have difficulty using terrorist and other unorthodox tactics deemed indispensable at certain stages of the conflict. A little-known cost of extended third-party involvement, is that it tends to raise the secessionists' expectations. Another related byproduct is that appeals raise the stakes of the conflict; the Centre is more likely to shy away from genuine talks and call in its allies, thus bringing more military and diplomatic pressure to bear on the secessionists.

One can conceive of several other costs of involvement, but the important question is, to what extent are the secessionists in a position to limit the damaging effects of involvement, above all the prime danger – dependence on the donor?

At this point it is worth remembering Peter Blau's classic model of the four strategies by which one can avoid or extract oneself from dependence on a third party. These strategies for independence – or 'de-dependence', if one could entertain such a term – are the following: (1) supply inducements which make the donor equally dependent; (2) obtain services elsewhere; (3) take by force; (4) do without the particular good provided. For the above to be attempted, the following prerequisites are essential: the existence of strategic resources to induce; availability of alternative sources of supply; coercive capability; an ideological framework justifying 'doing without'.[21]

Some movements can supply inducements, but the inducements are rarely of such a nature as to create interdependence, which is the basis of a lasting mutually advantageous relationship. As for alternative sources of supply, they are hardly ever readily available and free from analogous dangers to the recipient. Coercive capability is even more unrealistic. 'Doing without' is practically impossible.

To conclude, all forms of involvement, in particular third-state involvement on the secessionist side, are fraught with difficulties and tend to be costly to the secessionists. Among the obvious guidelines that one could suggest are that involvement should be pursued only if it is absolutely necessary; that material aid should have as many sources as possible, including aid from parties other than states; and that aid should be sought, to the degree possible, from parties committed for other than sheer economic or political gains that are almost by definition reversible.

Secessionist movements request different things, from different third parties, and in different ways. Several of them appear to be indiscriminate and catch-all in their appeals, and even erratic or arbitrary. However, the inbuilt costs of third-party, in particular state involvement, the limited capabilities of the secessionists, as well as the modest outcome appeals can have, makes most secessionist organizations selective in their choice of target and in the content of their appeals.

The fairly obvious targets for lobbying are the actors supportive of the Centre, or likely to support the Centre in a crucial manner, and parties already supporting the secessionists or one of the rival secessionist fronts. Secessionist movements place special emphasis on the former colonial power (if one exists), on neighbouring states, regional powers, the superpowers, well-known arms suppliers, organizations and states with vested interests in the region, relief organizations, prestigious international non-governmental organizations (INGOs), the regional international governmental organization and the United Nations. In most cases there is little contact with other separatist or revolutionary organizations in the vicinity, for fear of damaging the secessionist case by giving it too radical a hue and complicating or even downplaying the case by presenting it as one of many that have to be resolved within a state.

Other primary targets include first of all those that are considered to be within the 'solidarity universe' of the secessionist ingroup because of ethnic or national identity, religion, ideology, language, culture, race or history. Then there are those that are seen as likely supporters because they are well-known historical enemies of the Centre. This is the celebrated dictum of Kautilya: that the enemy of one's enemy is one's friend. Third, are parties that have supported secessionist or other liberation movements or who are known to be assertive and likely to use unorthodox methods. Such parties could be revolutionary or radical states, leaders known to be mavericks, or governments known for their eagerness to play a dynamic role in world affairs. Fourth, are parties that have a tradition of giving relief aid or mediating in armed conflicts. Fifth, are states that happen to be accessible for lobbying or international or regional centres from which larger audiences can be reached. Of course, parties that are sought after obviously include those who have indicated a degree of concern for the armed conflict at stake or who have explicitly voiced their sympathy for the secessionist plight.

In the selection of targets and in the acceptance of material aid, secessionist organizations are in fact more often than not pragmatic in their approach. They will accept aid even from disreputable sources. It is regarded as far greater folly to shun forthcoming aid from a disreputable source for the sake of an impeccable image or ideological purity than it is to accept such aid with its possible adverse consequences. Of course shady dealings are kept as secret as possible. The Centre is obviously keen to oblige. Equally, foreign journalists are in search of a story. However, the centre may lose its credibility by crying wolf too often, and at times inadvertently precipitate involvement by a third party by publicizing the secession and pointing to the logic of support by a particular third state.

Secessionist movements confronted by allegations of unholy dealings can react (and have generally reacted) in three fundamental ways. The most common method is simply to reject the accusations out of hand, as preposterous fabrications of the enemy (the 'desperate' and 'unscrupulous' Centre). Another characteristic, though less common, reaction is the blatant assertion that when the struggle is for sheer survival and self-determination, then even 'uniting with the devil' – Mazzini's memorable call for the unification of Italy in the previous century – is justified. 'A drowning man clings to a serpent' (as the commander of the Ottoman army had put it in the 1830s when the Sublime Porte was under dire threat and asked its arch-enemy Russia for aid) and can hardly be blamed for it. A third more common reaction is to embark upon some form of rationalization.

Justification through rationalization is essential for internal purposes (group identity, ideology, cohesion, morale), and is not only a question of international propaganda. Calling in the 'devil', say South African or white mercenaries, in an African context, is incompatible not only with the image and ideology which a movement wants to project, but also with its actual avowed beliefs and very identity. Thus the third reaction – rationalization – can also be seen as a sincere attempt to resolve 'belief dilemmas' and achieve a balance between the components of attitudes, beliefs and behaviour.

Belief dilemmas can be resolved by one of four modes of rationalization: denial, bolstering, differentiation and transcendence.[22] With denial, the attributed quality of the referent is repudiated. It is claimed that they are not in fact anti-communist, anti-white, anti-black or whatever. Bolstering does not eliminate the imbalance but only reduces it by way of introducing novel variables. It can be used to indicate that there has not been any degeneration of the secessionists' image or ideology. The rationale is of the following type: the purity of a liberation movement is in no way endangered by a strict business arrangement, or that interaction will change the other side for the better. (The other side will 'see the light' and be infused by virtue, as it were.) The technique of differentiation splits the referent into two parts, one of which is acceptable. For a secessionist situation, for example, the donor could be said to have good elements as well; and it is only with those – so the argument runs – that the secessionists do business. Transcendence, the fourth device, attempts to override the incongruence by placing the issue within a wider perspective, such as, say, that of a common struggle of the small states against attempts at intrusion by large or extra-regional states, or the big powers.

At first glance it seems that the devil acknowledgement, which sounds cynical, or the rejection, which fails to convince all but a few, are more appropriate solutions than the above attempts at moral alchemy and sophistry. But such a course is not always practicable. For denial to stick it must be plausible and defensible – which is rarely the case, for the Centre can muster more resources and have greater influence over third parties and world opinion. As for the devil approach, it is not always handy, for it can annoy a sponsor, despite the existence of a tacit understanding in such matters between the secessionists and the secretive sponsor.

Pragmatism in the selection of targets and acceptance of third-party aid calls for a diffuse or flexible ideology. However, few secessionist movements can hope to cause a stir internationally and attract wholehearted internal support by being ideologically slippery and uncommitted to a particular type of future society. The foundations of the future should be laid during the phase of the 'liberation struggle', – or so run the present-day nationalist myths. Thus, the professed ideology cannot but be a double-edged sword, both an asset and a scourge which separatists cannot do without.

The main techniques of persuasion in the secessionist repertoire are publicizing the case (that is propaganda), and positive and negative sanctions. The first technique evokes the affective and intellectual components of a third actor, while sanctions call for utilitarian considerations, that is, for calculations of costs and benefits.

Propaganda is used by secessionist movements at times with far greater skill and improvisation (in spite of their limited resources) than by governments, so much so that it can even backfire as being far too artful – as in the case of Biafra. This emphasis on publicizing the case, which is one of the basic functions of secessionist activity, is not unrelated to the obvious fact that it is after all secessionists who seek substantive change, including territorial change, which will *inter alia* affect other states as well, and the international system. Putting one's case across is thus of paramount importance.

Secessionist propaganda, like all forms of propaganda is prone to misrepresentation, repetition, persistency and the use of attention-seeking devices and psychological techniques aimed at exploiting the emotions of the target audiences. Falsehood, distortion and misrepresentation are known to be effective techniques, particularly in areas where information is rudimentary to non-existent, and where the pre-existing beliefs are necessarily oversimplified and tentative, based as they are on ambiguous, random and intermittent messages.[23] Of course, there are limits to the degree of distortion of events, as many a secessionist movement has come to appreciate (usually when it is too late). For a secessionist movement to make world-wide impact and attract the informed circles in third countries it must be in the position to present its case articulately and succinctly, making it appear as factual, rather than as argumentative or manipulative.[24] Inevitably, all forms of propaganda have inbuilt limitations. As with most forms of social communication, propaganda is not unidirectional, but a two-way process.[25] Propaganda which happens to accord with existing predispositions has the effect of strengthening them, whilst the propaganda which runs counter to existing attitudes has the opposite result, of reinforcing the original negative image.[26]

The main thrust of secessionist propaganda is the argument for the case for self-determination (whether it be independence or some extended form of autonomy). The sets of arguments used by secessionist movements are strikingly similar and tend to follow a uniform pattern. This is probably due to the fact that they try to conform to the existing requirements of the international legal system and reply to criticisms which are conventional and legalistic in character. The basic initial arguments of the secessionists are legal and historical: they include the argument of professed separate cultural identity (that they are a nation apart), the argument that they have suffered injustice and discrimination (and perhaps extreme physical violence) at the hands of the Centre, the argument of abortive attempts at a peaceful settlement, the argument of ingroup support and legitimization, the viability of an independent or semi-independent entity, the unwavering resolve for the armed struggle and lastly the argument of continued transactions to the benefit of the former unified state and the larger region. In most secessionist cases there is a tendency to overindulge in blatant sentimentalization and horrendous verbal and pictorial images of the extent of suffering and atrocities sustained by the group. Injustice and related notions, such as discrimination, are also fundamental to the secessionist repertoire, as are legal and historical arguments. The legal and historical arguments have

42

their counter-arguments and can be more easily undermined. After all, the respective states are the historical victors and are better placed to narrate history and furnish legal facts. Another common secessionist tendency is to present the case as unique and comparable only to anti-colonial liberation movements, that is to self-determination units.

Secessionist organizations try to be as comprehensive as possible in the presentation of their cases, setting forth all the possible arguments, instead of limiting themselves to those particularly suited to their case. In their eagerness to meet requirements and touch a responsive chord in their target's apparatus, they attempt to gear their line of argument and image to their audience – a tendency which at times borders on the ludicrous. Secessionist cases are presented by way of two basic variations: one is intended for parties without any pre-existing affective ties, those likely to be convinced by the merits, the justice of the case; the other is for those within the solidarity universe of the secessionists, that is those with ethnic, religious, cultural, linguistic, historical, racial or ideological affinities. For the first group the argument tends to go thus: 'We have a just case; you are well known to be principled champions of justice, therefore you will support us for justice to triumph and in order to create a more just and peaceful world.' For the latter category the argument is tinged with the suffering of a brother people: 'Your brothers are on the verge of being culturally extinguished and are victimized daily by aliens; our struggle is your struggle; it is your moral duty to intervene; abstention is a dereliction of duty.'

Whatever the merits of the secessionist case, the soundness of the arguments or the skill and credibility of secessionist ambassadors at large, secessionist fronts are handicapped by the very fact of being secessionist. Yet they do have one thing to their advantage: the propensity of man to side at times with the weak in a struggle and to attribute to the underdog a greater moral standing.[27]

Tangible inducements and negative sanctions are also fairly common persuasion techniques used by secessionist movements, mainly for third parties more likely to be convinced by instrumental rather than affective reasons.[28]

Over the years, secessionists have used an array of rewards or promises, perhaps realizing that they can be more effective than negative sanctions.[29] More convincing are inducements whose payment takes place on the spot, as it were, or whole reward is realizable in the immediate future and not linked with the independence or extended autonomy of the region in question. But few such regions, even those that are relatively advanced and rich, are wealthy enough to pay on the spot. Thus most secessionist organizations over-indulge in promises that seem hollow or a preposterous sell-out, or in undertakings which give them little credibility and of course limited influence. Most common forms of inducement are financial contributions, economic concessions, strategic concessions, political alignment, direct or indirect military assistance against the third parties' enemies, financing the third parties' allies, financing important projects and investment in third states, concessions to educationalists, missionaries and others, and promises in religious and cultural fields.

One reason for not over-indulging in the use of inducements is the well-known fact that, if they succeed, then 'payment' has to be made. The opposite is the case with negative sanctions; when they are successful the threat is simply not implemented.[30] This payment factor dampens the tendency to use inducements. Another problem with inducements is that they are often regarded by the other party as no more than disguised threats – the other side of the same coin. In addition, a promise to reward implies a threat of no reward if the other party fails to comply.[31] Another pitfall of inducements occurs when they are inappropriate in character. This applies to third parties more likely to intervene due to affective reasons. If such actors are given 'money' instead of appreciation their willingness and enthusiasm for support or mediation may decrease.[32] Finally, inducements should not fall short of expectations, and the target should be in urgent need of the particular reward; at best the target party should be interlinked and interdependent with the secessionist movement or its territory.[33]

Threats to deter or punishments to compel third parties to act in the way desired by the secessionists have also been made use of, particularly by rich territories. Using such methods is also part of the tough image secessionists are keen to project, which makes them appear as demanding rather than as pleading or selling out. The most common among the various negative sanctions used are sheer military force, or the threat of force; castigating a third party as hypocritical and immoral, exposing various alleged dealings of third parties, various actual or threatened curtailments (impoundings, nationalizations, mobilizations, closures, suspensions of activity and others); detention and imprisonment of personnel, hostage-taking, damage to property and installations, various forms of blackmail, etc., as well as more subtle techniques such as threats of realignment, switching sponsors and abandoning a patron who has capitalized on the secessionists, and the like. In secessionist as well other revolutionary situations, strong-arm tactics and scorched earth policies can be fairly credible, particularly if the movement is known to favour such tactics or to be desperate for a breakthrough.

Negative sanctions are often not convincing for a variety of reasons in secessionist as well as in other situations of conflict. The threat may

44

simply not be registered by the target, due to a communication problem. It may be misperceived or the sanction may be so severe or outrageous that it is not credible to the target. The secessionists may be regarded as bluffing, particularly if they are known to be unwilling or unable to proceed with the sanction. Another important reason is if the gains for non-conformity override the costs. Equally, the target party may be able to counter-pose an even greater and far more credible threat to the secessionists, or may be capable of avoiding detection and deceiving the secessionists.

Secessionist movements, particularly in their early stages, cannot construe credible threats which run to the very heart of their target. 'Compellence' (administering the punishment until compliance takes place)[34] when applied can have serious repercussions, making the secessionists appear as blackmailing and as terrorists. A 'carrot and stick' strategy may perhaps be more effective, but can rarely be used with conviction by secessionist organizations against an independent state. In addition, when applied, it is a strategy highly likely to create resentment and only temporary rather than reliable commitments.[35]

On the whole, it is true to say that inducements and negative sanctions are risky and rarely effective for the secessionists, particularly when they are obvious and direct. However, blatant and abortive inducements and negative sanctions do have at least one merit: they are a sign of great commitment on the part of the secessionists, which indicates that they are ready to take great risks and endanger values. It is a signal that the stakes have risen, a cry that the movement is *in extremis*.

Having pointed out some of the important features of secessionist international activity, it is now time to move on to an examination of the features of international involvement.

INTERNATIONAL INVOLVEMENT IN SECESSIONIST MOVEMENTS

The international system can influence internal wars in three different ways: by diffusion and encouragement, by isolation and suppression, and by reconciliation. Historically, there have existed four basic types of relationships between external parties and the two parties in conflict: what can be called 'international civil war', in which both parties receive external state support; the case of a 'holy alliance' where there is universal or great power support for the Centre; a 'concert', where third parties attempt to find a peaceful solution; and 'abstention', that is, refusal to become involved at all.[1]

TYPES OF INVOLVEMENT

In practice, third parties can be involved in a secessionist war as intermediaries; as partisan supporters of the movement as a whole; as supporters of one of the secessionist fronts, while being hostile or indifferent towards the others; and, of course, as favourable towards, or actively supportive of, the central government threatened by a secessionist movement.

Non-involvement, or passive neutrality, is almost impossible to attain, particularly with regard to universal or regional political IGOs which have a member state plunged in a war of secession. For them, as well as for many states, non-involvement is, in the oft-quoted remark of Talleyrand, a mysterious word not substantially different from involvement. Neutrality can be regarded as an actual policy of genuine non-involvement only with regard to states, regional political IGOs or INGOs concerned with other issues, geographically distant or possessing limited capabilities.

States, and to a somewhat lesser extent IGOs, have considerable difficulty appearing as honest brokers, as equidistant intermediaries. In most instances the secessionist front is not even considered an *interlocuteur valable* by the Centre. Therefore, seeking to mediate is considered a hostile act of interference (as with Nkrumah's attempt to mediate in the Sudanese secessionist war, or the initial reaction of Lagos to pressure for talks on the part of other African states during the secession of Biafra). The great difference in military capability is also a decisive factor weighing against third-party mediation, as the Centre believes it can subdue the secessionists by military means. The very nature of the conflict as seen by the Centre – one of vital interests such as territorial integrity, viability, authority and state prestige – makes the Centre strenuously resist external mediatory involvement as long as it can.[2] When talks do take place, following third-party mediation, the objective is rarely conflict settlement. For the Centre, but also to some degree for the secessionists, the aim is rather to produce 'side effects',[3] such as gaining valuable time, appearing conciliatory, improving intelligence gathering, publicizing their respective cases and discrediting the adversary.

When third parties fail in their attempts at talks, or when the talks are abortive, mediation is almost invariably perceived as partial. The Centre will see it as a form of recognition and legitimization of its adversary and as a ploy intended to freeze military activities for the benefit of the secessionists in order to save them from defeat. The secessionists, for their part, think it is intended to present the Centre as conciliatory and to give the Centre time so as to consolidate its position.

As Oran Young has pointed out, for a third party to be able to present itself as an intermediary it must, to begin with, appear as impartial, independent, salient to both parties involved, and be able to command their respect. These qualities should be reinforced by the personal qualities of the individuals who undertake such a role.[4] For mediation to take place for other than its side effects, it should be attractive to both parties, or at least attractive to one party, with the other going along on the basis that rejection would be unwise or too great an affront to the mediating third party. States which seek to act as intermediaries are of course aware that they are treading on thin ice, and usually start by presenting their good offices quietly and privately. Privately or publicly, the formula is usually of the following type: we want to mediate, both parties should arrive at a peaceful settlement on the basis of the territorial integrity of the state in question with due consideration to the substantive grievances of the secessionists which gave rise to the conflict. Yet even this formula can be repudiated without much ado by one or both of the parties concerned. This can occur if their positions are still wide apart. The Centre does not admit the importance and legitimacy of the separatist claims and the secessionists have not mellowed as yet, still being convinced that independence is attainable. The offer can also be repudiated if one (or both) of the parties in conflict have not fully assessed the costs of the armed confrontation, or because the actual costs of the armed violence have not yet reached a totally unacceptable level.

A third party can be considered partisan to the secessionists if its activity is intended to enhance, or has the effect of enhancing, the secessionist position, even if it is not clear whether the actual motivation to buttress the secessionist movement exists. What may cause problems, among other things, is if a third party supports one front of a secessionist movement, while it is decidedly hostile to another front or organization of the very same movement.

Partisan third parties are formally independent or autonomous actors. If they are not states, IGOs or their respective sub-units,[5] they are to be considered as third parties if their actions are voluntary, unpaid, or paid only nominally by the secessionists or their allies, and if it can be presumed that their activity is distinct and is regarded as such by the parties concerned.

There have been historical cases of truly unpaid volunteers,[6] perhaps the best-known post-war case being that of Count von Rosen in Biafra. On the whole, however, armed individuals, gunrunners and gundealers would fall foul of their distinguished profession should they choose, for whatever reason, to shun the lure of the almighty dollar and take to running a charity show for the destitute revolutionaries and separatists of this world. Of course the odd mercenary, well paid and well fed, like the notorious Rolf Steiner of Biafran and Southern Sudanese (and other) renown can always claim (which incidentally he did, and convinced nobody) that he was unpaid,[7] and hence independent. Other so-called independent volunteers are in fact no more than puny agents of a state or organization as in the classic case of the Belgian officers in Katanga during 1960–61.

Partisan involvement is basically of two kinds: tangible involvement or support and political–diplomatic or moral support. The second kind of partisan support is more congenial to governments (states) and political IGOs, and only to a few INGOs with great moral standing. The two types of involvement can exist independently of each other, although it is more rare to find political–diplomatic support on its own without some kind of tangible assistance, however meagre.

Tangible involvement can be seen as consisting of three types of material support: utilitarian aid or material aid, aid by way of access (access aid), and assistance by way of services rendered within or outside the secessionist terrain.[8] Some escalation ladders of aid to insurgents in general have been suggested, such as an eight-step ladder by Richard Little, which also includes verbal support, and more recently one by Bertil Duner which includes six echelons.[9] The exigencies of a secessionist war could be covered, among others, by an eight-step ladder, as follows:

1. simple transactional involvement;
2. humanitarian involvement;
3. non-military involvement;
4. military involvement without the inclusion of personnel;
5. involvement by personnel in a non-military capacity;
6. foreign combat unity nominally under a secessionist command;
7. direct military confrontation of a limited scale;
8. full-scale military intervention (invasion, war).

The last four steps can be regarded as intervention, that is, as 'physical' involvement.[10]

Political–diplomatic support includes verbal public statements, diplomatic pressure on the Centre and its allies, voting in IGOs, official contacts with the secessionists, etc. The most easily discernible forms of diplomatic support are verbal statements, which can range from an indication of concern for the war to *de jure* recognition of a secessionist entity, or recognition of a liberation movement. In this instance, a five-step escalation ladder can be outlined, as follows:

1. expression of humanitarian concern;
2. call for a negotiated settlement between the central government and the rebels without jeopardizing the territorial integrity of the state;
3. call for open-ended peace talks between the two parties concerned;
4. clear statement that the secessionists have the right to self-determination;
5. recognition of secessionists as a state or as a liberation movement.

Conventional wisdom holds that tangible support is far more important than political support. Words are cheap and readily available.[11] Admittedly, tangible support is crucial in a war of secession, in particular high-level assistance and material aid. However, political support and recognition are also highly coveted goals, particularly for a secession *stricto sensu*. Ultimately, it is numerous recognitions that will transform a secessionist entity (a unilaterally-declared state contravening the strict self-determination principle) into a state, despite the tenets of the declaratory approach. Interestingly, third states partisan to secessionists are more likely to provide high-level material support than high-level diplomatic support such as recognition. Apparently, for third states, the utterance of such 'words' is not regarded as 'cheap'.

THE INVOLVEMENT AND DILEMMAS OF STATES

Third parties that are states are the most effective of the various actors involved in secessionist situations. State partisan involvement can be the crucial factor, not only for the success, or relative success of a secessionist movement, but also for its failure.

Governments reacting negatively to secessionist appeals can either lack the capacity or the motivation (or both) to respond.[12] They can be either wholly unsympathetic or hostile to the particular secessionists, or otherwise consider involvement, or the kind, scope, level or magnitude of involvement requested, impracticable, unwise or untimely.

Sympathetic governments can withhold aid because it is too costly. Economic ties, including trade and investment with the state threatened by secession, are important impediments – the more so if there is some level of economic dependence or other form of dependence. Involvement may be controversial domestically, particularly if there are no obvious tangible gains or if the majority, or an important segment within that state is aligned to the state fighting a war of secession due to cultural, religious, linguistic, racial or other affinities. An important domestic constraint is the fear of a demonstration effect or cries of double standards – assisting other minorities, while rejecting self-determination or minority rights to one's own minorities. The fear of retribution and reprisals by the state threatened by secession is another major impediment, particularly if that state is powerful. Apart from armed clashes, an intervening state can run the gauntlet of attempts at destabilization by its neighbour. There are also the dangers of fishing in one's neighbours ethnic waters when one is equally vulnerable and thus likely to face retribution along the same lines. The possible international repercussions are also an important consideration in such circumstances, particularly the damage to close relations with traditional allies, or with states with which cordial relations have been forged gradually through years of effort.

Other factors weighing the scale against support are if the case for self-determination has serious flaws, if the secessionist movement is elusive or far too ambitious and, perhaps most importantly, if the insurgents appear far too weak militarily. Particularly if the movement is of doubtful legitimacy, riddled by warring factions, or does not appear to be economically viable as an independent state, it would be unattractive to prospective sponsors who would not relish the idea of supporting *ad infinitum* a politically and economically non-viable state. In still other cases secessionist appeals for aid may simply be inappropriate or unwise, as when a particular third state is already involved as a mediator or should preferably be kept in reserve as a future potential mediator.

Less evident, but no less important, are more abstract international systemic considerations which suggest non-involvement, limited involvement, or highly secretive involvement. Systems and relationships within

50

systems at other levels have shown a considerable degree of boundary maintenance by almost uniform adherence to rules of conduct based on social expectancy. In experimental settings individuals and groups have been induced to act against their own judgement or contrary to their own moral principles, in order to conform with the latent and unspecified, but clearly suggested social expectancy of a particular situation. Furthermore, the imminent destruction of one protagonist need not incite involvement, as seen in the well-known case of 'bystander apathy'.[13]

The extent to which explanations and causal links at one level can be applied to other levels of human relations is methodologically problematic, if not totally unacceptable. But it can supply useful insights if used with care as an illustration if similar and revealing parallels exist at other levels of interaction. Among the hypotheses that one can find particularly useful and applicable at the international level with regard to secessionists are the following. First, the existence of norms of social expectancy among the occupants or actors of a system of relationships, that is the predominance of 'role' and of 'the situation' over the individual inclinations of particular decision-makers. Second, is the element of risk which points to non-involvement so as not to endanger the survival of the actor considering intervention. Lastly, it appears that the greater the number of 'onlookers' the greater the diffusion of responsibility for the fate of the victimized.

One of the cardinal principles of international legitimacy in the international system is non-involvement by one member in the internal affairs of another member of the system. This ban is even greater when reinforced by analogous rules in regional organizations. It is thus hardly surprising that states supporting secessionist movements are invariably regarded as deviant and have to go to great lengths to justify their action. It is obvious that any state on its own, however powerful it may be, cannot easily defy the will of the other states. Individual sympathy for the secessionists is often submerged under the general will, which upholds the territorial integrity of independent states and condemns disintegration. Even when secessionist movements have a very sound case, such as the East Bengalis in 1971, with their 'mountain of corpses', other states do not feel the moral obligation to intervene individually or collectively or through IGOs, but react with the utmost caution, upholding almost instinctively the territorial integrity of the beleaguered 'sister' state. This had been the case even with India, the third state which at a later stage intervened militarily to assist the secessionist Bengalis of Pakistan.

In spite of the tangible and systemic reasons against involvement in support of secessionist movements a considerable number of states have become involved, though the overwhelming majority only marginally. This involvement can be distinguished into so-called 'push' involvement

51

and 'pull' involvement. The first is the result of an initiative by the intervening party in an attempt to defend its interests, while the second is the outcome of secessionist appeals and lobbying. States that finally do get involved, as C.R. Mitchell has pointed out, are often already there as a result of transactional and affective linkages that predate the armed conflict.[14]

It has been argued that the initial reluctance to support a secessionist movement may weaken, should the separatists formally declare independence.[15] This is only partially substantiated. A number of 'declare' secessions got far less than several 'incremental' secessions.

The motives for involvement, be they partisan or mediatory, have been analytically divided into instrumental (or otherwise utilitarian) reasons on the one hand, and affective reasons on the other. The corresponding involvement has been designated instrumental (or utilitarian) involvement and affective involvement.[16]

Instrumental motives are international political (including general strategic) considerations, short-term and longer-term economic motives, domestic motives (internal political reasons including the demonstration effect fears) and short-term military gains.[17]

Affective involvement in secessionist cases includes reasons of justice (being convinced of the soundness of a case for self-determination, be it for independence or for some form of autonomy), humanitarian considerations, ethnic, religious, racial or ideological affinity and apparently personal friendships between top protagonists.[18] At this juncture it is worth pointing out a distinction made by Herbert Kelman in his theory of persuasion. Kelman differentiated between identification and internalization.[19] Put simply, identification means persuasion based on empathizing, that is, for our purposes, identifying with the secessionist group or its leadership. Internationalization is persuasion derived from the inherent value of the claim, that is (for our concerns) the merits of the case for autonomy, independence or generally self-determination.

The basic axiom of instrumental or utilitarian involvement is that for risk-taking to be worthwhile, gains should outweigh costs. Ideally gains should be as cheap as possible, that is a large return for a small outlay. An instrumental gain or advantage can be literally 'payable on the spot', more or less as a business transaction. Then there are long-term gains and advantages, where payment is linked with the future independence of the 'grateful' independent state. A different situation that is not uncommon, is when third states gain simply by the fact that the armed conflict continues indefinitely sapping at their adversary's resources and diverting its military forces. Equally, aid can be used as a bargaining counter. In such cynical exercises, the independence of the secessionists or their reconciliation with the Centre is resisted by the patron.

The general tendency among commentators is that instrumental motivation tends to override affective reasons for involvement. Put differently, there can be exclusive instrumental motivation devoid of affective elements while affective motivation cannot stand on its own. Interestingly and predictably, intervening governments maintain precisely the opposite: that involvement on their part is completely lacking in any utilitarian considerations or ulterior motives; that it is based solely on the inherent justice of the case or on humanitarian concern.

According to the first view, the motive of all involvement is instrumental; all else is embellishment and window-dressing for various audiences. Thus, even in cases where involvement on religious, cultural, racial or even ethnic grounds makes sense, it is considered no more than a means to placate public opinion or gain a diplomatic point over another state. The essence is again instrumental. The same applies to professed reasons of justice or humanitarian considerations. The aim, it is claimed, is not humanitarian, or justice *per se*, but enhancing prestige, attempting to present oneself as virtuous or wanting to project a dynamic image or a willingness to act independently, irrespective of the economic sacrifices. Moreover, it is argued that it could not be otherwise, for tangible gains are after all what foreign policy is supposed to be about, what decision-makers are expected to pursue in the furtherance of national interest within an 'anarchic world society'. Put differently, governments will simply be unable to sell a policy of supporting secessionists if there are no obvious gains involved. Indeed, unprofitable involvements may even put their own tenure on power at risk.

The opposite view, that affective motivation is more common in involvements in secessions, can be reinforced by the need for cognitive consistency between actions and beliefs, behaviour and self-image. Even if, to begin with, the motives are purely instrumental in nature, the need for cognitive consistency may bring about a metamorphosis through continuous rationalizations and justifications. This can generate a dynamic of its own and continue, irrespective of gains or losses. Of course it could also be that support does not stop because the third party has invested so much in the secessionists that it does not want to give up before gaining some dividends.

In practice one can consider involvement as affective *prima facie* if it does not appear to fulfil or fulfils only marginally economic, political, domestic or military interests.

INTERNATIONAL GOVERNMENTAL AND
NON-GOVERNMENTAL ORGANIZATIONS

International Governmental Organizations (IGOs) are in general averse or indifferent towards secessionist movements. Until now the UN has intervened drastically only once, and in that case decidedly against a secessionist movement (in Katanga in the early 1960s). Regional political IGOs, such as the Association of South East Asian Nations (ASEAN) or the Organization of African Unity (OAU) tend to stand aloof, though they have not always been able to avoid discussions on the issue.

The potential for involvement by regional political IGOs exists when the state threatened by secession is not a member-state. Such IGOs have, of course, less influence than they would have had if the state in question was their member. The Organization of the Islamic Conference mediated in the case of the Moros and to some extent showed interest in the Eritreans and in the Turkish Cypriots. The League of Arab States, though guarded and 'correct', is not indifferent to the Eritrean plight. This was not apparent with other secessionist movements with better cases, such as Bangladesh and Kurdistan whose adversaries happened to be members of such IGOs. A qualified exception to this unmistakable trend is the case of Biafra, where the Commonwealth Secretariat as well as the OAU attempted to mediate on more than one occasion. (Note, however, that the secessionist Biafrans did not regard the OAU, or for that matter the Commonwealth Secretary-General, as impartial, but as decidedly against them.)

United Nations agencies, such as UNICEF or the UNHCR, have given relief aid but only in rare cases have such 'functional' IGOs been prepared to follow the unorthodox procedure of direct humanitarian aid to the secessionists without having secured the Centre's explicit, or even its tacit, approval.

The OAU position in matters such as intervention, territorial integrity and non-acceptance of the right of self-determination to secessionists does not diverge from that of the UN. In fact the OAU, as the IGO most confronted by secessionist claims, is even more firmly committed to the orthodox principles of international legitimacy. Any redrawing of African boundaries is considered totally unacceptable.[20] African unity is based on the self-determination of 'peoples', yet in practice 'territorial revision' is considered 'inconsistent with African Unity',[21] and its acceptance a 'major setback for unity'.[22] Indeed, any conflict away from the 'major task' – that of liberating Black Southern Africa and until the 1970s, Portuguese Africa – has been considered by the OAU and most African states an almost 'frivolous diversion from the central business'.[23] According legitimacy to the ethnic principle is seen as weakening the case against the partition of South Africa on ethnic grounds (the Bantustan scheme).[24] But probably the most important reason for this posture is the one that Nigeria put forward when warning Biafra's supporters: that all African states have their potential 'Katanga' or 'Biafra'. Thus, on the issue of secession there is unprecedented uniformity between conservative and radical African states. All stand against secession ('against balkanization') appearing to manipulate the principle of African unity for the status quo. Today, as a result, the OAU appears to many to be more of an 'alliance' of states to preserve the status quo and the rule of established governments, than a 'movement' as it was originally conceived.[25]

With the exception of the Biafran case, the OAU had meticulously avoided becoming involved in the other major secessionist wars of the continent.[26] It is also worth remembering that, even prior to the creation of the OAU, African states were not prepared to recognize secessionist entities as seen in particular in the case of the Katanga secession, which had no lack of sympathizers among African governments. In the mid-1960s when most of Africa was independent and the OAU formed, the African sub-system indicated a tendency to pursue, whenever possible, 'intrasystem solutions' over 'extrasystem solutions to African problems'.[27] Apparently, this trend was more evident in the 1960s and early 1970s than it is today.[28]

One can distinguish three types of non-governmental organizations (NGOs) which can be involved as partisans of secessionist movements:

1. transnational associations or international non-governmental organizations (INGOs);
2. domestic non-governmental organizations; and,
3. non-governmental organizations based in third states.

Domestic non-governmental organizations active in the secessionist region – the region under effective secessionist authority, or in the area claimed by the secessionist movement or active in other regions of the state – include, among others, settler organizations and groups, expatriate priests and missionaries and political organizations active in the state threatened by secession.

Non-governmental organizations active in third states consist of pre-existing or *ad hoc* cause groups created with the purpose of assisting the secessionists and generating a lobby.

For the most part NGOs supporting secessionist movements are non-profit-making institutions, though profit-making organizations have also appeared in exceptional cases in connection with separatists. Probably the best-known example to date of the latter is the case of the Union Minière du Haut Katanga, which was deeply involved in the secession of Katanga from Congo–Leopoldville (Zaïre). Among the non-profit-making institutions that have been involved through the years in secessionist situations, or who have lobbied to support secessionists, are human rights or minority rights organizations such as Amnesty International or the Minority Rights Group; relief organizations such as the International Committee of the Red Cross, Oxfam or Caritas Internationalis (the relief agency of the Roman Catholic Church); quasi-juridical groups such as the International Commission of Jurists; churches such as the Roman Catholic Church or the Anglican Church; religious organizations such as the World Council of Churches or the World Muslim League; missionary orders such as the Verona Fathers or the Holy Ghost Fathers; cause groups other than human rights groups, such as the Movement for Colonial Freedom or the ultra-conservative John Birch Society in the US; scientific institutions such as the Institute of Race Relations in London and of course various political parties and revolutionary groups. The latter include the armed secessonist fronts of another secessionist movement in the same or another state and pure revolutionary movements seeking power from the Centre.

NGOs can be involved as outright partisan supporters, as supporters in a subtle manner or even as mediators, as so-called 'unofficial diplomats'. Unofficial diplomats can move with greater ease than governments or IGOs, avoiding cries of *parti pris* and not embarrassing the government threatened by separatism. Their lack of clout is often compensated for by their discreet approach, their greater access and their potential to follow more effective novel approaches than those of the traditional arbitrator, conciliator or mediator. They can be the initiators of contacts and then act as moderators or as supportive consultants within a problem-solving framework. Today, given the notorious ineffectiveness of IGOs in inter-state as well as intra-state conflicts, NGOs may become more and more involved than had been previously the case.[29]

Profit-making organizations of a transnational character are by definition involved for reasons of profit or long-range interests. The official justification for involvement is that helping the secessionists is the price they must pay to stay in business. Non-profit-making NGOs intervening as intermediaries, or partisan supporters of the secessionists, do so ostensibly for reasons linked with the aims of the organization, be they religious, revolutionary, political, or humanitarian. Relief agencies are faced with the dilemma of not being able to perform their task without being characterized as supportive of the secessionists. The dilemma is far greater for the International Committee of the Red Cross (ICRC) which is, by its very statute, neutral and impartial. Most relief agencies take the view (at least officially) that their aid – when administered to secessionist-held territory – is purely humanitarian and not political. But as one researcher of NGO humanitarian intervention has put it, somewhat bluntly, such a distinction is propaganda.

Once a relief agency bypasses the central authority, it can perform, perhaps altogether unwittingly, several of the following functions, as pointed out by Laurie Wiseberg:

1. according legitimacy to the secessionists by dealing with them directly;
2. providing moral support;
3. publicizing the secessionist case by their appeals for funds for the starving or displaced or refugees;
4. providing directly or indirectly the secessionist movement with medicine, food, funds, currency or perhaps even fuel or means of transportation or communication, as a result of their inability to control the final destination of their supplies or the precise use of their funds;
5. serving as a cover for arms shipments;
6. providing access to the outside world.[30]

In practice relief operators often become personally involved with the plight of the secessionist population. Personally involved and committed are also, of course, the expatriate missionaries and the settlers, both of whom have vested interests to protect.

We have described above some of the salient features which characterize the international relations of secessionist movements. We have also discussed the normative framework in which these movements find themselves, and have traced the etiology of secession and separatism in general. It is now time to examine specific cases of secessionist movements in order to provide a clearer picture of the issues at stake and the dynamics involved.

5

KATANGA
(July 1960 – January 1963)

Le Katanga, pays d'ordre et de paix... a déclaré son indépendance
... uniquement pour échapper à l'esclavage et à la misère qui
furent partout les conséquences de l'emprise communiste et pour
que son peuple reste libre, dans un monde libre.

[L]e gouvernement Katangais n'hésiterait pas à modifier radicale-
ment sa politique à l'égard de la Belgique et à abandonner la
sollicitude constante qu'il a témoignée pour les intérêts belges...
avec une sincérité et un courage qui lui ont valu de nombreuses
critiques...

Moise Kapenda Tshombe
President of the State of Katanga

Congo–Leopoldville, the second largest African country, became independent under the name of Zaïre at on 30 June 1960. Eleven days later,
the country's south-eastern province, Katanga (today's Shaba), proclaimed
its independence. The Katanga secession lasted for thirty-one months
and was by far the gravest insurrection of the plethora of armed conflicts
that shook the newly-born state, calling in question the ability of arbitrarily
carved multi-ethnic states to survive and casting an ominous shadow over
the future of post-colonial Africa.

ETIOLOGY

Of all the African states that gained their independence in the 1950s and
1960s the Congo (Zaïre) was probably the least prepared for statehood.
The political parties appeared just a few years before independence – with
the exception of Abako[1] which was formed somewhat earlier – and were
all ethnically or regionally based, including those with a national appeal
such as Patrice Lumumba's Mouvement National Congolais (MNC).
And there was hardly any university graduate in the about-to-become
independent Belgian Congo. As a result, in the mid-1950s even the
African and Belgian harbingers of the eventual independence for the
Belgian Congo placed it at a far more remote date than 1960. Congo's

1. Congo–Leopoldville (Zaïre) and Katanga (Shaba)

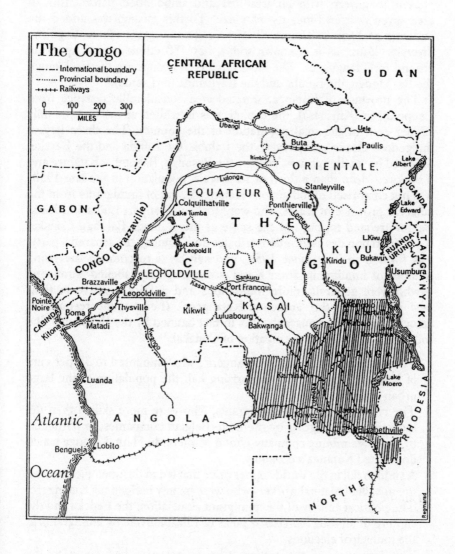

lack of preparedness was due above all else to Belgium, which had chosen to govern with an iron fist and unbounded paternalism an area seventy-seven times its own size. To this mishap was added the endemic problem of almost all African states – great ethnic–linguistic diversity. Zaïre, as it is known today, has 150 ethnic groups speaking around forty languages. The most numerous groups are the Ba-Kongo, the Ba-Mongo, the Baluba and the Ba-Lunda (or Lunda).[2]

The province of Katanga, situated at a considerable distance from Leopoldville (Kinshasa), the capital, was inhabited at the time by only 13 per cent of the total population of the country. The three largest indigenous ethnic groups were the Baluba, the Lunda and the Bayeke, followed by smaller groups, such as the Basonge, Bahemba, Batabwe and Tshokwe. More than a third of Katanga's, population in the late 1950s was not comprised of indigenous Katangese, but of immigrants from the adjacent province of Kasai, who were for the most part Lulua and Kasai Baluba (related to, but not the same as the Katanga Baluba). Conakat (Confédération des associations tribales du Katanga), the separatist party, was formed in November 1958, precisely as a reaction to the rising number of immigrants from Kasai – disparagingly labelled 'strangers' – who were generally more industrious and politically active in their new milieu than the 'authentic Katangese'. (Fedeka, the resourceful association of the immigrants, was in fact banned by the Belgians.) The following factors led to the creation of Conakat:[3]

1. The sheer presence of the 'strangers', who amounted to 38 per cent of Katanga's population, comprising half the population of the large urban centres.
2. The recruitment of the immigrants, who were more skilled than the indigenous Katangese, by the large Belgian companies, in particular by the huge mining company Union Minière du Haut-Katanga which dominated Katanga's economy.
3. A sudden fall in the world copper price that led to the unemployment of the unskilled manual workers who were mainly indigenous Katangese.
4. The political activity of the immigrant association, the Fedeka and the capture of all four *bourgmestre* posts of Elizabethville by immigrants in the municipal elections.
5. The influence of the settlers (the *colons*) who had come to the conclusion that their small number did not permit them to seek a solution similar to that of South Africa or the Rhodesias and that the only way to further their interests was by having native *évolués* spearhead the secession.

The aim of Conakat was the establishment of an 'autonomous and federated state', linked with the Congo, to be governed by 'authentic Katangese and all men of good faith'.[4] Initially, the indigenous Baluba together with a smaller group, the Tshokwe, participated in Conakat, but they soon left to associate themselves with the immigrants and form the Cartel Katangais, commonly known as Balubakat Cartel, which was lead by Jason Sendwe.[5] Conakat's separatism had its basis not only in xenophobia and the assertiveness of the immigrants who threatened their interests, but also in the menace posed by a radical and pro-unitarist central government to be led by Lumumba, Belgium's implacable enemy. Separatism was an inter-ethnic alliance of the Lunda, Bayeke and other conservative ethnic groups, including the Baluba chiefs. Conakat was supported by roughly half the population of Katanga, as seen by the election results of May 1960. To these should be added the *colons*, the Kata-Belges, who formed only 2 per cent of the population, and whose party, Union Katangais, was for a time formally merged with Conakat.[6]

The prospect of future disadvantage under an independent Congo was a major concern. Katanga was by far the richest Congolese province, with its immense mineral resources (the 'geological scandal', the 'Ruhr of Africa'), part of the well-known Copperbelt which continued into the Rhodesias. Conakat and the colonat raised the spectre of the milch cow in a unitary or tightly federal Congo as the one proclaimed by the Loi Fondamentale, the provisional Constitution of the Congo. In Katanga, there were at the time two dominant views within Conakat, one minimalist, the other maximalist. According to the first view, an even split between the provincial and central government, irrespective of percentage of population would suffice. The more ambitious claim was that since the viability of the Congo was hinged on Katanga, it had to become the economic and political pivot of the country.[7]

The precipitants that led Conakat nearer to secession included the following:[8]

1. The departure of the Balubakat (Association des Baluba du Katanga) from Conakat, which allowed a more uninhibited separatist policy and more extended collaboration with the colonat.
2. The total inability to block a unitarist or tight federalist Loi Fondamentale and the frustration of all the Conakat attempts to alter the Loi Fondamentale or at least diminish the control and economic administration of Katanga by Leopoldville.
3. The election results and its repercussions, in particular the rise of Lumumba, Conakat's arch-enemy, to power.
4. The rising influence of the Balubakat Cartel in the Centre and in

61

Elizabethville, which had come very close to Conakat in the elections and, in particular, the appointment of Sendwe, the Cartel leader as High Commissioner for Katanga, which meant that the provincial government's autonomy would be drastically curtailed by Leopoldville.

Lumumba's premiership and Sendwe's posting were the two final events that acted as the *coup de pioche* for secession. From then on for Conakat it was a question of finding the appropriate moment to declare independence. Apparently, at least two attempts were made prior to the independence of the Congo, but both were foiled by the Belgian administration still in command in Elizabethville. After independence, the opportune moment came with the Force Publique Mutiny which led to the Belgian military intervention in the whole of the Congo. Katanga's viability was not in doubt, due to its mineral resources and the assistance of the *colons*. The venture seemed almost assured of success, given the disarray of Leopoldville, the support of the Kata-Belges, the presence of Belgian troops and the final acquiescence of the initially reluctant Union Minière. Belgium also appeared sympathetic and had made the necessary amendment to the Loi Fondamentale to allow Conakat to form a government without the votes of the Cartel Katangais.[9]

In the case of Katanga, the external factor was of paramount importance, far greater than in most other secessionist movements imbued with a degree of ingroup legitimization. It is clear that without the colonat, the Union Minière and Belgium, secession would not have taken place, at least not at that time. Independence had in fact been conceived many years before by Ucol-Katanga (Union pour la colonisation–Katanga), the settler organization headed by a Kata-Belge named Thyssens. Then 'in a process like osmosis', as one author has put it,[10] the goal of independence became common to both *colons* and traditionally-inclined indigenous Katanganese. However, this is not to say that separatism had no African roots.[11] The idea of independence awakened echoes of historical consciousness in several Katangan ethnic groups, many of whom had a history of kingdoms well before the advent of Belgian colonial rule.[12] This Katangese sense of distinctiveness is also evidenced by the fact that the Balubakat Cartel initially followed Conakat on the issue of greater autonomy and greater share in the profits from the mineral resources.

INTERNATIONAL ACTIVITY

Katanga was led by a triumvirate consisting of Moise Kapenda Tshombe, the leader of Conakat, who was named President of the State of Katanga, Godefroid Munongo, named Minister of the Interior and Jean Baptiste Kibwe, dubbed Minister for Finance. Also influential were Evariste

Kimba, the Foreign Minister and two other ministers, Yav (Defence) and Samalenge (Information).[13]

Tshombe was a *primum inter pares* but his leadership was indisputable. His strong points were his image of moderation, his adroit balancing acts and, above all, his ability to deliver the goods indispensable to the secessionist movement due to his good connections among the *colons*, and among various circles in Belgium and elsewhere in the West.[14] The Katangese leaders were also equipped with sound traditional credentials. Tshombe was the son-in-law of the Lunda paramount chief, Munongo was cousin of the Bayeke paramount chief and grandson of Msiri, the dreaded Bayeke king of the nineteenth century.[15]

The moderates were Tshombe and Kimba. They favoured a solution short of complete independence, what came to be known as 'Katangalization'. Munongo, Kibwe and the *colons*, who were generally regarded as 'ultras', favoured independence. The second tendency appeared to be in the ascendency for most of the secession.[16] Katanga's ideology was unashamedly capitalist but with detectable elements of indigenous tradition. Munongo, Conakat's first president, who was apparently involved in Lumumba's death, was known to scorn the Western democratic system, craving for a traditional kingdom of Katanga similar to that of his grandfather, Msiri. For as long as it lasted however, Katanga claimed to be Africa's model of Western democracy.[17]

A special characteristic of Katangese decision-making, which sets it apart from other secessionist movements, is the element of the mainly Belgian settlers, the Katanga *colons*, the *colonat*. Such was the rapport between the Conakat leaders and the *colonat* that the second should be considered for all practical purposes as an integral part of the secessionist movement.

It was only after the declaration of independence that the influence of the *colons* began to diminish as the Katangese became more and more masters of the situation. But they continued to play an active role until they were finally expelled by ONUC (Organisation des Nations Unies au Congo), following a UN Security Council Resolution. The active *colons*, acting as advisers, were distinguished by ONUC into two categories: those *ex officio*, the so-called '*adeuxien*' – from the relevant paragraph (A,2) of the UN Resolution – and the *conseillers occultes*. The Katangese leaders themselves made a distinction between political advisers and 'technical advisers', but admitted privately that all were in fact political advisers. The most influential advisers among the colonat were apparently Tignée and Thyssens, the notorious *conseiller occulte* and head of Ucol-Katanga. In key positions were also overseas Belgians such as Colonel Champion and Major Weber, Professor Clémens (the author of the Katangan Constitution) and

Stuelens, the Katangese representative in New York. A French officer, Colonel Faulques, took over when the Belgian officers had to leave.[18]

From the outset, Katanga's international activity was of the highest level, replete with the trappings of the foreign policy of an independent state. There were four permanent representations abroad. The first to be set up was in Brussels, initially denominated the Katangese delegation to the Common Market (Delperkat) and later the Cultural and Economic Office (Ocekat). A permanent mission was set up in Paris towards the end of 1960, and one was set up in New York, in March 1961 (the Katanga Information Service, Katinfor). A mission was also set up in Brazzaville. There was a permanent liaison post in Usumbura and listening posts in Rhodesia, South Africa and Angola. Communications were coordinated by the Service de la Centralisation et de la Coordination du Renseignement (SCCR). Of great importance to international activity was the Information Division under Samalenge, where *colons* were prominent. Roving ambassadors included Tshombe himself, Kibwe, Kimba, Samalenge, Yav, Tshombe's two brothers, Thomas and Daniel Tshombe, and others.

The international relations of Katanga can be divided into four phases:

1. The Belgian phase, from independence on 11 July 1960 until early October 1960, when Belgian influence reigned supreme.
2. The period from mid-October 1960 until the Tananarive Conference of Conciliation in March 1961, when efforts were made to change patrons, in particular substituting France and French-speaking African states for Belgium.
3. The period of the anti-UN struggle, from the reversal of the Tananarive understanding (in the Coquilhatville Conference) until the presumed abandonment of secession with the Tshombe–Adoula agreement at Kitona in December 1961.
4. The year 1962 until the final collapse in January 1963, a year of feverish attempts to find supporters and counter the United States–UN diplomatic offensive, amidst gradual and steady isolation.

The first phase, Katanga's honeymoon with Belgium, ended, like many a honeymoon, in near divorce. Following the declaration of independence the Katangese embarked upon an ambitious international campaign in several capitals, concentrating mainly on Brussels, in order to secure recognition, more arms and mercenaries. Recognition was not achieved, but UN intervention in Katanga was staved off, and several states, including the United States – later to become Katanga's arch-enemy – made no secret of their sympathy for the secessionists. And the Western press immediately launched Katanga as a *cause célèbre*.[19]

The second phase saw a number of far-reaching changes which heralded worse days to come. The official Belgian contingent under Colonel Champion was replaced by forces of ONUC (Organisation des Nations Unies au Congo), headed by Conor Cruise O'Brien, with the mandate to use force, if necessary, to implement the withdrawal of all foreign political advisers and troops. Lumumba fell from power and was finally put to death by none other than the Katangese themselves. The Baluba took up arms and held the region north of Katanga, the region of Lulualaba, until the end of the secession, in what was in effect a secessionist-merger movement from a secessionist territory. But on the surface the scene looked reassuring enough for the Katanga leadership. Leopoldville, now under President Kasavubu and Mobutu, was so conciliatory towards Elizabethville that there was even talk of an Elizabethville–Leopoldville–Bakwanga (the capital of secessionist South Kasai) axis directed against the rival government of Stanleyville, which had been set up by the Lumumbists under Gizenga. The military power of Katanga was at its peak with the arrival of mercenaries and with Belgian officers heading the Katangese army. In March 1961 Katanga had its moment of supreme triumph at the conference held at Tananarive, Madagascar, where Leopoldville accepted the confederal formula presented by Tshombe. During this period relations with Belgium worsened, but Belgium was still regarded as holding the key to independence.[20]

In the third period the scene changed. The first blow for Katanga came in April 1961 at the second Congo conference held at Coquilhatville. Leopoldville rejected the Tananarive understanding and had Tshombe arrested and detained for two months. ONUC–Katanga became more assertive with three operations (Operations Rumpunch and Morthor in August and September, and a third operation in December 1961) to rid Katanga of the advisers. Relations with Belgium further deteriorated and Elizabethville now relied mainly on the support of the Rhodesians. The chain of events linked with Operation Morthor led to the death of UN Secretary-General, Dag Hammarskjöld, at the Ndola aircrash, and finally to the Kitona agreement of December 1961, when Tshombe appeared to be relinquishing secession. In fact he was once more resorting to a technique for which he was becoming notorious: to appear to consent and then to simply ignore his commitments.[21]

In 1962 Katanga once more rose from the ashes of Kitona only to fall a year later to the UN and Congolese forces with the active support of the Kennedy Administration. The new Secretary-General of the UN, U Thant, abandoned his predecessor's cautious line of non-intervention, launching a plan – originally a United States plan – for economic sanctions if the Katangese continued to defy the government of Leopoldville. As for the Katangese, they persisted with their campaign, aimed at denigrating the UN and the United States in the eyes of the West and threatening a scorched earth policy against Belgium and the Union Minière which by 1962 appeared less enthusiastic in its support.

The end finally came in January 1963. This time there was no last-minute trick available to the wily Katangese leader, though it is worth remembering that he survived, later emerging as Prime Minister of the Congo. Katanga fell to ONUC's 'Operation Grandslam'.[22]

The main thrust of Katanga's propaganda for its case was that Katanga was the 'shield of Africa against communism' and Lumumbism; that it was a model of democratic rule, prosperous and calm (as Tshombe had put it, 'un flot de prospérité et de bonheur au coeur de l'Afrique déchirée'[23]) and, above all, a model case of the ideal relationship and cooperation between Blacks and Whites ('la belle amitié');[24] and that, given its resources, a unitary or tight federal system of government would be unworkable, inevitably leading to Katanga's exploitation by Leopoldville. In contrast with other secessionist movements the Katangese did not use legal or historical arguments to propagate their case. They formulated, however, the other habitual arguments of secessionist movements, such as the legitimization argument (pointing to the election results and the participation of Baluba notables in the secessionist ranks), abortive attempts at peaceful settlement (the 'Tananarive spirit', abused by Leopoldville), and even the physical violence argument – despite the fact that there was little physical contact for most of the time with the Congolese army. In fact the atrocities which were said to be committed by the Baluba in the north of Katanga were identified with Leopoldville. Much was made also of an argument, less prominent in other secessionist movements; which was the argument of the benefits to the region and to Leopoldville of having an independent or confederated Katanga, which would be willing to assist all the states of Central Africa and beyond. Thus several schemes of economic association were presented.[25]

Katanga presented its case smoothly and with fervour, but had considerable difficulty in countering the accusations of its critics. These were, first of all, the role played by Belgium, and Belgian interests, particularly Union Minière and the *colons* – all of which smacked of neocolonialism and made them appear as proxies. Then there was the lack of support on the part of half of Katanga's population under the Balubakat Cartel which had openly rebelled in the northern part of Katanga and was in control there for most of the time, in spite of the punitive operations of the mercenaries. Third, was the scourge of the

66

mercenaries, the so-called '*affreux*' (the atrocious ones). Fourth, was support from disreputable sources such as Welensky and South Africa. Fifth, was the very important consequence of leaving the rest of the Congo economically non-viable and in general the issue of balkanization. Lastly, there was the matter of having been directly involved in the death of Patrice Lumumba, considered to be one of Africa's rising stars.

Katanga of course vehemently denied all the above, and in particular the Belgian and Rhodesian links, responding with bold, often ingenuous arguments. Over the matter of Lumumba's death, however, their claims lacked the usual polish and conviction.[26]

The Katangese were vociferous and, despite being fairly inexperienced to begin with, soon used almost every technique available to persuade sympathizers and dissuade adversaries. More than twenty-five years have elapsed since the Katanga case, but still it presents the most complete set of examples of inducements and negative sanctions ever deployed by a secessionist movement.[27]

Belgium, the primary target until early 1961, was invoked in the early part of the secession by such arguments as 'la belle amitié', common anti-Lumumbism and genuine anti-communism and of course the continuation of the existing economic relationship perhaps even in an institutionalized framework (between Katanga and Belgium or between Belgium and the whole of the Congo with Katanga acting as the guarantor). Such inducements were very early on coupled with threats and castigation. Variations of the main threat, that of realignment, were the following: the union of Katanga with the Rhodesians, the formation of a Central African confederation or community including entities outside Belgian influence, such as neighbouring Tanganyika (a British colony until December 1961) and substituting France, the Federation of Rhodesia, or even Britain, as patrons of Katanga. Such threats were fairly credible for there were traces of such attempts at realignment, most notably with Welensky and the French.

Castigation, the other classic secessionist technique, took the form of exposing Belgium as inconsistent, hypocritical and duplicitous, as instanced in its actions against the recognition of Katanga by other Western states and its attempts to insulate the secessionists from prospective sponsors and investors. Belgium, it was argued, did not honour its commitments and was indirectly supporting Lumumba and his communist allies, thereby running counter to the obvious wishes of the Belgian people and the Belgian king.

With the equivocal policies of the Belgian Foreign Minister, Spaak, which the Katangese deemed hostile acts, the din of threats rose to a crescendo. There were now even threats of destruction of Belgian property and investment. Words led to action. The Belgian consulate was vandalized in one instance, two envoys sent by Spaak were detained and Katanga demanded the removal of the Belgian consul of Elizabethville. Belgian concerns already in Katanga were not allowed to expand any further and their existing activity was curbed.

Appeals to the West in general and the United States in particular made ample use of the communist scare, using first Lumumba and then his heir, Gizenga, as the bogeymen, and presenting the new leadership in Leopoldville as incompetent and totally unable to curb the Lumumbist extremists. As the Kennedy policy evolved, offering full support to ONUC and Leopoldville, the Katangese, with the assistance of the Katanga lobby in the United States, unleashed a vociferous campaign aimed at denigrating both the UN and the Kennedy Administration, which were said to be terrorizing Katanga and handing over the West's 'bastion against communism' to the 'Russians', thus condemning Katanga to be 'the Hungary' of the 1960s. The United States was said to be unscrupulous and far from disinterested. Its motive was for short-term gains, such as eliminating Katanga's copper from the world market and taking over its minerals, particularly those essential for the space and nuclear industries.

The Francophone states of Africa also loomed large in Katanga's list of priorities. The basic objective was to incite the known sympathizers to recognize Katanga, first of all Congo–Brazzaville. For Filbert Youlou, the president of Congo–Brazzaville, two inducements were fairly well established. One was a financial contribution to a campaign of a referendum of great importance to Youlou, and the second, the financing of the huge Kouilou dam scheme, a project linked with the viability of Congo–Brazzaville and the survival of the Youlou regime. In fact, such was the extent of Tshombe's financial assistance to this small African state, that in Brazzaville he was called 'l'oncle à héritage'.[28]

Another highly important target was the Federation of Rhodesia, under the leadership of the outspoken Sir Roy Welensky. There, apart from anti-communism and ideological affinity, much use was made of the prospect of possible future economic and even political union. Financing, an inducement which had become Katanga's trade-mark, was also used. For instance, Tshombe gave financial support to the black African nationalists whom Welensky favoured.

For targets such as France and South Africa, there were, apart from the ideological appeals, various economic incentives.

The Katangese made sure that the Union Minière would keep in line. In fact its activity was restricted, its operation as a near-monopoly questioned, and, more dramatically, there were threats of closing it down altogether and even destroying its installations. Such threats were the speciality of Munongo and Kibwe, but they were soon picked up by Tshombe at a later stage, which obviously gave them greater credibility.

Probably the most successful and consistent strategy was the veritable hate campaign waged against the UN and ONUC. As the assertiveness of ONUC grew and there was no recognition, Katangan statements bordered on the hysterical. The total destruction of Katanga was threatened. Interestingly, this threat of mutual destruction was not completely devoid of credibility, for the Katangese appeared to be *in extremis*. Furthermore, as one author has put it, 'who could calculate the rationality of Munongo? Who could be certain one of the "ultras" in the European community might not find this melodramatic gesture profitable?'[29]

However, one particular threat of the Katangese was certainly not credible. This was Munongo's outburst in 1961 that they were prepared to switch immediately to the Soviet Union should the West not commit itself forthwith and with the incredible claim that this was no 'facile or perfunctory blackmail'.[30]

Rich Katanga was always suspected of using one more technique – bribery. At least one case did gain publicity. This was the attempt at bribery of Costa Rican officials for Costa Rica to recognize Katanga.[31]

INTERNATIONAL INVOLVEMENT

Belgium and the Union Minière were the main patrons of the Katanga secession. Others that supported the secessionists enthusiastically were the short-lived Federation of Rhodesia and Nyasaland and Congo–Brazzaville. Several conservative circles in the West and in Africa were sympathetic, and France, South Africa, Portuguese Angola and, in more guarded form, Britain provided support, diplomatic as well as material. Less decisive in the fall of Katanga were the radical African and Non-Aligned states. Of crucial importance were the UN and the Kennedy Administration which forged close links with Leopoldville, whose government they had been instrumental in setting up at the Lovanium Assembly in August 1961.

The involvement of Belgium can be distinguished into four phases, the first two of which correspond to the first two phases of Katanga's international relations. First, is the period of unreserved support, which stopped short only of recognition and of full-scale military intervention

69

against Leopoldville (akin, say, to India's intervention in support of secessionist Bangladesh in December 1971). In the second period, which lasted until the Belgian change of government in the spring of 1961, Belgium was more restrained and was accused by Tshombe of playing a 'double game' – supporting both parties in the conflict. The third period of involvement saw a gradual disengagement from Katanga which lasted until as late as November 1962. Finally, towards the end of the secession, relations had reached such a low level that they bordered on hostility.

During the first phase, and for most of the second, arms were involved, including combat and transport aircraft, spares, finance, foodstuffs, etc., and the Belgian troops that had intervened prior to the secession were placed at the disposal of Katanga, thus insulating the secessionists from the threat of the Congolese Army. When the Belgian troops left Katanga, Belgian officers seconded by the Ministry for African Affairs headed the Katanga Army (the Gendarmerie). Aid was channelled by Mistebel (Mission technique belge) headed by senior Belgian officials d'Aspremont-Lynden and Rothschild. In Brussels, mercenary recruitment was assisted by the Sureté and the Ministry for Defence, and Katangese cadets were educated in the Belgian Military Academy.[32]

On the whole, Belgian involvement with Katanga during 1960, and part of 1961, amounted to no less than the provision of the total panoply of state infrastructure to the as yet inexperienced secessionists. Brussels of course convinced very few when it claimed that it was merely protecting the Belgians and was prepared to provide 'technical assistance' to any part of the Congo that so desired it (requesting aid from Brussels was, of course, not the prerogative of provincial governments). Belgium acted for most of 1960 almost as if it recognized Katanga *de facto*. Tshombe was praised for his role in Katanga and the protocol offered to Katangese emissaries amounted to the one reserved for foreign dignitaries. The Eyskens government, and in particular Foreign Minister Wigny, argued against UN involvement and offered diplomatic support to Elizabethville. With the new government of Lefèvre, which had Spaak as Foreign Minister, diplomatic support began to diminish, though it still persisted until as late as November 1962. In 1962 Belgium pleaded against the use of sanctions and called for the halting of ONUC operations in Katanga.[33] These were counteracted by anti-Katanga initiatives, such as the joint Kennedy–Spaak communiqué on economic sanctions, and Spaak's landmark statement of December 1962, where Tshombe was described as 'no more a statesman but a powerful rebel'.[34]

Belgium's motivation was instrumental. It was, above all, the protection of its political influence as befitting a former colonial power.[35] In 1960 the Lumumba factor was decisive, as well as the activity of the vociferous Katanga lobby in Brussels. The initial extended involvement of Belgium was advocated by all major political parties, public opinion and big business. But this, according to van Bilsen, constituted 'a complete reversal of the former Belgian policy, which was based on the unity of a centralized Congo State in close relationship with Belgium'.[36] This novel policy was not necessarily to balkanize the Congo or destroy its unity, but rather to provide support to any part of the Congo 'which desired to escape the grip of the Lumumba movement, primarily Katanga'.[37] On the whole, Belgium appeared to favour a confederal or loosely federal Congo, and advised Elizabethville accordingly.[38]

Apparently Belgium had not actually planned the secession, as Lumumba claimed. But without its support Katanga would have collapsed in the first crucial months of secession. Thus, even though Belgium was not, strictly speaking, the instigator, its involvement can be regarded as closer to the 'push' instead of the 'pull' variant. The second type of involvement can be based mainly on the various Katanga appeals prior to secession, while 'push' involvement can be supported for at least three reasons: (1) that Belgium would have intervened anyway, though not necessarily for the reasons Tshombe had hoped; (2) that intervention predated the secession; (3) that the orders given to the Belgian paratroopers were markedly different from those given to the military in the other provinces.

Katanga's 'double-game' accusations[39] against Belgium sprang from the lack of recognition and Spaak's policy of disengagement from Katanga. The official rationale for non-recognition in the first months of the secession appeared in the telegrams sent by Foreign Minister Wigny to several Western powers. It was argued that recognition would render the rest of the Congo economically non-viable and a prey to communism (the Katangese, incidentally, were not aware of these telegrams). Another official justification for non-recognition was that it would lead to the discrediting of Tshombe as a neocolonialist stooge. In fact, non-recognition and the gradual switch of policy that followed later provided the means to safeguard Belgian interests in the rest of the Congo, and were aimed at preventing the *entrée* of other Western countries.[40] The Belgians obviously wanted to keep the Congo and its riches to themselves and non-recognition appeared to them a useful fig-leaf.

France provided Katanga with arms, including rockets and some combat aircraft and was apparently involved in mercenary recruitment. The French mercenaries, who were most effective in Katanga, were mainly former OAS men or legionnaires. Colonel Trinquier, of Algerian renown, was involved in recruitment and was offered the command of the Katanga army, a post which was finally taken by another old Algerian hand, Colonel Faulques, who headed the school of paracommandos and became chief of staff to the incompetent Katangese head of the army. The French assisted from their base in Brazzaville and permitted among other things, the use of their airspace in Equatorial Africa. (This was a privilege not accorded to the UN or United States aircraft when arms were urgently needed for ONUC.) France supported Belgium at the diplomatic level in the UN and elsewhere, the only state to do this openly. France condemned UN involvement, but otherwise stood aloof, keeping the Katangese emissaries at arm's length (though at one point a French envoy named Bistos stated that France could consider recognition).[41]

De Gaulle's 'unrelieved hostility' towards the UN,[42] which France refused to pay for its Congo operation, was apparently not unrelated to fears of a precedent for UN intervention in Algeria. Support for Katanga was motivated basically by a desire for an economic *entrée* and the fear of communist and radical inroads in the heart of Africa. De Gaulle's image of the world and of Africa, shared by his confidant and main adviser on Africa, Foccart, were apparently also a factor. The formidable, if somewhat simplistic, French leader defined the international system as comprised of mature Western democratic states, evil communist states and a universe of immature multi-ethnic states with no history and no firm guiding principles. This last group of states, which included the African states, could easily fall prey to communism and anarchy. The danger was even greater if such states were unfortunate enough to be saddled with that preposterous invention of 'les Anglo-Saxons', the federal system of government. Katanga appeared to be a resolutely anti-communist emergent nation which had broken with an non-viable federation only to find itself threatened by a host of dangers: Lumumba, the 'communist' Stanleyville Lumumbists and an inept UN, organ of the 'irresponsible Afro-Asians'.[43]

The Federal Government of Rhodesia and Nyasaland accorded Katanga, in the words of its prime minister, Sir Roy Welensky, 'all necessary and legally possible support'. Included in this were funds, foodstuffs, medicine, spare parts and assistance, such as asylum for Katangese leaders, a platform to issue statements, facilities for the transference of Katanga gold to Swiss banks, the refusal to assist the UN in any way, business as usual regarding trade and, most significantly, continuation of the vital copper exports which brought in Katanga's revenue. Had Salisbury, contrary to the ONUC claims, not assisted with arms and personnel, this would no doubt have been due to the restraints imposed by Britain and to the fact that the Federation's foreign relations were the exclusive responsibility of Whitehall.[44] Welensky's political support was total and uninhibited, spearheaded by the outspoken

Rhodesian premier himself, who made vitriolic statements and caustic remarks regarding the UN and its supporters, and advised the Macmillan government to recognize Katanga for 'the good of the Free World'.[45]

In the Rhodesian case, affective motives reinforced instrumental aims. Tshombe with his genuine anti-communism and anti-radicalism, and his stand on racial partnership, was a natural ally of the Federation, to the extent that the White Rhodesians, as one journalist had put it, were in a 'psychological state of shared siege with Katanga'.[46] At the same time, an independent Western-oriented Katanga could act as an effective buffer against African radicalism. There were also the prospects of cooperation or even of an economic association between Katanga and the Rhodesias which would in effect unite the Copperbelt. Welensky's association with Tshombe, whom he came to like personally, projected his image as the 'architect of racial partnership'. Ultimately, Welensky's uninhibited support for Katanga served his main aim – the survival of the Federation – by easing the pressure for dismantling it.[47]

British support was for the most part indirect and subtle, but nevertheless important. Furthermore, it appeared unwilling or at least unable to constrain Welensky.[48] Welensky, incidentally, has characterized the British attitude as restrained compared to his own, but as basically sympathetic towards Katanga, and not ruling out its recognition, at least in the early days of the secession.[49]

Britain provided assistance such as the discouraging of UN inspection of arms smuggling from Northern Rhodesia, the refusal of clearance to Ethiopian jet fighters reinforcing ONUC, the suspension of an order for bombs for UN aircraft, assisting Tshombe to escape during ONUC's Operation Morthor in September and providing the Katangese leaders with friendly advice.[50]

But probably the most crucial support was diplomatic, and there, again, it was fairly subtle. According to major critics of the Macmillan government at home and abroad, British support was at its highest in 1961 and 1962. London abstained or vetoed crucial UN resolutions, and in the aftermath of the abortive ONUC Operation Morthor in September 1961, provided Secretary-General Dag Hammarskjöld with a virtual ultimatum. On this and on other occasions, Whitehall publicized its criticism of the UN operations in the Congo to a far greater extent than appeared justified. However, Britain paid its share of expenditure to the UN and provided ONUC with some aid, albeit reluctantly.[51] The preoccupations of Whitehall in the Katanga affair were economic interests, the fear of 'communist' penetration on the doorstep of East Africa and the Rhodesias, and of course the question of North and South

Rhodesia. Indirect support may also have been a form of appeasement towards Welensky and the various overlapping conservative lobbies inside and outside parliament.[52]

Congo–Brazzaville, the small former French colony across the Congo river from Leopoldville, provided Katanga with assistance and diplomatic support. Congo–Brazzaville was the staging point for the various Katangan sorties to African and European capitals and the transit point for arms and mercenaries (via Point Noire and Brazzaville). President Filbert Youlou's support rivalled that of Welensky; prior to Lumumba's death, he had decided to recognize the secessionist state, apparently on a *quid pro quo* basis (recognition for Tshombe's financing of the Kouilou dam project). Recognition did not come but the abbé Youlou acted as if Katanga was recognized *de facto*: he invited Tshombe to participate in the Brazzaville Conference of 1960, treated him as a Head of State and in 1961 paid what amounted to an official visit to Elizabethville. Youlou introduced the Katanga case to the Brazzaville group and probably provided the initial link with the obscure but powerful French network operating under Foccart. Youlou shared Tshombe's ideology and pragmatism, but his much-publicized identification with Katanga was far from disinterested. Brazzaville stood to gain from a weak and fragmented Congo, particularly as Youlou had ambitions of leadership in central Africa. There were also the well-known financial benefits for anyone dealing with Tshombe.[53]

South Africa provided material aid such as funds and foodstuffs, and was probably also involved in arms supplies, including combat aircraft, and in mercenary recruitment. Trade relations continued smoothly and were in fact on the increase with the vital Katanga export, copper, reaching South Africa via the Rhodesias. Furthermore, Pretoria was highly critical of the ONUC operations in Katanga, rejecting U Thant's appeal for a South African embargo on copper from Katanga, and, in the end, refused to pay its share of ONUC expenditures. South Africa made no secret of its sympathy towards Katanga and a number of top-level Katanga delegations were met officially by South African ministers.[54]

South Africa's motives were mainly strategic considerations and the possibility of an economic penetration into Katanga's Copperbelt. Pretoria feared that Lumumba's radicalism could spread southwards in domino fashion reaching its very doorstep. In the short run, the case of Katanga provided an opportunity to criticize and obstruct the UN and the Afro-Asian countries that had already begun to mount their anti-apartheid campaign. This was also a time when the bantustan scheme was still very novel. A relationship with Katanga and the identification with a black African leader, Tshombe, could sell the policy to conservative Africans in South Africa and to the so-called moderate African states.[55]

74

Portugal's support for Katanga was hardly disguised. Angola, which incredible as it may seem, was designated a province of metropolitan Portugal, provided the route for arms, mercenaries and aircraft from South Africa and Europe, via Lisbon. The Benguela Railway, from Benguela and Dilolo in Angola to Katanga (Kolwezi–Jadotville–Elizabethville), was also a principal route for Katanga's vital exports of copper and other minerals (which brought the hard cash from Union Minière). The Portuguese denied overflight rights to UN planes, rejected the stationing of UN observers to check the arms and mercenary trail and refused to pay their share of ONUC expenditures to the UN.[56]

For the Portuguese, the wave of decolonization had suddenly (as in the case of Rhodesia) reached their borders. In fact by 1960 and 1961 the very first Angolan African raids took place with the use of the territory of Congo–Leopoldville as a springboard. No such activity was permitted from Katanga. Not only was Katanga a useful buffer, Western-oriented and conservative, but it was also a source of good business. With the extended traffic it had generated for Benguela Railway it saved the company from the brink of bankruptcy. And no doubt the Congo conflict as a whole provided Portugal with arguments to justify its policy of retaining its colonies indefinitely.[57]

The United States, under the Kennedy Administration, became Leopoldville's most important third-state supporter and the object of wrath for the Katangese. But before that in 1960 and for a great part of 1961, Washington's policy was contradictory, confused and at times on the verge of disaster, seeming to tilt more towards the Katangese side, though less so after the fall of Lumumba. The new consistently anti-Katanga policy was formulated gradually in the second part of 1961 by the Kennedy Administration.[58]

Acts of support for Katanga in 1960 and 1961 were mainly indirect. In 1960 they included, first, the refusal to accord military aid to Leopoldville upon Katanga's secession (which had then driven Lumumba to appeal to the Soviet Union). During the same period, Belgian policy in the Congo was defended and there was no criticism of Belgium's slow pace in withdrawing its forces. On the other hand the United States voted for the UN resolutions and was not against ONUC's entry into Katanga, though it obviously favoured the cautious non-interventionist approach of Dag Hammarskjöld over that of the other UN officials. On the whole, the approach of the Eisenhower Administration had been apparently to leave all options open, even the option of future active support for Katanga.[59]

The main consideration during the Eisenhower period had been the dreaded Lumumba and the fear of communist and Soviet influence in the heart of Africa. Kennedy's swing to the other side was justified on the grounds that if Katanga was permitted to become independent, the rest of the Congo would be economically non-viable and would lapse into anarchy or perhaps disintegrate; and that the danger of communism no longer existed with the death of Lumumba, the weakening of Gizenga and the rise to power of staunch anti-communists and supporters of the United States, such as Adoula (the United States choice) and Mobutu.[60]

Apart from Congo–Brazzaville, several other conservative states of the so-called Brazzaville group were sympathetic towards Katanga, most notably the Malagashy Republic, followed by Cameroon, the Central African Republic, Ivory Coast and Niger. Tunisia was also apparently not hostile to Katanga when Lumumba was still in power.[61]

Several Western states, such as Israel and the Federal Republic of Germany, were also mentioned in the press at this time in connection with Katanga, because German- and Israeli-made arms appeared in Katangan hands. Luxembourg was mentioned, because of at least one incident of a transit of arms through its territory, and Australia because some Australian nationals piloted the Katanga aircraft. More obvious was the voicing of support by Italy and Greece, which had communities of more than 500 settlers each in Katanga. The maverick Papa Doc Duvalier of Haiti also at one point appeared sympathetic.[62]

Of the non-independent entities and their leaders, sympathizers included the black Rhodesian leader Harry Nkumbula, Kaunda's rival who headed the conservative Northern Rhodesian African Congress, and South Kasai (the other secession in the Congo) under the leadership of the megalomaniac Albert Kalonji who later joined the other Congolese leaders at the Lovanium Assembly of national reconciliation in 1961.[63]

The relationship between the Katanga secession and the Union Minière du Haut-Katanga (UMHU) is the best-known case of symbiosis between a multinational corporation and a secessionist movement. The Union Minière paid all royalties, duties and taxes due to the central government to the Katanga government instead, arguing that it had no other choice if it wanted to stay in business. The company's financial contribution amounted to 60 to 80 per cent of Katanga's revenue and rose in 1962 as a result of further negotiations with Tshombe. Furthermore, the company provided a cover for mercenaries, the use of its workshops for the manufacture of arms, bombs and armoured cars and the assembly of aircraft, and presented Katanga with a radio station which was the most powerful in central Africa. In effect, Union Minière had placed its entire organization and network at the disposal of the secessionists, and provided the link which enabled the Katangese to contact influential business circles in Western Europe.[64]

According to Gérard-Libois, author of the most authoritative work

on the Katanga secession, the province could not have seceded without
Union Minière support, support which, incidentally, was only half-hearted
to begin with.[65] Secession was initially treated only as 'means of
blackmail' or as 'an alternative linked to an eventual catastrophe'.[66]
In the last stages of the conflict the companies that controlled the
Union Minière, in particular the Société Générale in Brussels, began
to have second thoughts.[67] It was then that Elizabethville switched
to its threat of destruction. These threats, it could be argued, gave
more credence to the company's claim that paying was the price
to stay in business. Even if the Union Minière had at any time
been under real threat, it is clear that both the company and
Katanga gained from their relationship. In fact after the secession
the company did not face any retribution. Katanga's experience may
be seen as pointing towards a more general conclusion, regarding a
secession's rapport with a multinational company: it can come about
only if it is highly profitable to the company active in secessionist-held
territory.

The best-known and most influential Katanga lobbies in the West were
those of Belgium, the United Kingdom, France and the United States.
In Belgium there was widespread sympathy in all the levels of society
and government, but most influential were the financial circles headed
by the Union Minière in Brussels and by the Société Générale (the
huge Brussels-based international concern which was the main parent
company in charge) and the other companies with interests in Katanga.[68]

The Katanga lobby in Britain was far less obvious that its Belgian
counterpart and certainly far less glamorous than the US Katanga lobby,
but it was no less effective. It was 'quiet but powerful'[69] and presents an
interesting example of the intricate links that exist between the City and
Westminster, particularly under Conservative governments. Politicians
championing the Katanga cause were at the same time former or actual
shareholders or directors of giant multinationals linked with Katanga;
directors of multinationals were former politicians. Particularly active
was Tanganyika Concessions, commonly known as Tanks, which was
one of the major shareholders in Union Minière and in other companies
linked with Katanga, such as Benguela Railways, and various companies
in the Rhodesian Copperbelt. Tanks hired a public relations firm, the
E.D. O'Brien Organization, which launched an imaginative and articulate
campaign aimed at those who mattered in Westminster and in the City. In
the House of Commons the British Katanga lobby could count on eighty
to ninety Tory backbenchers and there was a very vocal group also in the
Lords.[70]

The exact influence of the Katanga lobby on the Macmillan

Government is difficult to assess. According to Keatley it was the role of 'a powerful negative group' inhibiting the government from supporting the UN and the Kennedy policy.[71]

In France, the lobby was more limited. It covered the extreme right of the political spectrum and segments of the Gaullist Party. The sending of arms and mercenaries was its main concern. The main French *ad hoc* cause group was the Association France–Katanga.[72]

The US Katanga Lobby matched, and at times even surpassed, its European counterparts at least in flamboyance. This was partly due to the difference in political cultures between the New and the Old World. At the same time it is the normal reaction of the right against an Administration's seemingly unconventional course.

The Katanga Lobby in Congress included Republicans and Southern Democrats, all well-known conservatives, some of whom had even visited secessionist Katanga. The most influential *ad hoc* group to emerge was the American Committee for Aid to Katanga Freedom Fighters.[73] Their campaign was assisted by other pre-existing extremist groups such as Young Americans for Freedom located in Indiana, the John Birch Society (the spiritual successor of the McCarthy movement) and the anti-Maoist Committee for One Million.[74]

It is not clear whether American business, so often in the forefront of foreign policy towards the Third World, was involved in the Katanga lobby. American big business had very few investments in Katanga, the most notable one being Metal Climax which was half-owned by Rhodesian Selection Trust, one of the big four which controlled the Rhodesian Copperbelt. Could the opposite be true, that in fact big business was against Katanga as the secessionists and the Union Minière shrewdly alleged?[75]

The secession ended in January 1963 and has not reappeared, at least not so far. During Tshombe's brief *séjour* as Premier of the Congo (July 1964 – October 1965) Katanga was, ironically, placed firmly under the control of the central government. When the central government was threatened twice in the late 1970s (in 1977 and in 1978) by the Front de Libération Nationale Congolais (FLNC), which crossed the border from Angola and made Shaba (former Katanga) its base,[76] it appears that the Lunda in particular supported the revolution, – an indication, no doubt, that their ethnic sentiments remained alive.

The secession of Katanga was in many respects singularly fortunate. The resolutely anti-secessionist OAU was not yet in existence and the self-determination norm was still in its infancy. The former colonial power was, to say the least, sympathetic and so was Western Europe. The settlers and the multinational firm, Union Minière, were deeply involved on their side and there was widespread sympathy in conservative African states. Yet the venture failed and was instrumental in giving secession a bad name. It remained to be seen whether other secessionist movements with better cases and free of the neocolonialist scourge, which bedevilled the case of Katanga, could fare better. The next major secession to take place came four years later. Again it occurred in Africa (where already two movements, in the Southern Sudan and Eritrea, were simmering, little known to the outside world). Biafra was its name and it pledged itself to take Africa and world opinion by storm.

6

BIAFRA
(May 1967 – January 1970)

Biafra is prepared to accept aid from the devil because the first thing is survival.

Our aim all along has been to delay the enemy until the world conscience can effectively be aroused.

Europe found peace through Balkanization, why not Africa through Biafranization?

General Chuchuemeka Odumegwu Ojukwu
Head of State of the Republic of Biafra

Nigeria became independent in October 1960. Accompanying its independence was an almost mystical belief in its ability to ride all storms and rise to its full potential, as befitting the giant of Africa. Yet within a short time one crisis gave way to another and in January 1966 the inept Westminster type multi-party system of government was overthrown by a military coup. In July 1966 there followed another coup and, in less than a year, on 30 May 1967, the Eastern Region (Eastern Nigeria) declared itself independent, assuming the name of the Republic of Biafra. Apparently, the giant of Africa had feet of clay.

ETIOLOGY

Prior to the secession of Eastern Nigeria, other regional governments and groups had also toyed with the idea of secession. The list includes, among others, the Western Region, the Calabar–Onitsa–Rivers district in the south-east, the Tiv ethnic group in the Middle Belt, and above all the Northern Region dominated by the Hausa–Fulani.[1] In fact the ultimate secession of the Eastern Region was treated then as something of a paradox: the country's 'most modern, progressive, nationally-oriented people came to be the country's tribal insurgents, leading the way to Nigeria's fragmentation'.[2] Eastern separatism had arrived belatedly, becoming pronounced only by September and October 1966, that autumn

80

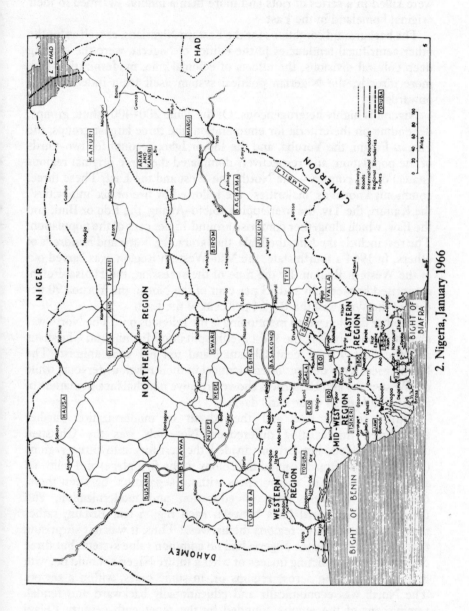

2. Nigeria, January 1966

81

of discontent, when thousands of Eastern Nigerians resident in the North were killed in a series of riots and more than a million swarmed to their original homeland in the East.

The background conditions for the Eastern Nigerians, as well as for the other centrifugal tendencies in the edifice of Nigeria, were the existing deep cultural divisions, the effects of colonial rule, modernization and, more directly, the Nigerian political system itself from independence onwards.

Nigeria is highly heterogeneous. Of the some 200–400 ethnic groups, depending on the criteria for enumeration, the three largest groups, the Hausa–Fulani, the Yoruba, and the Ibo or Igbo, account for two-thirds of the population, and respectively dominated the three original regions (states) of the country – the North, the West and the East. These three, commonly known as 'majorities', are followed by five or six 'minorities', the Kanuri, the Tiv, the overlapping Ibibio–Anang, the Edo or Bini, and the Ijaw, which altogether comprise around 15 per cent of the population. The rest include the Efik, the Igala, the Igbira, the Nupe and hundreds of others. In 1964 a fourth state, the Mid-Western Region, was carved out of the Western Region. By the time of the secession, the Hausa–Fulani comprised between 56 and 75 per cent of the North, the Yoruba 90 per cent of the West and the Ibo 64 per cent of the East.

Another division worth mentioning is the religious one. The North was almost wholly Muslim, the West evenly split into Muslims and Christians and the East 90 per cent Christian and ten per cent animist. The Northerners were devout, often fanatical in their religious fervour, while the Westerners and Easterners showed relative nonchalance in matters of religion (at least in those early days).[3]

British colonial rule and the advent of modernization further exacerbated the existing differences. Not only was the Christian dimension added, but Britain divided the territory into three regions (after having arbitrarily carved the colony in the first place) and followed a consistent policy of 'separateness without separation' between them, encouraging different rates of education and modernization, and favouring transactional links between each region and Britain, rather than between the three regions themselves.[4] Thus, it was not surprising that upon independence Nigeria had no common value system, but three dominant and conflicting images of what a future Nigeria should be, with little understanding across regions or, in some cases, within a region. The North was economically and educationally backward and feudal, reminiscent of the empire founded by the nineteenth-century Fulani scholar-conqueror Uthman Dan Fodio. The South was split between the Ibo (and other groups of the East) who were segmented, anti-authoritarian

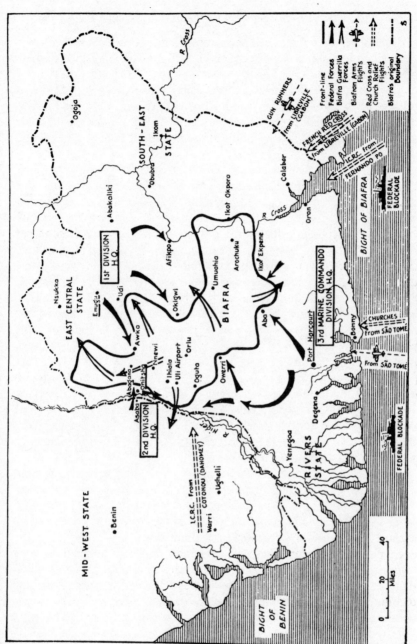

3. Biafra, October 1968

and achievement oriented, and the Yoruba, who were structurally more or less half-way between the Ibo and the Hausa–Fulani.[5]

Nigeria was to become a classic example of the positive correlation between modernization and politicized ethnicity. The politics of Nigeria's First Republic neither united nor accommodated the daunting diversity of the country, but added even more twists to the Nigerian Gordian knot of the 1960s. And the demands of both 'majorities' and 'minorities' increased as one crisis followed another, moving Nigeria nearer to the edge of the precipice: the 1962 Western crisis that saw the fall of the Action Group and of its revered leader, Chief Awolowo; the 1962–63 census crisis; then the 1964 election crisis in which the North managed to defeat an almost all-Southern alliance; and the *coup de grace*, the rigged Western elections of late 1965. The Northern Nigerians remained entrenched in the seat of government, one way or another, until the military coup of January 1966. Nigeria's strong man was Sir Ahmadu Bello, the Sardauna of Sokoto, and the central government was headed by Balewa, the Sardauna's deputy in the Northern party, the Northern People's Congress (NPC). Junior partners in government were the National Council of Nigerian Citizens (NCNC), founded by Dr Nnamdi Azikiwe (the mercurial 'Zik'), originally called the National Council of Nigeria and the Cameroons, and the splinter group from Chief Awolowo's Action Group, the United People's Party of Chief Akintola (later renamed Nigerian National Democratic Party).

Thus the political system was reduced to a three-actor game, with the Northern Region constitutionally assured of its dominant position and the other regions relatively content under the cardinal principles of Nigeria's First Republic, which were the tenet of regional security and the ethnic imperative. Bargains were struck that were ephemeral and coincidental, and corruption reached astounding proportions. At federal level there was little room for opposition or for the smaller ethnic groups. Effective mechanisms for adjustment to change were lacking. Thus overall legitimation eluded Nigeria, and Lagos could not become the dominant focus of political identification.[6]

The characteristics of the Nigerian body politic were the perfect recipe for turmoil, military coups and separatism. Not surprisingly the first coup, that of the idealistic majors in January 1966, was initially greeted with relief even among many Northerners, such was the disgust with Nigeria's First Republic. However, the new regime of Major General Ironsi soon ran out of favour, being labelled an Ibo regime. When Ironsi introduced a plan for a unitary system of government, riots ensued in the North and West, followed, a little later, by the Northern coup of July 1966. This coup was to set in motion the gruelling process towards ultimate secession.[7]

Biafra's precise secessionist allegiance still remains an area for speculation, but it is clear that secession had the support of the majority of the population of Nigeria's Eastern Region in 1967. No doubt the secessionist core consisted of the Ibo of the Eastern Region, who were nine million strong prior to the arrival of the refugees. The some five million non-Ibos (Ibibio, Efik, Annang, Ijaw, Ogoni, Ekoi, Yalla, Ukelle and others) varied in their support for secession, but it appears that in 1967 a significant number approved of this extreme solution, albeit with less enthusiasm than the Ibo.[8]

The Eastern Nigerians, and in particular the dominant Eastern group, the Ibo, were certainly hardly in a situation of disadvantage or inequality compared with the other major Nigerian ethnic groups. In fact in most respects – in education, economic affluence, government positions and others – the Ibo were, to use the Orwellian expression, 'more equal' than the other Nigerians. Their party, the NCNC, governed the Eastern Region and participated in the central government. However, the Ibo themselves felt that they were at a disadvantage, discriminated against and edged out of meaningful participation in the affairs of government. This paradoxical view can be explained in at least three ways. One is the argument of Ibo ambition and assertiveness, a cultural trait that did not permit the Ibo to be satisfied with less than total control of Nigeria. The second exegesis is the factor of oil resources.[9] This view is not implausible, for it appears that Ibo separatism first came to the fore in 1964, which was precisely the year that the potential of oil in the Eastern Region became apparent. The third argument delves into theoretical explanations such as 'rank disequilibrium' and 'relative deprivation', and thus calls for some elaboration.

The Ibo, originally a poor and backward linguistic group, had within the space of a few decades caught up with the most educated and advanced group, the Yoruba, and had come to be regarded as an ethnic group and as the one most geared towards modernization. Yet the Ibo continued to be negatively evaluated by the other large ethnic groups, and they remained the Nigerian outgroup *par excellence*. Events after 1964 did little to allay Ibo fears. To their original perception of rank disequilibrium was now added a sense of 'relative decremental deprivation', the frustration of the 'revolution of rising aspirations'.[10] The Ibo came to feel victimized and, never having forgotten how much Nigerian nationalism owed to their efforts (Azikiwe's NCNC had been the prime mover of Nigeria's nationalism), they felt themselves deprived of the main prizes of statehood.[11] Apprehension reached its peak following the July 1966 Northern coup and the mob violence in the North two months later that cost the lives of thousands of Easterners resident in the North.[12]

Biafra

The July Northern coup, which appeared to herald Northern domination or at least the suppression of the Ibos, was dramatized by the killing of several senior Ibo officers. Together with the September–October atrocities and the subsequent flood of refugees, these can be regarded as the principal events responsible for initiating the difficult passage towards secession.[13] Following the July coup the Eastern military governor, Colonel Ojukwu (placed there by the Ironsi regime), called for a loose association or confederation of four regions. In this he was joined by the North and West in the constitutional talks that started in Lagos. Initially only the mid-West advocated a tight federal system of government. Then the massacres of Easterners took place, and a wave of more than a million refugees swarmed into the Eastern Region. The Eastern delegation refused to attend the *ad hoc* constitutional assembly, where the North in fact made an astounding *volte face* (apparently due in part to British prompting) and sided with the mid-West for a tight system of government.

The yawning gulf opening up between Lagos and the East was momentarily arrested by a two-day meeting of Gowon, Ojukwu and the other Nigerian military governors at Aburi, Ghana. The well-prepared and articulate Colonel Ojukwu appeared to be carrying the day with his call to 'move slightly apart and survive' rather than 'move closer and perish in the collision'.[14] But what came to be known as the Aburi Accord came to naught as each party interpreted the agreement differently, and the Eastern hopes and expectations created by the Aburi meeting were dashed. From then on the downhill snowballing path to ultimate secession was inevitable as the East stuck to Aburi (or to its interpretation of Aburi), while Lagos appeared to be totally committed to a tight federal system of government to comprise twelve states.

From March onwards secession was awaited from day to day, so that when it was finally brought about three months later it was almost an anti-climax. This delay inevitably raises several questions, such as when the decision was taken, and why secession did not take place earlier in the aftermath of Aburi or at the end of March when Lagos cut off all communications and transactions with the East. Eastern critics of secession, and even Ojukwu himself after the war, claim that the decision to opt for independence was taken as early as August 1966, following the July Northern coup. The majority of commentators, however, including Biafran actors of the time, maintain that secession was simply an idea in the air (perhaps there even existed a contingency plan of sorts), and that it needed time to mature and was reversible even as late as the spring of 1967.[15] Among reasons that have been put forward for the delay in declaring independence are that there were still Northern troops

85

in the East; that the East was unprepared militarily; that Easterners were awaited to return from the rest of Nigeria, so as not to be left as hostages; that there was no consensus among top decision-makers; that time was needed to gain popular support among Ibos and non-Ibos in particular; that it was hoped that Nigeria and the FMG (Federal Military Government) under Gowon would simply collapse; and perhaps that a mutually agreed solution was still possible.[16]

The triggering event is considered to have been the twelve-state Decree which split the former Eastern Region into three states, confining the Ibos to their original poor and overcrowded homeland. The viability of Biafra was not in doubt, given its numerous and fairly educated inhabitants and the abundance of oil. By late spring 1967 independent statehood was considered feasible, even though no patron had been secured. The FMG was not deemed capable of mounting a decisive military offensive. Britain was considered unlikely to assist Lagos, because of the oil factor. No lengthy war was anticipated. The secessionists felt confident that they could withstand the Nigerians for the crucial time necessary to achieve independence internationally, and that come what may their sound case for self-determination was bound to prevail in the end.[17]

INTERNATIONAL ACTIVITY

The secession of Biafra lasted for almost a thousand days, from 30 May 1967 until 12 January 1970. The undisputed leader of Biafra was Colonel (later General) Chuchuemeka Odumegwu Ojukwu, the charismatic, Oxford-educated governor of the Eastern Region from the January 1966 coup onwards. Ojukwu had gradually come to personify the East's stubborn spirit of resistance to Northern encroachments, and he earned the place of leader of the East, and of the Ibo in particular, at a time when the role could not easily be fulfilled by the traditional leaders of Iboland, Azikiwe (the former President of Nigeria) and Okpara (the former President of the Eastern Region). Ojukwu's closest confidants were C.C. Mojekwu (the Commissioner for Internal Affairs), Dr Pius Okigbo and Francis Nwokedi. Others influential in foreign policy included Mbu (the Commissioner for Foreign Affairs), Dr Ibiam, Professor Njoku, Professor Dike and Chief Justice Mbanefo (all four Ambassadors-at-large and heads of Biafran delegations), Onyegbula (the Permanent Secretary for Foreign Affairs) and Chukwuemerije (head of the Directorate of Propaganda). Azikiwe, Okpara and other distinguished Eastern politicians assisted as representatives, particularly in 1967 and 1968.

Biafra, with its gifted and internationally-known politicians and other

86

celebrities, pursued a vociferous campaign exceeding even that of Katanga. From the start there were no less than five missions abroad (in Lisbon, Paris, London, New York and Dar es Salaam), and this number rose to eight or nine in 1969. Public relations firms were hired, emissaries sent throughout the world, and the Directorate of Propaganda used the services of some of the East's foremost literary figures such as Chinua Achebe and Cyprian Ekwensi.

Biafra appeared ideologically conservative during the first two years of secession. Its more radical image (encouraged by the leftist intellectuals who had joined the movement) was inaugurated only as late as June 1969 with Ojukwu's Ahiara Declaration, which set forth somewhat ambiguously the 'principles of the Biafran Revolution'. When it came to ideology, Ojukwu's *leitmotif* was that Biafra was attempting to fill 'Africa's ideological vacuum'.[18] But in moments of greater candour he admitted that 'in this struggle the first thing is to survive; after that we can begin to talk ideologies'.[19]

The avowed goal throughout the secession was independence, or as the Biafrans put it more diplomatically, 'internal sovereignty'. This was said to be the only realistic solution guaranteeing Biafra's ultimate aim – the survival, security and development of its people. However, on a number of occasions it appears that the secessionists would have settled for less in what would have been a process of 'genuine negotiations without preconditions'.

Biafra had few scruples about receiving aid from disreputable sources (though it attempted to keep such dealings as secret as possible). As Ojukwu stated at one point in 1968: 'Anybody who offers assistance for my people is a true friend. Biafra is prepared to accept aid from the devil because the first thing is survival.'[20]

The Eastern Region had already commenced its international activity prior to the final secession, probing African states and securing arms shipments with private dealers.[21] In 1967, upon its declaration of independence, Biafra attempted to penetrate the international system, but with very limited success. Ojukwu has claimed that there was no foreign policy as such during that period, but it was obvious that the Biafra strategy was to appeal for unconditional negotiations under international auspices in order to freeze, according to Stremlau, the existing two power centres in Nigeria.[22] In 1967 Biafra raised interest only in Africa, where a top-level committee was set up on the subject within the OAU, comprising five African heads of state.

The first seven months of secession passed through several phases. First there was the June 1967 period of 'phoney war' when among others, the oil companies were lobbied; then came the early July attack of the

Nigerian army and the first Biafran military setbacks, while oil payments and diplomatic recognition were not forthcoming. There then followed the momentary triumph of the Biafran forces with the dramatic mid-West military offensive, which signalled an equally impressive peace campaign in Africa. But the year ended with three months of military setbacks and increasing isolation.[23]

The year 1968 brought the greatest hopes and gravest dangers to the secessionists. By May their territory was reduced to being totally landlocked. The only links with the outside world were by plane from Lisbon to the Uli airstrip and through the lone telex line to Lisbon. By the beginning of September, Owerri (the capital city after the fall of Enugu) had fallen and Biafra's single lifeline, the Uli airstrip, was threatened. At the same time, this was the year of a number of international breakthroughs: four diplomatic recognitions (by Tanzania, Gabon, the Ivory Coast and then Zambia): French declarations on Biafra's right to self-determination, and by September French arms on a regular basis; appeals by the Pope and the World Council of Churches; peace talks under international auspices (the Commonwealth Secretariat in Kampala and the OAU in Niamey and Addis Ababa); and systematic relief flights in defiance of the federal blockade.

Biafra, internationally ignored in January 1968, had by June and July become a veritable *cause célèbre*. During this period international activity gained in importance, for it became clear that only with third-party support could Biafra avert the slow but relentless Nigerian military offensive. The first objectives were recognition by African states, funds and arms. Azikiwe visited several African heads of state, Ibiam (senior churchman and former Premier of Eastern Nigeria) took charge of the churches, and aggressive PR firms were hired to enlist international sympathy.[24]

The year 1969 held no major breakthroughs. Biafra became more defiant, but at the same time, several factors tarnished its image: its intransigent position regarding daylight relief flights; the so-called 'Kwale incident' concerning the killing of European employees of Agip, and the arrest of survivors for what appeared as ransom; and its refusal to engage in talks under the OAU mantle. The more defiant approach was inaugurated with the Ahiara Declaration and with the resurrection of Biafra's air force under Count von Rosen, a Swedish-born pilot, who made impressive sorties with a small fleet of Minicon aircraft bombing mainly oil installations. The primary target for backing was the United States under its new Nixon Administration (Nixon as a Presidential candidate had voiced support for Biafra in no uncertain terms). Several small states were approached for recognition, but the secessionists snubbed OAU attempts at mediation, even as late as December 1969 when Selassie proposed talks in Addis Ababa under OAU auspices.[25]

Propaganda was Biafra's foremost persuasion strategy. It 'ranked next only to the actual fighting'[26] and was generally praised by commentators of the time.[27] But upon closer scrutiny, this particular Biafran tactic was not that effective and often backfired.[28] What are beyond doubt, however, are its ingenuity and sheer volume. After all 'words were at times all that Biafra had in ample supply',[29] and in the propaganda field the Biafrans often 'seemed to be winning the war of words while losing the battle of arms'.[30] Propaganda was orchestrated by the Directorate of Propaganda (whose various committees reached as many as forty-one in number) and furthered by the special representatives stationed abroad heading the permanent missions, the roving ambassadors and the PR firms (to Biafra's annoyance, the firms themselves received far more credit than they were due). The companies involved in 1967 were the quiet Ruder and Finn of New York and the subtle External Development Services in London, and, in 1968 and 1969 the vociferous Markpress headed by Bernhardt in Geneva, and Robert S. Goldstein Enterprises in Los Angeles.[31] The basic themes of propaganda were genocide, the fact that Biafrans had been driven out of Nigeria, and self-reliance.[32] A distinction has been made between the genocide phase of the campaign, which lasted until spring 1969, and the self-reliance phase from then on.[33] In 1967 the propaganda was fairly discreet, while over the next two years it became more blatant, gradually losing its earlier lustre.[34]

Biafra's case for self-determination was a good one, and was presented for the most part very articulately.[35] The cornerstone of the argument was Biafran subjection to physical violence, in particular during the genocide phase of the campaign. This argument, which later backfired,[36] was based on the following grounds:

1. the pre-war massacres;
2. the act of launching a war against Biafra;
3. the avowed 'quick kill' objective of Lagos;
4. FMG's intransigence and reluctance to reach a peaceful settlement;
5. the indiscriminate bombing of civilians;
6. the alleged killings and intimidation of Easterners in the 'occupied territories';
7. the use of starvation as a 'legitimate weapon of war' by the FMG.

All these, they claimed, had irrevocably shattered the already delicate fabric of Nigerian society. The Biafrans were threatened by 'cultural' as well as 'physical extermination'.

The secessionists maintained that they had the unqualified support of all the Eastern ethnic groups. It was argued that the Ibos and non-Ibos were equal in the new state of Biafra, a region culturally, socially and economically 'intricately interwoven for decades'. And the Biafrans used all the other common arguments of secessionist movements, such as resolve (they would 'never yield' – should the Nigerians overrun their territory they would have to 'hold down physically every Biafran alive'), the abortive attempts at peaceful settlement, historical arguments (recent history, Northern secessionist tendencies, etc.), domination and injustice (the Hausa–Fulani avowed aim of continuing their 'interrupted conquest to the sea' – interrupted by the British colonizers), Biafran separate identity, some legal considerations (such as that the Gowon regime was illegal), and arguments concerning Biafra's viability and great potential for Africa as a whole (Biafra as 'a philosophy', a 'revolution', a 'pride to Africa' and to the 'Black Man' in his search for 'identity and recognition' free from the 'fetters of colonialism and neocolonialism').

The three main criticisms against the Biafran case were lack of support by the Eastern minorities, the Katanga stigma, and balkanization. The Biafrans cited various examples of prominent secessionists who were not Ibo, and proposed a plebiscite under international auspices to resolve the issue (implying, of course, that it was bound to turn out in their favour). The arguments dissociating Biafra from the Katanga stigma were more convincing: that the oil companies did not assist Biafra, and that several known critics of Katanga had pointed out the difference between the two secessionist movements, including a supporter of the FMG, President Mobutu.[37]

Countering the 'bogey of balkanization', as Ojukwu had called it, was a more awesome task for the secessionists. Balkanization was presented by the FMG in its dual sense, both as external balkanization – that all African states had their potential Katangas or Biafras – and as internal balkanization – the disintegration of the rest of Nigeria and what a setback that would be for African unity.[38] One can distinguish at least three approaches in Biafra's repertoire: the crude argument for public consumption, the unique anomaly or endoparadigmatic approach, and the revolutionary argument or exoparadigmatic approach.

The first mode of dealing with the issue was to reject the label altogether by arguing that the Biafran position did not constitute a secession but was a case of 'constructive desertion' – the Easterners had been forced to resort to independence. A more sophisticated version of this was that this was the 'frame of mind' dominant among Easterners who were shocked by the atrocities committed and fearful of genocide.[39] The second approach conformed with the African paradigm dominant within the OAU (sanctity of boundaries and African unity). It was persistently claimed that Biafra was a unique case: 'In the history of nations, no country has ever broken up simply because another did. Each case of dissolution of a political union has always been due to unique local factors.'[40] Biafra could act as a 'beacon for the furtherance of unity . . . never again will one section of the political community seek with impunity the total annihilation of another section . . . without contemplating the possible consequences of such an act'.[41]

Furthermore, the Biafrans argued, 'it would be tragic if Africa should consider the territorial structure of existing countries more sacrosanct than the safeguarding of the lives of persecuted communities in those countries'.[42] This last point provides a link with the final and most revolutionary argument, which runs as follows: the African boundaries were colonially imposed and arbitrary, producing artificial constructs which were conflict-prone and incapable of development. Thus the whole of Africa was kept 'under tutelage' by the developed states; the approach of larger wholes for their own sake (the 'elephantine theory of politics') could not 'enhance the African revolution, as it did not enhance Europe's development'.[43] And the Biafran leader concluded epigrammatically: 'For a time there were endless wars in Europe, incessant conflicts until the old European empires were dismantled, until the Balkans were Balkanized – then came peace . . . Europe found peace through Balkanization, why not Africa through Biafranization?'[44]

African states and the OAU were lobbied with the more subtle anti-balkanization arguments, and with the call for an 'African' solution to the conflict. It was also claimed that the territorial integrity and inviolability of African states was not at stake, for this basic principle of the OAU actually applied only to inter-state affairs, banning all attempts to enlarge the territory of one state at the expense of another; it did not apply to the disintegration of a state. The only solution was through a negotiated settlement between the two parties concerned. But the FMG was bent on 'smite to unite'. It could be convinced to reach a peaceful settlement only if several African states would recognize Biafra – recognition would in effect end the war. It appears that although the secessionists were partly successful in Africa, they lost faith in the OAU too soon for their own good. By late 1968 and throughout 1969 they snubbed the OAU, rejecting mediation attempts and resorting only to blunt accusations.[45]

France, whose support was sought in terms of arms, training and recognition to neutralize international support for Nigeria, was approached in a number of ways, in addition to using the basic arguments of the Biafra case. Biafra apparently sold itself as France's natural ally in West Africa which would counter British and now Soviet influence in

91

Nigeria. It appeared ready to join the French community and become culturally attached to France instead of Britain.[46] There was also an attempt (highly publicized for obvious reasons by Lagos) to sell the East's mineral resources, such as oil, to French concerns (for example to SAFRAP, the subsidiary of ERAP).[47]

Portugal's assistance was canvassed early on, apparently on the basis of a mutually beneficial business arrangement.[48] There was also a concentrated effort to enlist United States support and, more realistically, its mediation. The earliest argument was US investment, but soon the Soviet presence was used for its propaganda value; Biafra put itself forward as the 'Czechoslovakia of Africa'.[49] When Biafra's great hope, President Nixon, did no more than 'smother' Biafra 'with relief', as Ojukwu later put it,[50] the secessionists switched to moral blackmail.

As for Britain, when the secessionists could make no more use of the 'oil card' they presented their case at times with telling analogies (such as a hypothetical situation in which the English would run amok and slaughter 30,000 Scots, with the remaining Scots seeking refuge in their original homeland in Scotland) in their attempt to capture British public opinion over the head of the Wilson government. But very soon the Biafran leaders reverted to what they called the 'dirty language campaign', accusing the British government of practically everything and insulting prime minister Wilson.[51]

The Soviet Union – together with Britain Nigeria's primary supplier of arms against Biafra – was reproached for its posture. Apart from the numerous accusations against Moscow, there were also at times attempts to formulate a few Marxist-sounding arguments, such as that Nigeria was a 'pre-capitalist feudal empire' akin to Tsarist Russia, or that Biafra was a liberation movement and historically the progressive force.[52] But perhaps the most ambitious attempt to alter the Soviet position at the eleventh hour came with the missions of Paul Nwokedi (a noted Marxist) to Moscow.[53]

Of the Biafran approach towards the People's Republic of China little is known other than that Ojukwu and Radio Biafra used at times wording along Chinese lines, such as 'revisionist Russia'[54] and other such expressions which bordered on the ridiculous. For Israel, the Biafrans highlighted what they said was an obvious communality of fate between these two industrious peoples, using such emotive terms as 'persecution', 'genocide', the anguished 'return to the homeland' and the 'Muslim threat', and the Israelis were reminded that the Ibo had long been regarded as the 'Jews of Africa' (an expression coined by Azikiwe well before Nigeria's independence) – and predictably, General Gowon, the Nigerian President, was dubbed the 'Hitler of Africa'.[55]

Among the other main targets of the secessionist state were the oil companies – Shell–BP in particular, by far the most important company involved in the East. The secessionists claimed that Biafra was a successor state and that it would honour its predecessor's commitments. It is interesting to note that the Biafrans demanded only that amount of revenue that had been due to the former Eastern Region,[56] rather than the total amount as Katanga had required from Union Minière – very curious to say the least, particularly since Biafra styled itself as an independent state. Whatever the Biafran approach, the Nigerian attack and takeover of the oil terminal on the island of Bonny rendered the secessionist argument obsolete. As one author had put it, 'fact and law had conspired' to deny the Biafrans even the possibility of a legal bluff.[57] Biafra then switched to tougher tactics, such as threats of destroying company property if payment was not made and the detention in Enugu (the first Biafran capital) of top Shell–BP officials. As the same time, offers were made to at least one of the companies less involved in the East – the French SAFRAP. The bombing of oil installations by the Minicon aircraft in 1969 can also be seen as a negative sanction against the oil companies.[58]

Biafra embarked upon secession without having secured any sponsor and without any friendly neighbouring state to provide access and sanctuary. But it was gradually able to gain one supporter after another, become a *cause célèbre*, earn recognition from five other states, and generate an impressive relief airlift programme in defiance of the federal blockade. All this was above all the outcome of the appeal of its case and the ingenuity and skill of the secessionists and of various enthusiastic supporters, rather than being based on any tangible gains. However, the Biafrans made a number of mistakes that were fatal. Even more crucially, the FMG was able to secure far greater material support together with vital diplomatic support. It is worth mentioning some of the more outstanding Biafran mistakes or strategies that finally backfired, for they amply portray classic positions – many of them catch-22 situations – in which many a secessionist movement has found itself.

The genocide argument was very important in generating interest and support for Biafra. However, the genocide strategy had outrun its course by 1968 and begun to have a boomerang effect. As the Biafrans themselves realized, when the genocidal intentions of Lagos were shown to be unfounded (particularly with the British–Nigerian master-stroke of inviting an international observer team that found no clear indication of genocide), their case for independence became baseless.[59]

Starvation, an argument which to begin with was used more by the relief agencies and less by the Biafrans themselves, was a great attention catcher, bringing the tragic image of the starving Biafran child into Western households. But it was hardly the stuff that makes governments recognize an entity as a state. Even the five recognitions of Biafra were not the normal type of *de jure* recognition that then leads to formal inter-state relations.[60] As the Biafran Foreign Ministry commented in a confidential memorandum: 'The humanitarian approach has backfired. Ours now is the picture of a piteous starving sickly people non-viable and incapable of defending themselves from hunger and war.'[61] Furthermore, as one author has pointed out, humanitarian aid to Biafra, by virtue of being Western or Western inspired, was likely to raised suspicion in radical African quarters.[62]

Biafran publicity often seemed to be far too articulate, witty or vociferous for its own good. Equally, it was not able to keep the public relations firms well enough hidden in the background. For the sake of audibility Biafra was sacrificing its credibility, while in fact the Biafrans themselves were perfectly capable, in most instances, of performing their own PR activities.[63]

Being ideologically elusive was understandable and had its virtues, but it cheapened Biafra's image when it ranged from 'save Biafra for the Free World' to a struggle against 'imperialism and neocolonialism' from the West and Soviet 'social imperialism and revisionism'; and from abiding with pre-existing laws and obligations to being the 'Biafran Revolution', Africa's new-found beacon. The Ahiara Declaration created concern among Biafra's conservative friends, while Biafra's general lack of consistent revolutionary rhetoric or socialist phraseology made it suspect to socialists and radicals worldwide.

Biafra's position on mercy corridors, daylight flights, and inspections on the part of the FMG suggested a callous disregard for the Biafran people. It appeared that Ojukwu was holding his people hostage to secure recognition. This accusation was not completely unfounded, but there were many good reasons why Biafra could not accept more open relief routes. Among others, it would expose itself to aerial or land attacks and it would dangerously divide the relief flights from the arms flights, leaving the latter open to attack by the Nigerian Air Force. The Biafrans opted for what appeared to them as the lesser of the two evils, and in the process they tarnished their image and alienated their friends.[64]

The African states and the OAU were priority targets of Biafra in 1967 and the first part of 1968. But the Biafrans lost faith in them a little too soon, and began snubbing and even abusing the OAU as well as individual African states and their leaders.[65] Thus they were bound both to lose prospective supporters and to embarrass existing ones. They effectively limited their supporters in their natural milieu of Africa –

precisely those allies that could lend their case an aura of African and subsequently international legitimacy.

Biafra's intransigence was another major error, understandable though it may have been. After a while it was obvious that, to stand any chance of success, Biafra would have to play its ultimate card – to reject secession in favour of a confederal or loose federal system. It would probably have failed, but it would have created a stir internationally by calling the FMG's bluff at the eleventh hour.

Among other things that went wrong were many of the arms deals, and the issue of currency. It is well known that Biafra was often tricked by private dealers, having to pay exorbitant prices and getting faulty equipment or even no military equipment at all.[66] A sudden change of Nigerian currency was something that the Biafrans believed the FMG could not accomplish, and when it did occur they were left with sackfuls of useless bank-notes.[67]

INTERNATIONAL INVOLVEMENT

Third-party involvement in the issue was decidedly of the 'pull' genre: external parties were persuaded by the Biafrans to support them. Among the African states involved on the Biafran side were the four states that eventually recognized Biafra. These were, in order of recognition, Tanzania, Gabon, the Ivory Coast and Zambia. Other African states that made no secret of their concern for Biafra included first and foremost Sierra Leone, and then Uganda, Senegal, Ghana, Dahomey and, far more more discreetly, Tunisia. Also worth mentioning are Congo–Brazzaville, which was sympathetic in the beginning, Botswana and the three states that acted as mediators under the OAU framework: first Ethiopia and then Liberia and Niger, all three of which were in fact on the Nigerian side of the fence. The remaining African states were, to varying degrees, on the side of Lagos.[68]

Tanzania's greatest service to Biafra was recognition, which was the first that finally arrived, setting the stage for Biafra to enter the world scene officially. Before and after their recognition, Tanzania, spearheaded by President Nyerere himself, was actively seeking other recognitions for Biafra, including an arms embargo, a ceasefire and a peaceful settlement. Apparently the Tanzanians introduced the Biafrans to the Chinese and assisted Biafra with some funds and relief aid; Tanzania became the staging point for arms from China.[69]

Tanzania, which was the first state after the Second World War to recognize *de jure* a secessionist entity as an independent state, was motivated by affective reasons. In fact it stood to lose from its association with Biafra more than did any other of the four African recognizers, particularly economically. The Biafran policy was very much in accord with Tanzania's well-known policy under Nyerere to follow a line based on principle even to the detriment of economic and other interests. Tanzania was convinced of the soundness of the Biafran case for independence, and took the genocide argument seriously.[70] Unity by force was regarded as a contradiction in terms and a perversion of the aim of African unity. As Tanzania was wont to put it: 'The breaking up of Nigeria is a terrible thing. But it is less terrible than that cruel war.' All secessions, Tanzania argued, should be judged on their own merits and not sacrificed carelessly in the name of African unity.[71] Secondary reasons for Tanzania's attitude included opposition to the British, a general dislike of Nigeria as a pro-Western African state, and disillusionment with the conservative bent of the OAU.[72]

Tanzania's delay in recognizing Biafra was probably due above all to the fact that the disintegration of Nigeria, Africa's largest multi-ethnic state, was regarded as a setback for African unity.[73] In 1969 Tanzania's somewhat guarded attitude was no doubt not unrelated to General Gowon's tactful policy towards Nyerere and his apparent moderation in comparison with Ojukwu's intransigence, which foreshadowed Biafra's defeat.

The Ivory Coast supplied Biafra with arms from its own stocks (which France replenished), as well as funds. It also provided air transportation for the Biafran leaders and hospital facilities, and was instrumental in bringing about and sustaining French aid to Biafra. From the end of April 1968 the Ivorians, and foremost of all the Ivorian President, Felix Houphouet-Boigny, mounted a diplomatic campaign for a ceasefire, unconditional peace talks, an arms embargo, recognition and mediation. Among heads of state Houphouet-Boigny was seen by the Biafrans until the end as 'the most sincere, dedicated, practical and active supporter of the Biafran cause'.[74] It has been claimed by some that the Ivory Coast was acting as a French proxy, but it seems that it was in fact Houphouet-Boigny who convinced the French to support Biafra and later made sure that French enthusiasm would not wane.[75]

Important to the Ivory Coast's considerations was the fear of 'communist penetration' in post-Balewa Nigeria, which could open a gateway following the Soviet expulsion from Ghana and its 'checkmate' with the Chinese in Guinea. Another well-known Ivorian fear was the threat of Islam and Arabism, both of which were linked with Biafra's adversary. Abidjan disapproved of the federal system of government in the African context and was known to give lukewarm support to the professed ultimate goal of the OAU – African unity. Ever since Nigeria's formation the Ivory Coast had considered it threatening; thus Nigeria's balkanization was regarded as a blessing. But perhaps of equal importance was the official justification – humanitarian concern – which was very much in line with Houphouet-Boigny's image and known stance against violence. Ivorian involvement was probably closer to the affective pole. Abidjan stood to lose from its Biafran connection, particularly within the French community. Such considerations and internal disagreements were probably responsible for the extended time the Ivory Coast took to swing to the Biafran side. But once the decision was taken, the Ivorian leader appeared immune to the mounting criticism at home and abroad.[76]

Gabon's material and diplomatic support to Biafra was similar to that of the Ivory Coast, its single major contribution being that Libreville was the principal staging point for French arms ferried to Biafra. President Bongo's sudden conversion to the Biafran cause following a visit to Paris suggests French influence. Bongo also shared Houphouet-Boigny's ideological viewpoint, his apprehension regarding Arabism and communism, and his dislike for federations. It has also been noted that the Ivorian President was to some extent a kind of 'super-president' of Gabon, and was Bongo's mentor.[77]

Zambia was the fourth and last African state to recognize Biafra, and did so on 20 May 1968. It assisted Biafra with some relief supplies, two old cargo aircraft and an amount of foreign currency, but no arms or personnel, both of which were badly needed by the Biafrans. On at least one occasion, Zambia provided Biafra with a platform to hold a press conference in the UN.

Prior to the act of recognition Zambia had indicated considerable concern for the Biafran case, offering to mediate and playing a principal role among East African states and within the OAU, most notably in the 1967 OAU summit conference at Kinshasa. So obvious was President Kaunda's leaning in favour of the secessionists at this conference that he had to leave the so-called 'caucus of heavyweights' – the group of heads of state trying to come to grips with the Nigerian war. (This caucus led to the formation of the OAU *ad hoc* Consultative Committee on Nigeria.)[78]

Following its recognition of Biafra Zambia's political activity on behalf of the secessionists was significant. In fact, the longer the war persisted the more intense was Zambia's activity, spearheaded by President Kenneth Kaunda, thus compensating somewhat for its limited material support in comparison with that of the other three African recognizers.[79]

From the start of the conflict Kaunda was in contact with Nyerere (it is known that Zambia often follows Tanzania's lead on international issues).[80] Zambia, generalizing from its own experience, disapproved of British-made federations in Africa, and was known to dislike Nigeria's

First Republic for being conservative and corrupt and for being on friendly terms with Black Africa's arch-enemies South Africa and Rhodesia. Unlike the Tanzanian approach, Zambia's recognition was less of a political lever to induce Lagos to enter into negotiations.[81] It was above all, as Anglin has put it, 'an expression of frustration, a symbolic gesture of protest against man's inhumanity to man'.[82] Biafra was seen as having a sound case for independence irrespective of whether or not genocide had been committed. It sufficed that this was an attempt at unity to be 'founded on blood', rather than based 'on the consent of all parties concerned'.[83] Lusaka's attitude was very much along the lines of Kaunda's 'Humanism', Zambia's ideological blueprint for politics.[84] If Tanzania's persuasion can be characterized as one of internalization, and the Ivory Coast's as one of 'identification', Zambia was motivated by both rationales.

After the overthrow of the Juxon–Smith military regime in April 1968, Sierra Leone under Prime Minister Siaka Stevens began to show interest in the Biafran plight. There were calls for a ceasefire and unconditional peace talks, and mediation was offered. In 1969, and even as late as January 1970, Freetown threatened to recognize Biafra if negotiations did not take place.[85]

Siaka Stevens and his foreign minister were early converts to the Biafran cause. The Leonean prime minister had been lobbied by a close friend and business associate, the influential adviser to Ojukwu, Francis Nwokedi. There was keen interest for Biafra in Sierra Leone, for there was a large community of Ibos in Freetown. It could also well be that the Biafran case provided an opportunity for the new regime to play a dynamic and original role in world affairs. It has also been suggested that Freetown was using support for Biafra as a bargaining ploy to gain certain concessions from Britain. Pressure from Nigeria and its allies, including Britain, and to some extent internal opposition, were the main reasons for not recognizing Biafra. The official justification was that recognition was incompatible with a potential role as mediator (an argument also used by Uganda at the time).[86]

Uganda was one of Biafra's early hopes for recognition. It is well established that Obote seriously contemplated recognition in the late spring of 1968, but he postponed it as Uganda was to host the Kampala peace talks.[87]

Uganda's position was roughly half-way between the two extremes in East Africa, Tanzania and Kenya. The Ugandans called for a ceasefire and talks, and branded the Nigerian war as the 'shame of Africa' and Nigeria's policy as one of 'extermination of the Ibos'.[88] Uganda was influenced by Tanzania and Zambia as well as by the articulate Biafran emissaries, though it was against secession in principle, as shown by Obote's policy towards the separatist Baganda in Uganda.

Senegal was to be Biafra's greatest disappointment as far as recognition was concerned. Senghor, the President of Senegal, had been assiduously lobbied by senior Biafran emissaries and by Biafra's principal supporters, and a strong impression was given that Senegal would recognize Biafra in the spring of 1968.[89]

Senghor used harsh words about Nigeria in 1968, but nevertheless, he concluded that the solution to the problem should be some kind of confederal framework, safeguarding the 'integrity' of Nigeria but not leading to 'unity', and respecting the 'Biafran need for autonomy'. Senghor's highly intellectual approach to problems, as well as his general moderation, were no doubt instrumental in Senegal's general comportment. The fact that the majority of the country's population was Muslim was probably also a factor.[90]

Ghana's sympathy was less clear, and strictly speaking Ghana should be placed with the negotiators rather than with Biafra's partisans. But contrary to the case of Senegal, the FMG over-reacted to the most minuscule of evidence, regarding it as confirmation of Ghana's *parti pris*.[91] The FMG apparently felt assured beforehand of Ghana's partiality.

Among the reasons for Ghana's slight pro-Biafran bent were the fear of Soviet communist penetration (this was a time when the post-Nkrumah Ghana was caught up in anti-communist hysteria); the appeal of the Biafran case (note that there was a vociferous expatriate Ibo community in Ghana); and a certain rapprochement with conservative Ivory Coast. Houphouet-Boigny, one of the doyens of African 'pragmatism', was a close friend of the equally pragmatic Busia, the Ghanaean Prime Minister.[92]

Dahomey (today's Benin) was considered the member of the Conseil de l'Entente most likely to follow the Ivory Coast's lead and recognize Biafra.[93] This was not to take place, but Dahomey did on a number of occasions indicate its pro-Biafran inclination by offering to mediate and by agreeing to the use of Cotonou as a staging point for relief aid to Biafra by the International Red Cross, when the newly independent Equatorial Guinea denied the use of Fernando Pó. Dahomey had to face the wrath of its huge neighbour Nigeria, so was reserved in its statements, pointing out that relief flights could be undertaken so long as they conformed with the various Nigerian requirements.[94] Yet Zinsou, the Dahomean President, put forward the great African dilemma: 'Can one say . . . that the boundaries of colonization were so well made as to be irreversible, and in respect to them should thousands die?'[95] Dahomey's motives were humanitarian concern and Biafra's appeal as a case of self-determination (if Dahomey with its two million inhabitants could be independent, why not Biafra?). For the use of Cotonou there was also a financial incentive: there was payment on the spot by the International Red Cross to the economically stricken Dahomey.[96]

Among the reasons for restraint one could also cite the existence of a large Yoruba constituency in the country, the reaction of the FMG to the agreement with the International Red Cross, and perhaps the influence of Senghor and other Francophone African leaders. There was also a Dahomean 'hostage' community of several hundred thousands living in West Nigeria.[97]

Bourguiba, the Tunisian President, was known to be sympathetic to the Biafran case, but he was obviously restrained by the fact that his was a Muslim country and he was also apparently taken aback by Biafra's rising intransigence.[98]

Burundi and Rwanda were not particularly vocal throughout the conflict but were cited as potential recognizers. The President of Burundi, Micombero, at one point provided a Biafran delegation with aircraft. Rwanda supported Nyerere in the Addis Ababa summit of 1969, and called for UN intervention.[99] Congo–Brazzaville was also sympathetic until Ngouabi's left-wing coup, which placed the new People's Republic of the Congo firmly on the Nigerian side.[100] Botswana's President Khama came forward in 1969 at the UN General Assembly with a strong appeal for a joint UN–OAU initiative to end the conflict. There were also some reports that Botswana's territory was being used as a transit point for arms ferried from South Africa – something which was strenuously denied by Botswana.[101]

France was the nearest to a patron that Biafra could secure outside Africa. The first French statement of support came fourteen months into the secession, and arms appear to have been sent only by late September 1968, following Biafra's anguished cry to its sympathizers. The quantity of arms involved was only a fraction of the arms received by Nigeria from the Soviet Union and Britain. But arms shipments were regular[102] and sufficient for a limited war of attrition. The arms transfers were orchestrated by Foccart, de Gaulle's close confidant on Africa.[103] Apart from arms there was relief aid, including qualified medical staff and some foreign currency.[104] The French government argued that the Biafrans had the right of self-determination, and called for a ceasefire and negotiations in parity. De Gaulle in his statement of September 1968 did not even exclude the possibility of a French recognition of Biafra.[105] But this never materialized, and France left Biafra suspended in a 'curious diplomatic limbo'.[106]

Biafra

The reasons for French support have never failed to baffle commentators. None of the three main lines of argument is completely convincing: the all-instrumental approach (similar to the French motives with regard to Katanga a few years earlier); the official French claim that its policy was based on humanitarian reasons and on Biafra's sound case for self-determination; or the personal idiosyncrasies of the man at the helm, de Gaulle. But the main reasons for French involvement can be given under five headings:

1. economic interests, primarily oil;
2. humanitarian concern and French public opinion;
3. the peculiarities of French policy towards Africa;
4. the presence of de Gaulle;
5. foreign policy and political interests in that area of Africa.

The argument of economic gains is not very clear, for France had more interests of this nature in the rest of Nigeria, and when France began supporting the Biafrans, the latter were no longer in control of the oil territory. De Gaulle and his adviser Foccart had Africa as their *domain réservé* and apparently, in the case of Biafra, were influenced by Houphouet-Boigny, an old friend of France and a former cabinet minister in French governments. The Biafran case seemed to fit in well with the French President's perception of Africa, his views on the fate of British-made federations and his fear of the 'Soviet menace'. It also provided him with the opportunity of embarrassing the British ('les Anglo-Saxons', whom it is well known he had disliked ever since his war days). Finally, the weakening of Nigeria, the British-dominated giant of Africa in proximity to the small and weak French-speaking African states, was, needless to say, a highly welcome prospect.[107]

The reasons for French reluctance to go any further are more obvious. They include among others factors such as the extended economic interests of France in Nigeria proper; the lack of support from other Francophone African states; Nigeria's careful policy towards the French; the negative attitude of the Quay d'Orsay towards any such policy; and the intransigence of the Biafrans, which in the long run made defeat unavoidable. After de Gaulle's resignation, President Pompidou continued supporting Biafra despite his lack of commitment to the Biafran affair.[108] In general, French support may have been reluctantly nailed down to its unusual position for internal or international reasons; it may have been largely fortuitous or even meticulously calculated as the most appropriate policy given the circumstances at hand. What is certain is that it struck a balance between the forces for and against support. For the Biafrans French military aid was crucial, although after the war

Biafrans claimed that this French assistance was in fact detrimental to their cause, for it raised false hopes and also annoyed the British, making them more determined in their support of Lagos.[109]

Portugal's assistance to Biafra was significant, though it may not have included arms and similar high-level tangible support. From the outset of secession Lisbon acted as the coordinating base for the arms, mercenaries and relief which reached Biafra via São Tomé. When Port Harcourt fell in 1967 and Biafra was left with no outlet to the sea, Lisbon was the lone communication and transportation link with the outside world. The Portuguese connection was a strict business arrangement, but considerations with respect to Portugal's continued presence in Africa no doubt also played a role.[110]

The role of South Africa is far more obscure. Arms and funds were once reported to have been involved, but such reports may simply have been, as some have suggested, a propaganda stunt by the British Foreign Office keen to assist the Nigerian attempt to discredit Biafra. After the war Ojukwu noted, somewhat cryptically, that he had received no such aid, but that he would have been 'a fool' not to have accepted arms from South Africa had they been offered to him.[111] Pretoria claimed that it was involved only in relief aid. Prime Minister Vorster upheld that the Biafrans were justified in their struggle for self-determination. No doubt the South Africans relished the idea of Nigerian disintegration. Sustained violence in Black Africa diverted African resources, drew world attention away from South Africa, and lent ammunition to their claim that the black Africans (the 'kaffir', later called 'bantu') were totally incapable of peaceful self-government. The Smith regime of Rhodesia was also sympathetic towards Biafra but hard pressed as it was it could not spare any arms or funds.[112]

Israel provided relief aid, including medicine and medical teams and perhaps some foreign exchange or help in bringing about some of Biafra's better deals in the open arms market. In Israel the popularity of the Biafrans was great, but in the aftermath of the June 1967 War Israel was keen to gain the support of the African states, the majority of which naturally supported Nigeria. It was also interested in upgrading its relations with Nigeria.[113]

The People's Republic of China, which was introduced to the Biafran case by Tanzania, provided a small quantity of light arms from late 1968 or early 1969 onwards. The amounts involved were insignificant but certainly useful to the secessionists, who were short of arms and wanted to keep their military sources as diversified as possible. The New China News Agency encouraged the Biafrans in their fight against 'the crimes of Anglo-American imperialism and Soviet revisionism', but support did not begin as early as 1967, nor were 'Chinese-looking mercenaries' involved in Biafra, as Lagos claimed.[114]

Haiti should also be mentioned, for in 1969 it provided Biafra with its fifth and last recognition, though one of doubtful value which apparently was regarded even in Biafra as a joke. Apparently it was a quirk on the part of Papa Doc Duvalier, who was persuaded by Ikejiani, a Biafran emissary and old friend.[115]

The five Nordic countries, in particular Norway followed by Denmark and then Sweden, were concerned with the conflict and provided substantial relief aid. At one point in 1969 Norway even considered recognizing Biafra, and came first among the relief suppliers on the basis of percentage of GNP (Sweden came third, Denmark fifth).[116] Nordic aid reflected the deep humanitarian concern of the Scandinavian peoples, and the belief that the Biafrans had a good case for self-determination.[117] Instrumental in spurring such sentiments were the activities of Nyerere and in particular of Kaunda (both of whom were much respected in Scandinavia), and the actions of the Nordic churches which had been lobbied by Kaunda. The Nordic countries, however, did not go any further, so as not to jeopardize relations with Nigeria (in particular trade relations) and also because of a certain traditional deference for Britain.[118]

Among other states that indicated some concern and provided relief aid worth mentioning were Canada (fourth in relief aid on the basis of GNP) and Switzerland (second); the Netherlands, Belgium and Czechoslovakia (under Dubček) placed an arms embargo on their equipment being procured by Nigeria. The Federal Republic of Germany, Ireland, Italy, Colombia and some other Latin-American countries also showed some concern.[119]

The United States came first in absolute quantities of relief aid, but only seventh in proportion to its GNP. It also repeatedly voiced its concern about the conflict, and placed an arms embargo. Interestingly, during the Johnson Administration, when involvement was fairly limited and the whole attitude detached, Washington had to cope with the strong criticism of Lagos. But under Nixon when interest rose considerably, the USA was to suffer the indignation of the Biafran leaders. On the whole, US involvement in the conflict can be regarded as fairly evenly balanced until the later period, when it was distinctly pro-Lagos, particularly when Biafra lay the onus of settling the conflict (peacefully) on the Nixon Administration and Nixon did nothing about it. Thus, indirectly at least, the United States buttressed the Nigerian policy of a military victory.[120]

The main reason for Washington's humanitarian involvement was no doubt public opinion. American concern was so great that the issue virtually became a domestic one, second only to Vietnam.[121] Nixon, it should be noted, had already committed himself by a dramatic statement in favour of 'the Biafran people' during his presidential campaign. On the other hand, Washington would go no further for it considered Nigeria a British responsibility and felt confident that any Soviet influence could easily be counteracted without resorting to unorthodox methods such as assisting secessionists. Furthermore the United States, generalizing from its own civil war, was a believer in federalism, and was at no time speculating on Nigerian dismemberment with an eye on its oil, as the Soviet Union mistakenly conjectured.[122]

Among IGOs involved were the Commonwealth, under its Secretary General, and the OAU. The UN stood aloof and only UNICEF was involved from the UN family, assisting with relief. The OAU created an *ad hoc* consultative committee of five heads of state whose attempts at mediation culminated in two meetings in 1968, one in Niamey and the other in Addis Ababa, involving Nigerian and Biafran leaders. But the first attempt at mediation came from Commonwealth Secretary General Arnold Smith, and it led to the Kampala peace talks of May 1968 between the FMG and Biafra.[123] Church-related bodies were involved with relief and Pope Paul VI, who was known to have a special interest in Africa, made several appeals and attempted to mediate in the conflict in what appears to have been a personal decision on his part.[124] Among Non-Governmental Organizations (NGOs) involved as unofficial intermediaries, the Quakers were particularly noteworthy.[125]

One of the most memorable events of the Biafran episode was no doubt the airborne relief operation to the starving enclave. There were two main relief groupings that between them handled 90 per cent of relief aid to Biafra: operation INALWA (International Airlift West Africa) and Joint Church Aid (JCA), both of which operated by way of blockade-breaking night flights to the Uli airstrip (Annabelle Airport, as it was called). INALWA was operated by the cautious International Committee of the Red Cross (ICRC) and came to include as many as forty national Red Cross societies and some nineteen international voluntary organizations. It channelled relief through Fernando Pó in 1968 and through Cotonou in Dahomey in 1969, but stopped operations when one of its aircraft was shot down by the Nigerian Air Force. Joint Church Aid, which operated through São Tomé, was basically Church-related and came to comprise some thirty-two relief agencies, churches and secular groups. It was formed towards the end of 1968, by the principal organizations that had already been individually airlifting to Biafra. These were the following: Nordchurchaid, Caritas Internationalis, Das Diakonische Werke, Caritas Verband Deutschland, Joint Church

Aid–USA (consisting of Catholic Relief Services, Church World Service and the American Jewish Committee), and Canairelief, the Canadian relief agency. Two other independent operations also existed: Africa Concern, the relief agency formed by the Irish Holy Ghost Fathers, and the airlift of the French Red Cross via Libreville.[126]

In the early stages the relief agencies bought space in the gun-running planes to Biafra, but by mid-1968 the Church agencies, like the ICRC before them, were able to provide their own planes. Night flights to the Uli airstrip became more systematic, defying the federal blockade after Count von Rosen's successful night flight at a critical point in August 1968. The ICRC tried to be correct and impartial in accord with its charter and tradition, but to no avail. It faced severe criticism from both Nigeria and Biafra and, after deciding to suspend its operations, ended up having delivered far less than JCA. On the whole, however, the relief airlifts were able to alleviate starvation and were instrumental in rendering the Biafra case a *cause célèbre*.

The pro-Biafran lobby in the West was far more spontaneous than was the Katanga lobby. It included a far greater number of individuals from all segments of society, as well as ranging through the political spectrum from left to right. The following Western countries should be included among those with *ad hoc* pro-Biafran organizations, extensive fund raising, favourable press coverage (often from journalists who had visited Biafra), and appeals in their respective legislative institutions: Sweden, Denmark, Norway, the Netherlands, Switzerland, the Federal Republic of Germany, Italy, France, Belgium, Canada, Ireland, Great Britain and the United States. Particularly noteworthy from the various *ad hoc* groups that appeared in the West were the Britain–Biafra Association in London and the American Committee to Keep Biafra Alive in the United States. The Biafran lobby within the British Parliament included a hard core of some fifty to sixty Labour and Tory backbenchers of all shades of persuasion, as well as the entire Liberal Party. The Biafra lobby in the US Congress was also a mixture of conservatives and liberals, including such politicians as Edward Kennedy, McCarthy, Humphrey, McGovern, Mansfield and Mondale.[127]

In spite of all the support and enthusiasm that Biafra generated after its first year of relative obscurity, Nigeria managed to receive far more aid and the diplomatic support that really counted. It was, after all, an independent state, and though weak and unstable it was potentially powerful with much to offer to prospective supporters. And there was the balkanization domino effect that all African leaders dreaded. The Nigerian assessment in the aftermath of the war was that their success was due first of all to the Soviet military aid which prompted the equally important British support, and to the almost unanimous African support both directly and through the OAU – in particular the support of its neighbours, most notably Cameroon with its extended borders on secessionist territory.[128] It is worth noting that the quantities of arms secured by Nigeria were many times larger than those of the Biafrans. (For heavy arms it has been estimated that Lagos received as much as seventeen times the value of arms supplied to Biafra.)[129]

Two decades have elapsed since Nigeria's Eastern Region opted for independence. Despite the well-known ardent nationalism of the Ibo, active separatism has not reappeared in the various states of the former Eastern Region, though ethnic tension as such remains almost as rife in Nigeria as it was in the dramatic 1960s. Ojukwu was pardoned by President Shagari during Nigeria's so-called Second Republic, and he returned to Iboland in June 1982 to be greeted by a rapturous crowd (he was then for a time considered an important political contender).

Despite its good case and able leadership, Biafra failed. Its message was a clear warning to all secessionist movements; declaring independence was apparently not the appropriate strategy in such a hostile world. Interestingly, not much later no less than three secessionist movements found solutions that made the Biafran struggle appear obsolete almost overnight. These were Iraqi Kurdistan in March 1970, Bangladesh in December 1971 and Southern Sudan in early 1972. Yet as the years went by, the lesson of Biafra was to reassert its validity as something of a model case, both for the student of secession and for actual or potential secessionist movements.

7

THE SOUTHERN SUDAN
(1961–1972)

We have endured many times more deaths . . . than all the African freedom movements combined. And yet the OAU will not even allow our story to be told . . . Our poor land does not have the oil of Angola, the chrome of Zimbabwe or the diamonds of Namibia.

Major General Joseph Lagu
Head of the Anya-Nya
and the Southern Sudan Liberation Movement

Our struggle is older than the borders of Sudan . . . it is a fundamental struggle pitting an indigenous African culture against alien invading forces – Arabization and Soviet imperialism. The Anya-Nya is the vanguard of Africa's struggle against this new colonialism. . .

The Anya-Nya Struggle: Background and Objectives (circa 1971)

The Sudan, Africa's largest country (it is a little smaller than Western Europe), is one of its most diverse. It has been described as a 'microcosm',[1] 'crossroads', 'gateway' of Africa, and as a country that is 'intermediary',[2] with a 'multiple marginality'.[3] A fundamental division of the country that has serious political implications is the one between North and South, which has made authors speak of an 'Afro-Arab schism',[4] of a 'dichotomous duality',[5] of a 'dualistic imbalance', and of an 'uneven territorial dualism';[6] or, as the separatists put it more popularly in the early 1970s, of a country split around the twelfth parallel into two parts by a 'grass curtain'.[7]

When the Sudan became independent on 1 January 1956, 40 per cent of the population was Arab, as against a little above 50 per cent in the North. In spite of these statistics, the Sudan was then considered, and is still so today, as an 'Arab Country' and the North as the 'Arab North'. This is due to the fact that the Arab Sudanese are predominant in the country's affairs, making the Sudan, as one author has put it, '*de facto* an Arab state'.[8]

4. The Sudan and the Southern Sudan

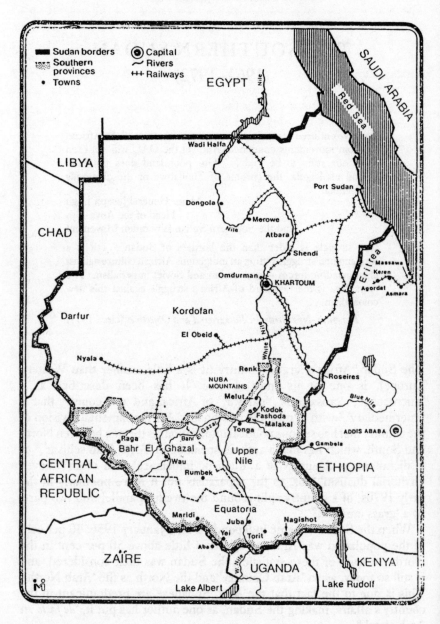

ETIOLOGY

The Southern Sudan, an area the size of France and the greater part of Britain put together, is inhabited by black Africans. The majority are animists and a minority are Catholics and Protestants. In 1956 the Southerners amounted to 29 per cent of the total population of the Sudan; that is, around three million. Today their numbers have doubled. Of the three main linguistic groups – the Nilotic, the Nilo-Hamitic, and the Sudanic – the most numerous are the Nilotic Dinka, well known for their ethnocentrism,[9] followed by the three other 'great Nilotic nations', the Nuer, the Shilluk and the Anuak and the largest Sudanic group, the Azande. The rest include the Nilo-Hamitic Murle, Didinga, Boya, Toposa, Latuka, Mundari, Kakwe and the Sudanic Kreish, Bongo, Moru, Madi and others. The Nilotics inhabit the provinces of Bahr el-Ghazal and Upper Nile, while the others mostly live in the province of Equatoria to the south.

During the period when the Sudan was an Anglo-Egyptian condominium (1899–1956), the South was administered separately by the British on the basis of the 'Southern Policy'. From 1930 to 1946 the British sealed off the South from Arab influence, to allow the Southerners to develop at their own pace and along their own lines. In effect the South was ruled in splendid isolation by the legendary 'Bog Barons', the British administrators, whose unmistakable paternalism was tinged with a fascination for the defiant tribesmen. This policy of separation was reversed in the course of the last decade of the Condominium when it became clear that the South was to be bound to the alien North as a future political entity.[10]

In the late 1940s and 1950s the gap in development between the two regions of the Sudan was striking, a prototype of centre and periphery in all conceivable aspects.[11] The Northerners and Southerners finally came together in the Juba Conference of 1947 which was organized by the British in order to decide the future of the Sudan. In Juba the Arab and African Sudanese viewed each other as strangers. The Southerners were fearful and suspicious of the far more developed Northerners. Yet, though uncertain about the precise future consequences of the conference decisions, the Southern leaders (handpicked by the British) finally gave their consent to a unified Sudan.[12]

Southern identity as a feeling of distinctiveness within the Sudan can be traced from the days of the incipient all-Southern feeling at the Juba Conference of 1947 to its maturity in the late 1960s when the separatist option was supported by the clear majority of Southerners.

In the 1950s it was an exclusive affair of the missionary-educated elite who formed the Southern Party, later renamed the Liberal Party and then the Federal Party. The basis of Southern distinctiveness was manifold. It was based on ascriptive symbols of unity such as race and culture, being black and African; on local religions and Christianity; on the distinct geophysical setting of the South; on a history of separate administration and before that on resistance to encroachments from the North. Of particular importance were two factors: the very existence of the Northern Sudanese as the 'outgroup' and the extent of underdevelopment and disadvantage in comparison to the North. This inchoate sense of an all-Southern identity led to negative stereotypes of the Northerners, who were seen as 'avaricious and domineering' merchants (*jallaba*) and soldiers (*mundukuru*), bent on exploiting them and selling them as slaves (*abid*, as the Northerners tended to call the Southerners). However, even by the mid-1960s, this feeling of Southern distinctiveness from the Northerners did not amount to a pervasive sense of community. For the Nilotics, the other black Southerners were regarded simply as 'other people' (*jur mathiang*) and only by the late 1960s as part of 'the same black people' (*wuok koccol*).[13]

The South was considerably underdeveloped, and its largely rural, poor and uneducated inhabitants were at a disadvantage compared to the more 'sophisticated' Arab Northerners. As one Southerner put it during the 1947 Juba Conference, his compatriots were like 'children in their relation with the grown-up Northerners'.[14] The latter blamed British policy for this state of affairs and did little about it, as the Sudan was preparing for independence and government was in Sudanese Arab hands. The Sudanese Arabs either dismissed, or paid lip-service to, the Southern demands for a federal framework. Characteristic of the way in which the Sudanese Arabs intended to run the country was the report of the Sudanization Committee of 1954. This went so far as to grant the Southerners only six of the some 800 senior administrative posts.[15]

The report of the Sudanization Committee in 1954 and many other real or imagined events – such as the telegram that Prime Minister Al-Azhari allegedly sent to the administrators in the South calling upon them to 'disregard the childish complaints of the Southerners' and 'persecute them, oppress them, ill-treat them'[16] – aroused considerable indignation towards Khartoum. Before long the growing fears and suspicions led to the first upsurge of violence which culminated in the Equatoria Corps mutiny of August 1955, four months prior to official independence – an ominous prelude of what was to come. Thus the Southern Sudanese cause registered its first victims, as Southern nationalist mythology was later to deduce.

When the Sudan became independent there was no genuine attempt to redress the striking imbalance between North and South and the extreme inequality and under-representation suffered by the Southerners. Soon it became obvious that in independent Sudan the Southerners were inexorably cast in the role of second-class citizens. Even the educated among them felt the brunt of discrimination and found their opportunities for social mobility decidedly stifled for the foreseeable future.

The underlying reason for the persisting inequality and differential treatment is no doubt Northern racial-cultural discrimination. The Arab Sudanese pride themselves on their Arab-Islamic culture and assumed Arab origins (in fact the majority are hybrid Arabs which may account for their passionate attachment to Islam and Arabism).[17] As a result they treat the black Sudanese and their African culture with contempt and intolerance 'unaware that other Sudanese might feel for their cultural heritage what they feel for their Arabness'.[18] Even in the highest echelons of power it was largely assumed that the South was in a state of 'cultural vacuum' ready to be filled by the 'great Arab-Islamic culture' of the North.[19] As historian Richard Gray concludes, the North was under the firm conviction that it was 'inherently superior to the South'.[20] Successive generations of Northern Sudanese leaders who have monopolized politics in Khartoum are of the belief that the Sudan is above all a Muslim and Arab country. For most of the years of Sudan's independent existence Khartoum has been unable to come to terms with the existing situation in the Sudan, with the obvious fact of the duality of the Sudan and with the need for a duality in parity.[21]

Upon independence the Liberal Party, which was soon superseded by the Federal Party, headed by Father Saturnino Lohure, pressed on for a federal system of government. In fact, prior to independence, Khartoum had promised to give full consideration to the Southern appeals, but attached no seriousness to the issue afterwards. The Southerners were allotted only three out of the forty-six seats of the constitutional committee. The Federal Party persisted with its attempt to remedy the situation through peaceful constitutional means calling for the establishment of a bi-national federal state along Canadian lines. Somewhat surprisingly, by 1958 the Southerners appeared to be very near to success. Aspirations surged only to be unceremoniously dashed by General Abboud's military coup, which apparently had the blessing of the two predominant Muslim religious orders, the Khatmiya and the Ansar (Mahdiya), which supported respectively the National Unionist Party (NUP) and the Umma, the two main parties of the Sudan. This sudden turn of events convinced the Southern Sudanese that they had fallen victim to the machinations of the 'perfidious' and 'dastardly'

Northerners.[22] This 'constitutional frustration', as one author has put it,[23] was essential in galvanizing the Southern elite into action with a gradual tilt towards enforced separatism. The forceful assimilation campaign of Abboud that followed, and the lack of any available democratic means to redress the situation, resulted in an exodus of Southerners to neighbouring African states and desertions from the Sudanese army. With all avenues to peaceful change blocked, the Southerners resorted to an armed struggle in the early 1960s.[24]

In a nutshell, it may be said that Southern nationalism and separatism were mainly the outcome of (1) the extreme level of inequality, (2) the threat of assimilation posed by the Arab Northerners, and (3) the intransigence of the regime in Khartoum to the claims of the Southern Sudanese for federal status, non-discrimination, and more equitable participation in the country's affairs.

INTERNATIONAL ACTIVITY

The separatist movement of the Southern Sudan during this decade can be divided into five periods:[25]

1. from 1962 until March 1965 the relative unity in the region was due to the Sudan African National Union (SANU) until this split into two factions;
2. from April 1965 until July 1967 the separatists remained in disarray despite attempts to rebuild unity, notably by the Azania Liberation Front (ALF);
3. from August 1967 until March 1969 the key role was played by the Southern Sudan Provisional Government (SSPG);
4. from March 1969 until July 1970 the opposition to Khartoum was fragmented into several groups, the most vocal of these being the Nile Provisional Government (NPG);
5. from July 1970 until March 1972 the unity established by the Southern Sudan Liberation Movement (SSLM) which led to the Addis Ababa Agreement.

The early bands of guerrilla fighters, although known collectively as Anya-Nya – probably derived from the Madi word for the venom of the Gabon viper – lacked unity and defied political control. With ivory as their sole 'export' asset, at least initially, the inadequately funded Southerners received limited external aid, and – unlike the Eastern Nigerians or the East Bengalis – they lacked the advantages of a large pool of well-educated and talented supporters. Furthermore, they had no unifying ethnic core or pre-existing common institutional or governmental apparatus. With such limited resources it was not surprising that the Southerners were unable to mount the kind of international campaign that could transform their rather obscure struggle into a veritable *cause célèbre*, as had the leaders of Katanga, Biafra and Bangladesh.

The separatist movement was dominated by a series of leaders, the better known of whom included William Deng, a former Dinka administrator; Father Saturnino Lohure, a Catholic priest from Equatoria who had headed the Federal Party; Joseph Oduho, a Latuka schoolmaster and one-time MP; Aggrey Jaden, a Pojulu former administrator; and Joseph Lagu, a Madi ex-officer in the Sudanese army. The two with the greatest sway were Lohure in the early phase, and Lagu towards the end: both owed much of their ability to wield authority to the fact that they could deliver external aid, from the missionaries and from Israel, respectively. Ethnic rivalries, personal ambitions, and personality clashes, as well as differences over tactics between the politicians and the Anya-Nya leaders, wasted the limited resources of the separatists and discredited the otherwise sound Southern case for self-determination. Perhaps the most publicized differences were those between the Dinka and the ethnic groups residing in the Province of Equatoria, with overall control of the movement appearing to swing from one to the other like a pendulum.

The Southern separatists had no clearly defined or revolutionary ideology, other than black nationalism. Under the Nile Provisional Government and the SSLM there was a certain amount of radicalism, but this was expressed mainly in rhetoric, and there was no comparison with the revolutionary ideology of nearby Eritrea. In fact the Southerners readily admitted, more than once, that they lacked a coherent ideology.

The ultimate aim of the separatists varied from one period to the next or between rival fronts during the same period.[26] SANU spoke moderately in terms of 'self-determination' but by 1964 was known to tilt towards complete independence. ALF called for an 'independent Azania' (the same name used today by the blacks of South Africa). The SSPG also sought independence and so did the NPG, which called for an 'independent Nile State'. The SSLM was more guarded, stating most of the time that its aim was self-determination and in view of the final outcome – autonomy – this was no mere propaganda. In fact instructions had been given to Lagu's plenipotentiaries to settle for a meaningful autonomy scheme as early as October 1970, but the process was deliberately obstructed by Joseph Garang, the Southern communist politician who was Numeiry's Minister for Southern Affairs until the abortive Leftist coup of July 1971.[27]

The Southern secessionist movement began in the 1960s in Uganda and Zaïre where various groups were formed. The group that was to prevail and provide a semblance of unity to the separatist ranks was the Sudan African Closed Districts National Union (SACDNU), soon renamed Sudan African National Union (SANU), headed by Lohure as patron, Oduho as president and Deng as secretary-general. Deng was the prime mover, but his influence gradually diminished when he made Geneva his base. The main targets of appeal of SANU were the neighbouring African states, various circles of academics, churchmen and missionaries in Britain and elsewhere in Western Europe and to a far lesser degree in the United States, the UN, the OAU, and INGOs such as the International Commission of Jurists. A small journal was published in Britain with the help of the missionaries. It was called *Voice of Southern Sudan*. There also appeared a readable booklet by Oduho and Deng (it was in fact mainly written by Lohure, the most revered figure at the time) which was published under the auspices of the Institute of Race Relations, London. Anya-Nya, the guerrilla force, appeared in 1963, functioning apparently as the military wing of SANU.[28]

When the Abboud regime collapsed, following a mass uprising in Khartoum which was partly related to the Southern issue, SANU split into two groups. One was SANU-inside, under Deng, which favoured accommodation with Khartoum on the basis of a federal framework for the Sudan, and the other was SANU-outside, under Jaden, which spurned the peace overtures of the new caretaker government of al-Khatim al-Khalifa. Finally peace talks did take place in Khartoum in March 1965 (the Khartoum Round Table Conference) with the initial participation of SANU-outside. But Jaden walked out of the Conference and the talks came to nothing for the Northern parties were not prepared to discuss a federal solution to the country's ills. SANU-outside fell to pieces in the spring of 1965 and for a time the secessionist movement was represented only by the Southern Front (SF), a political party set up in the Sudan upon the fall of Abboud and headed by the veteran politician, Clement Mboro.[29]

Among the various groups that emerged from SANU-outside, most notable was the Azania Liberation Front (ALF) formed by Oduho. There was also the evanescent Sudan African Liberation Front (SALF), under Jaden. SALF soon merged with ALF, but before long Oduho was at loggerheads with Jaden, his erstwhile antagonist and was able to expel him from the organization. Prospects were bleak when the main source of arms in the mid-1960s, the arms gleaned from the Simbas fighting Tshombe's Congo Government were no longer available, and even staunch supporters of the South, such as the Verona Fathers, appeared less forthcoming. Lohure left his base in Nairobi, where he had been acting for years as treasurer and arms supplier, and joined Oduho in the bush. But after a while the two men clashed and Lohure had Oduho arrested by a protégé of his, Colonel Joseph Lagu. In 1967 Lohure met his death in mysterious circumstances on the Ugandan side of the border. After that ALF collapsed.[30]

In the meantime, Jaden was active in building the so-called Home Front, and in August 1967 summoned the Angudri Convention, which heralded a new, more ambitious, attempt at unity and institution-building. In Angudri the Southern Sudan Provisional Government (SSPG) was created, with Jaden as president and 'ministerial portfolios' for Oduho and rising separatist leaders such as Kwanai and Mayen (formerly of the Southern Front), in what was an attempt at ethnic, regional and even denominational balance. The Anya-Nya, with General Taffeng as commander, was placed under the 'Minister of Defence'. The SSPG was little known to the outside world, not being able to mount any worthwhile campaign, but was instrumental in forging Southern nationalism at a time when lack of arms and funds threatened the movement with total collapse. But unity was not to last. Already Oduho and Lagu, by then a rising figure in the guerrilla ranks, and others, had left the SSPG, and by late 1968 and early 1969 the SSLM was in the throes of major crisis. Jaden lost his grip on the Provisional Government and ended up having to flee to Kenya.[31] Muortat Mayen then took over, calling a convention at Balgo-Bindi, which led to the establishment of the Nile Provisional Government (NPG), with Mayen as president and Wanji as 'foreign minister'. The NPG was mainly a Dinka affair and there were new splits and permutations in the secessionists' ranks. One of the foremost groups rivalling the NPG was the Anyidi Revolutionary Government (ARG), 'Anyidi' being the name of an old trading post linked with Southern resistance in the old days. It was headed by Taffeng with Jaden as 'foreign minister'. Oduho formed his own group, which he again called ALF, and there was also the Sudan–Azania Provisional Government, under an old stalwart of the movement, Ezibon Mondiri. As for Lagu, he was becoming his own man in the bush in Equatoria. To complicate matters even further there appeared an Azande separatist movement, the Sue River Revolutionary Government or Suer Republic under Michael Tawili. Southern fragmentation roughly coincided with Numeiry's takeover in Khartoum. The most vocal group during that period was the NPG, which reactivated the journal *Voice of Southern Sudan*, soon renaming it *Voice of the Nile Republic*, but most effective was Lagu's group which established contact with Israel.[32]

The final stage of the movement was inaugurated by Lagu's attempt to unify the Southern secessionists. Lagu, after securing Equatoria, took overall command of the Anya-Nya forces and soon the politicians collaborated, lest they be left out and condemned to impotence. The new united front was known by various names, but finally settled for the Southern Sudan Liberation Movement (SSLM). Arms from Israel began to flow in and there was a more vigorous and imaginative international campaign spearheaded by the Southern Sudan Association (SSA), set up in London before Lagu had taken over. The SSA chairman was Brian McDermot, a Briton, and the director was the late Mading de Garang, later confirmed as the SSLM representative in London. Other permanent representatives of the SSLM included Dr Lawrence Wol Wol in Paris, Dominic Mohamed in Washington, Angelo Voga in Kampala and Job Adier de Jok in Addis Ababa. There were two publications at the time, *Grass Curtain*, edited by Mading de Garang, and a pictorial news-sheet called *Anya-Nya*.[33]

The SSLM was able to raise the cost of the war for Khartoum, and was wise enough to grasp the opportunity of a settlement in the nick of time, when its arms routes were about to be cut off, mainly as a result of Emperor Haile Selassie's rapprochement with Numeiry and Amin's break with Israel (arms from Israel came through Uganda and Ethiopia).

On the Sudanese side, the architects of the settlement appeared to have been the former Southern Front politician, Abel Alier, who had taken over the Ministry for Southern Affairs after the execution of Garang, and the Northern intellectual Dr Gaafar Ali Buchheit, heading the Ministry for Local Affairs. The mediators were the World Council of Churches (WCC) and the All Africa Council of Churches (AACC) and, at the final stage of the negotiations, Haile Selassie. On the Southern side the negotiation process was handled by Mading de Garang, assisted by Lawrence Wol Wol.[34]

In those ten years of separatist activity the main argument available to the Southern Sudanese was that of Southern self-determination. With oil not yet found in the South (it was discovered in 1979), there was a dearth of available goods to use as credible inducements or negative sanctions. Of the few inducements that have come to light, worth mentioning are the harassment of the Simbas in exchange for arms from Zaïre and the alleged assistance afforded to General Amin in his overthrow of Obote in 1971. It has also been alleged that attempts were made to entice the United States by offering them bases to 'fight communism' and the like.[35]

The negative sanction used to discredit the supporters of Khartoum was the exposure of the extent of Soviet and radical Arab involvement with the Sudan, characterizing it as no less than complicity in genocide. This appeared also in its moral blackmail version, evident in various letters to African leaders, Obote in particular. The most dramatic appeals of this kind were the various open letters of Lagu to the Pope, Kaunda, Brezhnev and Kosygin. The exposure of the extent of Soviet aid was part of the worn-out argument of many a secessionist movement, the communist scare being an obvious attention catcher for Israel, South Africa and the West. Khartoum, it was argued, was handing over 'warm water naval bases' and air bases to the Soviet Union. Sudan was the 'Soviet Vietnam' and linked with a general Middle East conflagration. Under the circumstances the Southern Sudan could do nothing else but resist the Arab and Soviet menace.

Two arguments were the corner-stones of the Southern case for self-determination: the argument of physical violence and the argument of racial-cultural domination and assimilation by the 'Arabs' of the Northern Sudan. The two were interconnected. The Southerners, the victims of atrocities and genocide, were treated as 'abid' (slaves) without a culture worthy of respect and suffered a 'harsher form of colonialism', by virtue of being African and wanting to remain African.

Among the other arguments used were the historical argument of separate Southern identity and historical resistance to Arab encroachments, the legal argument, that they were in fact never truly consulted as to the fate of the Southern Sudan, and the argument that they were ready to negotiate and reach a peaceful settlement while Khartoum consistently tricked them and remained intransigent. Their struggle, the separatists claimed, did not attract the support of third parties, not even that of their African brothers, for they were not rich enough to entice support. But it sufficed that they had the support of the vast majority of the Southern Sudanese, as indicated by the rising number of recruits to the Anya-Nya ranks, and were determined to persist with their just struggle for liberation whatever the sacrifices.[36]

The issue of balkanization was handled in several ways. The Southern Front argued to some extent that no state had 'an absolute right to murder innocent people' and that the Southern Sudan was entitled to the 'inalienable right of all people to control their own destiny'. By the 1970s the argumentation became more radical under the NPG which appeared to imitate the Biafrans in style, though it could not match them in articulateness and ingenuity. The NPG argued that the Southerners were a separate nation, henceforth to be called Nileans. The other nation in the Sudan, the Arabs, were submitting them not only to 'racial subjugation', and 'domination' which amounted to 'imperialism and colonialism', but were also committing 'genocide' against the 'Nilean nation'. For them the only way to survive was by way of an independence struggle. The SSLM, for its part, claimed that their 'struggle was older than the borders of Sudan', hence the sanctity of African boundaries was not contested, that it

117

was 'a fundamental struggle pitting an indigenous African culture against alien invading forces – Arabization and Soviet imperialism'; that it was the 'vanguard of Africa's struggle against this new colonialism' and thus deserved the support of all Africans.[37] A book published at the time by the now discredited Oliver Albino went even further, arguing that there was a need for a Black African intergovernmental organization distinct from the OAU, for 'to sacrifice four million Africans to the Arabs on the altar of African unity may defeat the purpose of unity itself'.[38]

For most of the time Khartoum was able to muster a far more articulate and pervasive propaganda campaign, thereby obscuring and downgrading the Southerners, even though the Northern case was, for most of the time, a weak one. The two basic flaws of the Southern case for independence were its lack of viability as an independent state (its oil reserves had not yet been found), and the conflicts and lack of unity in the secessionist ranks which were not unrelated to inter-ethnic rivalries.

The Southerners reacted to criticism on these two grounds with predictable, but far from convincing arguments. Thus it was claimed that viability was not in doubt, for even smaller land-locked African states were known to be viable, that the area was huge and had great potential (timber, water, animal life), there could be several untapped resources, and that the South could become viable if it had a competent government of its own. It was argued that there was no great division between the ethnic groups. All shared the same African culture and race. Only political divisions existed, which tended to be exaggerated and which were after all normal, given the conflict with the Sudan. What was important was that the objective remained the same for all: a 'unanimous demand for independence' by way of an armed struggle as seen by the continued recruitments and the continuation of the struggle despite the limited funds and arms.

Other arguments in Khartoum's propaganda arsenal included external involvement (that of Tshombe and various imperialist forces including the CIA in the mid-1960s, and Israel for most of the time);[39] the various killings and atrocities within the Southern ranks particularly in the 1960s; the military weakness of the Southerners; the negative attitude towards the various peace offers, in particular to the Numeiry overtures, and of course the Biafran analogy.

The Southerners denied the first claim. As to the second allegation they maintained that only traitors were put to death. On the issue of military weakness they used various arguments, notably that their show of weakness was a mere guerrilla tactic, but they also capitalized on their role as a weak underdog to attract world sympathy. The overtures of Numeiry and others were treated as hypocritical (as 'sugar-coating'), in line with the 'traditional Arab tactic' of 'deceiving the Southerners' and misleading international public opinion. The Biafran analogy which was courted in 1968, when Biafra still appeared winnable, was rejected from 1969 onwards. Mading de Garang, in particular, listed as many secondary characteristics of the Biafran case as he could detect, and, taking them one by one, disclaimed any similarities with the struggle of the Southern Sudanese.[40] And the news-sheet *Anya-Nya* came out with a graphic attempt at dissociation:

Southern Sudan is not Biafra:
1. we are fighting a war of liberation of Black Africans from imperialism – Arab and Soviet;
2. we have no treasury abroad;
3. our only resources are human, ours are the only people in the world still captured and sold into slavery;
4. we employ no mercenaries, yet we are fighting Sudan's mercenary army – 3,000 Egyptians, 1,000 Soviets, Soviet-piloted aircraft;
5. we are Africans, fighting a war of liberation.[41]

Thus the Southerners went about pleading and protesting. Sometimes they were tentative, at other times aggressive, but at no time could they compete with the ingenuity and sheer volume of Biafran propaganda. At the end of the day however, this often timid and haphazard approach, born of necessity, had its virtues for the relatively simplistic Southerners could not easily be depicted as artful propagandists and manipulators of public opinion as their more famous contemporaries, the Biafrans were.

INTERNATIONAL INVOLVEMENT

The Southern struggle from 1962 to 1972 might be regarded as one more 'forgotten war', like most secessionist movements in Asia and Africa during the last thirty to forty years. The Southerners received negligible political support from other governments, although a little aid did arrive from Uganda, Ethiopia, Zaïre, and Israel, as well as from organizations linked with the expatriate missionaries that had been expelled by Abboud in 1964.

Israeli partisan involvement with the Anya-Nya is swathed in an aura of secrecy, but its existence is well established. Arms were brought by land, mainly through Uganda, and by air via Ethiopia. Also provided were funds, relief aid, assistance in military, medical and agricultural matters, and the training of Anya-Nya in Israel and perhaps also on Ethiopian and Ugandan soil. From late 1969 onwards, airdrops from a lone DC-3 took place regularly once a week. It appears almost certain that Lagu himself was trained in Israel and that Israeli officials visited Lagu's Headquarters.[42]

Sudan began accusing Israel of being involved in the South from the early 1960s, but there is no hard evidence to support this claim. It seems that the whole furore raised by Khartoum has all the elements of a self-fulfilling prophecy. Indeed, Khartoum was rendering a service to the Southerners by advertising the little-known war and pointing to how natural and advantageous Israeli involvement could be.[43] According to a good source (made known to the author), the secessionists first made contact with Israel at Lohure's base in Nairobi with the help of the missionaries, but actual aid in arms came much later in the aftermath of the Six Day War, or perhaps in 1969, following Numeiry's takeover, which had initially led to a radical Left regime. (Note the link: missionaries/Lohure (the Catholic priest), Israel, then Israel/Lagu (Lohure's one-time protégé).)

Israeli aid was not great but it was sufficient to create a military stalemate, though not enough to defeat the Sudanese Army. It was also crucial for the assertion of Lagu's leadership and the unification of the Southern secessionist movement under Lagu's group. It seems that Israel made the continuation of aid conditional on the formation of a unified front under Lagu.

The Israeli aim in supporting the Southern Sudanese was to sap the resources of the Sudan and of its Arab allies (most notably Egypt) and to strand an Arab army in the Southern marshlands. (Similar, as we shall see, were Israel's considerations in their assistance to another group of secessionists in an Arab country – the Kurds of Iraq.) As critics of Israel have put it, Tel Aviv's goal was to 'stab the Arabs in the back', to take advantage of the Arabs' 'soft underbelly'. Another obvious objective was to discredit the Arabs as much as possible in the eyes of Black Africa. In the days after the Six Day War, Israel was keen to make inroads in Africa at the expense of the Arabs (as Golda Meir had put it, if their neighbours would not be their friends, then perhaps their neighbours' neighbours would). Another reason for involvement, suggested by some, was that Israel was a good client of the CIA.[44]

It is not clear whether Israel was aiming at harassing and discrediting the Arabs *ad infinitum* by a perennial Southern struggle or whether it had in mind the creation of an independent client state of Southern Sudan. Anti-Lagu Southerners claimed at the time that Lagu had been encouraged to secede. (Note that when the Southerners wanted to sell their prospective agreement with Khartoum they advanced the argument that an Afro-Arab Sudan, rather than an Arab Sudan threatened by a secession, was more in the interests of Israel.)[45] But, on the other hand, it could be argued that Israel, well-known for its political acumen and power-political views, would have realized that the Anya-Nya was hardly on the verge of a successful secession and that Ethiopia or Uganda could mend their fences with Khartoum on a *quid pro quo* basis, as had often happened in the past.

Apparently Israel calculated that it was gaining on the cheap. With very little outlay – mainly a small amount of weapons captured in the Six Day War – it sapped Arab resources, redirected them, and at the same time discredited the Arabs. It was a worthwhile outcome for a bit of adventuring in the White Nile.[46]

Uganda's attitude in those ten years of the conflict was complex and fraught with contradictions. The leaders of SANU had considered Uganda as the state most likely to assist them in their own struggle for independence, but Milton Obote did not live up to these expectations. They received only limited support of an indirect nature, such as tolerating political activity or turning a blind eye to the use of Ugandan soil as sanctuary and as an arms trail. But after Obote had mended his fences with Khartoum in 1966, Uganda became hostile, to the extent that there were joint Ugandan–Sudanese sweeping operations along the borders to track down Anya-Nya fighters. When Numeiry rose to power in the Sudan there was again a rapprochement with Obote. No wonder that the Southerners were jubilant on Obote's overthrow – as Lagu put it at the time: 'good riddance to such Black Africans unworthy of the name'[47] – especially as Amin not only provided the Anya-Nya with some funds, as well as an external haven or springboard for their operations and training, but also allowed Israeli arms to be ferried through Ugandan territory.

Even during Obote's rule, Amin (then head of the army) had assisted the Anya-Nya. According to one account, the Israelis first approached Obote, and when he did not permit their aid to traverse Uganda they turned to General Amin – hence the so-called 'Israeli connection' which helped to precipitate Obote's first downfall. When Amin took power he openly supported the neighbouring secessionists, characterizing the policy of Khartoum towards them as 'barbarous' and akin to apartheid. At one point he even went so far as to threaten to use 'maximum force', if necessary, against the Sudanese forces for pursuing the Anya-Nya into Uganda.[48]

It was small wonder that Amin's actions and rhetoric, as well as his known association with Lagu and his kinship links with the Southerners, had the effect of raising the latter's hopes, including the possibility of an India–Bangladesh type of rescue operation. But the unpredictable Amin suddenly made a *volte face*, following a visit to Colonel Qaddafi in Tripoli. The Israelis were evicted from Uganda in March 1972, and it became clear that Amin was heading towards a *quid pro quo* arrangement with Khartoum, whereby he would stop aid to the Anya-Nya in return for Sudan breaking links with the exiled Obote and his supporters.[49]

The Ugandan pro-Southern position was not merely an off-shoot of the general Ugandan–Sudanese relations. There was an important body of support for the Southerners within the Ugandan army and administration, the opposition party, the Democratic Party, and elements within the ruling Uganda People's Congress. The Christian Churches, particularly the Catholic Church, were keenly interested and there was general sympathy among the various ethnic groups of the North which spilled over into Southern Sudan. These ethnic groups were the Lango, Acholi, Madi, Lugbara and Kakwa. Obote himself was a Lango, and Amin a Kakwa, with relatives in the Southern Sudan.[50]

During the Obote period in particular, there were few if any tangible gains for aiding the Southern Sudanese secessionists.[51] Uganda's limited involvement thus falls nearer to the affective pole. In the case of Amin, there was the close rapport with Lagu, perhaps Southern assistance during Amin's coup, and the Israeli factor. Amin of course claimed that his sympathy was purely affective. But he seemed ready to leave the SSLM out in the cold following his astounding change of political orientation after his visit to Libya.

It is possible to speculate on the various reasons against greater involvement. There was above all the fear of Sudanese retaliation, the fear of the demonstration effect within Uganda (the Buganda separatism) which makes Uganda an upholder of the sanctity of colonial boundaries and, according to one author, bribery may have been a factor.[52]

Ethiopian partisan involvement with the Southern Sudanese secessionists waxed and waned in accordance with the Ethiopian–Sudanese relations of the time. Relations were poor between the two countries and, on more than one occasion, brought them to the verge of war. This was due to disputed boundaries, Sudan's extended partisan involvement with the Eritrean secessionists, and because of the assistance of Ethiopia granted to the Southerners.[53]

At its highest, Ethiopian partisan involvement included sanctuary, bases for the Anya-Nya, the turning of a blind eye to arms traffic, from around 1965 until 1967–68, and from that period onward permission to the Israelis – the trainers of the Ethiopian Army – to use Ethiopian soil to train Anya-Nyas, and, in particular, ferry arms by airdrops, with Ethiopia as the staging point. Ethiopia, of course, denied that this was going on.

During the Abboud period, relations were unusually cordial and there was no assistance to the Southerners. In fact the Sudanese Army was trained in Ethiopia. But from the fall of Abboud onward (October 1964) relations worsened and both governments supported the other countries' secessionists. There were several attempts at reconciliation – one with the Ethiopian–Sudanese Agreement of 1965, a second with the Nairobi Agreement of eleven East and Central African states in the spring of 1966 and in early 1967, when Haile Selassie paid a visit to Khartoum – but none were successful.[54]

When Israeli involvement with the Southerners became regular, Ethiopian assistance became more consistent and continued until the Selassie–Numeiry Agreement of November 1971, according to which no assistance was to be given to the Anya-Nya or to the Eritrean Liberation Front. This was a severe blow for the Southern secessionists who had come to depend on arms via Ethiopia. Beshir has called it 'perhaps the most important agreement in the direction of solving the Southern problem'.[55] From the agreement onward, Ethiopia played a significant role as mediator in the Addis Ababa peace talks.[56]

Ethiopia's support for the Southerners was in retaliation for Sudan's aid and moral support to the Eritreans. It was a telling form of revenge and a bargaining chip in Haile Selassie's dealings with Khartoum. Contrary to Sudanese aid to the Eritreans, Ethiopian aid to the Southerners was not based on any affective or ideological links. Furthermore, secession as such was not condoned. Selassie, who dominated Ethiopia and regarded its foreign policy as his *chasse gardée*, was the foremost architect of the sanctity of the inherited African boundaries and, with secessionist problems of his own, was hardly likely to afford 'self-determination' any legitimacy. By the late 1960s, the Israeli factor may also have been prominent in the Emperor's considerations, for by then the United States appeared somewhat uninterested in its bases in Ethiopia.[57]

Historically, Ethiopia has always felt encircled by Islam and the Arabs. It defines itself as a Christian island beset by an Arab–Muslim sea. By the 1960s the Arab–Islamic encirclement often coincided with another menace for imperial Ethiopia – socialism and radicalism. Under the circumstances Israel was a natural ally. (And such a link could even draw on the Biblical tradition of the encounters between King Solomon and the Queen of Sheba.)

Zaïre, or Congo–Leopoldville as it was then called, was responsible for arms, sanctuary and other facilities for the Southern secessionists. This was during the mid-1960s at the time of the Simba revolt which challenged the Tshombe Government of Leopoldville. The Simbas received arms from the Soviet Union and Arab countries through the Sudan. There are several versions of how the Anya-Nya secured the Simba arms, but the most plausible one is that the Anya-Nyas disrupted the arms trails and engaged the Simbas in combat and then availed themselves of the arms. The Tshombe government may then have rewarded them for services rendered. The Zaïre connection was mainly a strict business arrangement, though Wol Wol, the prominent Southern diplomat, has termed Congolese involvement 'moral support',[58] which implies more than a strict *quid pro quo* undertaking. Whatever the Congolese motivation may have been, this much coveted source of arms was cut off when the Simbas were defeated.[59]

Among other states involved in the separatist war were Malawi and Kenya. Kamazu Banda the President of Malawi caused many raised eyebrows – surprising even the Southern Sudan supporters who had lobbied him – when he accused the Sudanese of 'butchering' Africans and related Sudanese behaviour to that of the South Africans and the Rhodesians. And Dr Banda added bluntly that it was only for want of funds that he did not raise an army to fight 'alongside the Africans against the Arabs' in the Sudan.[60]

Kenya appeared to tolerate Southern separatist activity until 1966 or thereabouts. Lohure, based in Nairobi, conducted the arms trail through Kenya and there were, from time to time, sympathetic noises from Kenyan ministers. But Kenyatta was careful as he had been with Biafra, and by 1966 his attitude had hardened markedly.[61] Tanzania, Chad and the Central African Republic were also known to be sympathetic to the Southern plight, but there is no evidence of any substantive aid, other than some limited relief aid to Southern refugees in their territory.[62]

No IGOs were involved, despite the repeated Southern appeals. An exception to this was the UNHCR which was involved with the large number of Southern refugees resident in neighbouring countries.

The World Council of Churches (WCC) and the All-Africa Council of Churches (AACC) successfully mediated in the conflict, the AACC acting as 'moderator' (in fact as chairman) in the Addis Ababa talks. The main churchmen involved were Canon Burgess Carr of the AACC (the moderator), and Leopold Niilus and Kodwo Ankrah of the WCC.[63]

Various other churchmen in Europe and Africa appealed for a peaceful settlement and some were involved in relief aid, particularly towards the end. The Vatican showed concern, particularly during the expulsion of the missionaries in 1964, and Caritas Internationalis, the Catholic relief agency, provided some relief aid. The Pope could not act as a mediator since the Vatican had links with the Verona Fathers (a Catholic order) and he was considered to be partial to the Southerners.

In the last years of the conflict some *ad hoc* groups sprang up, mainly in Britain and Scandinavia and elsewhere in Europe as well as in East Africa. But these groups were a mere shadow of those which had created such a furore in the West for Katanga and even more for Biafra. Most notable were the Southern Sudan Association in London and two groups in Kampala, the Makarere group and the Kampala Committee, which were concerned with channelling aid from Caritas Internationalis, Oxfam and other agencies to the Southern Sudan, which was then facing serious problems of malnutrition. Such relief aid reached its peak towards the end of the struggle when it had become of vital importance as funds and arms from Israel began to dwindle, following the Selassie–Numeiry accord of 1971.[64]

Through the years the most committed supporters of the Southern cause were the missionaries, who were expelled from the South by General Abboud with the charge of fomenting secession. Three groups of expatriate missionaries had worked in the South for decades. The most notable were the Verona Fathers and the Church Missionary Society of the Presbyterian Church. The first, a Roman Catholic order, were responsible for having proselytized the majority of the some quarter of a million Christians of the South.

The role of the missionaries in the South can be seen as encompassing two periods: the first until their expulsion in February 1964, and the second following the expulsion.

Prior to their expulsion, the main role of the missionaries was to shield, as it were, their Southern flock from the Abboud regime's excesses. There was assistance to secessionist leaders such as Oduho, Lohure and Deng, mainly by way of introducing them and the Southern case to Europe through the missionary network. They published articles, periodicals and booklets revealing the Southerners' plight under Abboud. They were also involved, it seems, with the publication of *Voice of Southern Sudan*.

The missionaries assisted with funds and propaganda, particularly after their expulsion. The Verona Fathers published a *Black Book* on the situation in the South and characterized Abboud's policy towards the Southerners as 'technical genocide'. The Church Missionary Society aided the Southerners in London and the Verona Fathers might have been instrumental in introducing the Southerners to the Israelis. Khartoum claimed that the missionaries were involved in arms supplies as well. This has not been confirmed, though the missionaries, the Verona Fathers in particular, were no doubt aware what use Lohure – a Catholic priest – was making of their cash.[65]

Several other parties were mentioned in connection with the Southern Sudan mainly by Khartoum and Sudanese authors, such as the United States, the CIA, Britain, British Intelligence, South Africa, the People's Republic of China, the Federal Republic of Germany, France and various parties of the Northern non-Arab Sudanese.

The United States was mentioned mainly in the mid-1960s in connection with the Tshombe–Simba affair. As for the CIA, it may have been vigilant, but it is not clear whether there was any actual form of assistance by the United States or the CIA.[66]

The Sudan reprimanded Britain on a number of occasions for interfering in its internal affairs, from allegations about British Intelligence[67] aiding the Southerners, to accusations based on the well-known sympathies of the Anglican missionaries. Of a different order altogether was the claim that Britain was responsible for having created the whole North–South Sudan conflict in the first place. Northern politicians in particular have spoken of a 'sinister imperialist conspiracy' on the part of imperial Britain. But as Howell argues, such a view would 'probably exaggerate the guile of British policy-making'.[68] There is very little historical evidence that at the time of the British takeover there was any assimilation *en masse* of the Southerners. Indeed, for decades the Southerners for the most part appeared to be resisting conquest and Islamization. With the exception of Arabic as the lingua franca, assimilation did not seem to be in order at least in the short run. Contrary to what the Northerners believed, the Southerners hardly felt that they were in a pre-cultural phase, or in a 'cultural vacuum' ready or eager to be 'civilized' by the Northerners.[69]

Nothing of substance has surfaced concerning the role of South Africa, despite the Northern claims which appeared mainly during the Numeiry period. The People's Republic of China was probably not involved, though there were some Chinese arms in Anya-Nya hands gleaned from the varied stocks of the Simbas and the open market in arms. A group around Mondiri appeared to favour a Chinese connection, and there seems to have been at one point some Chinese interest, but nothing seems to have come of it.[70]

The German Federal Republic which was accused of involvement during the trial of German mercenary Steiner vehemently denied this and no evidence of any aid has been established.[71]

France appeared to have given some promises to the Nile Provisional Government, but they came to nothing.[72]

Finally the USALF (United Sudan African Liberation Front) and various other black Northern Sudanese groups, such as the General Union of Nubas and the Beja Congress favoured a coordination of policy with the Southern Sudanese, for together with the Southerners, the blacks in the Sudan were in fact a majority. The Southerners, for their part, were not wholly uninterested but preferred to go their own way. This may have been due to the fact that the African Northerners, the majority of whom were Muslims, were largely considered as one with the Arabs.

The Southerners were also suspicious of the most prominent Northern African leader, the Reverend Philippe Abbas Gabboush, president of USALF.[73]

When the Arab Sudanese finally came to accept the Sudan's irretrievable Janus image and realized that their cultural vacuum thesis was erroneous (or at least that its golden moment was for ever gone) a peaceful settlement was possible. Thus only could the Southerners accept a solution short of independence. The result was the Addis Ababa Agreement, which gave them meaningful autonomy, an almost unique achievement in the annals of secession following the Second World War.

The Addis Ababa Agreement stood its ground for about ten years, as something of an 'evolving miracle'.[74] But as of 1982 and 1983 Numeiry began to undermine the accord. His undoing of this historic reconciliation culminated in the establishment of the *Sharia* (Islamic law) throughout the country. Many Southerners, including officers of the Sudanese Army took to the bush, others tried to convince Numeiry to alter his destructive course. Two guerrilla groups become active in the course of 1983, Anya-Nya II and the Sudan People's Liberation Army (SPLA), but before long the SPLA came to dominate the whole movement under the leadership of Colonel Dr John Garang de Mabior, with the veteran Joseph Lagu heading the political wing, the so-called Sudan People's Liberation Movement (SPLM). The SPLA does not seek independence for the South or even self-determination, but rather the annulment of the *Sharia* and the rejection of other forms of Islamic law. It also calls for the creation of a united secular and socialist Sudan. Support for the SPLA during Numeiry's last years in office came from Libya and Ethiopia, but after his downfall only from Ethiopia. The SPLA is far more articulate and bolder than the older secessionist Southern fronts of the first Sudanese civil war and is equipped with two very potent weapons: the oil factor (most of the oil found in the Sudan is in the Southern Sudan at Bentiu) and the Jonglei Canal. These are the two gigantic projects on which the country's economic recovery and viability is based. Both have been postponed indefinitely (by now they would have been fully operative) as a result of SPLA activity against Chevron, the main oil company involved, and against the French consortium building the canal. More generally, oil makes the South appear viable on its own (economic viability, remember, had been one of the greatest weaknesses of the Southern secessionist case in the 1960s and 1970s).[75]

Sadiq al-Mahdi, who headed the post-Numeiry democratic government, a coalition of his own Umma party with Mirghani's Democratic Unionist Party, was to begin with somewhat conciliatory towards the

Southerners and even met Garang, the SPLA leader, in Addis Ababa in 1986 at the time of an OAU meeting. But soon matters turned sour, and even though Mirghani's party later reached an agreement with the SPLA, Sadiq appeared bent on dealing with the SPLA militarily, taking advantage of the various Southern inter-ethnic rivalries (the SPLA is said to be largely Dinka-dominated). A more attenuated form of Islamic law was promised, but not the creation of a secular state as such. Today, under the military rule of General Beshir (following a coup on 30 June 1989), the main bone of contention, the Arab–Islamic character of the Sudan still remains, not permitting a truly Arab and African Sudan, the 'duality in parity' as introduced by the Addis Ababa Agreement.[76] Thus, as the 1980s draw to a close, the prospects for peace in the Sudan remain almost as remote as when Numeiry took his disastrous decisions in 1983.

8

IRAQI KURDISTAN
(1961–1975)

The Kurds have no friends
Kurdish proverb
Our hands and feet had ... been tied to Iran ... the mental
fixation had become total.
Kurdistan Democratic Party (1977)

In the aftermath of the First World War, Iraq was one of the entities that were arbitrarily carved out of the ruins of the Ottoman Empire by Britain and France. Feisal, the by now legendary leader of the Arab revolt against the Sublime Porte, was named king by the British. The 'Anglo-Arab monarchy' of Iraq was given its independence in 1932, but still remained under British tutelage until as late as 1958 and the violent coup of the Free Officers. An 'invented' country, Iraq lacked any cohesion, and despite its immense wealth and constant international support which seemed to herald an era of peace and prosperity for all its inhabitants, has often been on the brink of disaster. There were many reasons for this state of affairs not unrelated to the initial artificial birth of the state. The majority of Iraqis are Shia Muslims, but it is the substantial Sunni minority that has always been politically dominant. By far the most outstanding issue ever since the 1930s has been the Kurds of Iraq, who comprise as much as 25 per cent of the population and live fairly compactly in the north of the country, in 'Iraqi Kurdistan'.

ETIOLOGY

Kurdistan is a geographical expression denoting the region of five countries wherein reside the Kurds. The origin of the Kurds is little known. They regard themselves as descendents of the Medes, who had confronted the ancient Persians. Kurdish, which is Indo-European and related to Persian, has not evolved into a single mutually comprehensible language. There are two main dialects, Kurmanji spoken in northern

129

5. Iraq, Iraqi Kurdistan and Kurdistan

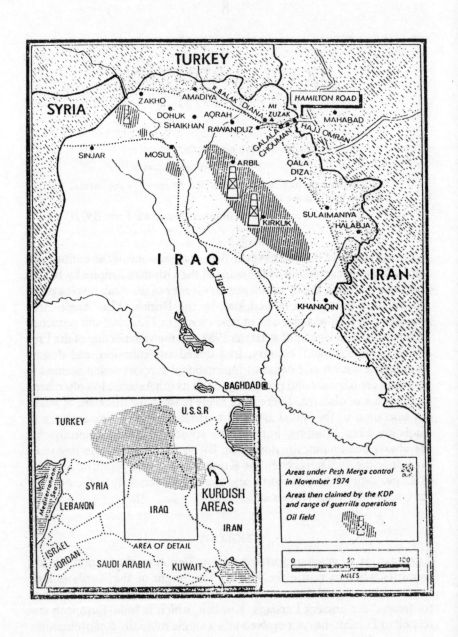

Kurdistan, and Sorani in southern Kurdistan, several sub-dialects and three different types of script, Arabic in Iraq and Iran, Hawar (Turkized Latin) in Turkey and Cyrillic in the Soviet Union. Three out of four Kurds are Sunni, the rest are mainly Shia (orthodox Shia and Alevi) and there are also some adherents of Yazidism (a *mélange* of religions including Zoroastrism). Tribal cleavages and the fragmentation into five states further enhances divisions. However, the Kurds defy assimilation and the overwhelming majority still live in Kurdistan, the region they have inhabited for at least three thousand years.[1]

The ethnic group called Kurds began to emerge gradually as a putative nation around the turn of the century. But by the time Kurdish nationalism could command a substantial following, they found themselves fragmented among five states – Turkey, Iraq, Iran, Syria and the Soviet Union – whose borders criss-crossed and divided historical Kurdistan. The great opportunity was missed in the aftermath of the First World War when the 'Sick Man of Europe' (Turkey) disintegrated. The Treaty of Sèvres provided autonomy for the Kurds with the clearly-stated prospect of independence in the near future. However, following the rise of Kemal Ataturk in Turkey, the treaty was scrapped and substituted by the Treaty of Lausanne in 1923, where no mention of the Kurds was made (or for that matter of the Armenians, who had also been provided for in the Treaty of Sèvres).

To enumerate the Kurds is something of a science in itself, an exercise in bypassing 'statistical genocide' and 'legal non-existence' and extrapolating from outdated censuses. In the late 1960s the numbers given were from five million to fifteen million. Today the numbers vary from around twelve million to twenty million, the most common figures of independent commentators being in the sixteen to seventeen million range. By whatever estimate, the Kurds are undoubtedly the fourth largest ethnic group in the Middle East after the Arabs, the Turks and the Persians (to whom they are close in numbers). Half of the Kurds reside in Turkey, a little less than one-third in Iran, around one-fifth to one-sixth in Iraq, and the rest in Syria and the Soviet Union.[2] Throughout the first part of this century insurrections took place in Turkey, Iraq and Iran. The centre of gravity appeared to shift from one to the other. Between 1925 and 1938 the most serious insurgencies were in Turkey, initially headed by the prototype Kurdish leader of this century, Sheikh Said of Piran. Then Iraqi Kurdistan, which had risen under Sheikh Mahmoud Barzinji in the 1920s, came to the forefront under a new leader, Mulla Mustapha Barzani, who was soon to personify Kurdish resistance. After that, it was the turn of Iranian Kurdistan, in what was probably the most dramatic episode in the Kurdish history of the first part of this century –

the short-lived Kurdish Republic of Mahabad in north-western Iran, a secession under the Kurdish leader Qazi Muhammed, propped up by the Soviet Union, which lasted for about a year (independence was declared on 22 January 1946 and the 'Republic' was overrun by the Shah of Iran on 16 December 1946). This was the nearest to *de facto* independence that the Kurdish nation had ever come.[3]

From the fall of Mahabad and Barzani's 'Retreat of the 500' into the Soviet Union (an episode which has now passed into Kurdish nationalist lore) the Kurds were silenced until 1958. In Turkey, Iran and Iraq, as well as in Syria, the Kurds were and still are the victims of inequality and discrimination so long as they are not prepared to shed their Kurdish identity and 'pass' into the majority culture. A case in point is Turkey, where, after the first few years of relative freedom under Ataturk in the early 1920s, the Kurds were designated 'Mountain Turks' who had 'forgotten their mother tongue' (and this remains the official definition to this day). From 1946 until the late 1970s and early 1980s, when the region saw major changes – the fall of the Shah, the Iran–Iraq war and the Evren regime in Turkey – it was only in Iraqi Kurdistan that the Kurds had developed into an armed secessionist movement coming to the verge of meaningful autonomy or even independence in what has been called by a prominent Kurdish leader, 'the longest, most sustained and most important political and military manifestation in the entire history of the Kurdish movement'.[4]

The various foes of the Kurds have traditionally claimed that the Kurdish real aim is pan-Kurdistan. Yet even though it is clear that the Kurds are not inclined towards assimilation with the dominant group of the state wherein they reside, they have not sought pan-Kurdistan. And in fact this is no mere tactic, but emanates from the realities of a fragmented and dispersed Kurdistan, which has not forged the bonds of a true pan-Kurdish struggle. For a moment, however, it appeared that Iraqi Kurdistan could create the nucleus of pan-Kurdistan from 1961 until 1975. But why Iraqi Kurdistan, and not any of the others, where in fact more Kurds reside?

Among the various reasons put forward to explain this phenomenon, the following are worth noting:

1. the percentage of Kurds as compared to the general population is larger in Iraq (20–25 per cent);[5]
2. the Iraqi Kurds were internationally recognized as a minority prior to the formation of the state of Iraq;[6]
3. Iraq was internationally weaker in comparison to Turkey or Iran; it was a newly-formed state without a well-established and effective state

apparatus, a tradition of statecraft or a substantial military force able to subdue insurgents by force;

4. the Iraqi Arabs were ethnically more distant from the Kurds than the Turks or the Persians; in addition, they were perceived by the Kurds as being, like themselves, a former subject race; as a result the Iraqi Kurds were highly unlikely to lose their cultural identity and be assimilated by the Iraqi Arabs;

5. Iraq, for its part, had recognized the Kurds prior to the secessionist war as a minority with certain rights *qua* minority;

6. located as they were in Iraq's northern mountains, the Kurds of Iraq were more concentrated than the other Kurds and physically less accessible to their adversaries;

7. the Iraqi Kurds had a charismatic leader in the person of Barzani;

8. there was apparently a greater fear of Arabism and pan-Arabism than the pan-isms of Turkey or Iran.[7]

In other words, the Iraqi Kurds more than any other group of Kurds in the 1960s and 1970s could conceive of an alternative to their situation. In addition to discrimination and attempts at assimilation of the Kurds, there was also the factor of oil and mineral resources in general which were in abundance in Iraqi Kurdistan (iron ore, natural gas and other as yet untapped resources such as coal, copper, gold, silver and perhaps even uranium). Oil in particular was the prime export and the main source of Iraq's national income. Baghdad disputed the fact that the oil in Kirkuk was in the area predominantly inhabited by the Kurds and was not prepared to share it with the Kurds, who, interestingly (and contrary to, say, the Katangese) demanded only a share proportionate to their numbers (and after the necessary deductions were made for defence, etc.). Iraq tried to inhabit the Kirkuk region with Arabs and disperse the Kurds. No doubt oil and the other riches of the area of Iraqi Kurdistan also made a future autonomous or independent Kurdistan attractive and the secessionist venture somewhat more feasible.

Given the history of Kurdish uprisings in Iraq and the intransigence of Baghdad, an extended militant separatist movement was probably inevitable. It could only be averted if the Iraqi Arabs were prepared to grant home rule to the Kurds and a favourable deal regarding oil. With the overthrow of the monarchy on 14 July 1958 this seemed a possibility. General Qassim reacted positively to the Kurdish appeals, summoning Barzani from his exile in the Soviet Union. The provisional constitution of Iraq called Arabs and Kurds 'associates in this nation', whose national rights were guaranteed. There followed a two-year period of grace until 1960 when there was unprecedented cultural and political activity on the

133

part of the Kurds. The Kurdish party was legalized and no less than fourteen Kurdish journals were published. It appeared to all that the Kurds had finally become the partners of the Arabs in a bi-national Iraqi state. But this was not to be. The 'Sole Leader', as Qassim styled himself, abruptly switched his policy, banning the Kurdish party and relieving Barzani of all his honours. He then appeared poised to deal with the Kurds militarily, but by that time, the Kurds had organized themselves in their mountain strongholds and were prepared to resist with arms.[8]

The first attack of the Iraqi army came in mid-September 1961 (hence the Kurdish 'September Revolution'). It is not clear whether at that stage the prospects of an external partner, most notably Iran, had been a factor in the Kurdish decision to resist with arms as the Kurdistan Democratic Party claimed later.[9] The situation was markedly different in the period 1970–74, following the 1970 peace agreement between Baghdad and the Kurds.

The peace agreement of 11 March 1970 was far-reaching. The agreement recognized the bi-national character of Iraq and committed the government to implement it within four years. It included the following concessions which went some way towards meeting the Kurdish demands of equality, home rule and partnership within Iraq:

1. It recognized that the Iraqi people consisted of two nationalities: the Arab and Kurdish nationalities;
2. The Kurds were to participate in the government, including the Revolutionary Command Council (the governing body of Iraq);
3. The Kurds were to be represented in the state bureaucracy and army in proportion to their numbers;
4. The vice-president of Iraq was to be a Kurd;
5. The administration, including the police and courts were to be manned by ethnic Kurds in the Kurdish provinces;
6. Kurdish was to be recognized in the areas where the Kurds were in a majority and it was to be taught together with Arabic in schools; Kurdish culture and education were to be promoted;
7. There was to be economic development in the Kurdish areas;
8. Most importantly, there was to be an autonomous Kurdish region with a legislative assembly of its own within four years.

Some of the above terms, such as the appointment of five Kurdish ministers in the cabinet, were immediately met, but others became the subjects of dispute. The thorniest problem was the delineation of the autonomous regions, above all the Kirkuk oilfield area, which Baghdad would not include in the Kurdish area. The plebiscite planned for October 1970 never took place and the legislative assembly was not the outcome of free elections but its members were hand-picked by Baghdad. Kurdish was not recognized as an official language and the policy of Arabicization appeared not to have been dropped.[10] As the situation grew worse there were even attempts against Barzani's life. The Kurds tried to reason with Baghdad, but the Iraqis went ahead with their emasculated version of the agreement, setting up in March 1974 a Kurdish Legislative Assembly under the dissident KDP member Hasem Akrawi. This turn of events does not necessarily imply that the Iraqis deliberately tricked the Kurds in March 1970, but they had certainly begun losing interest in power-sharing. It could perhaps be argued that a fundamental factor that weighed in favour of the hawks of Baghdad and made the 1970 concessions appear redundant was the 1972 pact with the Soviet Union.[11]

The fact that the March 1970 Agreement (which incidentally contained a number of secret clauses that further favoured the Kurds) was curtailed and that the whole process of reconciliation was seriously undermined by Iraq is not in doubt. What remains an open question is whether the disastrous – for the Kurds – last round of fighting in 1974–75 was avoidable. It appears that at that point the prospects of Iranian as well as United States support placed a limit on Kurdish tolerance and made an armed secessionist bid appear feasible. A more disturbing argument, put forward by critics of Barzani, is that after a time the Kurdish leader deliberately spurned attempts at reconciliation, having realized that self-rule (with or without the oilfields of Kirkuk) was bound to marginalize his role and render him obsolete in the new Iraqi Kurdistan envisaged by the Agreement.[12]

INTERNATIONAL ACTIVITY

The Arab–Kurdish armed conflict in Iraq has been a bewildering series of contradictory events, fits and starts, vacillations on both sides, lulls in the fighting and, incredibly, as many as five agreements.[13] At its height, the secessionist movement controlled 40,000 square miles with about 50,000 guerrillas.

The Kurds were led by the Kurdistan Democratic Party (KDP), under the leadership of Mulla Mustapha Barzani. The original organization, the Kurdish Democratic Party, was formed in 1946 on the suggestion of Barzani before he left for the Soviet Union. In 1954 it was called the United Democratic Party of Kurdistan; by 1960 it was known as the Kurdistan Democratic Party. In the first two or three years there was a clear split between Barzani, the President of the KDP, and the KDP Politburo headed by Ibrahim Ahmed (the Secretary of the KDP) and Jalal Talabani. The reasons for this rift were differences over tactics, Barzani's authoritarian leadership as opposed to collective decision-making, and the rural–tribal versus the urban–intelligentsia. There were also overtones of ideological as well ethno-linguistic differences (Sorani versus Kormanji speakers). The two factions which developed into two fronts, finally clashed in 1964 and Barzani asserted his leadership which remained undisputed until the final collapse of March 1975.[14]

The unified KDP as set up in 1964 consisted of a Revolutionary Command Council of forty-six and later sixty-two members, presided over by Barzani. Directly below this top organ were the KDP, the Revolutionary Army of Kurdistan popularly known as Pesh Merga (literally 'those facing death'), an executive organ set up and functioning more or less like a ministerial cabinet called the Executive Bureau which was presided over by Barzani, with Habib Karim and later Osman as secretaries with functions similar to those of prime minister.[15]

From 1964 onwards, Barzani's authority was paramount, not only in Iraqi Kurdistan, but also among the Kurds beyond Iraq. Barzani's authority among the Kurds can largely be attributed to his prowess as a military commander, which had established him as the national hero of Kurdistan, almost beyond reproach. His power base was the feared tribe of the Barzani, which had traditionally been led by his family. Barzani, for all his faults, his authoritarian and arbitrary rule and his stubbornness and harshness towards political rivals, was the only Kurdish leader capable of providing an effective guerrilla force and bridging the gap between the largely rural 'tribal' Kurds and the 'detribalized' townsmen and intelligentsia.[16] No doubt his ability to somehow procure arms and funds, even if not from sources approved by the intelligentsia, was also an important factor further enhancing his leadership.

The original party, the Kurdish Democratic Party, declared in its 1953 party conference that it was 'a Marxist–Leninist inspired party'. Relations with the Iraqi communists passed through various phases,[17] but it is fairly clear that the core of its intellectual leaders, men such as Ibrahim Ahmed, Talabani and Vanly, were clearly leftists. This orientation was reinforced by the Mahabad episode, the milestone of Kurdish nationalism, by Barzani's 'retreat of the five hundred' to the Soviet Union after the fall of Mahabad, and his sojourn there for eleven years. However, when Barzani took over the whole movement by the mid-1960s orienting the Kurds towards Iran and the West, the KDP remained radical only in rhetoric. Barzani was no socialist, but profoundly conservative, inclined at best towards some form of oligarchic reformism.[18]

The Iraqi Kurds meticulously avoided stating that independence was their goal, or that their ultimate aim was pan-Kurdistan. The goal appeared vague: from extended autonomy to a dual federation, or a loose federation akin to a confederation. Apparently, as admitted by Ibrahim Ahmed, the main determinant of the goal was based each time on a comparison of their 'strength' to that of the 'enemy'.[19] Vanly, the best-known Kurdish publicist, has put it differently: the Kurds have the inalienable right to self-determination as a people. This was not tantamount to independence, but could also mean autonomy or some kind of federal framework. Solutions short of independence can be the goal if the states concerned 'show that they deserve unity with the Kurdish people'. This would be the basis for the Kurdish people's 'final choice'.[20] Apparently, by the mid-1970s, when the stakes had risen, the aim was independence, as Barzani himself had occasion to point out.[21]

Prior to 1964, international activity was formally headed by a committee of three under Ismet Chériff Vanly. In 1964 the so-called 'Représentation générale à l'étranger' was formed, again under Vanly, based in Lausanne and directly responsible to Barzani. Its main duties were fund-raising, publicizing the cause and appealing to international organizations. By late 1966, the Représentation disappeared and for the next few years international activity was 'empirical, episodic, insufficient and uncoordinated'.[22] There were, from time to time, permanent representatives abroad, such as Akrawi in Cairo (in the first part of the 1960s). Among the roving ambassadors worth mentioning were Talabani, Vanly, Bedir-Khan, Osman and Shafiq Ahmed. For most of the second part of the 1960s and in the 1970s, the two main centres of Kurdish activity abroad were Lausanne, where Dr Vanly headed the Committee for the Defence of the Kurdish People's Rights, and Paris, where the veteran emir Dr Kamuran Bedir-Khan, considered the doyen of the Kurdish *émigrés* in Europe, headed the Centre d'Etudes Kurdes.[23]

The international relations of Iraqi Kurdistan can be divided into two overlapping phases. The first spans the first part of the 1960s until 1964 or 1965. During that period the primary targets were various 'progressive' Arab states, such as Nasser's UAR (Egypt) and Ben Bella's Algeria, the Soviet Union (the original ally in the 1940s) and apparently also Iran and Turkey. Barzani was also keen to attract Western public opinion and Western governments and for this reason invited Western journalists to the Kurdish mountain strongholds.

During the second phase of international activity, the Kurds appealed to the West and to the West's allies in the region (Iran, Israel, though perhaps not Turkey), with the ultimate aim of drawing in the United States. This was the line favoured by Barzani, but not appreciated by the radicals of the KDP. Soon contacts with the Soviet Union and various Arab countries began to be dropped, being regarded as of secondary importance.

By the 1970s there was something of a 'fixation' with Iran, and by implication with the United States. Contact with Iran had already been made as early as 1962, but apparently the Kurds were still wary of using the Iranians.[24] When other doors seemed closed, Talabani made a successful trip to Teheran in the spring of 1964. Barzani had no faith in the Shah, but was confident that the United States were acting as guarantors of the Shah's policy and would not permit any back-tracking. Like another conservative leader of the Middle East, President Sadat of Egypt, Barzani believed that the United States alone had the solution to his nation's problems. He also thought he was dealing with the President and Secretary of State of the United States, which in the event he was (though they had passed on the details to the CIA), so he was on safe ground.[25] Apparently he was unaware of the particular brand of politics for which Nixon and Kissinger were notorious throughout the Near East and beyond.[26] It also appears that the conclusion of the Soviet–Iraqi agreement of 1972 was an important factor in making Barzani go ahead with what to many Kurds was an 'unnatural alliance' with the Shah, whose feelings about Kurdish nationalism were well known since the days of the Mahabad episode.

As an armed separatist movement, the Kurds were in the rare position of being able to point persuasively to the existence of a nation. It was argued that the Kurds were a nation of many millions, the fourth largest ethnic group in the Middle East. They had been conquered again and again, but they had never been subdued or assimilated, nor even dispersed, having remained in their original homeland for over three thousand years. Yet they had not been afforded the right of self-determination, a right readily granted to much smaller and arbitrary entities, even though the stillborn Treaty of Sèvres after the Second World War had recognized such a right. In Iraq, where they were accepted as a minority with certain rights as such, they continued to be the victims of discrimination and flagrant injustice, and even more crucially, to be subjected to a policy of 'Arabization', as seen by the eviction of the Kurds from the oil-rich regions and the resettlement by Arabs. During the war period the Kurds fell prey to Iraqi 'terrorism', 'torture', 'executions', bombings of civilians, the use of napalm and gas, even against civilians, and other such atrocities, all amounting to no less than 'genocide'. Apart from these basic arguments in favour of separatism, the Kurds tended to make much of their military prowess and the single-mindedness of their struggle, as well as their 'progressive' ideology.[27]

138

The rejection of the 1970 Peace Agreement was justified in a fairly comprehensive manner on the basis of the argument of Iraqi duplicity.[28] The Kurds had greater difficulty repudiating the Iraqi claims of having become 'stooges' of the Shah, of the United States, of the Central Treaty Organization (CENTO) or the CIA, though they seemed to fare somewhat better against the charges of being involved in 'collusion with Israel' or of amounting to a 'second Israel'.[29]

The main IGO target at the time had been the UN, to which, in the 1960s alone, no less then ten missions had been sent.[30] For the UN and world audiences the main thrust of the Kurdish presentation of its case was to allude to gross violations of human rights and to genocide. It was argued that the UN Charter itself was in urgent need of revision which would allow petitions by minorities such as the Kurds based on the right of self-determination. Such a right would not necessarily lead to secession, but to various forms of federation, or to autonomy. Independence was appropriate if Iraq was not prepared to respect the previous schemes. Several states, including Cyprus in 1964, Mongolia, Ireland and Iceland were lobbied to raise the Kurdish issue in the UN, and unsuccessful attempts were made within the framework of the Council of Europe (for the Kurds of Turkey), and the Islamic Conference.[31]

In order to convince the Shah of Iran, Barzani offered to immobilize the Iranian Kurds in the event of their showing separatist tendencies. Indeed it appears that Barzani went so far as to have the Kurds from Iran detained and deported back to Iranian hands. In some cases they may have even been executed by their fellow Kurds of Iraq.[32]

The persuasion tactic used to woo the United States – which the Shah had undertaken to swing towards the Kurdish side[33] – was mainly to sell the Iraqi Kurds as the future trusted ally of the United States in the Middle East and the Gulf. Oil and the other mineral resources of Iraqi Kurdistan were also part of the attractive package for the United States, together with the time-honoured technique employed by many a secessionist movement, the communist–Soviet scare.[34] For the West, and for the United States in particular, as well as for parts of the Arab world, the Kurds were careful not to use any terrorist tactics, which would have tinged their cause with an alarmingly revolutionary hue. The most obvious target for threats of sabotage was the oil installations of Kirkuk, which was one of the contested regions.[35]

For Egypt and other Arab countries the argument put forward was that should Iraq reach a peaceful settlement accepting extended autonomy, Iraqi forces (including Iraqi Kurds) would be left free to assist in the conflict against Israel with more than a mere token force. Continued civil war could not but weaken even Iraq, one of the most powerful Arab states, thus limiting its ability to cope with United States influence at work via Turkey and Iran. Finally, a strong autonomous Kurdistan could function as an effective and reliable buffer. Alternatively, the Kurds, disillusioned with their natural allies, the progressive Arab states, would be left with no other choice but to align with the enemies of the Palestinian cause and the Arab world. In addition, when Egypt, Syria, or any other Arab state was at odds with Baghdad, the Kurds sold themselves as natural allies.[36]

Barzani appeared to have been in favour of developing connections with Israel which, under the circumstances, was a natural ally. In the 1960s, in particular, contacts were very low key and apparently mainly handled by non-Kurdish groups such as the Amsterdam-based International Society Kurdistan. The Kurds indicated that, despite their sympathy for the Palestinian cause, they also favoured an Israeli homeland in the Middle East. According to one account, as the years went by, Barzani began to be inclined towards a formal recognition of Israel. However, the Kurds were obviously aware that the Israeli connection was best kept as secret as possible.[37]

The end of this phase of the Iraqi Kurdish secessionist movement came with an unexpected twist of events – the agreement between Iran and Iraq, which left the Kurds out in the cold. Barzani did his utmost in the very last moment, going to Teheran to convince the Shah and appealing to the United States. Finally, it was decided to abandon the struggle on 18 March 1975. A mass exodus to Iran took place, the Shah having agreed with Baghdad to keep the borders open for a while.

The collapse of the Kurds was the result of various factors, most of which have been put forward by the Kurds themselves in their attempt to draw the appropriate lessons from the disaster. These factors are clearly of great relevance to other ongoing secessionist movements and to the understanding of armed secession in general. Obviously the prime Kurdish mistake was excessive dependence on arms from a single source (Iran) – a source which was, moreover, considered untrustworthy from the very beginning. Another error was the naive belief in the existence of a guarantor, while the United States had been drawn in reluctantly and had little stake in the conflict. The Kurds had almost no other alternative sources of supply from one point onwards, but did little to try to become self-sufficient. They did not even mobilize their own people, but left them passive onlookers and easy targets of the Iraqi Army in the over-crowded Kurdish enclave. This was in part due to the lack of any revolutionary appeal and the conservative and authoritarian attitude of Barzani and his chief associates. Lack of radicalism and mobilization, and the rumours of Iranian or United States involvement did little to raise interest in the Kurdish plight in the Middle East and the Third World. In fact

Barzani was hardly concerned with presenting the Kurdish case in the Third World and in socialist countries. Even general propaganda to the West appeared not to be a priority. Thus, no influential lobbies could be generated that could raise the issue from world platforms.

Another serious mistake was the inability or unwillingness of the Kurds to co-opt the Arab Left which was traditionally sympathetic to the Kurdish cause. In effect the Kurds had managed through their policies to insulate themselves from an array of potential supporters. They were 'cockily secure' in their belief in the US guarantee, acting on the basis of the assumption that aid from Iran and the US would never stop. This 'excessive self-confidence' bred by Iranian and US involvement was almost ridiculous and sapped at the precious few Kurdish resources as the secessionists created a bureaucracy and designated themselves as ministers and the like. More crucially, by 1974–75 they went so far as to switch to more conventional warfare when they lacked the means to engage the massive Iraqi forces now buttressed by the Soviets. Thus the Kurds collapsed. The fifth war (1974–75) had been the most lethal with probably more dead than in all the other Iraqi–Kurdish wars of the 1960s put together.[38]

INTERNATIONAL INVOLVEMENT

The Kurdish secessionist struggle in Iraq was for most of the time an obscure and forgotten war, like the contemporary conflict in the Southern Sudan. Yet at times it was able to attract the interest of some important powers in the region, namely, the Soviet Union, Iran and Israel. Towards the end, the secessionists found to their chagrin that they were identified with the 'reactionary forces' of the Middle East. As one Kurdish leader has put it, 'the situation was quite absurd: the Kurds, an oppressed people fighting a war of national liberation, were drawing support from imperialism and its agents whilst their oppressors enjoyed the moral and material backing of the socialist camp and the progressive forces'.[39]

Iranian aid was material, while Soviet involvement was almost exclusively diplomatic. Iran supplied funds, arms and other military equipment from around 1964. There were steady increases in arms supplies, the most pronounced ones being in 1969 and 1974–75. Tangible support also included relief aid, communications equipment, access facilities, sanctuary and hospital care. By 1974 Teheran handed the Kurds 122mm field-guns and anti-tank missiles, and the Iranian army shelled the Iraqis from across the border. Iranian infantry divisions may also have been involved in attacks from Iraqi soil (according to one report they were disguised as Pesh Mergas).[40]

So far as the Shah of Iran was concerned, the support which he gave the Kurds was entirely instrumental in nature, so much so that it can be regarded as the archetypal model of instrumental involvement on the part of a third state in support of a secessionist movement. There was not even the slightest possible hint of any sympathy for the Iraqi Kurdish cause, or support for a peaceful settlement that would benefit the Kurds (e.g., by an autonomy scheme). It is characteristic that the arms provided were barely enough for the Kurds to be able to continue the struggle – so long as the continuation was seen as profitable in Teheran – and carefully rationed not to allow any major success in the field. It has been reported that at times crates were sent that contained useless arms or even sand, and that the Kurds had to prove that they were in urgent need of ammunition each time. The ammunition provided was only enough for a few days' fighting.[41]

Iran provided aid to the Kurds in order to harass and weaken Iraq, Iran's traditional enemy. (Indeed, areas of Iraq were claimed by Iran.) More generally, support was a blow to the various forms of Arab nationalism and radicalism, such as Nasserism and Baathism. But above all the Kurdish issue was for the Shah a bargaining-chip. When Iraq was ready to abandon its claim to the Shatt-al-Arab waterway and accept the Ottoman–Persian Protocol of 1913, which set a mid-channel line, the Shah agreed to halt all aid to the Kurds. The agreement was signed in Algiers by the Shah and Saddam Hussein on 6 March 1975, during an OPEC meeting, following the mediation of Egypt and Algeria and apparently with Kissinger's blessing.[42] The Kurds were taken by surprise for the Shah did not forewarn them (only in the last days did Parastin, the Kurdish secret service, get wind of the agreement). Thus, the Shah abandoned the Kurds, whom his official press had acclaimed as their 'brothers' and as 'combative Aryans who are the spearhead of the Iranian nation'.[43]

It was often argued, by United States commentators in particular, that the Soviet Union was the one power that could truly benefit from the existence of an independent Kurdish state. What is beyond doubt is that ever since the days of the Mahabad episode the Soviets showed a keen interest in Kurdish affairs.

Soviet support was mainly verbal, though there might have been some trickle of material aid in the early 1960s. The Soviet press and media of the 1960s occasionally referred to the Kurdish plight in Iraq, and, according to the KDP, relations with the Soviet Union remained cordial until 1972. The Soviet Union put direct or indirect pressure on Iraq (through other socialist states, or radical Arab states) for a peaceful settlement and autonomy for the Kurds. On at least one occasion it warned Iran, Turkey and Syria not to use their troops to assist Iraq against the Kurds. The Soviet press occasionally criticized the Iraqi government for its treatment of the Kurds, and the Soviet Union in one instance attempted to place the issue on the agenda of the UN General Assembly. There was also once a Soviet draft resolution in ECOSOC. However, by the early 1970s Moscow's relations with Iraq grew warmer, culminating in the Iraqi–Soviet Treaty of Friendship and Cooperation of 1972. The Soviets then tried to mediate in the conflict and avoid a recurrence of the internal war, but ended up providing Iraq with the weapons and technical expertise to deal with the separatists.[44]

To claim that Soviet policy towards the Kurds was 'opportunistic' and 'schizophrenic'[45] is not too wide of the mark, if one looks at the Soviet attitude as a whole from the days of Mahabad in the 1940s (when Mahabad was propped up, later to be abandoned to the Shah),[46] though it is perhaps too long a period to expect any consistency on the part of Moscow. However, it is worth noting that Moscow was initially reluctant to supply arms to the Iraqis and continued to press for a peaceful settlement. But more importantly, the Soviet Union was the only major power to come to the fore and declare its support for the Kurds, through its press and otherwise, and with arguments taken from the Kurds' own propaganda arsenal (there were allusions to genocide and to the contravention of the legitimate rights of minorities).[47]

The United States had, for the most part, repudiated the repeated appeals of Barzani during the 1960s. But in the mid-1970s, Nixon and Kissinger were persuaded by the Shah to give arms and other material aid to the Kurds, and they instructed the CIA to carry out the project. The total aid involved was some sixteen million dollars, a small amount compared to the funds given by the Shah to the separatists. Kissinger, like the Shah, was not concerned with the Kurdish plight and did not want the conflict to be resolved in any way favourable to the Kurds. The aim was simply to weaken Iraq, a Soviet ally in the Middle East, and do the Shah a favour.[48] Most of the story came to light with the secret Pike Committee Report on CIA clandestine activities which was presented to the US House of Representatives. The Shah, according to the report, raised the issue of aid to the Kurds in May 1972 when Nixon visited Teheran. He asked Nixon to 'help him help the Kurds make life difficult for his Iraqi neighbour and enemy'. Nixon was initially reluctant, not wanting to become involved in operations 'which might prolong the insurrection and thereby encourage separatist aspirations, perhaps even provide the Soviet Union with an opportunity to make trouble ...'. Finally, a little later, the President was convinced, and gave the token amount of sixteen million dollars as a 'gesture' aimed at 'overcoming the old Kurdish leader's suspicions'. And the report notes that it was 'clear that the project was originally conceived as a favour to our ally [the Shah] . . . the US acted only as guarantor that the insurgents would not be abandoned by the Shah'.[49]

Israel provided some financial aid and small amounts of arms and ammunition, and apparently there was some training of Pesh Mergas by Israeli military experts, though it is not clear in whose territory. Obviously, all activity was highly secretive so as not to antagonize the Arabs any further. By and large Israeli considerations were similar to the ones that had prompted them to assist the Southern Sudanese, but a degree of sympathy need not be altogether discounted. Israel may be notorious for its power-political approach in its foreign relations, but it is also known for its strong emotionalism, which has often baffled commentators who are not aware that *Machtpolitik* is not tantamount to *Realpolitik*. It is worth noting that, apart from the Kurdish calls of Arabicization and genocide by Arabs, there are in Israel Jews from Kurdistan, with similar habits and customs to the Kurds, who apparently retain good memories of the Kurds. (Note that in the 1960s a Jew was appointed member of the Revolutionary Command Council of Iraqi Kurdistan.)[50]

Among Arab countries there was some interest for the Kurds in governmental circles in Nasser's UAR and Ben Bella's Algeria, the two Arab countries generally known for their liberal approach towards the Kurdish problem. Kuwait, whose territory was threatened by Iraq also showed interest, as did Syria with its well-known antagonism towards Iraq. Lebanon, Tunisia and Jordan were also not indifferent. In the early 1960s, Nasser was in favour of a decentralization solution and allowed the establishment of a permanent Kurdish mission in Cairo. Sadat, following his *rapprochement* with the Shah, was also not totally unsympathetic. But among Arab states, Syria should be credited with material support. When Iran abandoned the Kurds, Syria even suggested replacing Iran as the patron of the Kurds, such was the animosity of Damascus towards the 'brother' Arab and Baathist Iraq (seen also recently with the support for Iran against Iraq in the Gulf war).[51]

Turkey, with its huge Kurdish minority, was hostile to the Kurds with the exception of a brief period in the early 1960s when Iraq was under Qassim, whom the Turks disliked. Ankara then turned a blind eye to the use of its territory by the Kurdish separatists of Iraq.[52]

Mongolia, lobbied by the Kurds and no doubt receiving a green light from the Soviets, went ahead and requested the inclusion of the Iraqi Kurdistan problem in the UN General Assembly agenda on the basis of 'the policy of genocide carried out by the Republic of Iraq'. However, it later withdrew the motion.[53] Among other countries, Czechoslovakia voted for the Soviet Union's draft resolution on the Kurds in ECOSOC, while Yugoslavia, Senegal and Ethiopia abstained.[54] France provided an important service to the Kurds in 1968 by taking heed of Barzani's appeals and not providing Iraq with arms, which were intended for use against the Kurds.[55]

The UN was never seriously involved in the issue of Iraqi Kurdistan or the Kurds in general. There had been some early concern in the League of Nations during the 1920s, when Britain had occupied the Turkish *villayet* (province) of Mosul, which was inhabited mainly by Kurds, and had wanted to unite it with its mandate territory of Iraq. Subsequently, though, in the UN, only some low-key discussions have taken place on rare occasions in ECOSOC and in its Commission on Human Rights in Geneva (including its Sub-Commission on Prevention of Discrimination and Protection of Minorities which is comprised of formally independent experts). Among non-governmental organizations, the International Committee of the Red Cross in Geneva provided some relief aid, despite the lack of permission on the part of the Iraqi Government. Among other groups, the International League for the Rights of Man based in New York appealed to the UN, and the International Federation for Human Rights visited Iraq and Iraqi Kurdistan has provided Kurdish representatives with a platform to address the UN Commission on Human Rights.[56]

The Iraqi Kurds, despite the validity of their cause and their moderate (compared to other separatist movements) demands, did not manage to generate sustained interest internationally. Various small groups of academics and Kurdish students were active, particularly in centres such as London, Paris, Geneva, Lausanne, Amsterdam and several United States cities, but with very meagre results. Perhaps the better-known and most competent group was the Amsterdam-based International Society Kurdistan.[57]

After the collapse a proportion of the separatists remained to cooperate with the Iraqis in the limited autonomy scheme. Barzani went to Iran and then to the United States where he died in 1979. Others resumed the struggle, by then at a low ebb, from as early as 1976. During the recent Iran–Iraq war, guerrilla activity increased, with aid coming mainly from Iran and Syria. The two main organizations involved were the Patriotic Union of Kurdistan (PUK) headed by Talabani and the KDP (originally known as KDP–Provisional Command), headed by Barzani's two sons, Masoud, who tried to forge links with the intelligentsia, and Idris, who was more traditional (he died early in 1987). In the early 1980s there were two groupings, the Democratic National and Patriotic Front and the Democratic National Front headed by PUK and KDP respectively.[58] PUK endangered its position for a while when Talabani reached a 'political and security agreement' (said to be far-reaching) with the hard-pressed Saddam Hussein of Iraq in December 1983. In 1986, however, there was a reconciliation between PUK and KDP in Teheran in November.[59]

By the 1980s it was not only the Kurds of Iraq who were up in arms, but also the Iranian Kurds. They resorted to an armed separatist struggle after the fall of the Shah, when it became apparent that Kurdish autonomy was not on Ayatollah Khomeini's agenda. And, following the military takeover in Turkey, the sleeping giant of the Turkish Kurds has begun to awaken. It is the first time in the history of Kurdish nationalism that all the three main regions of Kurdistan are up in arms. And they face the determined armies and diplomacies of three powerful states – Iran, Iraq and Turkey – all deemed highly strategic. The Kurds were able to thrive on the Iraq–Iran war, but already one can see the signs of military cooperation between states against the Kurds, mainly on the part of Turkey and Iraq, which have already signed an agreement aimed against the insurgents. Iran, interestingly, was one of the sources of arms for the Iraqi and Turkish Kurds, while trying to subdue its own Kurds by military means.

To revert to the Iraqi–Kurdish relations, it seems that Baghdad is still convinced that the Kurds seek nothing else than secession (by way of autonomy) and to 'grab' the oil regions making Iraq non-viable. The Kurds on the other hand feel cheated and deprived of their rights and of their proportionate gains from oil (to which they regard themselves entitled by reason of their comprising one-fourth of the Iraqi population and living in the oil-rich territories). So long as these mutually distrustful perceptions continue, agreements may still succeed one another, the Kurds may again be defeated militarily, but the conflict will be far from resolved.

9

BANGLADESH
(March 1971 – December 1971)

General Yahya . . . unleashed the Pakistan army with open license to commit genocide on all Bengalis . . . Pakistan is now dead and buried under a mountain of corpses.

We will be eternally grateful to the . . . people of the USSR and India.

Tajuddin Ahmed, Prime Minister of the
Bangladesh government-in-exile

The geographical oddity called Pakistan, comprising two regions separated by 1,200,000 miles of Indian territory, came into existence in 1947. The original version of the 'two nations' theory – that in India there were two distinct nations, the Hindus and the Muslims – as conceived by the Muslim poet–philosopher Iqbal, envisaged a Muslim state only in north-western India. Even as late as 1940, when the two nations theory had gained ground under Mohammed Ali Jinnah and the Muslim League, the official position as stipulated in the famous Lohure Resolution was that wherever the Muslims formed the majority they should constitute 'independent states', not one Muslim state.[1] The final creation of one Muslim state to include two wings was formally put forward only a year prior to the independence of Pakistan. The two wings of Pakistan remained unified until December 1971, when Bangladesh became an independent state. In retrospect it seems incredible that the two regions held together for so long. It was popularly said that the only things that had held it together were Islam, the fear of India, and Pakistan International Airlines; this was not far from the truth.

ETIOLOGY

Not only were there few factors to hold Pakistan together, but the conditions prevailing favoured disunity rather than unity between the western region and the eastern region (East Bengal as it was known until 1956). Apart from the total physical discontinuity, with India, the arch-adversary, in between (in addition India almost completely

147

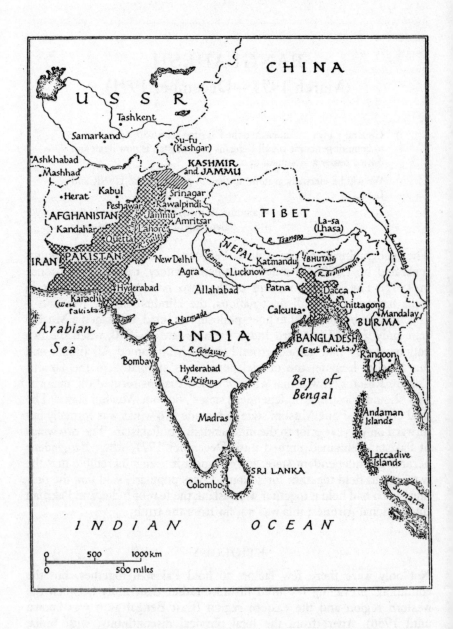

surrounded East Pakistan), there was a clear imbalance with regard to land, resources and people. Even more importantly, there were striking linguistic, cultural, physical and socio-psychological differences which made the West Pakistanis and the Bengalis two completely distinct peoples. Furthermore, the social structure of each region was different. To all these factors was soon added a great discrepancy in terms of wealth and development which came to have the unmistakable characteristics of a centre–periphery relationship. As demonstrated in particular by the flow of trade and investment, East Pakistan was a colony of West Pakistan in all but in name.[2]

The immense distance between East and West Pakistan created serious communication and transportation problems, and obviously did not facilitate physical contact between the inhabitants of the two regions. There was limited flow of labour and manpower from one region to the other, and it was practically impossible to forge an integrated economy. The different geophysical settings raised altogether distinct requirements for each region. The eastern region, with one-sixth of the territory, had 56 per cent of the total population (and one of the highest population densities in the world), and a climate which brought frequent cyclones and floods that devastated the countryside. It was relatively poor in natural resources, producing mainly jute (upon independence in 1947 all the jute mills were lost, for they were in Calcutta in India's West Bengal). Its jute exports were directed solely to West Pakistan (rather than overseas, where they would have achieved far better prices), and the East was West Pakistan's captive market in terms of imports, buying manufactured goods from West Pakistan instead of from, say, India where they were cheaper, and closer to hand.[3]

In the first years of independence the major grievance of the Bengalis was the language issue. Urdu, the language of a minority even in West Pakistan, was named as the only official language even though few Bengalis could speak it. Indeed, the great majority in the whole of Pakistan could not speak Urdu. Jinnah was adamant against Bengali demands to place their language on the same level, claiming that a Muslim state or nation like Pakistan should 'have one language and that language can only be Urdu and no other language'.[4] It was only in the mid-1950s that Bengali finally became an official language together with Urdu.

It was obvious to all those not emotionally involved in the birth of Pakistan that the country could not become a cohesive political community. As Hans Morgenthau had put it in 1956: 'Pakistan is not a nation and hardly a state. It has no justification in history, ethnic origin, language, civilization, or the consciousness of those who make up its population. They have no interest in common save one: fear of

Hindu domination. It is to that fear, and nothing else, that Pakistan owes its existence.'[5]

It was Islam and the Pakistani political system that were called forth upon the country's inception to achieve the impossible and forge a nation, or at least a state. But this was not to be. Jinnah, the charismatic leader who had greatly annoyed the Bengalis over the language issue, died a year after independence, and in a few years the main vehicle of Pakistani integration – the Muslim League – began to lose its power as Bengali stalwarts and others even in West Pakistan began to form rival parties on a regional basis. The most important party to emerge in the East was the Awami (People's) League led by the astute Bengali politician Suhrawardy, who had originally been opposed to Jinnah's partition scheme.[6]

As the Pakistani polity evolved it was clear that the majority – the Bengalis – would wield no authority in the Centre. Not only were they grossly under-represented in administration and the army, but also in government during Pakistan's first democratic phase from 1947 until 1958. The two exceptions were the two short interludes of Nazimuddin as Governor General in the early 1950s, and Sahrawardy as Prime Minister for a year in 1956–57. The Bengali leaders of political parties, such as Sahrawardy and Fazlul Haq (the 'Lion of Bengal'), were for the most part denied even the positions that were rightfully theirs in Dacca. When electoral victory entitled them to high offices, they were eventually deposed. Up until 1956 no Bengali was named governor of East Pakistan.[7]

The sense of inequality and discrimination was further heightened by a number of factors. The Bengalis, who upon independence had more educational institutions and were the better educated, were soon overtaken by the West Pakistanis. Upon independence their per capita income was 10 per cent lower than in West Pakistan; by 1959–60 it had grown to 30 to 36 per cent less, and by the late 1960s it was 60 per cent less. A number of other statistical figures, such as the amount of expenditure in the East relative to its contribution, are equally telling. General Ayub Khan, it is true, tried to remedy the situation during his first years in office, but the situation soon grew even worse. This was the core of the Bengali economic grievance: that the small differences that had existed upon independence increased dramatically with every passing year of independent Pakistan. There was also another less-publicized form of discrimination – the obvious racist sentiments of the Punjabi, who came to dominate Pakistan, a factor which came to the fore with tragic consequences in the spring and summer of 1971 and which in some measure explains the extent and ferocity of the Pakistani onslaught against the 'brother' nation of the Bengalis.[8]

Bengali separatism grew mainly in the 1960s during the era of General Ayub Khan, whose Punjabi military rule excluded any meaningful participation by the East Pakistanis. In the 1950s there was a demand for a level of autonomy, which was spelled out in the Twenty-One-Point Programme of Sahrawardy's Awami League in 1954.[9]

A turning point for Bengali nationalism and for the process towards separatism was the presentation in 1966 of the Six Points by Sheikh Mujibur Rahman, the successor of Sahrawardy as leader of the dominant East Pakistan party, the Awami League. The Six Points called for a loose federal system of government between East and West. Only foreign affairs and defence were to be reserved for the federal government, and it was to have no power of taxation. Each of the two parts of Pakistan was to have its own militia and its own separate currency or separate fiscal system. Needless to say, the Ayub regime strongly opposed any such developments.

As Ayub became more repressive, the West Pakistanis themselves began to agitate. In fact, ironically, the original turmoil that led to the elections of 1970 and then to the bloodshed and secession of 1971 came from West rather than East Pakistan, spearheaded by Zulfiqar Ali Bhutto's Pakistan People's Party. The situation changed drastically when Ayub decided to resign and his successor, General Yahya Khan, promised early elections on the basis of one man one vote. This amounted to a rejection of the sacred 'parity principle'[10] of Pakistan's 1956 Constitution, in that the East Pakistanis would now be assured of a majority and be entitled to govern the whole of Pakistan.[11]

Immediately after Yahya's undertaking the pre-election debate brought to the surface the extent of mutual distrust and hostility between Bengalis and West Pakistanis. On the eve of the elections a dramatic event further highlighted the extent of East–West Pakistan estrangement: a catastrophic typhoon-borne flood, costing the lives of over 200,000 East Pakistanis, to which Islamabad was seen to react with callous indifference. The elections followed in December 1970, and the result was stunning. It was an overwhelming victory for the Awami League, which had campaigned on the basis of the Six Points. The League secured 75 per cent of the Eastern votes, losing only two seats in the East's Assembly and winning an absolute majority in the National Assembly. First in the West and second overall came the Pakistan People's Party led by former Foreign Minister Zulfiqar Ali Bhutto. The election results set the scene for the acceptance of the Six Points by Islamabad; but the West Pakistanis were not prepared to give in. These events, which occurred over a very short period of time, can be seen as the precipitants that brought secession more sharply into focus.[12]

Initially Yahya tried to play the fair arbiter, but before long he sided with the intransigent Bhutto who, having realized that the election results would secure him no more than junior partnership in a Rahman-led government, was actively whipping up an atmosphere of frenzied fanaticism among the Western Pakistani masses. The summoning of the new Assembly, which was to take place in March, was postponed and extensive talks between the three protagonists began in Dacca. In the meantime there was an impressive military build-up in East Pakistan, supervised by the new governor General Tikka Khan (soon to be known as the 'butcher of Dacca'). While Rahman, Yahya and Bhutto talked the Bengalis demonstrated *en masse* calling for immediate independence. But Rahman resisted, calling only for a *hartal* (non-cooperation), which incidentally led to an impressive show of popular solidarity.[13] It was only after the harsh army crackdown of 25 March 1971 that the Awami League opted for secession. The declaration of the independence of Bangladesh was first heard by radio on 26 March, but was made official two weeks later on 10 April 1971.[14]

INTERNATIONAL ACTIVITY

International secessionist activity lasted for nine months from April until December 1971, when the Pakistan Army surrendered and the world was presented with a *fait accompli*.

The Awami League lacked the necessary radicalism and dynamism of a party heading a secessionist movement. Despite its astounding electoral victory it was not a structured mass party with deep roots, but was rather an amalgam of political notables who for the most part held conservative views. Thus it was not surprising that even at the late hour of March 1971, when Tikka Khan was supervising the military build-up in the East, Sheikh Rahman and the Awami League would still not opt for independent statehood, the furious Bengali millions notwithstanding. In general, the Awami League was trying to emulate the example of the Congress Party in India, but with limited success. At best it tried to follow the lines of Nehru's ideological blueprint, and regarded friendly relations with New Delhi as an imperative.[15]

Rahman, the Awami League leader, a less able politician than his predecessor Suhrawardy, was interned in West Pakistan throughout the secession. He was named president, with Syed Nazrul Islam taking over as acting president. The leading figure of the secession was Tajuddin Ahmed, named prime minister of the Bangladesh government-in-exile. Tajuddin was second in command to Rahman in the Awami League, and had led the pro-independence faction in March 1971 while Rahman

152

had resisted secession until the very end. Two other Awami League stalwarts, Mustaque Ahmed and Quamaruzzaman, were Minister for Foreign Affairs and Minister of the Interior respectively. Colonel Osmani, a retired officer, was made commander of the various disparate groups of guerrilla fighters known as 'Mukti Bahini' ('freedom fighters'). The Mukti Bahini rose to at least 150,000 strong, but their military performance was poor due to inexperience (the East Pakistanis had no tradition as a 'martial race' and were a very small minority in Pakistan officer corps). The terrain was also inappropriate for guerrilla warfare, being without mountains or forests save the Chittagong Hill Tracts, which were far too remote.[16]

The some nine parties of the left, such as the National Awami League, the communist parties and others, which had called for secession when the Awami League was still undecided, were not given an official role to play, though they pleaded for a unified front. These small parties, and the military commanders of the Mukti Bahini, were in no position to contest the government-in-exile – at least, not in the short run. The League was internally as well as internationally recognized as the legitimate representative of the East Bengalis, and more tangibly as the vehicle of forthcoming Indian support, without which the cornered Mukti Bahini guerrillas would have been unable to mount operations for long. Indeed, India made sure of channelling its aid only through the government-in-exile stationed on Indian soil.

Some half a dozen or so Bangladeshi diplomatic missions were sent abroad, two of which went to India (one to New Delhi, the other to Calcutta). The Government of Bangladesh had as its nominal base a liberated enclave town renamed Mujibnagar, but its real base was Calcutta. Justice Abu Sayeed Choudhury[17] organized and led the secessionist movement abroad as foremost roving ambassador (he was also European representative with a base in London, and head of the mission lobbying the UN). H.R. Choudhury was the representative in Calcutta, and Siddiqui was sent to North America. A great number of Bengali intellectuals assisted in the propaganda campaign. Academics Dr Mullick and Dr Mazharul Islam were active in India forming the Liberation Council of Bangla Desh Intellectuals, while others tried to gain the support of public opinion in the West, especially in Britain and the United States. Particularly active also were various student groups abroad and the some ninety diplomats of Pakistan who created an impact overseas by their declaration of allegiance to secessionist Bangladesh.[18]

From 10 August onwards the official goal was independence. Four conditions were set for a peaceful settlement: the release of Rahman, the withdrawal of the Pakistani Army from Bangladesh, the recognition of Bangladesh's sovereignty, and compensation for the damages incurred during the crackdown which had started in March 1971. All other formulas were said to be inapplicable in view of the massacres. However, it appears that at some point around September 1971 the Awami League, fearful of losing its grip on the more radical elements in the Mukti Bahini, had put out feelers to Pakistan for a possible reconciliation based on the release of Rahman, United States mediation and an autonomy plan for Bengal. Nothing came of this, however, and the secessionists ended up lobbying India more vigorously.[19]

The international activity of secessionist Bangladesh had little time to evolve into a true secessionist foreign policy in its own right. In fact, most of the missions to Europe, North America and elsewhere were sent somewhat belatedly from September 1971 onwards, and even then they were generally overshadowed by the powerful international campaign of their patron, India.

Bangladesh's primary target for support was India, to the exclusion of other possible alternatives.[20] This gamble, which did pay off in the end, was well justified. India almost completely surrounded East Pakistan (Burma, the other neighbouring country, showed indifference); it had received the refugees, was Pakistan's arch-enemy, had ethnic and other ties with the Bengalis, was a long-time sympathizer with their plight, and was a state that counted internationally. India was so powerful and so natural an ally that keeping it at arm's length would have been, to say the least, unrealistic. But it is not clear whether the Bengali government-in-exile actively sought the kind of support that India was prepared to give – a support which inevitably culminated in total military intervention. It has been suggested that even though Bangladesh's prestige was bound to suffer from outright military intervention on the part of India, the Awami League leaders considered it imperative after a while, for a protracted armed struggle would inevitably have spelt the demise of the League from the leadership of Bangladesh. It is not clear how India was approached, but no doubt use was made of the obvious advantages of Pakistani disintegration and a friendly Bangladesh – which incidentally nurtured no dreams of uniting with West Bengal as an independent state. But the astute Indian leadership needed little prompting in assessing the advantages of the situation, which soon appeared as the ideal opportunity to dismember Pakistan.

Appeals to other third parties were mainly for recognition, diplomatic support and humanitarian relief, an embargo on arms to Pakistan, and for pressure to persuade Pakistan to abandon its aggressive policy. Among such targets were first of all Britain, followed by the United States, France, the Soviet Union, the UN, Afro-Asian countries and the West in general.[21]

The main tactic used by Bangladesh for gathering international support was to present its arguments for self-determination, which were very convincing. Full details were given of the 'colonial' and 'imperialist' relationship between the two wings of Pakistan. As if that were not enough, the Punjabi 'military coterie' had spurned the people's verdict in the 1970 elections when they had clearly voted for the Six Points. Colonialism and treachery had led to the utmost brutality, to the 'butchery' and 'genocide' of an entire people – an act unprecedented in our times, an atrocious onslaught, well organized and executed by the Pakistan Army, leading to the killing of an incredible 'three million Bengalis',[22] perhaps the worst atrocity in so short a time-span in the history of mankind.[23]

Tajuddin Ahmed's words were the *leitmotiv* of Bangladeshi propaganda when he stated:

General Yahya himself left Dacca on the night of March 25 after having unleashed the Pakistan army, with an open license to commit genocide on all Bengalis . . . Pakistan is now dead and buried under a mountain of corpses. The hundreds and thousands of people murdered by the army in Bangla Desh will act as an impenetrable barrier between West Pakistan and the people of Bangla Desh . . . . These acts indicate that the concept of two countries is already deeply rooted in the minds of General Yahya and his associates, who would not dare commit such atrocities on their countrymen.[24]

Under the circumstances, former East Pakistan was under 'occupation' by a foreign army bent on the continuation of its 'colonial rule', this time perpetuated by sheer 'terror'. The leaders of the Pakistani 'military junta' were way beyond reason and could in no way be brought to their senses by their allies. Tajuddin Ahmed continued:

General Yahya's genocide is . . . without political purpose. It serves only as the last act in the tragic history of Pakistan . . . . Bangla Desh will be set back fifty years as West Pakistan's parting gift to a people they have exploited for twenty-three years.[25]

And, in conclusion:

Pakistan is dead and murdered by General Yahya – and independent Bangla Desh is a reality sustained by the indestructible will and courage of 75 million Bengalis who are daily nurturing the roots of this new nationhood with their blood. No power on earth can unmake this new nation, and sooner or later both big and small powers will have to accept it into the world fraternity.[26]

Islamabad provided an elaborate scenario of Bengali and Indian intrigue to dismember Pakistan by creating havoc in the East and murdering non-Bengali residents, in which they had to intervene to restore law and order and bring life back to normal. The real figure of some eight or nine million refugees was put at only two.[27] But such were the merits of the Bengali case that even international lawyers, reputed to be among the most conservative of scholars, were inclined to regard the secession of Bangladesh as the one possible exception to the rule against secessionist self-determination (though admittedly many of them claimed this *ex post facto*).[28]

INTERNATIONAL INVOLVEMENT

The case of East Pakistan, unlike all other secessionist movements with the exception of Katanga, was given wide publicity in the world media from the very beginning, in spite of Pakistani efforts to the contrary. Thus international opinion was aroused, placing limits on the extent of overt support to Pakistan. The world was shocked by the brutal assault of the Pakistan army. Yet when the moment came to stand up and be counted in the UN, the majority of states supported Pakistan against secessionism. In view of this paradox, the posture of India and that of the Soviet Union became critical. Without their sponsorship of Bangladesh, the Bengalis would not have succeeded in the aftermath of Biafra, at least not at that time.

India played the role of patron in a way far surpassing all other sponsors of secessionist movements after the Second World War. But India was not the instigator of the secession, as Pakistan liked to claim. In the first seven months of secession India provided the Mukti Bahini with sanctuary, an operational base to be used as a springboard, military and other technical advice, training, arms, funds and other material, and perhaps some limited artillery cover. It also assisted the government-in-exile to organize itself and helped make it appear as a credible alternative to the unpopular administration of East Pakistan. From as early as 26 March 1971 the Lok Sabba (Lower House) condemned Pakistan's action and extended 'whole-hearted sympathy and support' for the struggle of 'East Bengal' for 'a democratic way of life'. But the Indian Government appeared cautious and did not proceed with the recognition of the secessionist entity, nor did it publicly approve of Pakistan's disintegration. It simply called for a just political settlement on the basis of the election results.[29]

India's political, diplomatic and moral support gradually gained momentum. High-ranking officials were sent to literally all the continents. This included a tour by the Foreign Minister Swaran Singh, and an impressive tour by Prime Minister Indira Gandhi to six Western capitals in October and November 1971. The case of Bangladesh was well presented in the UN. Even more crucially, Soviet support for Bangladesh and for India's future military action were secured by the signing of the Indo-Soviet Friendship Agreement, which in fact amounted to a military security pact. At the same time, India was preparing the world at large and the Western powers in particular for the outcome of this conflict which was taking place on its very doorstep.[30] Indira Gandhi's warning while in Washington in November was transparent: 'We have acted with patience, forbearance and restraint. But we cannot sit idly if the edifice of our political stability and economic well-being is threatened.'[31]

On 4 December India declared war on Pakistan. Pakistan claimed that India had already intervened militarily prior to that date, and that in fact there had been some artillery cover for the Bengalis. Gandhi herself admitted that there had been extended border incidents in late November. But the full-scale military confrontation between the two countries was initiated by Pakistan in an ill-fated air attack, apparently in an attempt to emulate the Israeli pre-emptive strike against Egypt in the June 1967 war. On 6 December, two days after the declaration of war, India recognized the People's Republic of Bangladesh. The Pakistan Army surrendered within two weeks, and thus India presented the world with a *fait accompli*.[32]

India's initial caution and reluctance to recognize Bangladesh were apparently due mainly to the following factors:

1. the non-approval in principle of secessionist self-determination;
2. the fear of a demonstration effect and a precedent for India's separatist ethnic groups (the Nagas, Mizos, Kashmiris and others) who could then accuse India of applying double standards;[33]
3. the fear of pan-Bengali irredentism (West Bengali secession and union with Bangladesh);
4. their wish to avoid an international outcry;
5. not wanting to give rise to Soviet criticism, particularly in the period before the Friendship Agreement;
6. the fear of UN-sponsored action;
7. the fear of full-scale military intervention on the part of the People's Republic of China and possibly even the United States in support of Pakistan.[34]

In addition, it appears that New Delhi had retained some hope, at least in the beginning, that a united and friendly Pakistan, under the Awami League and the pro-Indian Sheikh Rahman, was possible. And India could not support Bangladesh unreservedly at a time when the situation was still fluid, with the Mukti Bahini in a weak position controlling only a very limited area. Finally, the world was still unprepared for and unacquainted with the magnitude of the refugee problem (India's official justification for becoming more involved).[35]

When overt military intervention did come about, the environment was more conducive for the following reasons among others:

1. the refugee problem – by then nearing eight or nine million Bengalis – was not only financially insupportable but was becoming very costly politically, upsetting the delicate balance of ethnic, religious and ideological forces in the neighbouring Indian states; [36]
2. the United States was not in a position to block India's attempt, for fear of Soviet intervention on the Indian side;
3. the People's Republic of China would not upgrade its military assistance to Islamabad for fear of a Soviet diversionary attack on the Sino-Soviet border, and also because of the physical inability of attack in the Himalayas at a time when all mountain passes were blocked by snow;
4. the Soviet Union was now ready to hold the diplomatic ring;
5. there was a fear that the longer the guerrilla struggle continued inconclusively, the greater would be the rise of the already existing anti-Indian factions and the loss of authority of the pro-Indian faction in the Awami League;
6. the Bangladesh lobby in India was clamouring on behalf of a case that was not only just, but concerned a people that had multiple affective links with India.[37]

It had become apparent that in the short term the Mukti Bahini could not mount an offensive against Pakistan's military machine and create a stalemate. India, on her part, was confident of achieving a swift military victory. What in the beginning had appeared to be an alarming situation, a vortex drawing in a reluctant India deeper and deeper, had become for New Delhi, due in great part to its adroit diplomacy, a unique opportunity to humble and weaken decisively its traditional enemy. It soon became apparent that Pakistan's disintegration was being presented to India on a silver platter. Indeed, it was the 'chance of the century' to dismember Pakistan.[38] The disintegration of Pakistan provided the unmistakable proof that Pakistan's *raison d'être* – the famous 'two nations' theory of Ali Jinnah – was, to say the least, suspect. India could not but relish the occasion to assist in discrediting the very essence of Pakistan that had been the subject of such acrimonious debate in the days before independence. Furthermore, the prospect of a friendly and obviously dependent Bangladesh appeared to herald an era of greater political and economic influence for India in the subcontinent. India's assessment was generally correct, at least in the short run. It gained a spectacular victory in foreign affairs and established itself as the undisputed power in South Asia. In addition, as had been calculated at the time, full-scale military intervention was to prove cheaper than feeding the refugees.[39]

For the first months of the conflict the Soviet Union, though critical of the atrocities and intransigence of Islamabad, was not ready to condone the disintegration of Pakistan, with which it had reached some level of understanding and cooperation following the Soviet mediation in Tashkent which had settled one Indo-Pakistani war. Of course, Pakistan disputed the sincerity of the Soviets and their wish to remain neutral, viewing their attitude as sheer hypocrisy.[40] But even after the August pact with India, the Soviets continued to call for no more than a political solution based on the electoral results that would preserve Pakistan's integrity (and note that Moscow meticulously avoided using the expression 'East Bengal', which the Indians had employed from the beginning of the secession). It was only in late autumn that the Soviet Union came out openly in support of Bangladesh. In the UN it effectively blocked a number of draft resolutions emanating from the United States and other allies of Pakistan, and it gave India diplomatic assistance and arms.[41]

The reasons for Soviet restraint were based on considerations such as the following:

1. the 'Tashkent spirit' which still existed despite Pakistan's close ties with China, and a certain commitment to the viability and integrity of Pakistan;
2. the hope of the retention of an integrated Pakistan with the anti-Chinese Sheikh Rahman at its helm;
3. a belief that Islamabad could still make a radical switch away from the policies of the hawks;
4. the fact that the situation was still fluid – even India was treading carefully – and that the Mukti Bahini's battle performance was unimpressive;
5. not wanting to condone an over-assertive India;
6. a reluctance to jeopardize the lives of Soviet technicians resident in Pakistan;
7. the fear of US and Chinese reaction on the side of Islamabad;
8. the wish to avoid displeasing Arab and Muslim states, which tended to side with Islamabad.[42]

Soviet support for Bangladesh hinged on India. Moscow could not but choose the powerful, stable and friendly India over the tottering and outrageous Pakistani military regime which would not listen to reason, even to the friendly advice of its allies the United States and the People's Republic of China, both of which called for a peaceful political settlement to the conflict. Moscow also calculated that neither Peking nor Washington would go so far as to intervene militarily against India; that India could easily inflict a devastating blow on its own against the Pakistan army; and that an independent Bangladesh was bound to be friendly towards the Soviet Union. No doubt the Bengalis had a good case. The Soviet Union is, at least theoretically, not opposed to secessionist self-determination, given its own constitution. Ever since the inception of Pakistan it had regarded it as an 'artificial state' and a 'non-viable absurdity' created by greedy imperialists. This view of Pakistan was abandoned during the *rapprochement* of the mid-1960s, but came to the fore again as Moscow became more annoyed with Islamabad's flirtations with Peking and with its role as a go-between for the *rapprochement* between Washington and Peking.[43]

In the case of India and the Soviet Union, both popularly known in Bangladesh as the 'liberators', power and political considerations no doubt loomed high, very much in accord with the image of their respective leaderships at the time. But affective reasons need not necessarily be considered as mere convenient justifications on the part of both New Delhi and Moscow. If there was any element of affective reasoning operable at all, one could suggest that India was nearer the 'identification' pole (ethnic–cultural–historical links with the East Bengalis) and the Soviet Union nearer to 'internalization' (the merits of the Bengalis' right to self-determination as such).[44]

Among other states which assisted Bangladesh, though in a more subtle manner, were first of all Britain and then France. Both called for a political solution based on the electoral results, and abstained on various pro-Pakistan draft resolutions in the UN.[45] Britain in particular bore the brunt of Pakistan's frustration, and was accused of being a behind-the-scenes primary ally of Bangladesh and India. Some of the accusations that Islamabad levelled at the British were apparently far-fetched, but there is little doubt where British sympathy lay (an interesting position in the aftermath of Biafra where, as we saw, Britain had actively supported the respective Centre). Britain suspended its development aid to Pakistan, but continued its arms supply to India and contributed relief aid to the refugees.[46]

Humanitarian concern ran high in Britain, where an impressive Bangladesh lobby both inside and outside Parliament had been created almost overnight. There were also the various old and new links with India which were greater and deeper than those with Pakistan (cultural, economic and to some extent also strategic ties).[47] On the other hand Britain could not go too far, due to its links with Pakistan and its moral duty as the architect, at least in part, of the partition of the Indian subcontinent. To recognize Bangladesh would be 'inopportune', claimed the British Foreign Secretary, particularly since India had not made a formal request to that effect.[48]

Some other states also came out in favour of Bangladesh, though in guarded fashion. Thus Bulgaria, Czechoslovakia, Hungary, Poland, Mongolia and Cuba followed India and the Soviet Union in voting against pro-Pakistan UN resolutions. The cue of Britain and France in abstaining was followed by Denmark, Chile, Afghanistan, Nepal, Malawi, Senegal, Singapore and Oman. Several of these states contributed to the debate by criticizing Pakistan in varying degrees. Others which also made critical remarks from time to time were Sweden, Yugoslavia, New Zealand, Malta, the Malagashy Republic, Gabon, Peru, and to a lesser extent Syria.[49]

UN involvement was very limited. It arrived belatedly and was decidedly on the Pakistan side. As in the case of Katanga, which had had far less convincing arguments for self-determination, the UN was not prepared to lend its approval or any legitimacy to a secession. Prior to the Indian military intervention, discussions had taken place in the Third Committee of the General Assembly, which could not properly tackle the humanitarian issue of the refugees for it was helplessly entangled with the political aspect. U Thant presented the Security Council with a vague memorandum in July 1971 without calling for any discussion of the problem.

With the outbreak of the Indo-Pakistan war, the Security Council became involved with a draft resolution favouring Pakistan, which was vetoed by the Soviet Union. The issue was referred to the General Assembly under the 'Uniting for Peace' formula, with a resolution proposed by Somalia. Again the resolution, which was put to the vote, favoured Pakistan, for it called for an immediate ceasefire and withdrawal of the troops of India and Pakistan to their respective territories, which meant that the secessionists would again be left alone to face the wrath of the Pakistan army. The votes cast were an incredible 104 in favour, with 10 abstentions and only 11 against (which in fact amounted to seven plus India, the others being Ukraine, Byelorussia and the Indian protectorate of Bhutan). Only after the Pakistani surrender was a strategy adopted by the Security Council calling for the strict observance of the ceasefire and the withdrawal of troops, though in the case of India not immediately, for fear of reprisals. The Bangladesh representative was not permitted to address the Security Council throughout the various extended debates.

161

(It is worth noting that even though Bangladesh had been recognized by the majority of states, it was admitted to the UN only on 17 September 1974, due to China's veto.)[50]

The two main supporters of Pakistan were the United States and the People's Republic of China, but both fell short of Islamabad's expectations by refraining from intervening militarily and by not sending any clear signals to New Delhi that they would directly assist Pakistan in the case of an armed conflagration. Both were, however, particularly vocal in the UN and attempted to help Pakistan through the Security Council, reprimanding India as the aggressor.

Nixon's policy on the Pakistan civil war achieved a unique distinction. It managed to dismay almost everyone: the US public and Congress, India, the Bengali secessionists, and its most 'allied ally' in East Asia, Pakistan. It probably satisfied only Peking. It was a half-hearted balancing act that lacked conviction and failed to convince, making the United States appear weakened and lacking in clout, and this at a time when their intervention in Vietnam was in full swing.

Nixon tried repeatedly to mediate in the conflict, and put pressure on Yahya who was apparently captive of the hawks (Bhutto and General Peerzada, the 'Rasputin of the Yahya regime'). In the words of Nixon in his report to Congress, 'the United States did not support or condone this action' – that is, the Pakistan Army's onslaught in East Pakistan. Washington ceased issuing and renewing licences for military shipments to Pakistan, and dropped new commitments for economic development loans. However, at least five million dollars' worth of arms and spare parts already in the pipeline continued to be sent until this finally dried up in November, as Nixon admitted following the outcry in the United States, India and elsewhere. When Indian forces entered East Pakistan and refused to comply with the UN resolutions to withdraw and reach a ceasefire, Washington suspended licences for the shipments of United States arms to India.[51]

The equivocal US policy of sympathy and diplomatic support for Pakistan was mainly dictated by the existing power relationships in the South Asian triangle, and above all by the tilt of the Soviet Union and China on either side of the conflict. The Nixon–Kissinger China policy, one of the most impressive and far-reaching of Nixon's policies, was just off the ground, with Kissinger's visit to Peking via Rawalpindi and Nixon announcing his plan to visit China. The main third party involved in arranging the dialogue had been Pakistan in the person of General Ayub Khan, whose mission was later undertaken by his far less formidable successor, Yahya. It also appears that Nixon and his entourage had had a distaste for India ever since his days as Vice-President in the 1950s when he was confronted by the acerbic Nehru and his adviser Krishna Menon. His contacts with Indira Gandhi had further reinforced his admiration for the Pakistani leaders – Ayub in particular – and Yahya appeared to him trustworthy and a friend of Washington. In addition to the above, it should be borne in mind that the United States has a tradition of opposition in principle to secessionist self-determination.[52]

Washington could go no further in its support for Islamabad due to fears of escalation into a super-power rivalry, to sharp criticism in the United States and in the West in general, and to the perception that the Pakistanis had overplayed their hand in the East and were intransigent beyond reason. For the record it is worth pointing out that in the years prior to the war the United States had found the Awami League claims reasonable and the situation in East Pakistan deplorable – so much so that Islamabad had on occasion indicated its irritation, at times even with statements bordering on the hysterical such as that a 'foreign power' (meaning the United States) was conniving to dismember Pakistan.[53]

The People's Republic of China, known at the time as an avid champion of liberation struggles, was placed in a dilemma by the Pakistan civil war. The pro-Chinese Bengali communists called upon China to recognize and support Bangladesh. Peking obviously did not relish supporting an oppressive military regime against a popularly elected one, but it had little choice. Pakistan was a close friend that had in the past risked its reputation in Washington to be friendly with Peking. India was a common adversary which was supported by the Soviet Union. Note that in the annals of secessionist wars and internal wars in general, it has been very rare for the two communist giants to support the same insurgent party at the same time. In addition, Rahman's Awami League was regarded as reactionary: it would simply substitute Western Pakistani domination for the exploitation by the conservative bourgeoisie, keeping the Bengali peasants under the 'yoke of capitalism'. To Chinese eyes this was not a true liberation struggle, even though many leftists including Maoists had joined the Mukti Bahini. Peking continued with its normal supply of arms to Pakistan but made it clear that it was not prepared to assist the Pakistanis with their army – though it is possible that Islamabad may have initially misread the signals of Chou En-lai, who was consistently urging a political settlement to the conflict. Thus, Chinese support for Islamabad was mainly diplomatic, and it continued some years after the independence of Bangladesh when Peking vetoed its admission to the UN.[54]

Of the various lobbies that sprang up for Bangladesh, rendering it a *cause célèbre* almost overnight, among the most vocal and influential were the US and British lobbies. In the United States the main centre of activity was the office of Senator Edward Kennedy, who was the chairman of the subcommittee on refugees of the Senate Judicial Committee. The Senate Foreign Relations Committee passed a resolution calling for the suspension of assistance to Pakistan. In Britain support inside and outside parliament was overwhelming, including several MPs and groups that had previously voiced their support for the Biafrans (as Pakistan was keen to point out).[55]

Various relief agencies assisted the refugees, and there were vociferous Bangladesh lobbies in Western capitals. The World Bank decided, much to Pakistan's frustration, to suspend development aid.[56] Among INGOs the International Commission of Jurists, after an on-the-spot investigation, reached the conclusion that the 'ruthless oppression and indiscriminate killings of civilians' had been perpetrated 'on a scale which was difficult to comprehend'.[57]

Bangladesh, the first successful secession after the Second World War, had a very good case for self-determination. However, with the benefit of hindsight it can hardly be regarded as a totally unassailable case for independence, nor as a unique case.

In the first place, Bangladesh is not economically viable, being the poorest country in the world sustained only by huge quantities of foreign aid. It is also notorious for its chronic political instability. After the killing of its first President, Rahman, there were further assassinations and coups, and the country was run by a military regime despite its lively democratic tradition. Today the masses of the Bengali people have to endure not only the periodical typhoons and floods, but also the callousness and corruption of the elite. There is also a case of a trapped minority, the Urdu-speaking Biharis who had been lukewarm supporters of separatism and are today discontented. And in addition to all this, there is at least one active separatist movement in Bangladesh – the obscure 'liberation front' of the Chittagong Hill Tracts.

But Bangladesh is an independent state, the only successful post-war secession, and it is fairly obvious that it can hardly be reunited with distant Pakistan. Up to the present time there has been no suggestion of another possible option – union with India; in fact, the contrary appears to be the case. Bangladesh, like Pakistan, is wary of the brooding presence of India. Because of this, relations between Bangladesh and its former tormentor, Pakistan, are, ironically, rather closer than they might otherwise have been.

THE MORO REGION

No struggle for national liberation will succeed without foreign support . . . Since we are Muslim, we are tied up not only with Mustapha and President Khaddafi, but with all Muslims and freedom fighters in the world.

Abul Khayr Alonto,
Moro National Liberation Front

The archipelago Republic of the Philippines gained its independence in July 1946. The islands had been 'discovered' by Magellan in 1523 and until 1898 were under Spanish rule. They were then ceded to the United States, and in the Second World War fell under Japanese occupation.

Ever since independence the Philippines has experienced one form or another of insurgency and crisis. Prior to the period of major unrest in the last days of President Marcos, and under Corazon Aquino, the two main insurgent groups were the Maoist New People's Army (NPA) and the Muslims residing in the south, the Moros. The Moro insurgency still rumbles on (as does the NPA), but it was at its peak from 1972 to 1977.

ETIOLOGY

The Moro problem has been described as a time-bomb set centuries earlier, when in the sixteenth century the Spanish conquistadores rolled back the tide of Islam that was spreading from the Sulu archipelago under the Sultanate of Sulu. The various Muslim ethnic groups that were already well established in parts of Mindanao and throughout the Sulu area strenuously resisted all attempts at conversion to Christianity, and did not regard themselves as Spanish subjects. (It was only in 1876 that the Sultan of Sulu recognized Spanish suzerainty.) This defiance, spearheaded by the fiercely independent Tausogs, earned the Muslims of the Philippines their name of Moros (Moors, pirates). When the United States took over in 1898 it had to send a series of expeditions against the Moros (the Moro wars), until the Muslims were finally subdued in 1914 and the Sultan of Sulu abandoned his claim to sovereignty, recognizing

165

7. Philippines and Southern Philippines

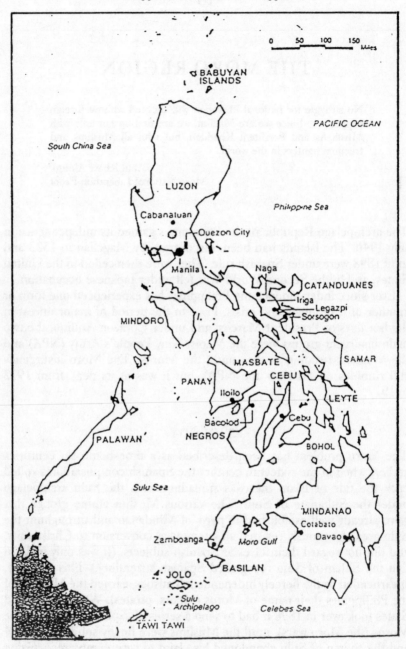

United States rule in 1915. Civil government was established in the Southern Philippines, but the territory was administered separately by the United States 'pacifiers' until as recently as 1936. Thus, until that date the Muslims of the Philippines enjoyed either *de facto* independence or self-rule, and were not subject to the administration of the Christians of the Philippines.[1]

The Moros of the Philippines numbered around two to three million inhabitants in the early 1970s, some 6 per cent of the total population of the country. Today they probably number four million. The region they inhabit and claim as their own, the Southern Philippines, comprises 39 per cent of Philippine territory and contains ten to fourteen million people, or a quarter of the population of the country. In the Southern Philippines they are a minority of one in three, or even less, being a clear majority only in the Sulu archipelago (Basilan, Jolo and Tawitawi) and in Lanao del Sur, one of the provinces of the large island of Mindanao. In the rest of Mindanao and in the island of Palawan, another southern island, the Moros range from 1 to 40 per cent at the most.[2]

Islam and all that it entails, coupled with history and location, gave rise to the Moro identity which to some extent united the some thirteen distinct Muslim ethnic groups. The most numerous Muslim ethnic groups are the Maranao of Lanao, the Maguidanao of the Catabato area, and the Tausog of Sulu. Others include the Samal, the Yakan, the Subanon, the Kalagan, the Badjao, the Ilanum, the Suluano and some others.[3]

The evangelizing character of both Islam and Christianity left little room for coexistence, let alone any form of unity, between Christian and Muslim Filipinos. For the Moros being Filipino means being Christian; the Muslims are a 'nation' apart. In addition to being a separate community, the Moro regions are the least developed areas of the Philippines, although they are rich in timber, gas and other natural resources (some oil was also discovered in the late 1970s). Ever since independence the Moros have been underprivileged, but their grievances were kept under control so long as Manila showed deference to their traditional Muslim leaders. Such leaders held office in local administrations and in the House of Representatives, were in charge of the Moro-inhabited areas of the Philippines, and in general were a law unto themselves. It appears that even as recently as 1968 or 1969 the dominant view of the Moro leaders was not in favour of secession; it was rather, as Noble has put it, simply wanting 'rewards for not seceding'.[4]

But matters came to a head as Marcos, who had taken power in 1966, began gradually to show his true colours, becoming increasingly authoritarian and eventually suspending the two-party system of government and proclaiming martial law. The Moros were faced directly with a centralized and domineering Philippines, now without the intermediary of their traditional Muslim leaders to offer them protection. They felt that their fate was sealed, that being Muslim was tantamount to perennial deprivation and powerlessness, and that they were under siege from the thirty-five million or so Filipinos who had no other aim than to put an end to their way of life through assimilation.[5]

Apart from the 'shrinking political arena' and continued underdevelopment, two other factors were conducive to the enhancement of Moro identity, encouraging the move towards eventual separatism. One was Islamic resurgence, reflecting worldwide Islamic revival. Imams from Arab countries began to teach in the Southern Philippines, and local traditional teachers and leaders became more outspoken; a new elite of Muslim intellectuals emerged, many of whom were graduates from Arab universities – al-Azhar in particular, the famous Islamic university of Cairo. Another crucial factor that coincided with this pride in being Muslim was the widespread migration of Christian Filipinos upon the encouragement of Manila. The Moros were swamped by the rising number of settlers who even appropriated their lands in total disregard of Islamic laws of property, finally dominating the agricultural sector.[6]

Several other events accelerated the separatist process, leading to the formation of various groups seeking autonomy or independence, the best known of which was the Muslim Independence Movement (MIM). Probably one of the better known of these events was the so-called 'Corregidor incident'. Muslim soldiers of the Philippine Army were put to death after having mutinied when they realized that they were to form part of a military contingent to invade and annex the neighbouring Malaysian (and Muslim) state of Sabah.[7] Another precipitant was the threat Manila posed to the authority of traditional Muslim leaders, particularly to that of the powerful and revered *datu* (chieftain) Udtog Matalam of Catabato. It was Matalam (whose son was killed at the time in a feud with Christian–Muslim overtones) who went on to declare the formation of MIM. Finally, extended acts of violence between Christians and Muslims dating from the 1971 elections onwards further mobilized the Moros. The clashes in 1971 resulted in a death toll of at least a thousand as the Muslims, known as 'blackshirts' (those linked with the MIM) and 'barracudas' (the private army of Ali Dimaporo, a Muslim congressman of the Nationalista Party), fought the 'ilagas' ('rats') – members of the Christian Ilongo ethnic group led by Governor Quibranza – and created havoc in the Southern Philippines.[8]

Two further incidents, both attributed to the Philippine authorities, should also be mentioned for they had a great impact among the Muslim community worldwide, leading to an increase in aid to the Moros. One was an onslaught by the Philippine Army in a mosque; the other an attack on and massacre of Muslims whose safe conduct had been guaranteed by the Philippine authorities.[9]

The proclamation of martial law is generally regarded as the triggering event for armed separatism, but this is only partly true. This measure was no doubt the last straw that convinced any Moro militants who still needed convincing. Armed violence was hardly spontaneous in the aftermath of martial law, for there were already large amounts of arms available from Libya and the Malaysian state of Sabah and training had taken place on Malaysian soil prior to 1972. Apart from the MIM, which had changed its name to Mindanao Independence Movement so as also to attract the Christians, there was a proliferation of guerrilla groups, such as Darul Islam which was active with the MIM in the Catabato region, Lamalip in Lanao, the Muslim Brotherhood in Jolo and the Green Guards of Zaboanga and Basilan. However, it is clear that armed violence rose markedly in October 1972, a month after the proclamation of martial law. The new front that was to dominate the Moro separatist movement was the Moro National Liberation Front (MNLF).[10]

INTERNATIONAL ACTIVITY

The MIM, formed in 1968, harnessed aspirations that the founder, Matalam, hardly recognized, anticipated or was in agreement with. Soon it was rivalled by the various other groups which had gone underground, but before the emergence of the MNLF it was Rascid Lucman of the MIM that dominated the movement and provided the critical link with outside sponsors. The MNLF, which took charge from late 1972 onwards and provided the movement with a semblance of unity, was created in Pulau Panghor of Western Malaysia from the youth section of the MIM, which was training on Malaysian soil.[11]

In its unified phase between 1972 and 1977 the MNLF was headed by Nurul Hadji (Nur) Misuari, a political scientist who had taught at the University of Manila, Hashim Salamat, an al-Azhar trained cleric, and Abul Kayer Alonto, a former law student and vice-mayor of Marawi City. Misuari is a Suluano who has links with the Chinese of the Sulu archipelago through his wife Desdemona Tan, a member of a prominent Chinese family. Salamat is a Maguindanao, and Alonto a member of a distinguished Maranao family. The MNLF was throughout a loosely-knit organization with parallel political and military structures. The political leadership comprised a thirteen-member central committee with Misuari as chairman, Alonto as vice-chairman and Salamat chairing its foreign affairs committee. The central committee was stationed abroad, first in the neighbouring Malaysian state of Sabah and then in Libya (apparently, of the triumvirate only Alonto remained in the Southern Philippines). The MNLF also had a political bureau, propaganda and intelligence bureaux, and provincial committees. The parallel military wing was the Bangsa Moro Army. Apart from Nur Misuari and his two seconds, other Moro spokesmen of the time were Syed Lingga, Abdulhamid Lukman who later defected, and Abdul Baki. The original Moro leader, Rascid Lucman, was to resurface later when the MNLF suffered a series of rifts.[12]

The precarious unity of the MNLF was maintained until 1977, after which time there were various splits. Of the original triumvirate, Salamat and Alonto left the MNLF, the first to form the Bangsa Moro Liberation Organization, stationed in Cairo. Moderate separatists in the Philippines rallied around the Moro Reform Liberation Front. The MNLF survived in amputated form under Misuari, assisted initially by the two older-generation leaders Rascid Lucman and Salipada Pendatun. These two headed the Bangsa Moro Advisory Council of the MNLF, stationed abroad. Salipada Pendatun later formed a third organization which was active in Saudi Arabia. Relations between the various fronts were poor, but it is not clear whether there were any armed clashes between them. (In the Islamic Ministers' Conference of Dacca in 1983, Misuari characterized the Salamat group as traitors and as an 'instrument of colonialism and the Marcos regime'.)[13]

The MNLF maintained that its ideology was Islamic socialism and not Marxism, in spite of the Marxist origins of its chief leaders, Misuari in particular. Misuari, who had been a member of the Kabataang Makabayan (the student group linked with the Maoist New People's Army), started as a protégé of Rascid Lucman of the MIM, but soon gained in stature by projecting himself as a radical Islamic thinker and skilful political leader, by demonstrating his ability to link the Moros with external supply sources – Libya, in particular – and by raising the interest of the Islamic world, thus replacing the older-generation conservative leader Lucman.[14]

The MNLF proclaimed independence as its official goal. But in the last years of the unified front, it appeared at times to be ready to settle for less. Thus, in the Jeddah talks with the Philippine Government, which took place in 1975 under the auspices of the Islamic Conference, the MNLF sought the establishment of 'an autonomous Bangsa Moro state' to consist of the islands of Mindanao, Sulu, Basilan and Palawan, which would be 'internally sovereign' but within the context of Philippine sovereignty. In the Tripoli talks which followed in December 1976 under Libyan chairmanship, the MNLF settled for only thirteen of the original twenty-one provinces sought, but this was claimed to be its ultimate concession. As Alonto had put it, their aim was the creation of a 'democratic federal state' with a separate army, and accepting this in the context of Philippine sovereignty was 'a big compromise' on their part.[15]

For international as well as Islamic audiences, the Moro secessionists used arguments such as the centuries-old historical rights of Moro nationhood; Filipino 'colonial domination', 'land grabbing' and 'Christianization'; various acts of 'inhuman behaviour', particularly against civilians, such as bombing with napalm which in the early 1970s, according to the MNLF, had reached the point of 'genocide'; the unequivocal support of the Moro people for a struggle for independence; insincerity on the part of Manila, Marcos in particular, who allegedly had a personal economic stake in the Southern Philippines; the image of a democratic, progressive and modern Muslim and Christian Southern Philippines organized as a federation; and finally, the claim to be able to continue the armed struggle until ultimate success was achieved.[16]

The MNLF was of the firm belief that no independence movement could succeed without external support, but was careful to limit its appeals mainly to the Islamic world. From 1968 until 1972 the nearby states of Malaysia and Indonesia were approached, and somewhat later Muslim and in particular Arab states and organizations were vigorously lobbied. It is worth noting that for all the MNLF's intransigence towards Manila, the secessionist movement was careful not to deviate markedly from the positions of its Muslim supporters – Libya, the Islamic Foreign Ministers' Conferences and the Islamic Secretariat.[17]

To such Muslim targets, the persuasion strategy was obviously Islam. Thus, the Moros were careful to reject the overtures of the various Marxist revolutionary groups active in the Philippines, despite the obvious short-term military returns that their support would bring (though it does appear that there was at times some local cooperation). The Moros were aware that any clear association with such groups would amount to a kiss of death, severing the coveted Arab and Islamic link.[18] The Moro case was thus presented in impeccable Islamic tones:

> We are not communist . . . but God-fearing People[19] . . . . Once our religion is no more our lives are no more . . . . We are born Muslims and we will die as Muslims . . . the ideological aspiration of our Revolution is no other than the paramount interest of our oppressed people, our homeland and Islam . . . between us and the Christian Filipino people there is an irreconcilable contradiction which no human contrivance can permanently resolve. The only

solution is our separation into two distinct and separate political entities.[20]

Other difficulties with the Moro case, which Manila of course was keen to point out, were the limited control of Southern territory,[21] the lack of unity on the ground, the gradual decline of the guerrilla army after 1977, the various splits on ethnic and personality grounds, the extensive foreign links, and above all the fact that the Moros were a minority in the very regions they claimed to represent and wanted to lead to quasi-independence. The result would have been minority rather than majority rule – the cardinal norm of democracy and self-determination. It was also argued that should the South be allowed to secede, Manila would be rendered economically almost non-viable, for its 'frontier territories' were its breadbasket and rich in natural resources.

The MNLF counter-argued that it was in complete control of the countryside and that the struggle would never end ('victory or death' was the battle cry). They played down their ethnic and other divisions, and claimed that 'the term Moro is a national concept that must be understood as all-embracing for all Bangsa Moro people'. They had far greater difficulty in dealing with the fact that they were a minority in the Southern Philippines. They retorted that theirs was not a religious war, that relations between Muslims and Christians were harmonious and that in fact enmity existed 'only between the Muslims and the Christians capitalists' who were exploiting their homeland and 'determining the policies' of the government in Manila. They recognized however, the fact, that they were 'becoming a minority in [their] own land'.[22]

The Tripoli Agreement of 23 December 1976 between the MNLF and the Philippine delegation (headed by Carmelo Barbero) provided for an autonomous region in thirteen out of the twenty-one provinces of the Southern Philippines, which was to have a legislative assembly, an executive council and Islamic law (*sharia*) courts. But there were many loopholes in the agreement and there was still the problem of a Christian majority in those provinces of the future autonomous region; indeed, only five of the thirteen provinces had a Muslim majority. In the thirteen provinces there were at most some four million Muslims and six and a half million Christians. The wily Marcos was quick to take advantage of the situation (the agreement had also split the secessionist ranks into those for and those against the scheme), calling for a referendum which, as the MNLF pointed out, had not been provided for by the Tripoli Agreement. The inhabitants of the region were asked whether they wanted extended powers under MNLF rule or autonomy under the firm control of Manila. Predictably, Marcos won the referendum (Misuari, faced with defeat at the referendum, called for a last-minute boycott). Marcos then went ahead with his version of autonomy, while the MNLF denounced it and resumed the armed struggle, but with much less conviction.[23]

INTERNATIONAL INVOLVEMENT

The Moro secessionists, despite their relatively weak case for self-determination and questionable legitimization among the Muslims of the Philippines, were able to raise the interest of the Arab and Islamic worlds and receive substantial tangible aid from very early on from two sources, Malaysia and Libya.

Malaysia denied any involvement, and on the whole its assistance to the Moros was *sui generis*. The federal government of Kuala Lumpur was apparently responsible for arms and other forms of tangible support prior to the full-scale secessionist armed struggle, from around 1968 until 1970 or 1972 at the latest. Yet for a number of years after 1972, aid continued from Malaysian territory, namely from the Malaysian state of Sabah with Kuala Lumpur apparently either unwilling or unable to curb it. At the same time the Malaysian Government was keen not to offend Manila within ASEAN (the Association of East Asian Nations) and, more importantly for the Philippines, not to create any difficulties from within the Islamic Conference.[24]

Islam was a factor influencing Malaysia's attitude, and the Philippines, with their claim to Sabah, made Malaysia and the Moros natural allies. When relations between Manila and Kuala Lumpur grew warmer, the federal government could still not curb Sabah's involvement, partly because of sheer practical constraints, but also for political reasons. Apart from the factor of great distance from Kuala Lumpur, Sabah under Tun Mustapha was considered the most stable of the Malaysian states, and it delivered critical votes for the alliance leadership of Kuala Lumpur. The very independent leader of Sabah was supportive of the federal government, but it was also clear that if provoked he could contemplate the secession of Sabah from the federation. On the other hand, the longstanding Philippine claim to Sabah provided the basis of a *quid pro quo* arrangement: Manila renounced its claim to Sabah in exchange for the cessation of Malaysian or Sabahan aid to the MNLF. In fact, this seems to have materialized with the good offices of Suharto of Indonesia, upon Marcos's initiative.[25]

Sabah, under the firm leadership of Tun Mustapha, was a consistent partisan supporter providing sanctuary, training grounds and an arms supply depot. It was a convenient conduit for arms from Libya and other Muslim supporters, being situated around fifty kilometres from the nearest Philippine islands. Tun Mustapha was a Muslim zealot who had ethnic and family links with the Moros and a common antipathy towards the Filipinos who threatened Sabah with annexation. He also cherished the aspiration of heading an independent state of Sabah which would include the Southern Philippines, along the model of the old sultanate of Sabah. This tangible support without restrictions was to stop with Tun Mustapha's fall from power in the latter part of 1975, thereby depriving the Moros of their major supply route.[26]

Libya furnished the MNLF with arms and other military hardware and also with financial aid. From 1973 until 1975 Libya was the MNLF's chief diplomatic and political supporter, often with dramatic statements at Islamic Conferences and at the UN. At the 1973 Islamic Conference Libya publicly admitted assisting the Moros, and urged the severance of diplomatic and economic relations with the Philippines in what amounted to a call for a kind of *jihad*. In 1976 and 1977 Qaddafi appeared less enthusiastic after the bold initiatives of President Marcos (who sent his foreign minister and then his famous 'secret weapon', his wife Imelda, to Qaddafi), which culminated in the Tripoli peace talks.[27]

Qaddafi's motives were officially declared to be support for Islam and its values, which were threatened by the Filipinos. It was generally acknowledged that the unpredictable Libyan leader, while referring to Islam and claiming to be its champion, mainly used it to serve his own political ends. Among the obvious goals were enhancing his image as a leader of stature in the Arab and Islamic worlds, replacing his hero Nasser who had died in 1970, and extending his own influence and that of the 'world revolutionary struggle' as he defined it. His by now well-known 'Green Book' propounding his 'Third International Theory' provides some insight into the Libyan leader's views on minorities and separatist movements in general. It is claimed fairly explicitly that minorities are nations with special rights and should be assisted in their struggle against domination by the other groups.[28]

Indonesia followed a correct non-interference line, despite some reports that arms were ferried to the Moros by the very independent governor of the Indonesian province of Makassar. Apparently Indonesia favoured a degree of Moro autonomy, but nothing close to independence (or extended autonomy),[29] and had offered to play the role of mediator in the conflict as well as assisting in the amelioration of Philippine – Malaysian relations.[30]

Among other third-party governments that voiced concern for the plight of the Moros and participated in joint ventures sponsored by the Organization of the Islamic Conference were Egypt, Saudi Arabia, Kuwait, Somalia and Senegal. Saudi Arabia apparently gave funds first to the MNLF and then to Pendatun's group, and Egypt assisted Salamat's group. But to Manila's relief, the Arab states were finally convinced not to go ahead with an oil embargo in the aftermath of the Middle East October 1973 war.[31] More recently, revolutionary Islamic Iran is reported to have become interested in the Moro case. It has deprived the Philippines of Iranian oil and is supposed to have established a beach-head in Mindanao.[32]

The IGO involved in the Moro secessionist conflict was the Organization of the Islamic Conference (OIC) through its Secretary-General and a quadripartite foreign ministers' committee mandated by Islamic Conferences of Foreign Ministers. The committee comprised the foreign ministers of Libya, Saudi Arabia, Senegal and Somalia, and the Secretary-General (first al-Tohamy and then his successor Amadou Karim Gaye) attended the Jeddah and Tripoli talks (the Jeddah talks were held under the OIC Secretary-General's auspices) and visited Manila, meeting with Marcos. The main Islamic Conference resolutions dealing with the issue were those between 1972 and 1977. The Jeddah Third Islamic Conference (1972) expressed concern. The Benghazi Fourth Conference (1973) was the toughest, expressing 'deep concern over the reported repression and mass extermination of Muslims in Southern Philippines', and urging the Philippines to stop these operations immediately. The Kuala Lumpur Fifth Conference (1974), much to Manilan relief, did not go further to demand Moro independence, but called for a peaceful political solution through negotiations with the MNLF 'within the framework of the national sovereignty and territorial integrity of the Philippines'. The next two conferences, in Jeddah and in Istanbul, urged the resumption of talks between the two parties. The MNLF has observer status in the OIC, but its days as an Islamic *cause célèbre*, when al-Tohamy, their champion, was Secretary-General of OIC, appear to be over – at least for the moment.[33] ASEAN, the regional IGO, did not at any stage become involved.[34]

After being outmanoeuvred by Marcos and left by Qaddafi and Sabah, the Moro movement, divided and disoriented, sharply decreased its activity. The guerrilla force, the Bangsa Moro Army, once no less than 50,000 strong, has dwindled to one-tenth of its size. But low-level guerrilla activity has continued, though, as the Marcos regime was losing its legitimacy, the centre of gravity was Manila where the mass uprising was growing. Other revolutionary forces, such as the New People's Army, now seem to be more prominent in the Philippines, and appear to be making inroads into traditional Moro territory.

Today, after the fall of Marcos and the establishment of Corazon

Aquino's rather shaky administration, a new chapter is opening in the turbulent history of the archipelago state. The Moro problem has still not been resolved and its settlement hardly appears to be Aquino's top priority, beset as she is by numerous difficulties and far more serious threats to her rule. Discontented Moro leaders, such as Nur Misuari (who incidentally made contact with the late Benito Aquino in Saudi Arabia when Marcos still held sway), are still in search of sponsors, as in the 1970s.[35] Guerrilla warfare could again reach the mid-1970s level if the various secret contacts said to be taking place between the MNLF and Philippine officials bear no fruit.[36]

ERITREA

The Arab nation, to which we Eritreans are linked with strong
ties of history and culture, will never be safe from the Zionist
and imperialist perfidy until it expels all of their influence from
the land of Eritrea.

Eritrean Liberation Front

Ethiopia is in the unique position of being the only African polity not to
have been colonized by the white man and having never been overcome
or conquered in its entire history, apart from the brief Italian occupation
between 1936 and 1941. In fact Ethiopia, or Abyssinia as it used to be
called, had defeated Italy, the encroaching colonial power in the famous
battle of Adowa in the year 1896 and during the European 'scramble for
Africa', under Emperor Menelik II, it was expanded through conquest,
doubling its size. From 1930 to 1974 Ethiopia was governed, indeed
totally dominated, by Emperor Haile Selassie I, in what was an autocratic
and feudalistic system, reminiscent of those which held sway in medieval
Europe.

Selassie, the absolute ruler, was deposed, following the so-called
'creeping coup' which started in February 1974 and ended in September
with the takeover by the PMAC (Provisional Military Administrative
Council) or Dergue (which means council or committee in Amharic).
Change, often violent, did take place and the empire-state was scrapped,
but the Shoan Amharic domination, characteristic of Selassie's regime,
does not appear to have been eradicated, at least not so far as the
various Ethiopian 'nationalities' are concerned. Indeed, after the rise of
the Dergue to power, and despite the intolerance and harshness against
any form of dissent (which has alienated most specialists on Ethiopia), the
centrifugal tendencies have multiplied and show no signs of receding. At
the pinnacle of Ethiopia's secessionist movements, which are today no less
than five,[1] stand the recalcitrant Eritreans.

ETIOLOGY

The Eritrean secessionist war is the longest African war and one of the

8. Ethiopia and Eritrea

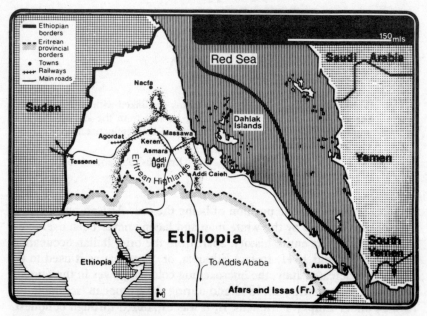

most persistent secessionist movements. This is in itself a major feat, for Eritrea had to struggle not only with a determined Ethiopia, Black Africa's most powerful state militarily, but also with the inherent weaknesses of its case for secessionist self-determination. Moreover, Eritrea itself has a record of appalling internal (fratricidal) wars.

Eritrea is one of a very few incremental secessions which were originally integral 'non-self-governing territories', hence a 'self-determination unit'. (Another less well-known case is the West Papuan movement in Indonesia's West Irian.) Eritrea was an Italian colony from 1889 until 1941. In 1941 the British took over administering the territory until 1952.

Eritrea's fate was decided at the United Nations in 1950 after prolonged debate. The Soviet Union, assisted by Czechoslovakia, called for independence on the basis of self-determination, while Britain and the United States tried to meet Selassie's demands for union by advocating a federal relationship. Italy, with its special interest in Eritrea, had little say and could not push forward with its goal for an Italian trusteeship that would later become an independent state. The UN decided to form a federation of Ethiopia and Eritrea, providing for a separate Eritrean Constitution, an Eritrean Assembly and an executive organ to administer the former colony. From 1952, when unification by federation took place, Selassie set out to achieve what he could not obtain through the UN – the

178

Eritrea

unqualified and total annexation of Eritrea to Ethiopia. The incorporation process was finalized by the 1960s. On 14 November 1962 the Eritrean Assembly, by then reduced to a mere rubber-stamp of imperial decisions, announced the end of the Federation. Eritrea had become one more province of Ethiopia, the fourteenth.[2]

The region of Eritrea comprises 9 per cent of Ethiopian territory, with 8–10 per cent of its population, that is about three or four million out of Ethiopia's present population of about thirty-four million inhabitants. Eritrea is distinguished into two main communities, the Tigrinya-speakers and the Muslims, most of whom are Tigre. The precise numbers of each community are unclear. Some authors claim that there is a rough equality between the two, but most believe that the Muslims have surpassed the Tigrinya-speakers by at least a 5 per cent margin. The Tigrinya-speaking Eritreans occupy the Eritrean highlands, are Christians (Ethiopian Orthodox, a Church related to the Copts) and have ethnic links with the Tigrinya-speakers of adjacent Tigray province (now also in the secessionist throes under the Tigray People's Liberation Front). They also have historical links with the dominant core of Ethiopia, the Amhara of Shoa province,[3] dating from before the Italian conquest. The Muslim Eritreans inhabit the Eritrean lowlands and the Red Sea coastline. Two-thirds are Tigre-speaking, which include the Beni Amer, and the Sahel tribes; the rest are Sahho, Bilayn (many of whom are Christians), Beja, Barya and the Afar or Danakil. The lowlands are also inhabited by the Kunama or Baza, who are Muslim, Christian and animist. The Muslim Eritreans have historical links with the Arab world.[4]

Eritrean nationalism is a product of the separate political existence of the region since 1889 and the callous and overbearing policy of Selassie's palace government. The colonial experience, first the Italians and then the British, laid the ground for a separate Eritrean society. Italian rule is regarded as being responsible for having laid the foundations of an integrated Eritrean economy and setting in motion the social process that was to lead to the emergence of a distinct Eritrean identity. British rule is credited with the political integration of Eritrea. But it was above all Selassie's rule which was instrumental in tying together the two distinct strands of Eritrean society, Christian and Muslim, and kindling Eritrean nationalism to the point of a mass movement for secession.[5]

In the late 1940s and early 1950s, when the fate of Eritrea was discussed (the Eritreans were not asked to express their wishes officially), independence was already one of the well-articulated goals, and probably the dominant view in Eritrea at the time, at least among the Muslims and some Christian circles. The Muslim League, together with the Liberal Progressive Party, a Tigrinya party, favoured independence. The

179

Unionist Party, the largest Christian party, favoured union with Ethiopia in order to render a blow to Italian influence which remained prevalent in Eritrea. Another party, which came to be called the New Eritrean Party, clamoured (with a little assistance from Italian settlers) for an Italian trusteeship which would then lead to independence. Upon union with Ethiopia, in 1952, Eritrean separatism emerged in two waves. To begin with in the 1950s and early 1960s it was largely a Muslim affair, headed originally by the Beni Amer, who are famous for their martial tradition. Later on, in the late 1960s, the Christian elite was able to mobilize the Tigrinya-speakers. By the mid-1970s the movement can be considered as truly legitimized by the vast majority of Eritreans.[6]

As time went by it was obvious that no historical, cultural or religious links with the Amharas could dissuade the Christians from joining the secessionist ranks, not even the old fears of Muslim domination in an independent Eritrea. Some form of separatism, though not necessarily independence, has been strongly supported by the great majority of Eritreans from the 1970s onwards.[7]

Only two ethnic groups in Eritrea are clearly against independence, and against the other lesser forms of separatism for Eritrea. They are the Afars and the Kunari. The main bulk of the Afars are not in Eritrea, but in other regions and in the neighbouring state of Djibouti. Until recently the Afars in general supported the successor regime to Selassie; now many of them are involved in the Afar Liberation Front, the latest Ethiopian separatist upsurge. The Kunari have supported Addis Ababa. A Nilotic group, they are traditional enemies of the martial Beni Amer, who spearheaded Eritrean separatism in the early days and dominated the various secessionist fronts. They have also been historically in conflict with the Beja as well as with the Christian Tigrinya-speakers. In addition, the Kunari claim that the various Eritrean fronts have ignored them and did not assist them when they were raided by the rival ethnic groups. (They even joined in the raids.) Thus the Kunari have not only favoured Addis Ababa, but have lent wholehearted support and even participated in its campaigns against the Eritrean secessionists.[8]

Seen as a whole, Eritrea does not qualify as an 'internal colony' of Ethiopia, nor are the Eritreans 'second-class citizens' of Ethiopia or underprivileged, as are other groups in Ethiopia, most notably the Oromo (formerly known as Galla, a disparaging name which they resent), who are the single largest group, comprising perhaps as much as 50 per cent of Ethiopia's population. This assessment however is only partly true. If one resists the well known 'ecological fallacy' – that aggregates indicate greater correlation than sub-units – then it can be seen that the Muslim lowlands inhabited by the Muslim Eritreans are a periphery not only of Eritrea, but of Ethiopia as whole, and that the Muslim Eritreans, like all the Muslims of Ethiopia, are an underprivileged group suffering discrimination. The Tigrinya-speakers together with their ethnic brethren of Tigray were the most advanced ethnic group in the whole of Ethiopia, second only to the Amhara or Amharized of Shoa province who have ruled the country for centuries. Yet the Christian Eritreans were also an aggrieved group in these terms, for they soon discovered that they were economically worse off than under Italian or British rule, and that Eritrea was irreversibly in decline.[9]

spark.

The rise of armed separatism was the direct result of the unflinching determination of Selassie to incorporate Eritrea and place it under his absolute rule. Federated Eritrea was, if nothing else, an anomaly within despotic Imperial Ethiopia, an island of pluralism and democracy within a feudal theocratic world. (Selassie also headed the Ethiopian Orthodox Church and considered his authority bestowed on him by God in the best autocratic tradition.) Obviously, such a thorn in the Ethiopian body politic had to be wrenched forthwith, lest it became infectious and threatened the rule of 'His Munificent Highness'. The following events during the ten years of federation rendered Selassie's aims transparently clear, and laid the foundations for the secessionist movement of Eritrea:[10]

1. The clash between the Eritrean authorities and Addis Ababa, which led to the resignation of the Eritrean Head of the Executive, Tedla Bairu, who was originally a believer in union with Ethiopia (he headed the Unionist Party) and the dismissal, a little later, of the speaker of the Assembly, Idris Mohammed Adam.
2. The banning of all parties, trade unions and even Eritrean newspapers.
3. The stringent measures taken against all dissidents and bloody crackdowns on more than one demonstration.
4. The replacement of Tigrinya and Arabic (the Muslim lingua franca) by Amharic as the official language of Eritrea.
5. The increased power of the imperial representative and the total control of elections for the Eritrean Assembly.
6. The suspension of the Eritrean Constitution, which was UN-sponsored, and the bringing of Eritreans before Ethiopian courts.
7. Other harsh and provocative measures which included the imprisonment of an Eritrean delegation that had gone to the UN in New York to protest, and the abolition of the Eritrean flag.

Selassie's unilateral abolition of the federated status of Eritrea was the last straw, but technically it was not the triggering event for the decision to seek independence by the use of arms. As early as 1958, independence had been advocated by the Eritrean Liberation Movement

(ELM) created in Port Sudan under the leadership of Muhammad Said Idris Nawad. In 1960 the Eritrean Liberation Front (ELF) was formed in Cairo, inaugurating the guerrilla struggle in September 1961, some ten months before Selassie's act of incorporation. The armed insurrection was launched in Eritrea proper by Ahmed Idris Awate, a renowned *shifta* (outlaw) leader from the days of Italian rule. Awate, who was a Beni Amer related to the leader of ELF, Idris Mohammed Adam, died in 1962, but his few hundred guerrillas continued to grow throughout the 1960s.[11]

In 1970, as armed violence grew, Selassie opted for a military solution, declaring a state of emergency in December. The secessionist ranks swelled in tandem with Selassie's repression and military onslaught. The Dergue, which followed the deposition of Selassie, persisted (after some brief initial wavering) with Selassie's policy on the Eritrean issue, demonstrating, as one author has aptly put it, that 'irrespective of who happens to be in control of the central government in Addis Ababa and regardless of the cost in lives or money, Ethiopia's perceived national interests do not alter'.[12] The 'primary objective', according to Mengistu Haile Mariam, the present Ethiopian leader, 'is to affirm Ethiopia's historical unity and to safeguard her outlet to the sea and to defend her very existence from being stifled'.[13]

INTERNATIONAL ACTIVITY

The ongoing armed struggle of the Eritrean secessionist movement has passed through innumerable vicissitudes since its official inauguration.

An initial striking characteristic of Eritrean secessionist politics is its lack of unity. By far the most pervasive source of discord has been the Muslim–Christian divide. To this must be added the ethnic–linguistic divisions, which were permitted to persist by the zonal system of semi-independent guerrilla groups that dominated the first phase of the war. There were also differences over tactics; ideological differences, often linked to a generation gap (the second-generation leaders being more radical and leftist); the attempts to democratize decision-making; and the role played by third-party sponsors.

As a result, for much of the life of the secessionist movement, there have been at least two rival fronts, or two dominant fronts among three, four or even more groups. During the 1970s in particular there were protracted fratricidal armed clashes as the warring factions rose, ebbed and permutated. The two dominant fronts, the ELF and the EPLF (Eritrean People's Liberation Front), which have been traditionally at loggerheads, were also intolerant of criticism in their midst, in particular of that emanating from two well-known dissident groups: the 'menka movement' within the EPLF calling for greater democratization and the 'fallul movement' in the ELF calling for radicalism.[14]

The ELF was set up by Idris Mohammed Adam, a Beni Amer who was the former Speaker of the Eritrean Assembly, with the participation of other well-known political figures such as Ibrahim Sultan Ali, the former leader of the Muslim League, Woldeab Woldemariam, the leader of the General Union of Eritrean Workers, Osman Saleh Sabbe and Tedla Bairu, the former head of the Eritrean executive. Despite the inclusion of prominent Christians, the ELF remained Muslim-dominated. During the second part of the 1960s, it incorporated the defunct ELM and accommodated, at least temporarily, the rising numbers of discontented Christian highlanders. Idris Mohammed was president, Bairu vice-president and Sabbe secretary-general. A new organizational structure was set up under Idris Mohammed following a meeting at Adobha in the late 1960s but discontent was rife as a result of the autocratic leadership of Idris Mohammed. The ELF soon split into two. One faction, the ELF-General Command, persisted for a while under Idris Mohammed. The other faction, the ELF-General Secretariat, was headed by Sabbe. Then, in 1970, a third front appeared – the Popular Liberation Forces (PLF).[15]

The PLF, led initially by Woldeab, was comprised mainly of Christian highlanders who had been disillusioned with the ELF's Muslim inclination and lack of radicalism. The PLF had hardly been formed, when, in 1972, it made an incongruous common front with Sabbe's group in what was generally regarded as a marriage of convenience which could not last. The PLF was Christian-dominated and radical, while Sabbe was conservative and the prime proponent of Eritrea's Muslim image internationally. From 1972 until 1975, Sabbe appeared to be leading the PLF, though he was nominally only the head of the PLF Foreign Mission stationed abroad. In 1975 Sabbe merged with the ELF Revolutionary Council (as the former ELF General Command was then called). The PLF did not endorse the PLF Foreign Mission's action, but formally split with Sabbe a year later. As for Sabbe's new alliance (with the ELF–RC), it lasted even less. Thus by the late 1970s there were three fronts. By far the most prominent was the Eritrean People's Liberation Front (EPLF, the former PLF) followed by the ELF–RC and the smallest group, the ELF/PLF (Eritrean Liberation Front/Popular Liberation Forces), led by the veteran Sabbe. There was also mention of other groupings in the late 1970s and early 1980s, such as Adem Salih's Eritrean Liberation Forces and a splinter group from Sabbe's ELF/PLF, the ELF/PLF Revolutionary Council under Osman

Agib (who was later assassinated) and Ali Birhatu. In 1982 the ELF–RC leader, Ahmed Nasser, was overthrown by Abdullah Idris, who headed the conservative wing of ELF and was assisted by Saudi Arabia and the Sudan. For a time there appeared to be some kind of alliance with Saudi backing between the three conservative factions led by Sabbe, Abdullah Idris and Adem Salih. However, the only front in Eritrea with a guerrilla force worth mentioning in the 1980s was the EPLF, whose strong man in the last ten years has been Essayas Afeworki.[16]

As the years went by, both the ELF and the EPLF were able to a considerable extent to shed their original justifiable labels of being respectively the Muslim and Christian front. The ELF professed to be generally nationalist and mostly Islamic in ideology, while its successor, ELF–RC, has inclined more towards radicalism, mainly Arab radicalism, rather than Marxism as such. The EPLF has been the major radical Marxist front with a fairly successful radicalization on the ground, mobilizing and educating as well as indoctrinating the peasantry and making women play an active role in the guerrilla ranks. The EPLF activity in this regard, and its attempt to be as self-sufficient as possible, is the very antithesis of the Kurdish movement in Iraq under Mulla Mustapha Barzani and has earned the praise of many radical intellectuals world-wide. The EPLF has also the onerous task of presenting the Eritrean secessionists as more radical and genuinely Marxist than the Dergue regime.[17]

Leadership was always a problem in Eritrea, as no leader could gain the stature necessary to unite all the secessionist fronts. Among the first generation leaders the most influential in the first decade of the movement were Idris Mohammed and Sabbe, but perhaps the most respected was Woldeab Woldemariam, who articulated Eritrean nationalism in the 1950s from Radio Cairo. In the 1970s the most prominent leaders were again Sabbe and second-generation leaders such as Ahmed Nasser, Ibrahim Toteel and Abdullah Idris of the ELF– RC and Ramadan Mohammed Nur and in particular Essayas Afeworki of the EPLF. Eritrea never had a generally accepted and popular leader of the movement, though Sabbe, with his diplomatic skills and ability to bring in Arab aid at times, appeared to be controlling the movement, as the man with the money.[18]

Independence has been the goal of the Eritrean secessionist movement ever since 1961 when the armed struggle was initiated. The rising radicalism of the Eritreans permitted them to speak also in terms of a general 'liberation' of all the nations of Ethiopia which would open the road for an Ethiopian confederation. More recently there appears to be a shift from 'independence as a pre-condition' for talks with Addis

Ababa to a somewhat more lenient position, advocating talks without
preconditions and a referendum – to be supervised by an international
commission – setting forth three options, independence, federation or
regional autonomy. This is the EPLF position. The ELF position on a
referendum of this sort is not very clear. It is known to have condemned
the idea, but also to have accepted it in principle. This leniency on the part
of the Eritreans, which was first manifested briefly in 1974 with the rise of
the Dergue, has not been reciprocated by Ethiopia. In 1976 the Dergue
set forth a Nine-Point Peace Plan for Eritrea, offering full participation
and speaking somewhat vaguely of 'regional autonomy which takes due
account of objective realities in Ethiopia', but after that backed down
when the Eritreans rejected the proposals as inadequate and as a mere
'show of ideological debate'.[19]

However, despite the Dergue's intransigence and its persistence with
the military solution to the problem, there have been some secret
talks between the secessionist leaders and senior Ethiopian officials.
Apparently, the first approach was with General Aman Andom, an
Eritrean who favoured a political solution along federal lines. But Aman
Andom, who was Mengistu's adviser and who briefly headed the Dergue
upon Selassie's fall, was condemned for his views on Eritrea, deposed
and executed. Secret negotiations took place again in the period 1977–78
between the Dergue and Afeworki of the EPLF and to some extent with
the ELF. In the 1980s the ELF under Ahmed Nasser was involved in
secret talks in venues such as Rome, Beirut, possibly Damascus, and
somewhere in East Germany. The ELF talks were denounced by the
EPLF, which was also suspected about the same time of being involved
in talks. It is not clear whether this willingness for talks on the part of
Eritrea in the 1980s, at a time when the Dergue remained intransigent,
was the result of military setbacks, pressure from various third parties
or some other reason. In the case of the EPLF, in particular, ideological
affinity with the Dergue may also have been a factor at least in the
1970s.[20]

Arab states and organizations have been the main targets of tangible
and political–diplomatic support. For most of the period under discussion,
support was sought from the radical Arab states and from the socialist
world. But when the Dergue finally switched away from the United States
and Israel (respectively in late 1976 and 1978) and embraced the Soviet
Union, Eritrea's pool of potential sponsors was drastically limited to the
conservative Arab states.

In the early 1960s, the first Eritrean centre for international activity
was Cairo, soon followed by Damascus, and Baghdad. Other centres
were Khartoum, Mogadishu, Tripoli and Aden. Eritrean offices have

sprung up in most Arab states and in some Western capitals, such as Rome (its main western office), London and New York. The main routes for arms have been through Sudan and South Yemen (via the Red Sea Islands), whenever Khartoum or Aden were friendly with the Eritreans. Throughout the twenty-five years of secessionist activity, Sabbe was the most effective Eritrean spokesman, much respected by many Arab leaders, despite the fact that his role in the Eritrean resistance was very controversial.[21]

Among non-Arab targets the following should be noted: the UN – considered the world body responsible for Eritrea, as well as the body answerable for abandoning Eritrea – the OAU, the Organization of the Islamic Conference, Muslim and African states, the two former colonial powers – Italy and Britain – various Western states and, among socialist states, primarily the Soviet Union, Cuba and the People's Republic of China.[22]

The cardinal argument of the Eritrean secessionists is no doubt the international law argument, according to which the Eritrean case is not one of secession, but rather one of self-determination on the part of a former colony in accordance with the generally-accepted principles of the OAU (sanctity of inherited colonial boundaries) and the UN. When the UN took the decision – contrary to the norm of self-determination – it at least federated Eritrea with Ethiopia, regarding it as a distinct entity, with a separate constitution, a different – democratic – system of government, a separate executive and parliament, that is not as a territory liable to be annexed by Ethiopia. The UN resolution on Eritrea was an international instrument not to be violated. Thus, Ethiopian 'annexation' is in clear defiance of the world body. As for Eritrean acquiescence at the time, this was given under duress. Apart from subtle pressure, on that very day in 1962, Ethiopian Army units surrounded the building of the Eritrean Assembly forcing the Eritreans to accept the dissolution of the dual federation. Furthermore, the Eritrean Assembly was by the 1960s no longer representative of the Eritreans. Intimidation by Addis Ababa had resulted in most representatives and members of Eritrea's executive organ being hand-picked, while the real leaders had abandoned office and were in exile. It goes without saying that Ethiopia is not a state like other states in Africa, but an 'empire', which had in fact participated in the nineteenth-century 'scramble for Africa'. Thus the case of Eritrea was not different from that of Namibia, or the former Portuguese colonies which finally gained their independence.[23]

Such argumentation placed the Eritreans in a different category from the other secessionist movements in Ethiopia. The Eritreans argued that there was 'a basic difference' between the 'Eritrean national question' and the 'question of nationalities inside Ethiopia' because each had different causes. Hence the resolution could not be the same. And the EPLF rounded up the anti-balkanization argument in the following terms: 'The claim of "Ethiopian disintegration". . . besides being anti-Leninist has no basis in fact. There is no revolutionary logic that says that peoples [nations] should be colonized and oppressed so that a certain big country may not 'disintegrate'. The Ethiopian–Eritrean relationship is 'essentially a colonial relationship'. Thus the struggle is 'an historically legitimate and just national struggle'.[24]

The arguments for secession also include the following: the killings and atrocities by the 'decaying feudalist autocratic rule of Selassie' and later on by the 'fascist military dictatorship' of the Dergue; 'oppression', 'domination', 'black colonialism' and Amhara 'military occupation' during both regimes; the legitimization of the 'national liberation struggle' by all Eritreans irrespective of religious or cultural differences, for Eritrea was a nation with roots dating from the very dawn of history; democracy and progressiveness and astounding social-economic and educational 'achievements' within 'liberated Eritrea'; the indomitable will for independence whatever the costs and as long as it takes; and finally, that Eritrea met all the criteria for a viable independent state.[25]

The Eritreans, of course, played down the resistance of the Afars and in particular of the Kunari, who in any event were not a large group. In response to the argument that Ethiopia without Eritrea would be landlocked, the Eritreans offered various solutions, such as a corridor to the sea or some kind of future political link after Eritrean independence. The argument that they were in collusion with ultra-conservative forces was brushed aside as preposterous, and the claim that they presented themselves as a would-be Muslim state was said to be an absurd one, which, they maintained, only applied long ago when it was used as an opportunistic tactic. The Eritreans, the EPLF claimed, were equally divided between Christians and Muslims, but the numbers and the division were of no importance. When it came to the issue of lack of unity, each front accused the others and of course played down the others' power or extent of support among the 'Eritrean masses'. The Nine-Point scheme for autonomy presented by the Dergue was characterized as inadequate and as a 'fraudulent tactic' aimed at gaining time and depriving the Eritreans of international support.

To the Arabs, Eritrea was presented (particularly in the 1960s) as a Muslim entity threatened by the 'infidel' Selassie (and later by the Dergue) in collusion with Israel, 'Zionism and US imperialism' (an 'Arab homeland' under the dire threat of 'Zionist and imperialist perfidy').

Independent Eritrea would constitute an Arab bastion in this highly sensitive area and would render the Red Sea an 'Arab lake'.[26]

Radical Arab targets have been presented with the claim of ideological affinity. But the events of the last ten years have provided Eritrea with the appropriate arguments for conservative Arab targets: that the Soviet foothold in Ethiopia was bound to extend with the Dergue's assistance northward into the Sudan and eastward into the Arabian peninsula and the Gulf. Eritrea sold itself as the conservative Arabs' last hope to arrest the communist and Soviet tidal wave from its new base in Addis Ababa. Even the self-reliant Marxist EPLF tempered its revolutionary rhetoric when dealing with profoundly conservative Arab states, such as Saudi Arabia. Thus Afeworki, in his attempt to gain Saudi support, sold himself as a nationalist rather than a socialist and played down the Marxism of the EPLF. Sabbe and the ELF tried to buttress their Muslim credentials by claiming that the vast majority, perhaps as much as 80 per cent of the Eritrean population, was Muslim, and that the goal of the secessionist movement was to establish a Muslim state.[27]

Socialist targets, and in particular the Soviet Union, were presented with ideological affinity, anti-Americanism, anti-Zionism and the prospects of political and strategic influence in a future independent Eritrea. Predictably, the Eritreans reminded them of the strong stand for Eritrean independence taken by the Soviet Union and Czechoslovakia at the UN in 1950. The Eritrean struggle was an anti-imperialist one, against the alliance of Selassie with Washington, which incidentally had brought about the UN decision in the first place. This 'act of annexation' was committed, argued the EPLF, 'in the era of imperialist domination of the world under the auspices of the leading imperialist power, the US, to serve the geographic and strategic interests of monopoly capital and the expansionist interests of the Ethiopian feudal ruling classes in Eritrea'.[28] When it finally became clear that Moscow was backing the Dergue against Eritrea, the Eritreans demonstrated their astonishment at what they considered a highly unnatural alliance. The Dergue, they claimed, was in fact not revolutionary or Marxist. Among other things, it persecuted all the progressive and revolutionary forces, not only in Eritrea, but in the whole of Ethiopia. The aim of the Dergue was to exterminate the revolutionary Eritreans, thereby vouchsafing Amharic domination and United States and Israeli imperialism, as in the days of the Emperor. It was hoped that the Soviet Union would soon realize its grave error, which made it appear so starkly unprincipled and opportunistic, and revert to its older policy of sympathy for the Eritreans, a policy which was above all consistent with its ideology and its avowed goal of endorsing liberation movements. On the whole, however, the Eritreans, despite their bitterness over Soviet policy, tried to avoid levelling strident accusations of imperialism against the Soviet Union.

The presentation of the Eritrean case for Western audiences is of a more recent vintage, similar to the arguments presented to the conservative Arab rulers, though stripped of course of its Muslim–Arab overtones. Thus, it is claimed, among other things, that Ethiopia constitutes a 'new Afghanistan'; that, under the circumstances, the West, the United States in particular, should back the Eritreans against the Soviet Union; and that the time has now come to remedy the 1950s 'mistake' of 'handing over' the Eritreans to Selassie.[29]

INTERNATIONAL INVOLVEMENT

The considerable material aid made available to the Eritreans came largely from Arab sources. During Selassie's rule in the 1960s and the first part of the 1970s, radical Arab states assisted the Eritrean secessionists, first Egypt and later Syria, Iraq, South Yemen and lastly Libya. After the rise of the Dergue it was the conservative states which became involved, mainly Saudi Arabia and Kuwait. The Sudan was also involved, one way or another, almost throughout the Eritrean secessionist struggle. Outside the Arab world, interest was shown in the early days by the Soviet Union and Cuba.

The two most consistent partisans have been Syria, followed closely by Iraq. Both Baathist governments were openly supportive of Eritrea. Radio Damascus, followed by Radio Baghdad were used for passionate Eritrean broadcasts. Arms, funds and military training were also involved. Syria, in particular, has been praised by the Eritreans for having been the first country to 'give military backing to the Eritrean Revolution', and Selassie had in fact charged Syria with intervention. Syria and Iraq varied their support from one Eritrean front to the other. Thus, for example, in the 1980s, when Iraq abandoned Nasser's ELF, switching to Sabbe's ELF/PLF (and then to Sabbe's rivals in the ELF/PLF), Syria once again assisted the ELF.[30]

After Syria and Iraq, the Sudan takes third place of prominent partisan supporter, though there have been vacillations over the years. Under Abboud, the Sudan was not involved, but on his fall, the Sudan was the venue for political activity, a sanctuary and base of operations, conduit of arms, and perhaps the source of a quantity of funds or arms. Before the Numeiry coup there was, from time to time, some clamping down on aid on a *quid pro quo* basis with Selassie. Numeiry's attitude was confusing, going as it did from a period of extended assistance in his first two years of office, to a period of virtual hostility in 1971, following the understanding

189

with Selassie (at the time of the Addis Ababa Agreement on the Southern Sudan), and from overt support (material and political) in 1976 and 1977, to a far more cautious line and attempts at mediation between the Dergue and the Eritreans. A mediatory stance appears to have been the Numeiry policy in his last years in office, though the Eritreans could still count on sanctuary and right of passage. After Numeiry's fall, the situation seems much the same, and apparently still worries the Dergue, which, at least until 1989, continued to be the main backer of the Sudan People's Liberation Army fighting Khartoum.[31]

Libya openly assisted the Eritreans with arms and funds during the first part of the 1970s, but from then on switched to a mediatory stance and by 1977 stopped aid altogether. The People's Democratic Republic of Yemen (PDRY) was involved in funds, arms, a conduit of arms (second only to the route through the Sudan) and sanctuary; it served also as a base for political activity, mainly during the Selassie period.[32]

Saudi involvement was relatively insignificant during the Selassie period, consisting mainly of some funds, but with the rise of the Dergue it rose spectacularly so as to be regarded by the 1980s as the prime 'banker' of the Eritreans. It has also been involved in internal Eritrean affairs, trying to unite the various fronts under the conservative pro-Islamic elements of the movement such as Sabbe. Among the Gulf states, the greater financial contribution comes from Kuwait.[33]

Egypt under Nasser was the first supporter of the Eritreans even before the 1960s, when Woldeab used to make his fiery statements from Radio Cairo. There were camps near Alexandria for the training of Eritrean guerrillas and Eritreans were sent to the Soviet Union to follow military courses. Support stopped with Nasser's sudden famous friendship with Selassie in 1963. When the Dergue took over there was some interest on the part of Sadat, who detested leftist revolutionaries and all radicals. Among other Arab states worth mentioning are Lebanon (site of one of the primary bases of Eritrean propaganda), Algeria and, after the rise of the Dergue, Morocco and Tunisia.[34]

Worth noting also is the training and material aid provided by Palestinian fedayeen organizations: al-Fatah to the ELF and the PLF, during the Selassie period, and the Popular Front for the Liberation of Palestine (PFLP) to its ideological brother the EPLF. But the Palestinians became lukewarm after the fall of Selassie. Other revolutionary organizations of the Arab world, such as the Popular Front for the Liberation of Oman, as well as other Arab NGOs, have indicated their support for the Eritrean struggle.[35] The Arab League has not been indifferent. The Eritreans have attended League summits as observers and the League has apparently intervened to unite the Eritrean fronts.

190

But on the whole the Arab League has refrained from challenging the OAU position on Eritrea in accordance with its policy of following the OAU lead in African matters.[36]

Arab involvement was based on a mixture of affective and instrumental motives. The second were probably more pronounced and included the desire to establish the Red Sea as an 'Arab lake', as well as fears of the Selassie–Israel–United States connection and later of the Marxist Dergue and the Soviet presence. The obvious affective motive is of course the pro-Arab and Muslim posture of several Eritrean fronts.[37]

It is worth looking in slightly more detail at the considerations of at least four Arab states: Egypt, Syria, Saudi Arabia and the Sudan.

Egypt under Nasser during the period in which the Eritreans received assistance coincides with Nasser's ambitious Pan-Arabist campaigns, which led to the brief union with Syria and to various attempts at destabilizing conservative Arab regimes. With Pan-Arabism in full swing (Nasser regarded himself as the personification of this ideal),[38] the case of Eritrea, though strictly speaking not Arab, appeared to fit in well with Nasser's scheme of things. It was a struggle against imperialism and the outcome of 'United States imperialism' in collusion with 'reactionary Ethiopia', the friend of Israel. Eritrea's independence would make the Red Sea an Arab lake and expand the Arab influence further into Africa (the traditional dream of Cairo to expand its influence to the south along the course of the Nile). The Egyptian leader, then at the very peak of his power and influence in the Arab world, had no qualms about becoming involved in Ethiopia's internal affairs. Involvement against conservative regimes that were a barrier to the expansion of revolutionary Arab nationalism was legitimized. As Nasser had put it, the frontiers of his propaganda ended only where they did not 'arouse an echo'.[39]

When Syria first began assisting the Eritreans, it was after the successful Baathist coup of 1963. In that heroic period of Syrian Baathism between 1963 and 1966, when the Baath was still under the leadership of its chief theoreticians and founding fathers, Michael Aflaq and Salah Bitar (then the Prime Minister), the motives were probably mainly ideological affinity and Pan-Arabism. From 1966 onward, as the star of General Assad began to rise, with his authoritarian Alawi-dominated regime, aid to Eritrea should be placed within the Syrian leader's greater ambitions of making Syria a regional power and controlling as many forces in the Middle East as possible. Of course rivalry with Iraq was also a factor, and this was reciprocated by Iraq who usually supported a different Eritrean group from the one sponsored by Damascus.[40]

Saudi assistance was no doubt part of the general policy of open-handedness, not only to Muslim states or to those with a sizable Muslim minority, but also to revolutionary or secessionist movements that appear to them as Muslim and threatened by 'infidels'. This is even more of an imperative should the threat be from a communist regime assisted by the Soviet Union. Thus Saudi aid rose spectacularly with the rise of the Dergue and with Soviet assistance against the Somalis and then against the Eritreans. Riyadh was of course apprehensive of the Christian and radical elements of Eritrea, particularly of the EPLF, but its almost paranoid fear of the Soviet Union and communism has not permitted an indefinite suspension of aid so as to purge the Marxist elements. Note that the Saudis hold the curious belief that the twin evils of this world are 'Zionism and Communism', and that there is a tacit alliance between the Soviet Union and Israel to destabilize the Middle East, weaken Arabism and overthrow the Saudi monarchy, which sees itself as the custodian of Islam and genuine Arabism.[41]

Sudanese aid is no doubt motivated to a certain degree by the fact that Addis Ababa has traditionally lent support to the Southern Sudanese. However, it appears that it is far less of a calculated move to have a bargaining counter, as has traditionally been the case with Ethiopian support for the Southern Sudanese guerrillas. It is above all a question of cultural affinity with the Eritreans, who are regarded as largely Muslim and speakers of Arabic, and who have ethnic kin across the border into the Sudan. The general public sympathy for the Eritrean cause in northern Sudan places limits on Khartoum's ability to reach and then implement a *quid pro quo* arrangement with Addis Ababa.

Among other states of the 'Arc of Crisis' (as the Middle East including the Horn of Africa has been dubbed by Brzezinski), Iran under the Shah showed some interest for a very brief period, but the present long arm of Muslim fundamentalist Iran does not so far appear to be very interested in Eritrea.[42] Of the states of Black Africa, only Somalia, a member of the Arab League by the 1970s, showed an interest, largely based on the dictum that the enemy of one's enemy is one's friend. Somalia was fairly open in its support, obviously wanting to sap its great enemy's resources and more crucially to divert the Ethiopian army to the Eritrean front.[43] In addition, as is well known, Somalia is one of the very few states that, for obvious reasons of its own (Somalian irredentism concerning the Somali-inhabited regions of Ethiopia, Kenya and Djibouti), is in principle in favour of secessionist self-determination, without which it considers the self-determination norm as devoid of its very substance and main area of application. The Eritreans raised the interest of only one more Black African state, Mozambique under the late Samora Machel, who allowed the Eritreans to open a permanent office there.[44]

Outside the region, Cuba, the Soviet Union and the People's Republic of China showed sympathy for the Eritrean cause throughout the period 1961–74 when Selassie was at the helm. Cuba provided arms and training. (Ahmed Nasser, the former ELF leader was a Cuba trainee.)[45] When the Dergue took over, Cuba, together with the Soviet Union, assisted the Ethiopians in defeating the Somalis who intervened, at first, successfully, in the Ogaden. Havana was not willing to assist in the Eritrean campaign, but pressed for a political settlement and repeatedly tried to mediate. From then on it is not clear whether the Cubans finally did lend assistance to the Dergue, whose main supporter in its Eritrean campaign was, of course, Moscow.[46]

The Soviet Union which had supported Eritrea's independence in 1950 might have given some material support to the Eritreans through the intermediary of its Arab allies. Before switching to the Dergue, it attempted to mediate in the conflict and presumably did not particularly relish the prospect of crushing the Eritreans, whose leading group, the EPLF, appeared to be 'progressive' and Marxist.[47] More recently it appears to be disillusioned with the Dergue and presses it to reach a compromise.

Selassie's skilful foreign policy and artful manoeuvring, together with his political clout in the OAU and elsewhere, discouraged several potential supporters or obliged others supporting the Eritreans to switch their policy, as in the case of the People's Republic of China, PDRY (South Yemen), the Sudan and, in the early 1960s, Egypt. The radicalization of the Eritrean movement and its dissociation from a Muslim identity was another factor that made several supporters lukewarm. Saudi Arabia, as already noted, demanded the limitation of the Christian and radical elements in order to continue with its assistance. Libya appeared to change its policy of support because it viewed the Dergue as progressive and came to accept the argument that Ethiopia as a whole was more Muslim than the Eritreans. For others, the prospect of a revolutionary Marxist Ethiopia was far too enticing to continue aiding the Eritreans against Addis Ababa.[48]

The OAU was not involved in the Eritrean question. Apart from the Arab League, with its discreet interest, the Islamic Conference Organization has not been totally indifferent to the Eritrean plight. The Afro-Arab Solidarity Organization admitted the Eritreans to membership at its Cairo Conference,[49] but perhaps of greater interest has been the case of the various armed movements within Ethiopia itself, which have at times supported the Eritreans morally or cooperated with them militarily. Thus, now and again, the possibility has emerged of some type of pan-secessionist alliance involving the Eritreans and recent rising secessionist movements such as the movement of the inhabitants of neighbouring Tigray province (the Tigray People's Liberation Front

193

which cooperated for a while with EPLF, but later clashed with it), the Afar Liberation Front in the Danakil plains adjacent to Eritrea and, to a lesser extent, the more geographically distant Oromos (Oromo Liberation Front) and the Somalis of Ogaden (Western Somali Liberation Front). In the late 1970s there was even the prospect of an alliance between all the anti-Dergue forces, secessionist as well as revolutionary, but the intricate alliances and ideological debates between the Eritreans and other revolutionary and secessionist movements, in particular with the Tigrayan TPLF, are so complicated that they cannot be dealt with here.[50] It is worth remembering, however, that the Eritreans' basic argument is that theirs is a different case altogether, and this obviously puts limits to any coordination with the other movements.

Special reference should also be made to the Italian Communist Party, which, from the days of Selassie, was an ardent supporter of Eritrea and has been involved in attempts to promote a negotiated settlement between Addis Ababa and the Eritreans. More generally, outside the Middle East, the Eritrean cause has sympathizers in several Western European countries, particularly Norway and Sweden, but also in Britain and France. The British Labour Party programme for 1982 endorsed the referendum proposal of the EPLF and committed a future Labour Government to assist the Eritreans financially. The French Socialist Party has repeatedly voiced its support for an independent Eritrea, but President Mitterand and his socialist government have so far taken no action.[51]

Eritrea has been unable quite to achieve the status of a *cause célèbre*. This is due primarily to its being silenced internationally during the early years of the struggles, by the resourceful foreign policy of Haile Selassie. Then, in the first years of the Dergue, the veil of silence was lifted for a time, as the secessionists gained control of the larger part of Eritrea. The resilience of the secessionists is due not only to the interest of Arab countries, which they have successfully lobbied, but also to the impressive mobilization of the Eritreans, particularly by the EPLF. The Eritreans suffered inconsistency on the part of their sponsors, but managed to obtain external aid most of the time by relying on several sponsors simultaneously – sponsors that could be alternated.

Yet the prospects for a peaceful settlement or for independence or autonomy are not good. The Dergue is as determined as Selassie to follow the old principle of Ethiopia *Tikdem* (Ethiopia first) and to persist with a military solution to the problem. Obviously the situation would alter drastically should Moscow become disillusioned with Ethiopia. In the 1980s Addis Ababa has periodically announced the imminent collapse of the secessionists. Yet the Eritreans refuse to succumb and, at the close of the 1980s, are somehow still in business. Their cause had obvious flaws, but one thing is certain: the Eritreans, whether Muslim or Christian, Tigre-speaking or Tigray-speaking, favour independence, or at least some form of extended and secure self-rule (extended autonomy or loose federation), and there is no lack of recruits to the cause. And the main supporter of Addis Ababa, the Soviet Union, is not apparently as forthcoming as before, realizing that a political and not a military solution should be the aim of the Ethiopians if they want to resolve the conflict.

- Soc. level - alliance of EPLF w/ TPLF
- state level - overthrow of Dergue
- inter-state - collapse of Moscow / support.

195

12

CONCLUSION

Secessionist movements seek some form of territorial separatism – from autonomy to complete independence – and in this aim they encounter strong resistance from their respective central governments, and from the majority of states and IGOs. Yet, in spite of the odds, and an international normative system which frowns on secession, separatist movements persist unabated, having become a permanent feature of the contemporary world scene.

For the process from regional assertiveness to separatism to be set in motion three elements must exist in time and place. First, there must exist a community or a society, that is a self-defined human collectivity (an ingroup) which is distinguishable and dichotomizes itself from the Centre (the outgroup). Second, there should be an actual or at least a perceived present, past or future inequality or disadvantage in the existing unified state. And thirdly, there must exist territorial contiguity, that is a distinct and integral territory in which ingroup habitation manifests a discernible degree of compactness over a period of time. Only if all three exist can a fully-fledged and legitimized separatist movement emerge. From their pristine form, these three attributes interact, to defuse or reinforce each other.

Secessions have sprung from separate communities, that is from groups with an ascriptive basis, as well as from societies which are separate from the community or society of the Centre. Ascriptive-communal identity can be divided into five types: ethno-national identity (ethnic identity, based on the restrictive definition of ethnic group which is founded on common language); national identity, in which the basis is not linguistic; religious identity, racial identity and sub-ethnic or 'tribal' identity. Societies are based on territory and a different ideology from that of the Centre. Two types of separatist societies have emerged: those which have a distinct history of separate administration from the Centre and those whose secession would split a nation in two. In the first type of society, which is more common, there is a working alliance of ethnic groups which claim to be able to run a multi-ethnic society.

The type of identity does not provide, to begin with, any reliable clue as

196

to the secessionist propensity or the capacity for resilience and protracted struggle. The distinction of the 'longest war' is claimed by ethno-nations, such as the Iraqi Kurds and the Karens of Burma, by groups with an attenuated (if any) ascriptive identity, such as the Southern Sudanese, as well as groups with no common ascriptive identity, such as the Eritreans. It is the precise political situation which lends salience to one or the other separate identity and to its endurance. In the Ethiopian and Sudanese setting, being a Christian Tigrinya-speaker or Dinka respectively was not a realistic rallying point from which to generate a secessionist movement. It was only under an all-Eritrean or an all-Southern Sudanese banner that the separatist option could make a lasting impact. Finally, it is numerical minorities (the East Bengalis notwithstanding) and not numerical majorities that seek separatism.

Inequality, disadvantage or deprivation appear in two forms in secessionist situations: as absolute-cumulative, that is, as inequality in all conceivable spheres, and as marginal and relative. An in-between case also exists. This is when a group is the most privileged in a state with the exception of the group at the Centre, as with the Tigrinyas of Ethiopia, in the provinces of Tigray and Eritrea. Marginal or relative disadvantage (when there is preponderance in some areas and not in others) amounts to rank disequilibrium. Note, however, that to date no absolute topdogs, or topdogs only with regard to culture and central political power, not even those in a numerical minority, have developed into active secessionists.

Our sphere of analysis, and in particular the seven secessionist cases that we have examined in detail, tend to confirm the hypothesis that the more a group within a distinct territory nears the point of being considered an ethnic group or a nation, the lesser the role played by inequality in spurring secession; or, to put it differently, the lesser the required degree of inequality (consider the cases of the Ibo, French Canadians, Tamils, Sikhs and Basques). Conversely, the more the group lacks ethnic identity, the greater the role played by inequality, and the greater the required degree of inequality. It has to be no less than absolute cumulative disadvantage (as in the case of the Southern Sudanese, the Muslim Eritreans, the West Papuans and others).

The first part of the hypothesis is not discredited by the fact that many ethno-nations, such as the Bengalis or the Kurds were also influenced by the existence of inequality. The second part is put to the test by the American Confederacy and by the secession of Katanga. It is worth noting, however, that in the cases of both the Confederacy and Katanga, much was made of the disadvantage factor and of the distinctiveness of their society, in addition to their difference in ideology from their respective central governments. Perhaps, in view of these two cases, one could add to the second part of the hypothesis the following caveat: or at least the intransigence of the Centre.

A number of background conditions foster and facilitate the process of inequality and community formation, as well as territorial compactness. Prominent in our case studies – all cases of the developing world – were modernization and, prior to that or in line with it, colonization. With developed states on the other hand, ethnic identity and separatism may be an outlet for the malaise generated by the dehumanizing post-industrial society and an alternative to the ineffective and callous bureaucratic state.

Once communal politics come to the fore with the formation of a sectarian and regional political organization, various events can function as precipitants of separatism and, its most extreme form, secession. They are mainly the actions and reactions of the Centre in its relations with the community or society in question, in the latter's active quest for change. In most instances the Centre determines the final choice of the ingroup and its gradual, though not relentless drift from no more than a search for greater participation and justice, to autonomy and then to independence. This is because the Centre has the prerogative, at least in the early stages, and can in most cases defuse or accommodate ingroup assertiveness by way of various strategies, provided they are seen as genuine by the group concerned and not applied when it is too late. Otherwise, they are bound to be regarded as superficial palliatives intended to appease, manipulate or deceive rather than as genuine measures designed to meet the periphery group's call for self-determination. Harsher strategies, such as induced or forced assimilation, subjugation and the like, are under present circumstances ineffective in the long run and in many instances can turn mere autonomists into fully-fledged secessionists almost overnight. Thus it is not an overstatement to argue that when the 'orphans of the universe' resort to secession, or to an armed struggle for secession, it is more often than not due to the Centre's lack of imagination, moderation or simple ability to adjust to change.

The final decision to secede – declare independence or begin an armed struggle – can be a last resort or an opportune moment. The last resort version is more evident when opportunity considerations (feasibility) are not apparent, as with the Southern Sudanese and the East Bengalis and, we could add, the West Papuans or the Nagas of India. Probably the best example of the opportune moment is Katanga. Other cases stand somewhere in between, with the Biafrans perhaps slightly nearer to opportunity; the Iraqi Kurds (in 1961) nearer to last resort; and the Moros, the Eritreans and Iraqi Kurds (in 1974) somewhere in

[handwritten: due to rising expect— or sign of move about why]

[handwritten margin note: N.D. 1969]

the middle, having plenty of external aid but with their respective Centres armed to the teeth.

Several case studies present a well-known phenomenon, which is often the prelude to revolution. There is an apparent change for the better by the Centre, making expectations rise, only to be dashed as a result of another sudden *volte face* on the part of the Centre, sometimes due to a change of government. This was the case with the Ibos in 1966 and in January 1967; with the Kurds from 1959 to 1961; the Bengalis of Pakistan in 1970 and early 1971; and the Southern Sudanese in 1958. It has happened also during secessionist wars, hardening the will of the secessionists to resist the Centre. Examples include the Katangese in the first part of 1961 (Tananarive and Coquilhatville conferences); the Southern Sudanese in late 1964 and early 1965 (prior to and during the Round Table Conference); and the Eritreans (briefly) on the fall of Selassie in late 1974.

Whatever the precise reasons for violent secession, secessionist movements, whether declared or incremental, are by their very act of secession thrust onto the international scene and become, nominally at least, an issue of international concern. In the first instance they are a source of worry to states bordering the secessionist territory.

International activity in the case of Biafra, the Southern Sudan and Iraqi Kurdistan was derivative. It developed later than secessionist activity at the two other settings, the internal level and the conflict (two-party) level. In the case of the Katangese, Moros and Eritreans, international activity was prominent from the beginning, spurring activity at the other two levels.

Secessionist organizations, like all actors in armed conflicts, respond to situations in ways that they see as beneficial to them on the basis of available incoming information and their interpretation of that information. It is misleading to regard them as following a random or irrational course. (This is in fact often the result of judging the situation from its final outcome.) Of course the situation is one of acute crisis and it cannot be free from misperception. Often there is initial enthusiasm and hope which is destined to be dashed. Biafra and Katanga, particularly during their first months, are characteristic examples of this frame of mind prompted by frustration. At the same time, they are good examples of the stubborn spirit of resistance and grim determination, which is the hallmark of most secessionist movements.

In secessionist movements internal disagreements are endemic and splits can occur despite the unabated external threat. Secessions *stricto sensu* appear more united, but this is partly due to their relatively limited time span, as with Katanga, Biafra and Bangladesh. Apart from the

199

official reasons given for the various splits that occur – differences over objectives and strategy – other reasons seen in the seven cases are the following: ethnic or religious conflicts as with Eritrea and the Southern Sudan; personality rivalries as with the Southern Sudanese, Eritreans and Kurds; ideological differences, as with the Eritreans and Kurds; the political–military split, obvious in the case of the Kurds and the Southern Sudanese; a different foreign sponsor, as in the case of the Southern Sudanese and the Eritreans; a serious failure in strategy, whether political or military, as in the case of the Moros and the Iraqi Kurds.

Leadership can be based on its claim to traditional authority, particularly in the early stages of a conflict, as with Matalam and Lucman among the Moros, Barzani among the Kurds, and in the case of the Katangese leaders. But as the secessionist situation we have examined is one of revolutionary violence, a charismatic revolutionary leader soon appears. In the final analysis, leaders assert their authority if they perform; that is if they are able to deliver the basic secessionist goods without which the armed struggle will simply crumble. This may often result in a leadership based to a considerable extent on a specific external sponsor, as in the case of Sabbe of Eritrea, Misuari of the Moros, Lagu of the Southern Sudan and Tshombe of Katanga.

The ideological credentials of secessionist movements are ambivalent. All can be characterized as simply nationalistic – with the exception of the Eritreans from the late 1970s onwards and the Katangese – on either side of the ideological spectrum. One can also discern a tendency to follow the general ideological trend of the time; 'democracy' and the 'Free World' in the early part of the 1960s, 'socialism' and 'non-alignment' by the 1970s. Consistency between professed ideology and the ideology of the partisan third party is difficult to achieve. The most consistent in this regard of the seven cases examined here were Katanga and the Moros. But in most instances secessionists have to accept aid wherever it comes from. This has been admitted by several secessionist leaders, even during the armed struggle. The standard justification has been that, faced with the struggle for sheer survival, one hardly has the luxury of choice.

Secessions *stricto sensu*, try as they may, have difficulty appearing flexible with regard to their goal; not so incremental secessions. The latter not having formally declared that they are independent states can be more flexible and adapt their goal more easily to changing circumstances. They are seen as more moderate, if not by the state directly concerned (the central government), at least by third parties that could play an active role.

With the obvious exceptions of Eritrea and to some extent the Moros, it appears that declared secessions are in the first instance more likely to gain international attention and extended third-party support. But if we look at other declared secessions such as the Republic of the South Moluccas, Nagaland and Papua Basena (West New Guinea), this is far from clear. Furthermore, with the three *causes célèbres* that we have examined, Katanga, Biafra and Bangladesh, by the end of the struggle only the last had greater support than that given to the Centre. With Biafra and Katanga, as well as Eritrea and the Moros, the most internationalized of incremental secessions, the respective Centres were able to muster greater aid for themselves, at the same time picking off, one by one, the secessionists' allies.

This discussion leads us to one of the fundamental questions of secessionist situations: the indispensability of third party, in particular third-state involvement, and its precise effect. On the one hand there is the position taken openly by the Moro National Liberation Front – that no struggle for national liberation can succeed without foreign support – and put into practice by the majority of secessionist movements. The antithetical thesis entertained by the EPLF (Eritrea) and by the Kurdistan Democratic Party (in its various self-criticisms after its defeat) is as follows: no struggle for national liberation will ever succeed unless a secessionist movement can live without and shun foreign involvement; that is, as long as it can remain self-reliant and continue with the armed struggle.

The vital, indeed indispensable, goods for all secessionist movements are: arms, funds, sanctuary and access. If these fall below a certain level, even the most autarchic of secessionist fronts has to choose between either abandoning the struggle (as did the Kurds in the spring of 1975), or making appeals for extensive aid (as did the Biafrans in September 1968). Being able to avoid external involvement for an extended period depends much on the kind of terrain controlled by the secessionists: whether it is physically inaccessible, and whether it has, or can be made to produce, certain goods, which can be used to procure arms and funds.

Secessionist movements may choose a vigorous international activity or a low profile. They can be selective in their targets of appeal, as were the Bengalis, the Moros and the Katangans, or catch-all, as the Eritreans, the Kurds, the Southern Sudanese and, above all, the Biafrans. A quiet approach in international activity may not be the result of choice (based, perhaps, on a realization of the dangers of third-party involvement), but may be imposed on the secessionists by circumstances such as lack of sympathizers, lack of means and capability, as in the case of the Southern Sudan and Iraqi Kurdistan.

Probably the most obvious danger of external state involvement is dependence on the donor, which leaves the secessionists running the risk of being left out in the cold, as illustrated by Iraqi Kurdistan in 1975, the Southern Sudanese in 1971–72 (to some extent), the Eritreans and the Moros. Extended involvement often leads to an unrealistic stance on the part of secessionist movements, as with Biafra and Katanga. Furthermore, the involvement of third states can escalate the conflict. The Centre may abandon all attempts at reconciliation and seek external aid in order to defeat the secessionists militarily. With its pre-existing foreign links as a state, as well as its ability to offer more to prospective supporters, it is almost invariably able to generate more aid on its behalf.

Targets of secessionist appeals are the superpowers, former colonial powers, neighbouring states, the Centre's known enemies, states within the solidarity universe of the secessionist movement (by ethnic, religious, racial or ideological affinity), regional and world IGOs, and generally all those that have the capability to provide support or are known to be sympathetic as well as states supporting their adversary, the Centre.

Inducements as well as negative sanctions are used to solicit support or neutralize support for the Centre. Yet the ability to provide inducements as well as negative sanctions is often limited, with the exception of Katanga, a particularly rich region. Thus the main techniques of persuasion remain, above all, the argumentation of the case and the claim to affinity with other states on ascriptive or ideological grounds, both of which point to the classical technique of almost all secessionist movements, that of moral blackmail, however subtly presented.

A good case for secession or extended autonomy should be able to counter, to a considerable extent, the various important arguments against secession. It should be able to manifest (a) a high level of suffering at the hands of the Centre (domination–exploitation–assimilation plus direct violence), (b) the existence of a community or harmonious separate society and (c) a realistic image of a more peaceful and advantageous leadership emerging from separatism with regard to both parties to the conflict. The case should appear as factually sound and not as one based solely on rhetoric. The secessionist movements which we have examined have tended to overindulge in the argument of direct violence, which can backfire, as with the Biafrans and the Moros, with regard to genocide. All, with the exception of Katanga, used historical and legal arguments which are by definition dubious, appear as artful pettifogging and can be countered by analogous arguments on the part of the respective Centres, which after all are the historical victors. Other characteristics include presenting the movement as a liberation movement of 'a nation' (or of a 'nation at its birth'), and above all as a unique case, not comparable to other secessionist movements, but comparable only to anti-colonial movements (a claim that can be made with some conviction only by Eritrea, West New Guinea and perhaps Tibet, for the period we have examined at least). Finally, there is a chameleonic syndrome: having to present oneself each time differently for the eyes of each beholder, which was most strikingly the case with the Biafrans and the Eritreans.

In the seven secessionist movements which we have examined, a great number of states were found to be involved. In many instances there were only unsubstantiated accusations of involvement on the part of the governments of the respective states threatened by secession, or press reports of dubious credibility. If we eliminate the unclear cases, we still have as many as seventy-three governments, all involved one way or another with secessionists, that is a number which represents half of the existing independent states in the world today. True, many were involved only marginally, but no doubt secessionist movements were able to generate more interest than one would expect at a time when the international normative framework considered them deviants *par excellence*. This finding however is somewhat circumspect. For one thing, the respective Centres threatened by secession could muster far more aid, with the exception of Bangladesh and Katanga in the beginning. Secondly, it should be remembered that the seven cases examined were among the most 'internationalized' of secessionist wars. In other words they are in fact not representative of post-war secessionist movements.

Many of the seventy-three states were involved in more than one secessionist movement as supporters, which gives us some 115 cases of involvement (115 diads of states and secessionist movements). Of the seventy-three, more than one-third were involved in more than one secessionist attempt; twenty-five were in two, seven in three (Israel, the Soviet Union, Egypt, Kuwait, Senegal, Ethiopia, Czechoslovakia), and one, France, in four. Biafra earned the most supporters, followed by Eritrea, while the Southern Sudanese, the Moros and the Kurds had the fewest.

Of the seventy-three states involved, nearly half had no previous link with the area, colonial, regional or otherwise. The overwhelming majority were involvements of the 'pull' variant; the secessionists had actively solicited and won the support of third states, but the degree of support secured was rarely sufficient to satisfy the secessionists. All sorts of states took part; developed states of the West, Eastern bloc states, and Third World states of various inclinations and ideological hues. Though hardly conclusive, it appears that Western states or underdeveloped states of Western inclination are ahead with regard to tangible aid, while non-aligned states come first with regard to high-level diplomatic support. This result is mainly due to the Biafran and Eritrean cases. Otherwise

203

there was a fairly even distribution, if the number of states in each group are taken into account.

Of the great powers, the Soviet Union and the People's Republic of China appear to have relatively few scruples about supporting secessionist movements, though it should be remembered that the first actively opposed Biafra and switched to supporting the respective Centres in two out of the three cases that it had previously supported. The United States, on the other hand, is in principle against secession and secessionist movements. It was opposed to Bangladesh and Katanga, it was the provider of arms for Manila, and as for military aid to the Iraqi Kurds and relief aid to Biafra, these hardly amount to endorsement of the respective secessionist movements.

The position of the former colonial power is particularly delicate in secessionist situations, for both parties to the conflict tend to seek its support (an exception were the Moros who did not seek United States aid). Of all the former colonial powers which we have examined, only one, Belgium, became a patron of a secessionist movement, but had to back down at the end. Britain, after some initial wavering in the Nigerian secessionist war, gave the wherewithal for Lagos to crush Biafra and was indifferent towards the Southern Sudanese, the Iraqi Kurds and the Eritreans. Britain did support Bangladesh, but mainly indirectly. Egypt supported Khartoum against the Southern Sudanese, the United States continued its military aid to Manila after the secessionist war had erupted, and finally Italy, though sympathetic to the Eritrean plight and a supporter of Eritrea's independence in the late 1940s, kept a low profile, avoiding any meddling in the affair.

All secessionist territories have an international border or an outlet to the sea which allows them to seek sanctuary, access and establish arms routes. Of the some eighteen states that could be considered as neighbours to such territories (that is to the seven secessionist regions we examined), two intervened militarily (one at the highest possible level), eight gave extended aid such as arms and military training over ·an identifiable period and two gave limited support. Only six out of the eighteen remained neutral or unfavourable. Of these, three (Indonesia, Turkey and the Central African Republic) experienced some difficulty in curbing arms trails organized by the secessionists. Rarely did a neighbouring state assist the Centre militarily.

Of the seventy-three states involved in the seven cases, a somewhat greater number provided diplomatic rather than tangible support (aid, assistance, access), which suggests the old dictum that 'words are cheap'. But upon closer scrutiny, one sees that most of the diplomatic support is of a low level, whereas tangible support is of a high level. In fact, in almost half the instances of tangible support, arms were involved. Diplomatic support of an extended level appeared only in about 20 per cent of the total, and as for the various types of recognition (which tend to go together with diplomatic support), they were limited in number. In almost 40 per cent of the cases, both types of involvement were present, but when only one or the other took place, diplomatic support had the edge over tangible involvement. It is worth noting that two movements, Eritrea and the Southern Sudan, do not conform to the preponderance of diplomatic over tangible support.

Of some thirty-two instances of involvement in arms supplies, a very small number of states went even further up the scale of involvement. There has been only one full-scale military intervention in support of a secessionist movement – that of India. Belgium and (less evidently) France included personnel involved in military operations, both states to Katanga. Others are not so clear regarding personnel. Military training was also provided by India, Belgium and France, as well as by Israel towards the Southern Sudan, by Iraq and Syria for the Eritreans, Libya and Malaysia for the Moros and perhaps China for the Biafrans. Iran supported the Iraqi Kurds with artillery by initiating border incidents against Iraq, as did India with Bangladesh prior to its military intervention. Of the seventy-three states involved with secessionist movements, eight could be seen as sponsors or patrons: Belgium towards Katanga, France towards Biafra, Israel towards the Southern Sudanese, Iran towards the Iraqi Kurds, India towards Bangladesh, Libya towards the Moros, and Syria and Iraq towards the Eritreans. Of the eight patrons, four were there at the side of the secessionists right from the start, four came belatedly (France, Israel, Iraq and, somewhat controversially, Iran). With few exceptions, all states involved tangibly denied or played down their involvement even when confronted with persuasive evidence.

'Premature' *de jure* recognition, in defiance of the world consensus at the time, was provided only by six states: the four African states and Haiti in the case of Biafra, and India in that of Bangladesh. At least seven governments did consider recognizing a secessionist entity: Congo–Brazzaville and Belgium in the case of Katanga; Norway, Sierra Leone, Uganda and Senegal in the case of Biafra; and the Soviet Union with regard to Bangladesh (in view of its early recognition following India). Whether France actually considered recognizing Biafra, or not, is unclear, while the Federation of Rhodesia was not of course legally in the position to recognize Katanga. Congo–Brazzaville, Belgium, South Africa, and perhaps Portugal, through Angola, could be seen as having almost recognized Katanga *de facto*, while many Arab states recognized the Eritreans as a liberation movement, and some did the same for the

Moros. Malawi and Uganda under Amin appeared to recognize the Southern Sudanese as a liberation movement. France with its peculiar position towards Biafra can be seen as having recognized the Biafrans as a liberation movement, and this applies also to China, with regard to Biafra.

Involvement is motivated far less by instrumental considerations than is generally suggested by most commentators on secession and civil war. In fact involvement is as much due to affective motives as to instrumental–utilitarian ones. In a third of the cases instrumental considerations prevail; in another third affective considerations appear to predominate; whilst in the last third there is a mixture of the two, the one reinforcing the other (in which cases it is unclear which is of more significance for the involvement decision and the continuation of involvement). Finally, there are slightly more cases of pure affective involvement than of pure instrumental involvement. It should be pointed out though that in two movements, Katanga and Iraqi Kurdistan, involvement was almost totally instrumental, particularly in the case of the Iraqi Kurds. In the other five cases there is either a balance between the two types of motivation or, in most, a clear preponderance of affective considerations. As for the 'interveners', small states are more prone to affective motivation, with the exception of Israel and Belgium. Medium states indicate an instrumental bent, while the three great powers were almost wholly spurred by utilitarian considerations, probably most unequivocally the United States, which opposes secession on principle, and, contrary to the Soviet Union and China, lacks any commitment to revolutionary change, being after all one of the primary status quo powers.

There is a slight tendency for instrumental motives to be more linked with tangible involvement, and for affective considerations to lead to diplomatic support and some form of recognition. This tendency is clearer in the event of high-level tangible involvement, but not in high-level diplomatic support. When the secessions we studied are examined one by one, all, with the exception of the Moros, demonstrate a link between tangible support and instrumental motivation. This is not the case with diplomatic support and affective motivation to which only the Southern Sudan, Biafra and Bangladesh conform, while Eritrea (because of the Arabs) presents a balance, motivated by a combination of instrumental and affective considerations.

Restraints for state involvement are for the most part instrumental in nature (loss of tangible values), regardless of the type of motivation for involvement (be it instrumental, affective or a mixture of the two). It appears that affective reasons do not usually act as restraints to instrumental involvement. But in two instances at least it appears that affective involvement was contained, partly by affective reasons to the contrary (Egypt with regard to Eritrea/Ethiopia, and perhaps Tanzania towards Biafra/Nigeria). In a number of cases there was a kind of balance between motives and restraints, both instrumental, which allowed involvement only up to a certain point at the level where there were large returns for a small outlay. The classic instance, of course, is for instrumental reasons to put a brake on actual or planned involvement which is based on affective considerations.

Most important among instrumental motives and instrumental restraints were considerations of an international political nature, namely the international political configuration of the region, strategic gains, the existing constellation of states for and against the secessionists, the position of allies, great and middle powers and friends, and relations with the state (government) threatened by secession. Of affective motives, the most important seem to have been humanitarian considerations, though in many cases such considerations led only to low-level involvement. Among restraints of an affective nature, prominent were the greater attractiveness of the state threatened by secessionist violence. This is often due to change of government, regime, policy, ideology or manifest moderation, or a mixture of these, with a corresponding realization of various weaknesses in the secessionist case, often accentuated by the movement's intransigent stance.

Of the involvements motivated wholly or partly by instrumental reasons, as many as four-fifths were influenced largely, or at least partially, by international political considerations. A little less than a quarter were influenced by domestic pressure for involvement, followed by one-seventh for military reasons, and a further one-seventh for short- and long-term economic considerations. The relatively minor importance of long-range economic considerations, which counters the neocolonialist 'folk image', should be stressed. In fact it would seem that only in one case were such economic motives (economic penetration) almost the sole instrumental motive for involvement (the case of France towards Katanga).

Among the easily discernible restraints (the majority of which were instrumental in nature), first came international political considerations. These restraints were equally distributed numerically into: (1) actual or anticipated reaction on the part of the Centre (the state threatened by secession); (2) pressure on the part of influential states; (3) the reaction of peers and regional actors. It is worth noting here that the greater military preponderance of the state threatened by secession was a restraint only for those states in the vicinity, not for those beyond 'striking

207

capability'. Such international political considerations were followed by domestic restraints, meaning either domestic pressure or domestic antipathy towards involvement (or greater involvement), or the fear of the demonstration effect internally. Apparently, purely economic restraints (i.e., those endangering economic interests in the Centre or its allies) were few. This lack is probably due to the fact that it is often subsumed under other factors, or so subtle that it cannot be easily discovered by commentators, for most commentators tend to search for economic motives when it comes to involvement and not for economic motives against involvement.

Of the affective considerations, 40 per cent were partly or wholly influenced by humanitarian considerations, which tended to overlap with the 30 per cent influenced by reasons of justice (a good case for self-determination or extended autonomy). In somewhat fewer cases, religious affinity–solidarity was obvious (mainly Muslim solidarity and only in one case marginally Christian solidarity). Ideological affinity played an even lesser part (mainly Marxist revolutionary, but also Arab socialism and, in at least one case, conservative ideology). Ethnic identity appeared to be as high as reasons of justice, often overlapping with the relatively few cases of racial solidarity. Finally, there were a number of instances in which personal friendship between the secessionist leaders and third-party decision-makers played a role.

International political considerations were the main motive for states involved in arms supplies to secessionists (in all but four of the thirty-two cases). In one-third of the instances of involvement, ideology seemed to play a role, followed by religion and ethnic identity. With regard to high-level diplomatic support, again international political considerations appeared to dominate, followed by humanitarian reasons, reasons of justice and religion.

Two factors of particular importance regarding motivation have been deliberately left until this point, since they do not easily fit into the affective–instrumental scheme of things. One is the unpredictable variable of an eccentric or maverick leader with great ambition and (sometimes) messianic aspirations. At least six such leaders were at one time or another involved in supporting secessionist movements: Qaddafi, Amin, Welensky, Papa Doc Duvalier, Tun Mustapha and, of course, Charles de Gaulle. The second factor is perhaps more useful. It is the extent to which the old Kautilya dictum applies; that the enemy of one's enemy is one's friend. In almost half of the instances of involvement in arms supplies, the intervening state was the Centre's enemy, seeking revenge or retaliation. But when it came to high-level diplomatic support and *de jure* recognition, this did not appear to play a role (with the exceptions of India against Pakistan, and Belgium against Lumumba's Congo in 1960).

Another important issue is the reliability of the donor, be he a sponsor or more generally an arms supplier or a high-level supporter diplomatically. Interestingly, one cannot establish, in the seven secessionist cases which we have examined, any relationship between the affective–instrumental dichotomy and reliability. This also applies to the eight sponsors, where again the general type of motivation does not provide any clue as to reliability or non-reliability. When affective and instrumental motivation are both split into specific motives, there are some correlations, though they are mainly weak ones. Thus, the following influences were linked with unreliable sponsors: domestic pressure for involvement, military considerations, long-range economic concerns, affinity with Marxist ideology, and apparently, even the new bandwagon of Muslim solidarity. More reliability-prone motives appear to be the following: the few instances of non-Marxist ideological affinity, humanitarian considerations, reasons of justice, and personal friendships. In other words 'identification' and 'internalization' (empathizing with all or with certain of the secessionists, or believing in their case) make for the most reliable of partisan supporters. This also emphasizes the need to present a good case for self-determination – as well as that of having a good case to begin with.

Being the enemy of the state threatened by secession (and presumably aiming at self-protection or revenge) is not a good indicator of reliability. Seven enemies of the Centre proved reliable, and as many as six did not. Duration and reliability suggest a link. Predictably, the longer the wars the greater the number of deserters, the major reason for abandonment being the sudden amelioration of relationships with the government of the Centre, often on a *quid pro quo* basis. Completely reliable supporters do not exist, for even the most intractable and seemingly interminable of inter-state conflicts have had their thaws and settlements.

The potential of success for secessionist independence movements after the Second World War is slim. More successful are attempts at autonomy, federal status or other such limited forms of devolution. Violent secessionist movements which have declared independence (secessions *stricto sensu*) are faced, sooner or later, with military defeat, unless the Centre somehow redefines its position, something which has not happened so far in the period following the Second World War. The chances of the secessionists compelling the Centre on their own are almost non-existent, given the ability of the Centre to generate more supporters when in dire threat. In fact, should such an improbable event take place – the secessionists overwhelming the

209

governmental forces militarily – it is more likely that they will cease to be secessionists and instead will attempt to capture power in the Centre (i.e., in government). This was suggested in the case of Chad and might have been the case with Biafra in July 1967, had the Biafrans continued with their offensive and entered Lagos. Basically, geographically-isolated, perhaps sea-separated secessionist movements can probably be counted on not to switch to 'dominance reversal' when victorious on their own. As matters stand today secessionist independence can be achieved only if there is total military intervention on the part of a third state, which has the result of defeating or otherwise neutralizing the Centre, and if this *fait accompli* is followed by numerous diplomatic recognitions of the secessionist state, provided of course that the intervenor has made it clear that it has no intention of annexing the secessionist state.

Total intervention and numerous recognitions are a rarity. At a minimum the case of the secessionists should be particularly sound to justify third-party intervention and a diplomatic recognition which is contrary to the stringent anti-secessionist normative principles. For total external state intervention to take place, success must be assured. This means that the intervening state should be in a stronger position militarily than the state directly threatened by secessionist violence. Furthermore, such intervention appears to take place if there is no other conceivable manner in which the conflict might be resolved. Gains should be evident, particularly international political gains. In practice this means no less than the following: that the issue at stake is none other than the secession or the secessionist movement itself. That should be the reason for the inter-state conflict, or the main problem in that phase of an historical inter-state conflict. This last element is highly unlikely, and emerges only in the case of Bangladesh. Apparently it is more common with another type of secessionist movement – one we have not examined – the secessionist–merger movement, where the infusion of ethnic affinity may to some extent obscure a strict cost–benefit analysis on the part of the potential intervenor, raising the level of acceptable costs and risk-taking.

It is possible, looking at the forty-odd years which have followed the Second World War, to suggest a number of guidelines for the future, regarding secession. (This is, of course, assuming there is no dramatic paradigm shift at the inter-state level.)

With regard to the etiology of separatism it can be said that, once a separatist process has begun (i.e., when a potentially legitimized separatist leadership emerges in a situation conducive to the separatist process), it can only be arrested if the Centre redefines its position and accords extended autonomy and power-sharing to the regional separatist group.

That is only if the Centre is prepared to meet the real needs of the separatists, transforming the existing territorial–political system into an advantageous one for them.

When the conflict develops into an armed confrontation, the potential for internationalization arises. In most instances internationalization favours the Centre, at least in the longer term, for the international system is in general disinclined to assist separatists, or assist them beyond a certain crucial point. For the secessionists there are two basic weapons: military prowess, that is, military striking capability (the ability to inflict serious damage upon the Centre in the field, thus raising the costs) and being able to present an exceptionally good case for extended autonomy or independence. Under present conditions, attracting large-scale intervention of the India–Bangladesh model is highly improbable. The best a secessionist movement can realistically hope for is some kind of autonomy or federated status and a degree of power-sharing with the Centre.

The time of the secessionist state has not yet come, despite the several examples of effective small states and ineffective large states. But consociationalism and autonomy as the only way of accommodation within a multi-cultural state has come of age. As the case of the Southern Sudan between 1972 and 1982 indicates, a mutually arrived at settlement after years of violence and bitterness is possible if it splits the difference. On the one hand there is no acceptance of independence as such for the secessionist movement. Territorial integrity is upheld. At the same time there is no assimilation of the secessionists, or attempt on the part of a central government to dominate the separatist community or society. The maximalist aims of both parties are rejected. But the real needs of the parties concerned are met. Real change has been achieved with no group being worse off in the end.

NOTES

INTRODUCTION

1. The term Centre will be used in this study as shorthand for the government of a multi-ethnic state or state with centrifugal tendencies.
2. See Appendix 1 for indicators of legitimization and indicators of credibility of threat.
3. For a categorization of revolutionary and 'liberation' (self-determination) movements, together with examples see A categorization of Nationalist Movements on p. 246.

CHAPTER ONE: ETIOLOGY

1. Walker Connor, 'Nation-Building or Nation-Destroying?', *World Politics* xxiv (April 1972), pp. 320–1; Hakan Wiberg, 'Self-Determination as an International Issue', in I.M. Lewis (ed.), *Nationalism and Self Determination in the Horn of Africa* (London, 1983), pp. 43–4.
2. Guenther Roth, 'Personal Rulership, Patrimonialism and Empire-Building in the New States', *World Politics* xx (January 1968), p. 204.
3. Connor, op. cit., p. 336.
4. Karl W. Deutsch, *Nationalism and Social Communication* (New York, 1966). In sociology the better-known integration theory is the diffusion-erosion model put forward by Smelser and by Eisenstadt.
5. J.M. Blaut, 'Nationalism as an Autonomous Force', *Science and Society* i (Spring 1982), pp. 1–23; Ekkehart Krippendorff, 'Minorities, Violence and Peace Research', *Journal of Peace Research* xvi (1979), pp. 34–46; Michael Lowy, 'Marxists and the National Question', *New Left Review* 96 (March–April 1976), pp. 81–100.
6. For Thomas Kuhn's celebrated paradigms' approach, see his seminal *The Structure of Scientific Development* (Chicago, 1970) and *The Essential Question* (Chicago, 1977).
7. Clifford Geertz, 'The Integrative Revolution: Primordial Sentiments and Civic Politics in the New States', in C.E. Welch Jr. (ed.), *Political Modernization* (Belmont, Ca., 1967), pp. 167–77, 183.
8. Nicos Poulantzas, *L'état, le pouvoir, le socialisme* (Paris, 1978), pp. 102–33; Samir Amin, *The Arab Nation* (London, 1978), pp. 10–11, 81; Blaut, op. cit., pp. 2, 20–3.
9. Donald Rothchild, 'Ethnicity and Conflict Resolution', *World Politics* xx (October 1969), pp. 596–616; Ian Lustick, 'Stability in Deeply Divided Societies: Consociationalism versus Control', *World Politics* xxxi (April 1979), pp. 325–45.
10. Arend Lijphardt, 'Consociational Democracy', *World Politics* xxi (January 1971), pp. 207, 211–25; Arend Lijphardt, 'Political Theories and the Explanation of Ethnic Conflict in the Western World: Falsified Predictions and Plausible Postdictions', in Milton J. Esman (ed.), *Ethnic Conflict in the Western World* (Ithaca, 1977), pp. 46–64; Eric A. Nordlinger, *Conflict Regulation in Divided Societies* (Cambridge, Mass., 1972).
11. Leo Kuper and M.G. Smith (eds), *Pluralism in Africa* (Berkeley, 1969), pp. 27–38; M.G. Smith, *Corporations and Society* (London, 1974). See also other articles in Kuper and Smith (eds), op. cit., particularly those by M.G. Smith, Leo Kuper and Pierre van den Berghe.
12. For other ways of classifying theories relevant to sub-nationalism and communal conflict see: Michael Banks and C.R. Mitchell, 'Conflict Theory, Peace Research and the Analysis of Communal Conflicts', *Millennium: Journal of International Studies* iii (Winter 1974–75); Chong-Do Hah and Jeffrey Martin, 'Towards a Synthesis of Conflict and Integration Theories of Nationalism', *World Politics* xxvii (April 1975).
13. Karl W. Deutsch, *The Analysis of International Relations* (Englewood Cliffs, 1968), pp. 196–96; James S. Coleman, 'The Political Systems in Developing Areas', in Gabriel A. Almond and James S. Coleman (eds), *The Politics of Developing Areas* (Princeton, N., 1970), pp. 532–76; Geertz, op.cit., pp. 167–77.

Notes

14. See among others Ernest Haas, 'The Unity of Europe Reconsidered', *Journal of Common Market Studies* v (June 1967), pp. 320–1; Roger Hansen, 'Regional Integration: Reflections on a Decade of Theoretical Efforts', *World Politics* xxi (1969), pp. 242–56; Paul Taylor, 'The Concept of Community and the European Integration Process', *Journal of Common Market Studies* vii (1968), pp. 83–101; R.J. Harrison, 'Neofunctionalism', in Paul Taylor and A.J.R. Groom (eds), *International Organization: A Conceptual Approach* (London, 1978), pp. 253–68; Juliet Lodge, 'Loyalty and the EEC: The Limits of the Functional Approach', *Political Studies* xxvi (1978), pp. 232–48.

15. See for a good review of theories of revolution Jack A. Goldstone, 'Theories of Revolution: The Third Generation', *World Politics* xxxii (April 1980), pp. 425–53.

16. See among others the following important works: Ted Robert Gurr, *Why Men Rebel* (Princeton, N.J., 1970); James C. Davies, 'Towards a Theory of Revolution', *American Sociological Review* xxvii (February 1962), pp. 5–19; Mancur Olson, *The Logic of Collective Action* (Cambridge, Mass., 1965); Chalmers Johnson, *Revolutionary Change* (Boston, 1966); Samuel P. Huntington, *Political Order in Changing Societies* (New Haven, 1968), pp. 263–343; Charles Tilly, *From Mobilization to Revolution* (Reading, Mass., 1978); Theda Skocpol, *States and Social Revolutions* (Cambridge, 1972).

17. See, among others, the following seminal works on inter-group conflict: Ralph Dahrendorf, *Class and Class Conflict in Industrial Society* (London, 1959), chapter 5; Lewis A. Coser, *The Functions of Social Conflict* (New York, 1954); Mujafer Sherif, *Group Conflict and Co-operation* (London, 1966); John W. Burton, *Conflict and Communication* (London, 1969); Johan Galtung, *Peace: Research, Education, Action. Essays in Peace Research*, i (Copenhagen, 1975); Adam Curle, *Making Peace* (London, 1971); Morton Deutsch, *The Resolution of Conflict* (New Haven, 1973); and Raymond Mack and Richard C. Snyder, 'The Analysis of Social Conflict: Towards an Overview and Synthesis', *Journal of Conflict Resolution* i (1957), pp. 212–48.

18. For a bird's-eye-view of the literature see: Konrad Lorenz, *On Aggression* (New York, 1966); Erich Fromm, *The Anatomy of Human Destructiveness* (Greenwich, Conn., 1973); Albert Bandura, 'On Social Learning and Aggression', in Edwin P. Hollander and Raymond G. Hunt (eds), *Current Perspectives in Social Psychology* (New York, 1976), pp. 116–28; and Ashley Montagu (ed.), *Man and Aggression* (London, 1973), in particular articles by Montagu, J.P. Scott and Leonard Berkowitz.

19. For a distinction into three paradigms see: A.J.R. Groom and Alexis Heraclides, 'Integration and Disintegration', in Margot Light and A.J.R. Groom (eds), *International Relations: A Handbook of Current Theory* (London, 1985), pp. 53–8; Alexis Heraclides, 'From Autonomy to Secession: Building Down' in A.J.R. Groom and Paul Taylor (eds), *Frameworks for International Cooperation* (London, forthcoming). For two paradigms instead of three see: Crawford Young, 'The Temple of Ethnicity', *World Politics* xxxv (July 1983), pp. 660–1; Anthony D. Smith, 'Conflict and Collective Identity: Class, *Ethnie* and Nation', in Edward E. Azar and John W. Burton (eds), *International Conflict Resolution* (Brighton, 1986), pp. 64–73.

20. See for an introduction John Stone, 'Introduction: Internal Colonialism in Comparative Perspective', *Ethnic and Racial Studies* xx (July 1979), pp. 255–9.

21. Michael Hechter, *Internal Colonialism* (London, 1975), pp. 9–43; Michael Hechter and Margaret Levi, 'The Comparative Analysis of Ethnonational Movements', *Ethnic and Racial Studies* xx (July 1979), pp. 260–74.

22. Krippendorff, op. cit., pp. 34, 38. For the Marxist approach to nationalism see note 5 above. For a very liberal neo-Marxist approach see Horace B. Davis, *Toward a Marxist Theory of Nationalism* (New York, 1978).

23. Johan Galtung, *The True Worlds: A Transnational Perspective* (New York, 1981), p. 260.

24. For the scholars mentioned see bibliography. For a sample of these works see the following volumes: Nathan Glazer and Daniel Moynihan (eds), *Ethnicity* (Cambridge, Mass., 1975); Wendell Bell and Walter E. Freeman (eds), *Ethnicity and Nation-Building* (Beverly Hills, 1974); Cynthia H. Enloe, *Ethnic Conflict and Political Development* (Boston, 1973); Esman (ed.), op. cit.; Harold R. Isaacs, *Idols of the Tribe: Group Identity and Political Change* (New York, 1976); Joseph Rothschild, *Ethnopolitics: A Conceptual Framework*

(New York, 1981); Anthony D. Smith, *The Ethnic Revival* (Cambridge, 1981); Donald L. Horowitz, *Ethnic Groups in Conflict* (Berkeley, 1985).

25. Geertz, op. cit., p. 170.
26. Rothschild, op. cit., pp. 14–15.
27. Immanuel Wallerstein, 'Ethnicity and National Integration in West Africa', in Pierre L. van den Berghe (ed.), *Africa: Social Problems of Change and Conflict* (San Francisco, 1965), p. 481; Immanuel Wallerstein, 'The Two Models of Ethnic Consciousness: Soviet Central Asia in Transition', in Edward Allworth (ed.), *The Nationality Question in Soviet Central Asia* (New York, 1973), p. 168; Samuel P. Huntington, 'Civil Violence and the Process of Development', *Adelphi Papers*, no. 83, IISS (London, 1971), pp. 2, 10–11, 14; Robert Melson and Howard Wolpe, 'Modernization and the Politics of Communalism: A Theoretical Perspective', in Robert Melson and Howard Wolpe (eds), *Nigeria: Modernization and the Politics of Communalism* (East Lansing, 1971), pp. 3–20; Milton J. Esman, 'The Management of Communal Conflict', *Public Policy* xxi (Winter 1973), pp. 49–71; Alvin Rabushka and Kenneth E. Shepsle, *Politics in Plural Societies* (Merill, 1972); Orlando Patterson, 'Context and Choice in Ethnic Allegiance', in Glazer and Moynihan (eds), op. cit., pp. 305–49.
28. Milton J. Esman, 'Perspectives on Ethnic Conflict in Industrialized Societies', in Esman (ed.), op. cit., p. 372; Richard L. Sklar, 'Political Science and National Integration – A Radical Approach', *Journal of Modern African Studies* v (1967), p. 6.
29. Esman, op. cit., p. 378; Donald L. Horowitz, 'Multiracial Politics in the New States: Toward a Theory of Conflict', in Robert J. Jackson and Michael B. Stein (eds), *Comparative Politics* (New York, 1971), p. 168.
30. Henri Tajfel, 'Social Categorization, Social Identity and Social Comparison', in Henri Tajfel (ed.), *Differentiation between Social Groups* (London, 1978), pp. 61–76; Henri Tajfel, *The Social Psychology of Minorities*, Minority Rights Group, Report no. 38 (London, 1978).
31. For the happy slave situation see: Curle, op. cit., pp. 4–5; Banks and Mitchell, op. cit., pp. 258–9.
32. Tajfel, op. cit., 9–14; Horowitz, op. cit., pp. 269–70.
33. For other similar categorizations see e.g. Rothschild, op. cit., pp. 155–9; Cynthia H. Enloe, 'Internal Colonialism, Federalism and Alternative State Development Strategies', *Publius* vii (1977), pp. 147–60; Michael Banton, *Race Relations* (London, 1967), pp. 68–76; Claire Palley, 'The Role of Law in Relation to Minority Groups', in Anthony E. Alcock et al. (eds), *The Future of Cultural Minorities* (London, 1979), pp. 127–60.
34. For a more detailed explanation of the denial–acceptance distinction and for its relevance to 'ethnic' conflict resolution see Alexis Heraclides, 'Conflict Resolution, Ethnonationalism and the Middle East Impasse', *Journal of Peace Research* xxvi (May 1989), pp. 198–203.
35. Rothschild, op. cit., p. 6.
36. For Galtung's approach see note 23 above and the corresponding sentence in the text. For Rothschild, Birch, Trent, Muhgan, and Nafziger and Richter see Bibliography at the end of the book. For the other authors mentioned in detail in the text see notes 37–40 below.
37. Ivo D. Duchasek, *Comparative Federalism: The Territorial Dimension of Politics* (New York, 1970), pp. 67–8; Ivo D. Duchasek, 'Antagonistic Cooperation: Territorial and Ethnic Communities,' *Publius* vii (Fall 1977), pp. 8–9, 15.
38. A.D. Smith, *The Ethnic Revival* (Cambridge, 1981); Anthony D. Smith, 'Towards a Theory of Ethnic Separatism', *Ethnic and Racial Studies* II (January 1979), pp. 21–35.
39. M. Crawford Young, 'Nationalism and Separatism in Africa', in Martin Kilson (ed.), *New States in the Modern World* (Cambridge, Mass., 1975), pp. 60–7.
40. Horowitz, *Ethnic Groups in Conflict*, pp. 229–81.
41. For classical definitions of minority see among others: Louis Wirth, 'The problem of Minority Groups', in Ralph Linton (ed.), *The Science of Man in the World Crisis* (New York, 1945), p. 347; Charles Wagley and Marvin Harris, *Minorities in the New World* (New York,

214

Notes

1958), pp. 4–11; Francesco Capatorti, *Study on the Rights of Persons Belonging to Ethnic, Religious and Linguistic Minorities* (New York, United Nations, 1979), pp. 5–15.

42. F.S. Husle, 'Ethnic, Caste and Genetic Miscegenation', *Journal of Biosocial Sciences*, Supplement I (July 1969), pp. 31–2; Wsevolod W. Isajiw, 'Definitions of Ethnicity', *Ethnicity* i (July 1974), pp. 111–12.

43. See among others the following: Richard A. Schermerhorn, 'Polarity in the Approach to Comparative Research in Ethnic Relations', in M. Kurokawa (ed.), *Minority Responses* (New York, 1970), pp. 1–2; Abner Cohen, 'Introduction', in Abner Cohen (ed.), *Urban Ethnicity* (London, 1974), pp. ix–x; Fredrik Barth, 'Introduction', in Fredrik Barth (ed.), *Ethnic Groups and Boundaries* (Boston, 1969), pp. 9–38; Paul Mercier, 'On the Meaning of "Tribalism" in Black Africa', in Pierre L. van den Berghe (ed.) op. cit., pp. 485–501; Walker Connor, 'A Nation is a Nation, is a State, is an Ethnic Group, is a . . .', *Ethnic and Racial Studies* i (October 1978), pp. 377–400; Pierre L. van den Berghe, 'Ethnic Pluralism in Industrial Societies: A Special Case?', *Ethnicity* iii (1976), pp. 242–55. See also reviews by James McKay and Frank Lewins, and by Charles Keyes cited in Bibliography.

44. For the concept of nation see among others the following classical modern works: Rupert Emerson, *From Empire to Nation* (Cambridge, Mass., 1960); Karl W. Deutsch, *Nationalism and Social Communication*, pp. 17–28, 97, 170–1; Elie Kedourie, *Nationalism* (London, 1966), pp. 13–15, 58; Ernest Gellner, *Nations and Nationalism* (Oxford, 1982), pp. 3–36.

45. For the fluidity of boundaries see works cited in note 43 as well as Wallerstein, 'Ethnicity and National Integration in West Africa', in Pierre L. van den Berghe (ed.), op. cit., pp. 472–7.

46. Geertz, op. cit., p. 170.

47. Stanley Lieberson, 'Stratification and Ethnic Groups', in Anthony H. Richmond (ed.), *Readings in Race and Ethnic Relations* (Oxford, 1972) pp. 200–1. A social class, a 'criminal class', a group of former slaves (the Spartacus model), etc., would, upon creating an independent state, generate all the distinctive divisions that make up a society. This would not be possible with other collectivities, such as for instance groups based on gender, though the idea is not are supposed totally inconceivable, as seen with the legendary Amazons who are supposed to have resided in Pontos, Asia Minor, prior to ancient Greek colonization.

48. See for this expression Ali A. Mazrui in 'Pluralism and National Integration', in Kuper and M.G. Smith (eds.), op. cit., p. 339.

49. Emerson, op. cit., pp. 95–6.

50. Another reason for making such claims is the attempt to meet international law standards of legitimacy.

51. Rank-disequilibrium is a situation of dominance or ascendancy in one domain but not in another, for example great political clout but not high educational level, as with the Hausa–Fulani of Nigeria, or economic strength but limited power, as with several Chinese or Indian communities in south-eastern Asia. For this concept which inspired many large-scale empirical researchers in International Relations, see Johan Galtung, 'A Structural Theory of Aggression', *Journal of Peace Research* i (1964), pp. 95–119.

52. For structural violence see Galtung's seminal 'Violence, Peace and Peace Research', *Journal of Peace Research* vi (1969), pp. 170–2.

CHAPTER TWO: THE INTERNATIONAL NORMATIVE FRAMEWORK

1. James Crawford, *The Creation of States in International Law* (Oxford, 1979), p. 89.

2. Paragraphs such as these have become a leitmotiv in UN resolutions.

3. Lee C. Buchheit, *Secession: The Legitimacy of Self-Determination* (New Haven, 1978), pp. 12–36; A. Rigo Sureda, *The Evolution of the Right of Self-Determination* (Leiden, 1973); Hector Gross Espiell, *The Right to Self-Determination: Implementation of United Nations Resolutions* (New York, United Nations, 1980): Vernon van Dyke, 'Self-Determination and Minority Rights', *International Studies Quarterly* xiii (September 1969), pp. 226–33; Rupert Emerson, 'Self-Determination', *American Journal of International Law* lxv (1971), pp. 466–7. See also the article by Adrian Guelke, 'International Legitimacy, Self-

Determination and Northern Ireland', *Review of International Studies* ii (January 1985), pp. 37–52.

4. Buchheit, op. cit., p. 7; Michael Reisman, 'Somali Self-Determination in the Horn', in I.M. Lewis (ed.), *Nationalism and Self-Determination in the Horn of Africa* (London, 1983), p. 168.

5. Sureda, op. cit., pp. 25–6.

6. Buchheit, op. cit., p. 6.

7. Crawford, op. cit., pp. 99–100; Emerson, op. cit., p. 464; Leo Gross, 'The Right of Self-Determination in International Law', in Martin Kilson (ed.), *New States in the Modern World* (Cambridge, Mass., 1975), pp. 136–44.

8. Ian Brownlie, *Principles of Public International Law* (Oxford, 1973), pp. 575–8; Hakan Wiberg, 'Self-Determination as an International Issue', in Lewis (ed.), op. cit., p. 45; Higgins, in van Dyke, op. cit., p. 225.

9. See for example Espiell, op. cit., pp. 11–12. Another UN rapporteur who wrote a study on self-determination with similar conclusions is Cristescu.

10. Emerson, op. cit., pp. 459, 465; van Dyke, op. cit., pp. 229–44; Sureda, op. cit., pp. 53–81, 110–11, 227; Crawford, op. cit., pp. 89–113; Wiberg, op. cit., pp. 49–51.

11. Buchheit, op. cit., pp. 73–107; Reisman, op. cit., pp. 151–60; Sally Healy, 'The Changing Idiom of Self-Determination in the Horn', in Lewis (ed.), op. cit., pp. 97–101; James Mayal, 'Self-Determination and the OAU', in Lewis (ed.), op. cit., pp. 85–7.

12. Ibid., pp. 87–9.

13. Van Dyke, mentioned in Ved P. Nanda, 'Self-Determination and International Law', *American Journal of International Law* lxvi (1972), p. 327. The United Nations position on this matter has been stated epigrammatically by U Thant: 'So far as the question of secession of a particular section of a Member State is concerned, the United Nations has never accepted and does not accept and I do not believe it will ever accept the principle of secession of a part of its Member state.'

14. Paul Taylor, *The Limits of European Integration* (London, 1983), pp. 269–75.

15. Joseph Silverstein, 'Politics in the Shan State: The Question of Secession from the Union of Burma', *Journal of Asian Studies* xviii (1958), pp. 43–57.

16. See the Preamble and Article 5, para. 3 of the Yugoslav Constitution.

17. Buchheit, op. cit., p. 127; Wiberg, op. cit., p. 53, p. 65 note 28.

18. Nanda, op. cit., pp. 328–34. Nanda points to seven features of Bangladesh that would qualify it as an exception to the ban against secessionist self-determination: physical separation; political dominance; marked religious–cultural–ethnic difference; significant regional disparity in economic growth; the electoral results as a mandate for extended autonomy; a brutal suppression akin to genocide or selective genocide; the economic and political viability of a future independent Bangladesh.

19. Higgins, quoted in Buchheit, op. cit., p. 131.

20. Crawford, op. cit., p. 215; Wiberg, op. cit., pp. 54–60.

21. Sureda, op. cit., pp. 265–93; Crawford, op. cit., pp. 218–28.

22. Buchheit, op. cit., pp. 98–9; Chan Heng Chee, *Singapore: The Politics of Survival* (Singapore, 1971), pp. 3–10.

23. Crawford, op. cit., pp. 16–25; Brownlie, op. cit., pp. 89–95. The case for the older 'constitutive approach' to recognition was put forward by international lawyers of the stature of Hans Kelsen and Hersch Lauterpacht, see e.g. Lauterpacht's classical *Recognition in International Law* (Cambridge, 1947), pp. 1–78.

24. Brownlie, op. cit., p. 94; J.E.S. Fawcett, *The Law of Nations* (Middlesex, 1971), pp. 49–53.

25. Lauterpacht, op. cit., p. 46; Davis J. Ijalaye, 'Was Biafra at any Time a State in International Law?', *American Journal of International Law* lxv (1971), p. 559.

26. Crawford, op. cit., p. 257.

27. Richard Falk, 'Janus Tormented: The International Law of Internal Law', in James N. Rosenau (ed.), *International Aspects of Civil Strife* (Princeton, N.J., 1964), pp. 194–209; Lauterpacht, op. cit., pp. 176–7; Rosalyn Higgins, 'Internal War and International Law', in C.E. Back and Richard A. Falk (eds), *The Future of the International Legal Order*

(Princeton, N.J., 1972), vol.III, pp. 86–7. The factual test includes extended armed conflict; occupation and administration by the insurgents of a large portion of national territory; hostilities conducted under the rules of law by a responsible authority; and circumstances which make outside states define their position as of necessity.

28. Falk, op. cit., pp. 210–40; Higgins, op. cit., pp. 81–121.
29. Bert W.A. Röling, 'The Legal Status of Rebels and Rebellion', *Journal of Peace Research* xiii (1976), pp. 150–4.
30. Tom J. Farer, 'The Regulation of Foreign Intervention in Civil Armed Conflict', *Recueil des Cours*, Hague Academy of International Law, cxlii (1974), vol.II, pp. 367–402; Ian Browlie, 'Humanitarian Intervention', in John Norton Moore (ed.), *Law and Civil War in the Modern World* (Baltimore, 1974), pp. 217–28. A case in point was the salutary Tanzanian intervention in Amin's Uganda, see Noreen Burrows, 'Tanzania's Intervention in Uganda: some Legal Aspects', *The World Today* (July 1979), pp. 306–10.
31. Higgins, op. cit., pp. 92–7; Farer, op. cit., p. 335; R.J. Vincent, *Nonintervention and International Order* (Princeton, 1974), p. 236; Buchheit, op. cit., p. 38.
32. Richard Little, *Intervention: External Involvement in Civil Wars* (London, 1975), p. 33.
33. Charles R. Beitz, *Political Theory and International Relations* (Princeton, 1979), pp. 83–8.
34. Richardson, mentioned in Little, op. cit., p. 29.
35. Ibid., pp. 18, 24.
36. Istvan Kende, 'Twenty-five Years of Local Wars', *Journal of Peace Research* viii (1971), pp. 5–22; Istvan Kende, 'Wars of Ten Years (1967–1976)', *Journal of Peace Research* xv (1978), pp. 227–41.
37. Robert O. Matthews, 'Domestic and Inter-State Conflict in Africa', *International Journal* xxv (1970), p. 467.
38. Michael Stohl, The Nexus of Civil and International Conflict', paper at the European Consortium for Political Research, Workshop on Social Conflict (Brussels, 1979), p. 25.
39. Buchheit, op. cit., pp. 29–30.
40. Nicolas Politis, 'Le problème des limitations de la souveraineté et la théorie de l'abus des droits dans les rapports internationaux', *Recueil des Cours*, Hague Academy of International Law, vi (1925), vol.I, pp. 5–121.
41. Buchheit, op. cit., pp. 20–30.
42. S. Calogeropoulos-Stratis, 'La libre détermination et le Tiers-Monde', *Hellenic Review of International Relations* ii (1981), pp. 231–2.
43. Buchheit, op. cit., p. 17.
44. Espiell, op. cit., p. 14; Nanda, op. cit., p. 336.
45. Crawford, op. cit., pp. 86, 100.
46. Onyenoro S. Kamanu, 'Secession and the Right of Self Determination', *Journal of Modern African Studies* xii (1974), op. cit., pp. 355–76; Reisman, op. cit., pp. 161–72 Nanda, op. cit., pp. 321–36; Umozurike in Buchheit, op cit., p. 213.
47. Buchheit, op. cit., p. 213.
48. Scelle, in Buchheit, ibid., p. 213; Robert Redslob, 'Le principe des nationalités', *Recueil de Cours*, Hague Academy of International Law, xxxvii (1931), vol.III, pp. 35–8.
49. Peter Russell and Storrs McCall, 'Can Secession be Justified? The Case of the Southern Sudan', in Dunstan M. Wai (ed.), *The Southern Sudan: The Problem of National Integration* (F. Cass, London, 1973), pp. 95–118.
50. Buchheit, op. cit., pp. 216–49.
51. Beitz, op. cit., pp. 112–15.
52. See Buchheit, op. cit., pp. 43–5.
53. A.J.R. Groom, 'Getting our Double Standards Right on Intervention', mimeo, University of Kent (Canterbury, 1980).
54. Falk, op. cit., pp. 243–4.
55. Farer's criteria include, among others, administration of territory by the rebels, violation of human rights by the incumbent, involvement of foreign combat units and that the challenge is 'coherent and political'. Farer, op. cit., pp. 297–406.
56. Beitz, op. cit., p. 92.

57. John W. Burton, 'The Relevance of Behavioral Theories of the International System', in Moore (ed.), op. cit., pp. 99–101.

CHAPTER THREE: THE INTERNATIONAL ACTIVITY OF
SECESSIONIST MOVEMENTS

1. Arnold Wolfers, *Discord and Collaboration – Essays on International Politics* (Baltimore, 1962), pp. 3–24.
2. See, in particular, John Burton, *World Society* (Cambridge, 1972) and John W. Burton, A.J.R. Groom, C.R. Mitchell and A.V.S. De Reuck, *The Study of World Society: A London Perspective*, International Studies Association, Occasional Paper, no. 1 (Pittsburg, 1974); also Robert O. Keohane and Joseph S. Nye (eds.), *Transnational Relations and World Politics* (Cambridge, Mass., 1971). In the 1980s this general approach is one of the three competing paradigms in International Relations, the others are neo-realism and structuralism or the world system approach (which is an extension of *dependençia* theory).
3. Astri Suhrke and Lela Garner Noble, 'Introduction', in Suhrke and Noble (eds), *Ethnic Conflict in International Relations* (New York, 1977), p. 5.
4. George Modelski, 'The International Relations of Internal War', in James N. Rosenau (ed.), *International Aspects of Civil Strife* (Princeton, N.J., 1964), pp. 20–1; Richard A. Falk, 'Janus Tormented: The International Law of Internal War', in Rosenau, ibid., p. 223.
5. Samuel P. Huntington, 'Civil Violence and the Process of Development', *Adelphi Papers*, no. 83, IISS (London, 1971), p. 13.
6. James MacGregor Burns, 'Wellsprings of Political Leadership', *American Political Science Review* lxxi (March 1977), pp. 273–4.
7. See Max Weber's classical presentation of the bases of authority in *The Theory of Social and Economic Organization*, Talcott Parsons (ed.) (New York, 1964), pp. 328–9.
8. For the concept of idiosyncracy credit see Edwin P. Hollander, 'Conformity, Status, and Idiosyncracy Credit', in Edwin P. Hollander and Raymond G. Hunt (eds.), *Classical Contributions to Social Psychology* (New York, 1972), pp. 365–6. For the role of personality in politics see Fred Greenstein, *Personality and Politics* (Chicago, 1970), pp. 41–57; Robert E. Lane, *Political Life* (New York, 1965), pp. 99–100; and Ole Holsti, 'Foreign Policy Formation Viewed Cognitively', in Robert Axelrod (ed.), *Structure of Decision* (Princeton, N.J., 1976), pp. 365–6.
9. For the durability factor see Judy S. Bertelsen, 'An Introduction to the Study of Nonstate Nations in International Politics', in Judy S. Bertelsen (ed.), *Nonstate Nations in International Politics* (New York, 1977), pp. 3–4.
10. Leon Festinger, quoted in Morton Deutsch, *The Resolution of Conflict* (New Haven, 1973), p. 357.
11. For the theory of cognitive dissonance and other similar approaches which explain this frame of mind see Leon Festinger's classical *A Theory of Cognitive Dissonance* (Stanford, 1957); Robert Abelson and Milton Rosenberg, 'Symbolic Psycho-Logic: A Model of Attitudinal Cognition', *Behavioral Science* iii (January 1958), pp. 1–10; Elliot Aronson, 'Dissonance Theory: Progress and Problems', in Robert P. Abelson et al., *Theories of Cognitive Dissonance: A Sourcebook* (Chicago, 1968), chapter I; Milton Rokeach, *Beliefs, Attitudes and Values* (San Francisco, 1975).
12. Harold D. Lasswell and Abraham Kaplan, *Power and Society* (New Haven, 1950), pp. 78–80; Lane, op. cit., pp. 97–162.
13. John Burton, *Deviance, Terrorism and War* (London, 1979), pp. 140–58.
14. John W. Burton, 'Resolution of Conflict', *International Studies Quarterly* xvi (March 1972), p. 8.
15. Suhrke and Noble, op. cit., p. 3.
16. Modelski, op. cit., p. 20.
17. See for example C.R. Mitchell, 'Civil Strife and the Involvement of External Parties', *International Studies Quarterly* xiv (June 1970), pp. 169–73.
18. Ibid., pp. 175–9. For a more recent statement of costs see Rothschild, op. cit., p. 181;

Notes

and for an early statement of this problem see Karl W. Deutsch, 'External Involvement in Internal War', in Harry Eckstein (ed.), *Internal War* (London, 1964), pp. 109–10.

19. Mitchell, op. cit., pp. 176–8.
20. Rothchild, op. cit., p. 181. See also in particular Arnfinn Jorgensen-Dahl, 'Forces of Fragmentation in the International System: The case of Ethnonationalism', *Orbis* ii (Summer 1975), pp. 665–6.
21. Peter M. Blau, *Exchange and Power in Social Life* (New York, 1964), pp. 118–21, 124. See also David A. Baldwin, 'Power and Social Exchange', *American Political Science Review* lxxii (December 1978), pp. 1229–42.
22. Robert P. Abelson, 'Modes of Resolution of Belief Dilemmas', *Journal of Conflict Resolution* iii (1959), pp. 244–51.
23. For the issue of perception see the classical volume of Jerome S. Bruner and David Krech, Jr. (eds.), *Perception and Personality* (Durnham, 1950), in particular the articles by Bruner and Postman as well as by Else Frenkel-Brunswik. For the International Relations literature on this see Axelrod (ed.), op. cit; Robert Jervis, *Perception and Misperception in International Politics* (Princeton, 1976); Herbert Kelman (ed.), *International Behaviour* (New York, 1965); J.C. Farrell and A.P. Smith (eds.), *Image and Reality in World Politics* (New York, 1968).
24. Irwing Janis and M. Brewster Smith, 'Effects of Education and Persuasion on National and International Images', in Kelman (ed.), op. cit., p. 214.
25. Raymond A. Bauer, 'The Obstinate Audience: The Influence Process from the Point of View of Social Communication', in Hollander and Hunt (eds.), *Current Perspectives in Social Psychology*, op. cit., pp. 335–44.
26. Lasswell and Kaplan, op. cit., p. 113.
27. Jorgensen-Dahl, op. cit., p. 674.
28. See for example: J.C. Garnett (ed.), *Theories of Peace and Security* (London, 1970); Thomas Schelling, *The Strategy of Conflict* (London, 1963); Thomas Schelling, *Arms and Influence* (New Haven, 1966); David A. Baldwin, 'The Power of Positive Sanctions', *World Politics* xxiv (October 1971), pp. 19–38; Richard Rosecrance, 'Reward, Punishment and Interdependence', *Journal of Conflict Resolution* xxv (March 1981), pp. 31–46.
29. Schelling, *The Strategy of Conflict*, p. 177; Baldwin, op. cit., p. 28.
30. Ibid., p. 28; Schelling, op. cit., p. 177.
31. Baldwin, op. cit., p. 25.
32. Morton Deutsch, op. cit., p. 389.
33. Rosecrance, op. cit., pp. 31, 34, 43; Baldwin, op. cit., p. 23.
34. Schelling, *Arms and Influence*, pp. 70–2.
35. Baldwin, op. cit., pp. 23–31.

CHAPTER FOUR: INTERNATIONAL INVOLVEMENT IN SECESSIONIST MOVEMENTS

1. George Modelski, 'The International Relations of Internal War', in James N. Rosenau (ed.), *International Aspects of Civil Strife* (Princeton, 1964), p. 31; Astri Suhrke and Lela Garner Noble, 'Spread or Containment: The Ethnic Factor', in Suhrke and Noble (eds.), *Ethnic Conflict in International Relations* (New York, 1977), pp. 213–15.
2. Arthur Lall, *Modern International Negotiation* (New York, 1966), pp. 132–62.
3. For the various side effects of negotiations see Fred Charles Iklé, *How Nations Negotiate* (New York, 1964), pp. 43–58.
4. Oran R. Young, *The Intermediaries: Third Parties in International Crises* (Princeton, 1967), pp. 85–105.
5. In some instances sub-units of states, IGOs or even large INGOs appear to have taken initiatives independent of their parent state or organization.
6. Perhaps the most celebrated historical example to date of real independent volunteers in a secessionist war is the case of the Philhellenes (in whose ranks was no less a figure than Lord Byron) who assisted the Greek secessionist movement of the 1820s.
7. Rolph Steiner, *The Last Adventurer* (Boston, 1978).

8. For a typology of tangible involvement see Table, p. 248.
9. Richard Little, *Intervention: External Involvement in Civil Wars* (London, 1975), pp. 9–10; Bertil Duner, 'The Many-Pronged Spear: External Military Intervention in Civil Wars in the 1970s', *Journal of Peace Research* xx (1983), p. 60.
10. For details on the proposed eight-step ladder of involvement with secessionist movements see pp. 248–9. Intervention is used in its original restricted international law definition of 'dictatorial' physical intervention, and not in its broader meaning as often used in International Relations theory (as activity aimed at influencing the authority structure of a third state). For this broader use we will use instead the more non-committal term involvement.
11. See, for instance, Little, op. cit., p. 9.
12. Mitchell, 'Civil Strife and the Involvement of External Parties', *International Studies Quarterly* xiv (June 1970), p. 172.
13. See among others the following seminal experiments: Solomon Asch, 'Effects of Group Pressure upon the Modification and Distortion of Judgement', in Dorwin Cartwright and A. Zander (eds.), *Group Dynamics* (New York, 1953), pp. 189–93; Mujafer Sherif, 'Experiments in Norm Formation', in Edwin P. Hollander and Raymond G. Hunt (eds.), *Classic Contributions to Social Psychology* (New York, 1972), pp. 319–29; Stanley Milgram, *Obedience to Authority* (London, 1974); Henri Tajfel, 'Experiments in Intergroup Discrimination', *Scientific American* ccxxiii (1970), pp. 96–102; Bibb Latané and John M. Darley, 'Bystander Apathy', in Edwin P. Hollander and Raymond G. Hunt (eds.), *Current Perspectives in Social Psychology* (New York, 1976), pp. 140–52; Craig Haney and Philip G. Zimbardo, 'Social Roles and Role-Playing: Observations from the Stanford Prison Study', in ibid., pp. 266–74. See also Irving Janis, 'Groupthink', in ibid., pp. 406–11.
14. Mitchell, op. cit., pp. 184–90.
15. Judy S. Bertelsen, 'The Nonstate Nation in International Politics: Some Observations', in Judy S. Bertelsen (ed.), *Nonstate Nations in International Politics* (New York, 1977), p. 255.
16. Suhrke and Noble, op. cit., pp. 226–30; Joseph Rothschild, *Ethnopolitics* (New York, 1981), p. 186.
17. For other ways of categorizing instrumental motives see Martin Edmonds, 'Civil War and Arms Sales', in Robin Higham (ed.), *Civil Wars in the XXth Century* (Lexington, 1972), p. 208; Rothschild, op. cit., pp. 184–7; Selwyn D. Ryan, 'Civil Conflict and External Involvement in Eastern Africa', *International Journal* xxviii (1972–73), pp. 489, 496–8.
18. For other ways of categorizing affective motives see Rothschild, op. cit., pp. 184–5; Robert O. Matthews, 'Domestic and Inter-State Conflict in Africa', *International Journal* xxv (1970), p. 464.
19. Herbert C. Kelman, 'Compliance, Identification and Internalization: Three Processes of Attitude Change', *Journal of Conflict Resolution* ii (1958), pp. 53–4.
20. James Mayall, 'Self-Determination and the OAU', in I.M. Lewis (ed.), *Nationalism and Self-Determination in the Horn of Africa* (London, 1983), pp. 77–91; Sally Healy, 'The Changing Idiom of Self-Determination in the Horn of Africa', in ibid., pp. 93–109; James Mayall, 'African Unity and the OAU: The Place of Political Myth in African Diplomacy', *The Year Book of World Affairs* (1973), pp. 128–33; Onyenoro Kamanu, 'Secession and the Right of Self-Determination: An OAU Dilemma', *Journal of Modern African Studies* xii (1974), pp. 355–76.
21. Mayall, 'African Unity and the OAU', p. 130, and generally note 20 above.
22. Benyamin Neuberger, 'The African Concept of Balkanization', *Journal of Modern African Studies* xiv (1976), pp. 523–9.
23. Mayall, 'Self-Determination and the OAU', p. 82.
24. Ibid., pp. 82–3; Neuberger, op. cit., p. 524.
25. See above, note 20.
26. Note that the OAU involvement in Chad took place in the early 1980s when the conflict was not more separatist.
27. William Zartman, 'Africa as a Subordinate State System in International Relations',

Notes

International Organization xxi (Summer 1967), p. 559.

28. S.N. MacFarlane, 'Intervention and Security in Africa', *International Organization* vx (Winter 1983–84), pp. 53–73.
29. For the role of unofficial diplomats as consultants see C.R. Mitchell, *Peacemaking and the Consultant's Role* (London, 1981); also Maureen R. Berman and Joseph E. Johnson (eds.), *Unofficial Diplomats* (New York, 1977).
30. Laurie S. Wiseberg, 'Humanitarian Intervention: Lessons from the Nigerian Civil War', *Human Rights Journal* vii (1974), pp. 78–9.

CHAPTER FIVE: KATANGA

1. Abako was the party of the ethnic Ba-Kongo, which had pan-Ba-Kongo tendencies. It was headed by Joseph Kasavubu ('King Kasa'), Congo's first President. *Dossiers du Centre de Recherche et d'Information Socio-Politiques* (henceforth *CRISP*), Brussels, *Congo 1960*, vol.I, pp. 225–34; Catherine Hoskyns, *The Congo since Independence January 1960–December 1961* (London, 1965), pp. 1–84; Jules Gérard-Libois, *Katanga Secession* (Madison, 1966), pp. 7–89; René Lemarchand, 'The Limits of Self-Determination: The Case of the Katanga Secession', *American Political Science Review* lvi (January 1962), pp. 404–6; Crawford Young, 'The Politics of Separatism: Katanga 1960–1963', in Gwendolen M. Carter (ed.), *Politics in Africa: 7 Cases* (New York, 1966), pp. 166–75; Colin Legum, *Congo Disaster* (Middlesex, 1961). See also the personal account of the Congolese politician, Thomas Kanza, *Conflict in the Congo* (Middlesex, 1972).
3. Gérard-Libois, op. cit., pp. 11–27; Lemarchand, op. cit., pp. 410–15; Young, op. cit., pp. 172–5.
4. Ibid., p. 225.
5. Ibid., p. 231.
6. Ibid., p. 232; Gérard-Libois, op. cit., pp. 7–89; Lemarchand, op. cit., pp. 404–6.
7. Ibid., pp. 406–9; Young, op. cit., pp. 174–7. See also the autobiographical accounts of the British Ambassador in Leopoldville and the first UN representative in the Congo respectively: Ian Scott, *Tumbled House: The Congo at Independence* (London, 1969); and Rajeshwar Dayal, *Mission for Hammarskjöld: The Congo Crisis* (London, 1976), p. 107.
8. Hoskyns, op. cit., pp. 68–74.
9. Kanza, op. cit., p. 96; Young, op. cit., pp. 180–2; Lemarchand, op. cit., pp. 411–14; Gérard-Libois, op. cit., pp. 39, 45, 83–9, 280–1; Pierre Davister, *Katanga – enjeu du monde* (Brussels, 1960), pp. 55–7; A.A.J. van Bilsen, 'Some Aspects of the Congo Problem', *International Affairs* xxxviii (January 1962), pp. 47–8.
10. Lemarchand, op. cit., p. 415.
11. Gérard-Libois, op. cit., pp. 278, 283–4.
12. Van Bilsen, op. cit., p. 47.
13. Gérard-Libois, op. cit., p. 201.
14. Conor Cruise O'Brien, *To Katanga and Back* (London, 1962), pp. 119–20; Kanza, op. cit., pp. 43–5. According to Jason Sendwe, the Balubakat leader, Tshombé's charm was not unrelated to the fact that he had a large Swiss bank account. Conor Cruise O'Brien has claimed that the Katangan leader was one of the 'best politicians money can buy'. O'Brien's choice of words was probably not accidental.
15. Hoskyns, op. cit., p. 280.
16. Gérard-Libois, op. cit., p. 286; Davister, op. cit., p. 102; Dayal, op. cit., p. 107; O'Brien, op. cit., pp. 119–21.
17. Young, op. cit., p. 187; Hoskyns, op. cit., p. 280; Ali A. Mazrui, 'Moise Tshombé and the Arabs', *Race* x (January 1969), pp. 285–304.
18. Lemarchand, op. cit., p. 415; O'Brien, op. cit., pp. 128–32, 182–4; Young, op. cit., pp. 174, 187–8; Gérard-Libois, op. cit., pp. 19–20; Hoskyns, op. cit., pp. 28–81, 397.
19. *CRISP, Congo 1960*, pp. 718–19, 738–40, 968–9; Institut Royale des Relations Internationales, *Chronique de Politique Etrangère* (henceforth *CPE*), xiii (July–November

The Self-Determination of Minorities in International Politics

1960), p. 761; Davister, op. cit., pp. 118–23, 129, 210–11; Young, op. cit., pp. 183–5, 189; Hoskyns, op. cit., pp. 161–5, 284–5.

20. *CRISP, Congo 1960*, pp. 44–5, 235, 295; *CRISP, Congo 1961*, pp. 215–19, 222–3, 235–6, 294–5, 664–5.

21. Gérard-Libois, op. cit., pp. 198, 213; Hoskyns, op. cit., pp. 395–408; *CRISP, Congo 1961*, pp. 267–8, 293–300, 512–52; Rosalyn Higgins, *United Nations Peacekeeping 1964–1967: Documents and Commentary. The United Nations Operation in the Congo (ONUC) 1960–1964* (London, 1980), pp. 395–404. See also Sir Roy Welensky's autobiographical account, *Welensky's 4000 Days* (London, 1964), pp. 240–1.

22. Stanley Hoffman, 'In Search of a Thread: The UN in the Congo Labyrinth', *International Organization* (Spring 1962), pp. 349–50; Ernest Lefever, *Crisis in the Congo: A United Nations Force in Action* (Washington D.C., 1965), pp. 22–4; Ernest Lefever, *Uncertain Mandate: Politics in the UN Congo Operation* (Baltimore, 1967); Dayal, op. cit., passim; Evan Luard, 'The Civil War in the Congo', in Luard (ed.), *The International Regulation of Civil War* (London, 1972), pp. 108–24.

23. Tshombé, in *L'Essor du Katanga* (Elizabethville, 6 July 1962).

24. O'Brien, op. cit., pp. 224–5, 289–90.

25. For a dose of the articulate Katangan presentations of their case see: *CRISP, Congo 1960*, pp. 718–19, 738–9 and *Congo 1961*, pp. 32–3, 60–2, 94–5, 249, 281–2, 667–8; *The New York Times* (14 July 1960); and *Le Soir* in 1960 (31 July –1 August; 3 and 5 August; 9–10 October and 9 December).

26. Munongo, who was probably directly involved in Lumumba's death, stated bluntly that he was hardly sorry for his death; that naturally Katanga would be accused of his death, and to this his answer was simply 'prove it'. (See *CRISP, Congo 1961*, p. 665).

27. For more details see Alexis Heraclides, 'The International Dimension of Secessionist Movements' (University of Kent, Ph.D. thesis, 1985), pp. 218–24.

28. *CRISP, Congo 1961*, p. 302; Tshombé in *Le Monde* (21–22 August 1960); Gérard-Libois, op. cit., pp. 176–7.

29. Young, op. cit., pp. 202–3.

30. Munongo, in *Africa Diary* (July 1961), p. 20.

31. *The New York Times* (4 January 1962).

32. Jules Gérard-Libois, 'L'assistance technique belge et la République du Congo', *Etudes Congolaises* ii (1962), pp. 1–11; Gérard-Libois, *Katanga Secession*, pp. 95–106, 114, 160–4, 171, 185–6; Higgins, op. cit., pp. 211–43; Hoskyns, op. cit., passim; *CPE* (July–November 1960), pp. 713–19, 743–52, 758–9, 819–21, 910–11; Pierre Wigny, 'Belgium and the Congo', *International Affairs* xxxvii (July 1961), pp. 273–84.

33. See above, note 32.

34. *The New York Herald Tribune* (9 August 1962); *L'Essor du Katanga* (10 August 1962); *Africa Diary* (December 1962), p. 914; *CRISP, Congo 1962*, pp. 420–1.

35. Hammarskjöld imparted to Kanza that the Belgians told him that they knew best how to deal with 'their Congo', which they were not prepared to place on the same footing as they would 'Nkrumah, Nasser, Sékou Touré or even Youlou across the river'. See Kanza, op. cit., p. 224.

36. Van Bilsen, op. cit., p. 48.

37. Ibid., p. 48.

38. *CPE* (July–November 1960), p. 847; *Le Monde* (8 October 1960).

39. Tshombé to Davister, in Davister, op. cit., p. 129; Tshombé in *CRISP, Congo 1960*, pp. 968–9.

40. *CRISP, Congo 1960*, p. 721. Eric Rouleau, 'Tribalisme et haut finance', *Le Monde* (7–8 January 1962); and Eric Rouleau, 'La Guerre des lobbies', *Le Monde* (9 January 1962); Gérard-Libois, op. cit., pp. 104–6, 127–8.

41. Hoskyns, op. cit., pp. 287, 447; Gérard-Libois, op. cit., pp. 165–9, 180, 184, 201, 226–7; *CRISP, Congo 1961*, pp. 302–4; *Le Monde* (21 September 1960).

42. Higgins, op. cit., p. 270.

43. Ibid., p. 270; Hoskyns, op. cit., p. 287; Lefever, *Uncertain Mandate*, pp. 113–14; *CRISP, Congo 1961*, p. 302.

Notes

44. Welensky, op. cit., pp. 213–66; the account of Lord Alport (the British High Commissioner in Salisbury), *The Sudden Assignment* (London, 1965), passim; Scott (the British Ambassador in Leopoldville), op. cit., pp. 44, 60. See also the account of UN officials in Dayal, op. cit., pp. 269, 272; and O'Brien, op. cit., p. 275 and the international press of the time: e.g. the *Sunday Telegraph* (21 January and 17 September 1961); *The Times* (21 January, 31 August and 18 September 1961). Lord Alport claims that one of the duties of his assignment as High Commissioner in Salisbury was precisely to restrain the Rhodesian Prime Minister. See Alport, op. cit., p. 104.
45. Welensky, op. cit., pp. 213–66.
46. *Observer Foreign News Service*, no. 17647 (29 December 1961).
47. Welensky, op. cit., p. 241.
48. Alport, op. cit., p. 104; O'Brien, op. cit., pp. 181, 228, 271–4, 285, 305; Hoskyns, op. cit., pp. 409–10; Higgins, op. cit., pp. 268–70.
49. Welensky, op. cit., pp. 266ff; Alport, op. cit., p. 103.
50. Lefever, *Uncertain Mandate*, p. 125; Higgins, op. cit., pp. 269–70.
51. Hoskyns, op. cit., pp. 409–10; Dayal, op. cit., pp. 164, 187, 238–9, 269–74, 276; Lefever, *Crisis in the Congo*, pp. 98–9; Higgins, op. cit., pp. 268–70.
52. Higgins, op. cit., pp. 268–9; Alport, op. cit., pp. 95, 164.
53. *CRISP, Congo 1961*, pp. 267–9, 277, 301–3; Gérard-Libois, op. cit., pp. 135, 143, 176–7, 221; Hoskyns, op. cit., pp. 258, 288.
54. See the Report of UN representative Gardiner, *CRISP, Congo 1962*, pp. 398–9, 405, 410. Also the following: *The Observer* (16 April 1962); Hoskyns, op. cit., pp. 147, 453; Gérard-Libois, op. cit., pp. 175–6.
55. Ibid., pp. 175–6.
56. *CRISP, Congo 1962*, p. 399; Hoskyns, op. cit., pp. 388, 467; Gérard-Libois, op. cit., p. 282.
57. Hoskyns, op. cit., p. 284; Gérard-Libois, op. cit., p. 175 note 139.
58. Higgins, op. cit., pp. 263–8; Lefever, *Uncertain Mandate*, pp. 82–7; Welensky, op. cit., pp. 220, 380. For more details consult Richard Doyle Mahoney, 'The Kennedy Policy in the Congo 1961–63' (Johns Hopkins University, Ph.D. thesis, 1980).
59. Higgins, op. cit., pp. 263–8; Dayal, op. cit., pp. 35, 45.
60. Lefever, *Uncertain Mandate*, p. 82; Hoskyns, op. cit., p. 286; *The New York Times* (14, 15, 21 December 1961).
61. *The Times* (20 August, 28 October 1960); *Le Monde* (4, 24 August 1960; 14 December 1961); Dayal, op. cit., p. 222.
62. Hoskyns, op. cit., pp. 117, 168, 177, 270; Higgins, op. cit., p. 270.
63. *CRISP, Congo 1961*, pp. 56–7, 244–9; Gérard-Libois, op. cit., pp. 69, 94, 138; Dayal, op. cit., pp. 164–6.
64. *CRISP, Congo 1962*, p. 409; Gérard-Libois, op. cit., pp. 206, 227–8, 283–4; E. Glinne, 'Le pourquoi de l'affaire Katangaise', *Présence Africaine* (June–September 1960), p. 59.
65. Lemarchand, op. cit., p. 414; Gérard-Libois, op. cit., pp. 283–4.
66. Glinne, op. cit., pp. 55–8; Lemarchand, op. cit., p. 414.
67. See above, note 65.
68. Young, op. cit., pp. 182–3; Hoskyns, op. cit., pp. 140–1.
69. *The Observer* (26 November 1961); *The Guardian* (6 September 1961).
70. See above, note 69; *The Observer* (3, 10, 17 December 1961); *Le Monde* (7–8, 9 January 1962).
71. *The Guardian* (6 September 1961).
72. *The Christian Science Monitor* (11 December 1961); Hoskyns, op. cit., p. 287.
73. The American Committee was set up in December 1961 under the chairmanship of a black pro-segregationist author named Max Yergen.
74. *The New York Times* (8, 14, 15, 19, 21, 28, 29 December 1961; 10, 12, 24 January 1962; 27 February 1962; 28 March 1962; 14 June 1962; 3 August 1962).
75. Tshombé in *The New York Times* (19 July 1960) and *The Times* (25 July 1962); Rouleau, op. cit.; *Le Soir* (7–8, 26 August 1960); *The Financial Times* (9 August 1960).

76. Five states came to the support of the inept and thoroughly corrupt Mobutu regime: France, Belgium, the United States, Morocco and Senegal.

CHAPTER SIX: BIAFRA

1. Tekena N. Tamuno, 'Separatist Agitations in Nigeria since 1914', *Journal of Modern African Studies* viii (1970), pp. 565–77.
2. Paul Anber, 'Modernization and Political Disintegration: Nigeria and the Ibos', *Journal of Modern African Studies* v (1967), pp. 165–6.
3. Tamuno, op. cit., p. 564; K.W.J. Post, 'Is there a Case for Biafra?', *International Affairs* (February 1966), pp. 17–28; A.H.M. Kirk-Greene, 'The Cultural Background of the Nigerian Crisis', *African Affairs* cclxii (1967), pp. 5–7; Ulf Himmelstrand, 'Tribalism, Regionalism, Nationalism and Secession in Nigeria', in S.N. Eisenstadt and Stein Rokkan (eds), *Building States and Nations*, vol.II (Beverly Hills, 1973), pp. 431–8; Chukwuemeka Onwubu, 'Ethnic Identity, Political Integration and National Development: The Igbo Diaspora in Nigeria', *Journal of Modern African Studies* xiii (1975), pp. 402, 407.
4. Anber, op. cit., pp. 168–70; Tamuno, op. cit., pp. 564–5; A.H.M. Kirk-Greene, *Genesis of the Nigerian Civil War and the Theory of Fear*, Scandinavian Institute of African Affairs, Report no. 27 (Uppsala, 1975), pp. 12, 17; E. Wayne Nafziger and William L Richter, 'Biafra and Bangladesh: The Political Economy of Secessionist Conflict', *Journal of Peace Research* xiii (1976), pp. 92–3, 95–7; S.U. Ifejika, 'Mobilizing Support for the Biafran Regime: The Politics of War and Propaganda' (York University, Canada, Ph.D. thesis, 1979), pp. 116–19.
5. Anber, op. cit., pp. 168ff; Michael Vickers, 'Competition and Control in Modern Nigeria: Origins of the War in Biafra', *International Journal* xxv (1970), pp. 603–5, 631–3; Himmelstrand, op. cit., pp. 435–47; Ulf Himmelstrand, 'Tribalism, Nationalism, Rank-Equilibration and Social Structure: A Theoretical Interpretation of Some Social–Political Processes in Southern Nigeria', *Journal of Peace Research* vi (1969), pp. 81–103; Onwubu, op. cit., pp. 408–10; Claude S. Phillips, 'Nigeria and Biafra', in Frederick L. Shiel (ed.), *Ethnic Separatism and World Politics* (Lanham, 1984), pp. 151–60; P.C. Lloyd, 'The Ethnic Background to the Nigerian Crisis', in S.K. Panter-Brick (ed.), *Nigerian Politics and Military Rule: Prelude to Civil War* (London, 1970), pp. 7–8; James O'Connell, 'Authority and Community in Nigeria', in Robert Melson and Howard Wolpe (eds.), *Nigeria: Modernization and the Politics of Communalism* (East Lansing, 1971), pp. 649–58; James S. Coleman, 'The Ibo and Yoruba Strands in Nigerian Nationalism', in Melson and Wolpe, ibid., pp. 69–80.
6. Kirk-Greene, op. cit., pp. 12–13, 17–19; Vickers, op. cit., pp. 206–33; Richard L. Sklar, 'Contradictions in the Nigerian Political System', *Journal of Modern African Studies* iii (1965), pp. 201–13; K.W.J. Post, 'The Crisis in Nigeria', *The World Today* (February 1966), pp. 43–7; Perbati Sircar, 'The Crisis of Nationhood in Nigeria', *International Studies* (New Delhi) xx (July 1968–April 1969), pp. 245–69; K. Whiteman, 'Enugu: The Psychology of Secession 20 July 1966 to 30 May 1967', in Panter-Brick, op. cit., pp. 117–18; Billy Dudley, 'Nigeria Sinks into Chaos', *The Round Table* lvii (January 1967), pp. 42–3; James O'Connell, 'Political Integration: The Nigerian Case', in Arthur Hazlewood (ed.), *African Integration and Disintegration* (London, 1967) pp. 172–5; John de St. Jorre, *The Nigerian Civil War* (London, 1972), passim.
7. See above, note 6.
8. Anber, op. cit., p. 176; Lloyd, op. cit., p. 3; Whiteman, op. cit., pp. 113–15; Onwubu, op. cit., pp. 408–10; Ross K. Baker, 'The Emergence of Biafra: Balkanization or Nation-Building?', *Orbis* xxii (Summer 1968), pp. 530–3; S.K. Panter-Brick, 'The Right of Self-Determination: Its Application to Nigeria', *International Affairs* xl (April 1968), pp. 262–6; Charles R. Nixon, 'Self-Determination: The Nigeria/Biafra Case', *World Politics* xxiv (July 1972), pp. 479–82; Stanley Diamond, 'Reflections on the African Revolution: The Point of the Biafran Case', *Journal of Asian and African Studies* v (1970), pp. 21–7; Margery Perham, 'Reflections on the Nigerian Civil War', *International Affairs* xlvi (April 1970), pp. 231–46. See also two personal accounts by former Biafran officials:

Notes

Raph Uwechue, *Reflections on the Nigerian Civil War* (New York, 1970), pp. 52–4; and Ntieyong Akpan, *The Struggle for Secession, 1966–1970* (London, 1970), pp. 24, 114–15.

9. Victor Diejomaoh, 'The Economics of the Nigerian Conflict', in Joseph Okpaku (ed.), *Nigeria: Dilemma of Nationhood* (Westport, 1972), pp. 30–3; Anber, op. cit., p. 177; O'Connell, op. cit., p. 182.

10. Onwubu, op. cit., pp. 404–13; Coleman, op. cit., pp. 69–80; Himmelstrand, 'Tribalism, Nationalism and Rank-Equilibration', pp. 81–99.

11. Conor Cruise O'Brien, 'A Critical Analysis of the Nigerian Crisis', *Pan-African Journal* i (Winter 1969), p. 36; C.C Wrigley, 'Prospects for the Ibos', *Venture* xxi (August 1969), pp. 29–32.

12. Kirk-Greene, op. cit., p. 21.

13. Ojukwu's statements in A.H.M. Kirk-Greene, *Crisis and Conflict in Nigeria: A Documentary Sourcebook* (London, 1971) (henceforth *DS*), vol.I pp. 198–9, 213–14, 306–9, 335, 363–7, 432–4, 449–53; John J. Stremlau, *The International Politics of the Nigerian Civil War (1967–1970)* (Princeton, 1977), pp. 36–55; Whiteman, op. cit., pp. 122–5.

14. Okukwu in *DS*, vol.I, p. 335.

15. Uwechue, op. cit., p. 51; Ojukwu to Stremlau, op. cit., p. 39; Lloyd, op. cit., p. 11; Ifejika, op. cit., pp. 220–7.

16. Ojukwu to Stremlau, op. cit., p. 36; Akpan, op. cit., pp. 69–72; Whiteman, op. cit., p. 112.

17. Nixon, op. cit., pp. 476, 497; Stremlau, op. cit., pp. 39, 44, 49, 53–4; Susan Cronje, *The World and Nigeria* (London, 1972), p. 44; Morris Davis, 'Negotiating about Biafran Oil', *Issue* iii (Summer 1973), p. 26. See also the account of the British High Commissioner in Lagos, Sir David Hunt, *On the Spot: An Ambassador Remembers* (London, 1975), pp. 178–9.

18. The Ahiara Declaration, *DS*, vol.II, pp. 376–93; Stremlau, op. cit., pp. 328–30.

19. General Chuchuemeka Ojukwu, *Biafra: Selected Speeches and Random Thoughts* (New York, 1969), vol.I, pp. 198–204; *Africa Research Bulletin* (henceforth *ARB*) (November 1968), p. 1240BC.

20. *West Africa*, no. 2686 (23 November 1968), p. 1393; Markpress, *Biafran Overseas Press Division: Press Releases* (henceforth *BOPD*), GEN–381, 386 (October 1968); Ojukwu to Stremlau, op. cit., p. 223.

21. Hunt, op. cit., pp. 172, 178–9; Akpan, op. cit., pp. 144–9; Cronje, op. cit., pp. 20–1, 255–6; Morris Davis, *Interpreters for Nigeria: The Third World and International Public Relations* (Urbana, 1977), pp. 42–5, 48–50; Billy Dudley, 'Nigeria's Civil War: The Tragedy of the Ibo People', *The Round Table* lviii (January 1968), p. 28.

22. Stremlau, op. cit., pp. 66–7.

23. For more details and extended bibliography see Alexis Heraclides, 'The International Dimension of Secessionist Movements' (University of Kent, Ph.D. thesis, 1985), pp. 316–21, 734–6.

24. Ibid., pp. 321–8, 736–9.

25. Ibid., pp. 328–33, 739–43.

26. Joseph C. Anafulu, 'An African Experience: The Role of Specialized Libraries in War Situation', *Special Libraries* lxii (January 1971), p. 33.

27. Olajide Aluko, 'The Civil War and Nigerian Foreign Policy', *The Political Quarterly* xlii (April 1971), p. 181.

28. Davis, *Interpreters for Nigeria*, pp. 48–55, 108–16, 120–49, 157–76; Cronje, op. cit., pp. 210–224; A.H.M. Kirk-Greene, 'Bibliography' in *DS*, pp. 482–95.

29. Ibid., pp. 482–95; Davis, op. cit., p. 54.

30. Lord Shepherd in Davis, ibid., p. 142.

31. Davis, ibid., pp. 48–55, 108–116, 120–49, 157–76; Morris Davis, 'The Structuring of International Communications about the Nigeria–Biafra War', *Peace Research Society, Papers* xviii, The London Conference (1971), pp. 62–3, 70–1; Anafulu, op. cit., pp. 32–40; Ifejika, op. cit., pp. 449–55; Stremlau, op. cit., pp. 110–17.

32. Ifejika, op. cit., pp. 318–23.

33. Stremlau, op. cit., p. 112.

225

34. Anafulu, op. cit., p. 34; Davis, *Interpreters for Nigeria*, pp. 48, 162–7.
35. For the voluminous Biafran presentation see e.g. Ojukwu's *Biafra*, vols I and II; Ojukwu and other Biafran officials' statements in *DS* (in particular vol.I, pp. 427–44, vol.II, pp. 247–272); the *BOPD* press releases; and the various pamphlets published by Biafra such as the 7–volume 'Nigeria Crisis 1966', 'The Case for Biafra', and others, available in London at the Institute of Commonwealth Studies (hence forth *ICS*) and at the Royal Commonwealth Society.
36. When it became apparent that the FMG had no genocidal intentions. .
37. Ojukwu in *DS*, vol.II, p. 194.
38. Stremlau, op. cit., pp. 84, 91.
39. See for instance the pamphlet 'Biafra Deserves Open World Support' (1968); *BOPD*, GEN-478; and *Biafra Newsletter* (10 November 1967, 12 January 1968).
40. Ojukwu in *DS*, vol.II, pp. 263–4.
41. Ibid., p. 199.
42. Ibid., p. 264; Chijioke Dike, 'Le Biafra et les grandes puissances', *Revue française d'études politiques africaines* (January 1970), pp. 69–78.
43. Ojukwu, *Biafra*, vol.II, pp. 192–4.
44. Ibid., p. 195.
45. Akpan, op. cit., pp. 179–80; Ross K. Baker, 'The Role of the Ivory Coast in the Nigeria–Biafra War', *African Scholar* I (1970), pp. 5–8; Jacques Batmanian, 'La politique africaine de la Côte d'Ivoire de son accession à l'indépendance, à la fin de la guerre civile au Nigéria' (University of Paris I, doctorat d'état, 1973), pp. 302–4.
46. Uwechue, op. cit., chapter I; Daniel Bach, 'Le Général de Gaulle et la guerre civile au Nigéria', *Canadian Journal of African Studies* xiv (1980), pp. 260–1; Walter Schwarz, 'Foreign Powers and the Nigerian War', *Africa Report* (February 1970), p. 13; Stremlau, op. cit., pp. 224, 226.
47. Ibid., p. 224; Cronje, op. cit., pp. 216–17.
48. Ojukwu, *Biafra*, vol.II, p. 180. According to unconfirmed reports valuable data of the OAU Liberation Committee were handed over to the Portuguese as part of the deal. See *West Africa* (2 December 1967), p. 1562.
49. Davis, *Interpreters for Nigeria*, pp. 48–55. See also various issues of *Biafra Newsletter* and various Biafran pamphlets with suggestive titles such as 'Russia's War vs American Business', 'Nigeria: A Communist Beach-Head in Africa', 'Russia Consolidates her Foothold in Nigeria' (in *ICS*).
50. Ojukwu to Stremlau, op. cit., pp. 293–4.
51. Davis, op. cit., pp. 42–8, 120–49. See also above, note 35.
52. See above, note 35.
53. Cronje, op. cit., pp. 277–8.
54. Ibid., p. 275.
55. Ojukwu, *Biafra*, vol.II, pp. 217–18, 255, 271; Ojukwu's letters to Premier Golda Meir and President Shasar of Israel Pol.021/81 (3 October 1969, 26 February 1969) in *ICS*.
56. Davis, 'Negotiating about Biafran Oil', pp. 26–9.
57. Ibid., p. 30.
58. Ibid., pp. 29–30; Cronje, op. cit., pp. 30–1; T.O. Elias, 'The Nigerian Crisis in International Law', *The Nigerian Law Journal* v (1971), p. 5.
59. Stremlau, op. cit., pp. 320–1; Davis, 'The Structuring of International Communications about the Nigeria–Biafra War', p. 69. Against this view see Aluko, op. cit., p. 181.
60. David A. Ijalaye, 'Was "Biafra" at any Time a State in International Law?', *American Journal of International Law* lxv (1971), pp. 551–9; Francis Wodie, 'La sécession du Biafra et le droit international public', *Revue générale de droit international public* lxxiii (1969), pp. 1035–44.
61. Quoted in Stremlau, op. cit., p. 320.
62. Kaye Whiteman, 'The OAU and the Nigerian Issue', *The World Today* (November 1968), 450.
63. Davis, *Interpreters for Nigeria*, passim; Cronje, op. cit., pp. 211–12.
64. *BOPD*, GEN-472. See also *West Africa* (12 July 1969), p. 821; (20 July 1968), p. 850;

(2 August 1969), p. 909; and (13 December 1969), p. 1529. As well as Ojukwu's letters to Senator Edward Kennedy dated 21 March, 13 and 17 December 1969 (available on microfilm at *ICS*).

65. Uwechue, op. cit., p. 142.
66. Stockholm International Peace Research Institute, *The Arms Trade with the Third World* (Middlesex, 1975), pp. 246–7; Georges Thayer, *The War Business: The International Trade of Armaments* (New York, 1969), pp. 165–8.
67. Ibid., pp. 167–8; Stremlau, op. cit., p. 232.
68. For more details see Heraclides, op. cit., pp. 383–94, 762–67.
69. Stremlau, op. cit., p. 237; Cronje, op. cit., pp. 197, 377; Douglas G. Anglin, 'Zambia and the Recognition of Biafra', *The African Review* i (June 1975), pp. 102–36.
70. Nyerere in the OAU in *DS*, vol.II, p. 438; Anglin, op. cit., pp. 103–6; Cronje, op. cit., p. 295; Ijalaye, op. cit., p. 555.
71. See above, note 70.
72. Ibid., pp. 555; *Africa Confidential*, no. 9 (26 April 1968), p. 5.
73. See above, note 70.
74. Batmanian, op. cit., pp. 337–8, 397–8; Baker, op. cit., pp. 5–8; Uwechue, op. cit., p. 97; Akpan, op. cit., pp. 177, 179–80.
75. Batmanian, op. cit., pp. 302–4, 310–65, 396–405, 650–7, 669–70; Baker, op. cit., pp. 5–8.
76. See above, notes 74 and 75.
77. Cronje, op. cit., p. 300; Baker, op. cit., p. 7; Stremlau, op. cit., pp. 137–8.
78. Anglin, op. cit., pp. 108–14; Gemuh E. Akuchu, 'The Organization of African Unity Peacemaking Machinery and the Nigerian–Biafran Conflict' (University of Denver, Ph.D. thesis, 1974), pp. 126–7, 136, 141.
79. Anglin, op. cit., pp. 129, 133–5; C.H. Mike Yarrow, *Quaker Experiences in International Conciliation* (New Haven, 1978), p. 212.
80. Akuchu, op. cit., pp. 126–7, 136, 141; Anglin, op. cit., pp. 104–36; Stremlau, op. cit., pp. 90–2.
81. Anglin, op. cit., pp. 103–8, 119–25.
82. Ibid., p. 119.
83. *DS*, vol.II, pp. 220–1.
84. Anglin, op. cit., pp. 107–8, 119–25.
85. *West Africa* (11 January 1969), p. 2693 and (11 October 1969), p. 1229. Consult also Kogbara to Onyegbula, 'Secret Mission Report', 013 Secret (30 July 1969) and telegram Pol. 96/37 (7 May 1969), both in *ICS*.
86. Kogbara to Onyegbula, op.cit; Stremlau, op. cit., p. 354 note 144.
87. *Uganda Argus* (21 May 1968).
88. Ibid.; Akuchu, op. cit., p. 141.
89. Dike to Stremlau, op. cit., p. 140; *Africa Confidential*, no. 16 (9 August 1968), p. 2.
90. Senghor's interview in *The Christian Science Monitor* (9 May 1969); Senghor's 'Introduction' to Uwechue's book, op. cit., p. iv; and *West Africa* (20 April 1968), p. 451.
91. Olajide Aluko, 'Ghana and the Nigerian Civil War', *The Nigerian Journal of Economic and Social Studies* xii (November 1970), pp. 343–60; Olajide Aluko, 'Ghana's Foreign Policy', in Aluko (ed.), *The Foreign Policies of African States* (London, 1977), pp. 75–9, 81–2.
92. See above, note 91.
93. *Africa Confidential*, no. 16 (9 August 1968), p. 2.
94. *ARB* (January 1969), p. 1299A and (August 1969), p. 1499B. Also see *West Africa* (18 January 1969), pp. 81–2; (8 February 1969), p. 165; (12 April 1969), p. 426; (9 August 1969), p. 941.
95. President Zinsou of Dahomey in Whiteman, op. cit., p. 551.
96. Stremlau, op. cit., pp. 286–7.
97. Philippe Decreane, 'Repercussions of Nigerian Crisis in Dahomey', *Africa Quarterly* vii (October–December 1967), pp. 212–14.
98. Uwechue, op. cit., pp. 140, 142–3; Cronje, op. cit., p. 306.

99. *ARB* (September 1967), p. 856BC; Uwechue, op. cit., pp. 142–3; Stremlau, op. cit., pp. 181, 353.
100. *West Africa* (11 May 1968), p. 561; (6 July 1968), p. 793; (11 October 1969), p. 1217.
101. *ARB* (August 1969), p. 1500B; *The Jet* (26 September 1969).
102. Apparently the arms supplies dwindled only twice, once in late 1968 and again in spring 1969.
103. France denied having armed Biafrans and technically this was not totally untrue given the fact that most of the arms for Biafra were procured by the Ivory Coast and Gabon, though of course with French loans.
104. Bach, op. cit., pp. 266–7; Cronje, op. cit., pp. 196–7; Zdanek Cervenka, *A History of the Nigerian War* (Ibadan, 1972), pp. 103–4; Batmanian, op. cit., pp. 310, 361–5, 401; Schwarz, op. cit., pp. 13–14; François Debré, 'Le conflit nigéro-biafrain', *Revue française d'études politiques africaines* xxxix (March 1969), p. 41; Perham, op. cit., p. 241.
105. De Gaulle, in *DS*, vol.II, p. 329; French statement in ibid., pp. 245–6.
106. Cronje, op. cit., p. 203; Bach, op. cit., pp. 260ff.
107. See above, note 104.
108. Ibid., pp. 204–5; Uwechue, op. cit., pp. 96, 98; Bach, op. cit., pp. 265, 268–70; Stremlau, op. cit., pp. 229, 231 (note 58).
109. As Stremlau points out in ibid., p. 233, trade with Nigeria continued throughout the war and the French financial contribution to Lagos accruing from such transactions was far greater than the cost of the arms to the Biafrans.
110. René Pelissier, 'São Tomé: Outpost of Portuguese Colonialism and Lifeline to Biafra', *Africa Report* (January 1970), p. 27; George Shepherd, 'Civil War and the International Arms Traffic', *Africa Today* xiv (December 1967), p. 5.
111. Ojukwu to Stremlau, op. cit., p. 223; Joseph E. Thompson, 'American Foreign Policy Toward Nigeria 1967–1970' (The Catholic University of America, Ph.D. thesis, 1974), p. 221.
112. Aluko, op. cit., pp. 180, 186; Stremlau, op. cit., pp. 233–4.
113. Ibid., pp. 235–6; *ARB* (January 1970), p. 1652; Kogbara to Onyegbula, 'Report', op.cit. (in *ICS*).
114. Bruce D. Larkin, *China and Africa* (Berkeley, 1971), p. 186; *ARB* (September 1968), p. 1190BC; *Africa Confidential*, no. 20 (11 October 1968), p. 5; Stremlau, op. cit., p. 237.
115. Hunt, op. cit., p. 197; Cronje, op. cit., p. 377 and note 61. To add a piquant note, according to *West Africa* (5 April 1969, pp. 373, 397), 'Papa Doc' recognized Biafra to get back at the British for Graham Greene's novel on Haiti (obviously *The Comedians*).
116. Camille Olsen, 'Les pays Scandinaves et le Biafra', *Revue française d'études politiques africaines* lii (April 1970), pp. 77–111.
117. It is worth remembering that three out of the five Nordics gained their independence through a unilateral act of independence (secession): Norway from Sweden in 1905, Iceland from Denmark in 1918, and Finland from Russia in 1919.
118. Olsen, op. cit., pp. 83–7, 97, 108–10.
119. See for more details Heraclides, op. cit., pp. 402–10, 772–3.
120. Thompson, op. cit., passim; Roy M. Melbourne, 'The American Response to the Nigerian Conflict, 1968', *Issue* iii (Summer 1973), pp. 33–41; Cronje, op. cit., pp. 225–51; Richard Sklar, 'The United States and the Biafran War', *Africa Report* (November 1969), pp. 22–3.
121. See above, note 120.
122. See above, note 120.
123. For the role of the OAU see in particular Akuchu, op. cit., passim; Whiteman, op. cit., pp. 449–53; Cronje, op. cit., pp. 281–319. For the role of the Commonwealth Secretary-General see Secretary-General Arnold Smith's *Stitches in Time* (London, 1981).
124. Laurie S. Wiseberg, 'Christian Churches and the Nigerian Civil War', *Journal of African Studies* vii (Fall 1975), pp. 312–13.
125. Yarrow, op. cit., pp. 179–260.
126. Wiseberg, op. cit., pp. 317–26; Wiseberg, 'The International Politics of Relief: A Case Study of the Relief Operations Mounted During the Nigerian Civil War (1967–1970)'

Notes

(University of California, Los Angeles, Ph.D. thesis, 1973), chapters 2, 4 and 5; Wiseberg, 'Humanitarian Intervention: Lessons from the Nigerian Civil War', *Human Rights Journal* vii (1974), pp. 67–74; Thierry Hentsch, *Face au blocus; La Croix-Rouge internationale dans le Nigéria en guerre* (Geneva, 1973), passim; Clarence C. Clendenen, 'Tribalism and Humanitarianism: The Nigeria/Biafra Civil War', in Robin Higham (ed.), *Civil Wars in the XXth Century* (Lexington, 1972), pp. 179–83; Alvin Edgell, 'Nigeria/Biafra', in Morris Davis (ed.), *Civil War and the Politics of International Relief* (New York, 1975), pp. 58–68.

127. For the US lobby, see above, note 120. For the British lobby see, in particular, Cronje, who was an active member of that lobby, op. cit., pp. 63, 172–82, 222–4 and the various booklets and pamphlets published by the Britain–Biafra Association in London (available in *ICS* and the Royal Commonwealth Society, London).

128. Aluko, 'The Civil War and Nigerian Foreign Policy', pp. 177–90; Aluko, 'Nigerian Foreign Policy', in Aluko (ed.), op. cit., pp. 186–8.

129. Bach, op. cit., p. 267 note 16.

CHAPTER SEVEN: THE SOUTHERN SUDAN

1. Muddathir'Abd Al-Rahim, 'Arabism, Africanism, and Self-Identification in the Sudan', *Journal of Modern African Studies* viii (1970), p. 233.

2. Mohamed Omer Beshir, *Diversity, Regionalism and National Unity*, Scandinavian Institute of African Studies, Report no. 54 (Uppsala, 1977), p. 35.

3. Ali A. Mazrui, 'The Multiple Marginality of the Sudan', in Yusuf Fadl Hasan (ed.), *Sudan in Africa* (Khartoum, 1971), pp. 240–55.

4. Dunstan M. Wai, 'Revolution, Rhetoric, and Reality in the Sudan', *Journal of Modern African Studies* xvii (1979), p. 72; George W. Shepherd Jr., 'National Integration and the Southern Sudan', *Journal of Modern African Studies* iv (1966), p. 194.

5. Mazrui, op. cit., p. 169.

6. Angelo L.L. Loiria, 'Political Awakening in Southern Sudan 1946–1955: Decolonization and the Problem of National Integration' (University of California, Los Angeles, Ph.D. thesis, 1969), pp. 1–128, 382.

7. Editorial, *Grass Curtain* (London) i, no. 1 (1970), p. 3.

8. Oluwadare Aguda, 'Arabism and Pan-Arabism in Sudanese Politics', *Journal of Modern African Studies* xi (1973), p. 177; Abd Al-Rahim, op. cit., pp. 116–17.

9. Lilian Passmore Sanderson, 'Education in the Southern Sudan', *African Affairs* lxxix (April 1980), p. 161.

10. Robert O. Collins, *Shadow in the Grass: Britain in the Southern Sudan, 1918–1956* (New Haven, 1983). The British who were *de facto* in charge of the Southern Sudan toyed for a time with the idea of uniting the region with British East Africa.

11. R.K. Badal, 'The Rise and Fall of Separatism in Southern Sudan', *African Affairs* liiv (1976), pp. 464–73. See also note 15 below.

12. See the Proceedings of the Juba Conference, Appendix in Dunstan M. Wai (ed.), *The Southern Sudan: The Problem of National Integration* (London, F. Cass 1973), p. 190.

13. See note 15 below.

14. See above, note 12.

15. Shepherd, op. cit., pp. 196–8; Badal, op. cit., pp. 463–73; Richard Gray, 'The Southern Sudan', *Journal of Contemporary History* vi (197?)), pp. 108–19; Paul Ladouceur, 'The Southern Sudan: A Forgotten War and a Forgotten Peace', *International Journal* xxx (Summer 1975), pp. 407–8; John Howell, 'Politics in the Southern Sudan', *African Affairs* lxxii (April 1973), pp. 163–9; John F. Howell, 'Political Leadership and Organization in the Southern Sudan' (University of Reading, Ph.D. thesis, 1978), pp. 32, 183–4; Per Olav Reinton, 'Imperialism and the Southern Sudan', *Journal of Peace Research* viii (1971), pp. 239–46; Mohamed Omer Beshir, *The Southern Sudan: Background to Conflict* (London, 1968), pp. 67–71.

16. Dunstan M. Wai, *The African–Arab Conflict in the Sudan* (New York, 1981), p. 58.

17. Abd Al-Rahim, op. cit., p. 243.

229

18. Aguda, op. cit., p. 188.
19. Wai, 'Revolution, Rhetoric and Reality in the Sudan', pp. 73–4.
20. Gray, op. cit., p. 117.
21. Alexis Heraclides, 'Janus or Sisyphus? The Southern Problem of the Sudan', *Journal of Modern African Studies* xxv (June 1987), pp. 213–14, 231.
22. Howell, 'Politics in the Southern Sudan', op. cit., p. 171; Cecile Eprile, *Sudan: The Long War*, Conflict Studies, no. 21 (London, 1972), p. 18.
23. Peter Woodward, 'Analyzing Sudan's Nationalist Movements', *Seminar Paper* AP/80/3, Institute of Commonwealth Studies, London (1980–81), p. 2.
24. Godfrey Morrison, *Eritrea and the Southern Sudan*, Minority Rights Group, Report no. 5 (3rd edn, London, 1976), pp. 16–17; Wai, *The African–Arab Conflict in the Sudan*, passim; Lawrence Wol Wol, 'Réflexions sur la conscience nationale au Sud-Soudan' (University of Bordeaux III, doctoral thesis, 1971), part 2; Dunstan M. Wai, 'Political Trends in the Sudan and the Future of the South', in Wai, (ed.), op. cit., pp. 147–8.
25. The corresponding phases of Sudan's political history from 1958 to 1972 are as follows: Abboud's military rule (November 1958 – October 1964); the second parliamentary phase (October 1964 – May 1969); the Numeiry regime (from May 1969).
26. See various issues of *Voice of Southern Sudan* (London), *Voice of the Nile Republic* (London), and *Grass Curtain* (London); Joseph Oduho and William Deng, *The Problem of the Southern Sudan* (London, 1963); Oliver Albino, *The Sudan: A Southern Viewpoint* (London, 1970); Lagu's article in *Grass Curtain*, I, no. 4 (April 1971); the pamphlet 'The Anya-Nya Struggle, Background and Objectives'. Several petitions of the various Southern groups are to be found mainly in private collections. The Southern files were destroyed following the Addis Ababa Agreement. See for details of various petitions Heraclides, 'Janus or Sisyphus?', pp. 215–28 and 'The International Dimension of Secessionist Movements' (University of Kent, Ph.D. thesis, 1985), pp. 445–82.
27. M. Louise Pirouet, 'The Achievement of Peace in Sudan', *Journal of Eastern African Research and Development* vi (1976), pp. 119–20; John Howell, 'Horn of Africa: Lessons from the Sudan Conflict', *International Affairs* liv (July 1978), p. 429.
28. Interviews of the author with Peter Kilner and Dr Richard Gray. See also the following: Howell, 'Political Leadership. . .', pp. 188–94; Robert O. Collins, *The Southern Sudan in Historical Perspective* (Tel Aviv, 1975), pp. 165–6; Shepherd, op. cit., pp. 203, 207; J. Bowyer Bell, 'The Conciliation of Insurgency: The Sudanese Experience', *Military Affairs* xxxix (1975), pp. 106–7; Keith Kyle, 'The Southern Problem in the Sudan', *The World Today* (December 1966), pp. 512–15.
29. *East African Standard* (Nairobi) (17, 18 February and 1, 9, 10, 12 March 1965); *Voice of Southern Sudan* (February 1964 and February 1965); Howell, 'Political Leadership. . .', pp. 172–3; Kyle, op. cit., pp. 515–16; Wol Wol, op. cit., p. 279; Edgar O'Ballance, *The Secret War in the Sudan, 1955–1972* (London, 1977), pp. 65–85.
30. See above, note 29, as well as the 1966 and 1967 issues of the Southern daily *The Vigilant*. For General Lagu's testimony regarding the arms from the Simbas see his 'A Southerner's View of the Sudanese Settlement', *New Middle East* xlix (October 1972), p. 17.
31. Collins, op. cit., pp. 88–9; Wol Wol, op. cit., pp. 291–2; O'Ballance, op. cit., pp. 97–9; Howell, 'Political Leadership. . .', pp. 248–52.
32. Wol Wol, op. cit., pp. 292–4; Wai, *The African–Arab Conflict in the Sudan*, pp. 113–14; Howell, 'Political Leadership. . .', pp. 253–65.
33. *Grass Curtain*, I, no. 1 and II, no. 1; the pamphlet 'The Anya-Nya Struggle', op.cit.; the news-sheet *Anya-Nya*, nos. 1–6. From the secondary literature see in particular Pirouet, op. cit., pp. 115–45; O'Ballance, op. cit., pp. 132–41; Wai, *The African–Arab Conflict in the Sudan*, pp. 142–66.
34. Wai, op. cit., pp. 142–66; Pirouet, op. cit., pp. 115–45.
35. John Howell and M. Beshir Hamid, 'Sudan and the Outside World, 1964–1968', *African Affairs* lxviii (1969), pp. 302; Shepherd, op. cit., p. 208; Howell, 'Horn of Africa', p. 429; David Martin, *General Amin* (London, 1974), pp. 24, 43–5.
36. See above, note 26.

Notes

37. See above, note 26.
38. Albino, op. cit., pp. 6–8.
39. One propaganda stunt on the part of Khartoum was the well-publicized trial of mercenary Rolf Steiner, who had assisted the Anyidi Revolutionary Government, and in his testimony implicated Israel, the Verona Fathers and a host of others.
40. Mading de Garang (ed.), in *Grass Curtain*, I, no. 4 (1971), pp. 30–1.
41. The news-sheet *Anya-Nya*, No. 3 (May 1971), p. 8.
42. Peter Kilner, 'Better Outlook for Sudan', *The World Today* (April 1970), p. 186; Howell, 'Horn of Africa', pp. 428–31; Pirouet, op. cit., pp. 140–1; Martin, op. cit., pp. 44, 158–9; George Ivan Smith, *Ghosts of Kampala* (London, 1980), p. 68; Wol Wol, op. cit., pp. 335–6; Cecile Eprile, *War and Peace in the Sudan (1955–1972)* (London, 1974), pp. 140–1.
43. Wai, *The African–Arab Conflict in the Sudan*, p. 139.
44. See above, note 42. For the comment on the CIA, see Howell, 'Horn of Africa', p. 434 note 40.
45. Pirouet, op. cit., p. 140.
46. Ibid., p. 140; Howell, 'Political Leadership. . .', p. 288.
47. See Lagu's letter in *Drum* (Nigerian edn) (March 1971).
48. Martin, op. cit., pp. 25, 43–4, 159; Smith, op. cit., pp. 78–9; Howell, op. cit., pp. 243, 265, 432–4; and above, note 42.
49. Howell, op. cit., pp. 292–3; O'Ballance, op. cit., pp. 127–8; Pirouet, op. cit., pp. 139–41.
50. Wai, *The African–Arab Conflict in the Sudan*, pp. 131–2.
51. Howell, 'Political Leadership. . .', p. 290.
52. Wai, op.cit., p. 132. One could envisage the ethnic groups of northern Uganda wanting to link up with an independent Southern Sudan.
53. Howell and Hamid, op. cit., pp. 303–4, 309–10; Morrison, op. cit., pp. 25–6; David Hamilton, 'Ethiopian–Sudan Border Issues', *Africa Research Bulletin* (February 1968), pp. 975–7; Howell, 'Horn of Africa', pp. 431–3; Pirouet, op. cit., pp. 134–7.
54. See above, note 53.
55. Beshir, quoted in Howell, 'Horn of Africa', p. 432.
56. Author's interview with McDermot, Chairman of the Southern Sudan Association. Also see Pirouet, op. cit., pp. 134–7.
57. See above, note 53.
58. Wol Wol, op. cit., p. 325.
59. Howell and Hamid, op. cit., p. 302; Selwyn D. Ryan, 'Civil Conflict and External Involvement in Eastern Africa', *International Journal* xxviii (1972), p. 469; Shepherd, op. cit., p. 208; Kyle, op. cit., p. 519.
60. Author's interview with McDermot. For two versions of President Banda's statement see *Straits Times* (Kuala Lumpur) (19 September 1968) and *Egyptian Gazette* (1 July 1968).
61. Howell and Hamid, op. cit., pp. 304, 309; Wol Wol, op. cit., pp. 326–7; *Africa Confidential*, no. 20 (October 1965), p. 4; O'Ballance, op. cit., pp. 77–8. See also the autobiography of the Northern politician and onetime Premier, Ahmed Mohamed Mahgoub, *Democracy on Trial* (London, 1974), pp. 204–6.
62. *The New York Times* (11 August 1965); *Africa Research Bulletin* (July 1968), p. 1117BC; Mahgoub, op. cit., pp. 204–6.
63. Pirouet, op. cit., pp. 120–37.
64. Ibid., pp. 120–37.
65. Morrison, op. cit., p. 17, Sanderson, op. cit., pp. 158–60; *Le mois en Afrique* (January 1966), pp. 35–6; *Africa Diary* (25 April – 1 May 1966), p. 2838; *Observer Foreign News Service*, no. 21788 (6 September 1965) and no. 22388 (28 February 1966).
66. Howell, 'Horn of Africa', pp. 428–9, 434 (note 40).
67. The Southern communist politician, Joseph Garang, when Minister for Southern Affairs under Numeiry, had accused the Southern Sudan Association chairman, McDermot, of being an agent of British Intelligence or of the CIA. McDermot, of course, denies any

such involvement, but, in interview with the author, would not totally exclude the possibility of some CIA interest in the Southern affair.

68. Howell, 'Politics in the Southern Sudan', p. 164.
69. Gray, op. cit., pp. 111–15; Shepherd, op. cit., p. 198; Wai, 'Revolution, Rhetoric and Reality in the Sudan', pp. 72–5; Robert O. Collins, op.cit., passim.
70. Oduho, in *Croissance des Jeunes Nations* (June 1966); *Africa Confidential*, no. 8 (12 April 1968), p. 3 and no. 14 (12 July 1968), p. 7; Ryan, op. cit., p. 471.
71. *Egyptian Gazette* (4, 6 January 1970); *Newsweek* (10 May 1971); *The Sunday Times* (1 March 1970); *Arab Report and Record* (16–30 April 1970), p. 247.
72. Interview of the author with McDermot. See also *Le Nouvelle Observateur* (8–15 March 1967, 17 August 1970).
73. Philip Abbas, 'Growth of Black Consciousness in Northern Sudan', *Africa Today* xx (Summer 1973), pp. 29–43; Bona Malwal, *People and Power in Sudan* (London, 1981), p. 184; *Voice of Nile Republic* (15 March 1970); *Grass Curtain* (April and July 1971).
74. *Sudanow* (March 1981), pp. 12–14.
75. For the events of the ongoing second Sudanese civil war see the following: Charles Meynel, 'Sudan – North and South', in *Uganda and Sudan*, Minority Rights Group, Report no. 66 (London, 1984), pp. 22–7; Andrew Mason, 'Southern Sudan: A Growing Conflict', *The World Today* (December 1984), pp. 520–7; Richard Greenfield, 'Two Months that Shook Sudan', *Horn of Africa* viii (1985), pp. 5–20; Ann Mosely Lesch, 'Confrontation in the Southern Sudan', *The Middle East Journal* xl (Summer 1986), pp. 410–28 and 'View from Khartoum', *Foreign Affairs* (Spring 1987).
76. See Heraclides, 'Janus or Sisyphus?', pp. 227–31.

CHAPTER EIGHT: IRAQI KURDISTAN

1. Israel T. Naamani, 'The Kurdish Drive for Self-Determination', *The Middle East Journal* xx (Summer 1966), pp. 280–4; C.J. Edmonds, 'Kurdish Nationalism', *Journal of Contemporary History* vi (1971), pp. 87–99; Ismet Chériff Vanly, *Le Kurdistan irakien: entité nationale* (Neuchatel, 1970); Martin Short, 'The Kurdish People', in *The Kurds*, Minority Rights Group, Report no. 23 (1977 edn), pp. 4–11; Uriel Dann, 'The Kurdish National Movement in Iraq', *Jerusalem Quarterly* ix (Fall 1978), pp. 131–7; Dana Adams Schmidt, 'The Kurdish Insurgency', *Strategic Review* ii (Summer 1974), pp. 54–5; Charles G. McDonald, 'The Kurdish Question in the 1980s', paper in the Conference on Ethnicity, Pluralism and Conflict in the Middle East, Tel Aviv University (9–10 May, 1984), pp. 2–6.
2. According to a 1980 estimate the Kurds are placed at 17.2 million, 8.7 million in Turkey (out of some 45 million at the time), 4.5 million in Iran (out of 48.2 million) and 3 million in Iraq (out of 13.1 million). See Richard Sim, *Kurdistan: The Search for Recognition*, Conflict Studies, no. 124 (London, 1980), p. 3. For similar more recent estimates see McDowall, *The Kurds*, Minority Rights Group, Report no. 23 (London, 1985), p. 7.
3. Archie Roosevelt Jr., 'The Kurdish Republic of Mahabad', *Middle East Journal* i (July 1947), pp. 242–69; Ismet Sheriff Vanly, 'Kurdistan in Iraq', in Gérard Chaliand (ed.), *People without a Country: The Kurds and Kurdistan* (London, 1980), pp. 153–63; McDowall, op. cit., pp. 9–13.
4. Vanly, op. cit., p. 153; Sim, op. cit., pp. 1–21. See also above, note 1.
5. In Turkey the Kurds comprise 18 to 20 per cent of the population, and in Iran about 8 per cent.
6. The League of Nations acknowledged their existence when the issue of Mosul was discussed there and there was also an Iraqi–British declaration in 1922 recognizing 'the rights of the Kurds who live within the frontiers of Iraq to establish a Government within those frontiers'.
7. Naamani, op. cit., pp. 259, 287–91; C.J. Edmonds, 'The Kurdish War in Iraq: The Constitutional Background', *The World Today* (December 1968), pp. 512–14; Short, op. cit., p. 4.
8. See above, notes 1 and 7, and the following: Vanly, 'Kurdistan in Iraq', pp. 165–7;

Notes

McDowall, op. cit., pp. 18–20; George S. Harris, 'The Kurdish Conflict in Iraq', in Astri Suhrke and Lela Garner Noble (eds.), *Ethnic Conflict in International Relations* (New York, 1977), pp. 70–2.

9. For the Kurdish claim after the war, see International Relations Committee of the Kurdistan Democratic Party, 'The Road of the Kurdish Liberation Movement', in *Know the Kurds* (henceforth *KK*), v (November 1977), pp. 50, 74–5. For scepticism see Harris, op. cit., p. 73 and Dann, op. cit., p. 142.

10. In the Iraqi context, Arabicization implies altering the population ratio by population transfers, rather than induced or forced assimilation as in the case of the Sudan.

11. Sim, op. cit., pp. 11–12; McDowall, op. cit., pp. 20–2.

12. Ibid., p. 22.

13. For a useful summary of the five peace agreements see Charles Benjamin, 'The Kurdish Nonstate Nation', in Judy S. Bertelsen (ed.), *Nonstate Nations in International Politics* (New York, 1977), pp. 79–86. The total of real fighting within 15 years amounts to some five years.

14. C.J. Edmonds, 'The Kurdish National Struggle in Iraq', *Asian Affairs* (June 1971), pp. 153–4; Harris, op. cit., pp. 74, 78–9; Benjamin, op. cit., pp. 77–8, 87; Dann, op. cit., pp. 136, 139–40; Short, op. cit., pp. 11–12; Edgar O'Ballance, *The Kurdish Revolt 1961–1970* (London, 1973), pp. 87, 121, 158.

15. Vanly, *Kurdistan Irakien*, pp. 240–52.

16. According to Naamani, Barzani, who was a brilliant guerrilla fighter, was a flawed hero; his interests were parochial, he had 'no sweep, no horizon, no grandeur'. See Naamani, op. cit., p. 294. See also Edmonds, 'Kurdish Nationalism', pp. 95, 101; Benjamin, op. cit., pp. 77–8; David Adamson, *The Kurdish War* (London, 1964), pp. 17–8; *KK*, pp. 28–33; McDowall, op. cit., p. 19.

17. Since its formation in 1934 the Communist party of Iraq recognizes the Kurdish rights.

18. Edmonds, 'The Kurdish National Struggle in Iraq', p. 151; Dann, op. cit., p. 137; Naamani, op. cit., p. 294; Short, op. cit., p. 4; Vanly, 'Kurdistan in Iraq', p. 163; Sim, op. cit., p. 10.

19. Ibrahim Ahmed (the then KDP Secretary-General) to Adamson, op. cit., pp. 91–2; Barzani in *Newsweek* (22 July 1974); *Kurdish Review* (November 1974), pp. 26–8; *Pesh Merga* (August–December 1976), pp. 5–11; Anthony McDermott, 'The Current Crisis', in *The Kurds*, Minority Rights Group, op. cit., pp. 22–3; Gershon Solomon, 'The Kurdish National Struggle in Iraq', *New Outlook* x (March–April 1967), pp. 7–8; Benjamin, op. cit., pp. 78–86.

20. Vanly, 'Kurdistan in Iraq', pp. 205–6.

21. Barzani in *Newsweek*, op. cit.

22. Vanly, *Kurdistan Irakien*, pp. 126–7, 251–2.

23. Ibid., pp. 285, 318; Adamson, op. cit., pp. 13–14, 23–5; Dann, op. cit., p. 139; Edmonds, 'Kurdish Nationalism', pp. 105–6.

24. *KK*, p. 57; McDowall, op. cit., p. 22; Vanly, 'Kurdistan in Iraq', pp. 184–92.

25. Ibid., pp. 182–92; O'Ballance, op. cit., pp. 83, 119–20.

26 According to the Pike Report (the report of CIA activities submitted to the House of Representatives), Secretary of State Kissinger justified not answering Barzani's telegram of 10 March 1975 thus: 'secret service operations are not missionary work'. Quoted in Vanly, 'Kurdistan in Iraq', p. 189.

27. See above, note 19, and the two works of Vanly, mentioned in Notes 1 and 2 above. For a useful summary of the Kurdish arguments see Short, op. cit., pp. 13–14.

28. See above, note 19.

29. For the Iraqi accusations levelled against the Kurds see the following: McDermott, op. cit., p. 20; Short, op. cit., pp. 12–13; Naamani, op. cit., p. 292; Harris, op. cit., p. 83. For the Kurdish handling of these accusations see for instance Vanly, *Kurdistan Irakien*, pp. 287, 290–1, 293–4; *Pesh Merga* (August–December 1976), pp. 5–11.

30. Vanly, *Kurdistan Irakien*, pp. 307–8, 318; Edmonds, 'The Kurdish National Struggle in Iraq', pp. 152–4; *KK*, p. 57; O'Ballance, op. cit., pp. 80, 134, 151.

31. McDowall, op. cit., p. 27; Vanly, *Kurdistan Irakien*, pp. 307–9.

233

32. Sa'ad Jawad, *Iraq and the Kurdish Question* (London, 1981), p. 297; Naamani, op. cit., p. 285.
33. Mohammed Heikal, *The Return of the Ayatollah* (London, 1981), p. 102; *KK*, pp. 50, 55–6.
34. Barzani to Schmidt, op. cit., p. 56; Barzani to *Newsweek*, op. cit.; McDowall, op. cit., p. 21; Harris, op. cit., p. 88; Benjamin, op. cit., p. 90.
35. Schmidt, op. cit., p. 56; Harris, op. cit., pp. 74–5; Gershon Solomon, 'Peace with the Kurds', *New Outlook* xiv (May 1970), p. 39; *The Financial Times* (20 August 1974); O'Ballance, op. cit., pp. 92–3.
36. *KK*, p. 59; Naamani, op. cit., p. 291; Short, op. cit., p. 5.
37. Jawad, op. cit., pp. 300–3; Vanly, *Kurdistan Irakien*, pp. 290–2; Naamani, op. cit., p. 292.
38. *KK*, pp. 50–60; Vanly, 'Kurdistan in Iraq', pp. 190–2.
39. Ibid., p. 190.
40. McDermott, op. cit., pp. 19, 22; Harris, op. cit., pp. 79–80, 83, 86; *KK*, pp. 50–60; Short, op. cit., pp. 4–5; Sim, op. cit., pp. 13–14; McDowall, op. cit., p. 22.
41. *KK*, pp. 53–61, 69; Vanly, 'Kurdistan in Iraq', pp. 184–9; Harris, op. cit., pp. 83, 86; Heikal, op. cit., p. 108; Benjamin, op. cit., p. 92; Schmidt, op. cit., p. 58.
42. According to one view the Iraqi–Iranian rapprochement was orchestrated by Sadat with Kissinger's blessing in order to isolate Syria during a new phase in the Middle East conflict. See *L'Express* in Vanly, 'Kurdistan in Iraq', p. 185.
43. The Shah told Heikal, the distinguished Egyptian journalist, that he did not wish 'to reactivate the Kurdish question', but 'wanted to give the government in Baghdad a slap in the face'. Thus, he said, he had spent some 300 million dollars for the Kurds. See Heikal, op. cit., p. 108.
44. Naamani, op. cit., pp. 292–3; Edmonds, 'Kurdish Nationalism', pp. 102, 105; Short, op. cit., pp. 5, 13–14.
45. Naamani, op. cit., p. 292.
46. Roosevelt, op. cit., passim.
47. Vanly, *Kurdistan Irakien*, pp. 314–19.
48. McDowall, op. cit., pp. 20–1; Benjamin, op. cit., pp. 90, 93–4; Sim, op. cit., pp. 14–15; Vanly, 'Kurdistan in Iraq', pp. 184–5, 190; Schmidt, op. cit., p. 56.
49. According to the Pike report the aim was to 'sap the resources' of Iraq, but not for the Kurds to prevail. See Vanly, 'Kurdistan in Iraq', pp. 186–7.
50. For limited Israeli involvement see Vanly, *Kurdistan Irakien*, pp. 289–92; Benjamin, op. cit., p. 91. For higher level involvement see Jawab, op. cit., pp. 300–3; Sim, op. cit., p. 15; McDowall, op. cit., pp. 20–1; *The Economist* (8 September 1979), p. 20.
51. *KK*, p. 59; Vanly, *Kurdistan Irakien*, pp. 283–5; O'Ballance, op. cit., pp. 80, 107–8, 132–3; McDermott, op. cit., pp. 20, 23; Jawad, op. cit., pp. 278–87.
52. Naamani, op. cit., p. 283; Jawad, op. cit., pp. 292–4; Harris, op. cit., p. 75; *International Herald Tribune* (18 May 1979).
53. Vanly, *Kurdistan Irakien*, pp. 317–18.
54. Ibid., p. 316.
55. Benjamin, op. cit., pp. 89–90.
56. Vanly, 'Kurdistan in Iraq', pp. 158–63, 180; Vanly, *Kurdistan Irakien*, pp. 251, 318–21.
57. Naamani, op. cit., p. 293; Dann, op. cit., p. 144; Edmonds, 'Kurdish Nationalism', pp. 105–7.
58. Other groups include the Socialist Party of Iraqi Kurdistan (IKSP), later known as the Unified Socialist Party of Kurdistan, the Kurdish Socialist Party (Pasok) and the Popular Democratic Party of Kurdistan.
59. Sim, op. cit., pp. 4–9, 15–16; McDowall, op. cit., pp. 24–5, 29; MacDonald, op. cit., pp. 24–5; *International Herald Tribune* (18 May 1987).

CHAPTER NINE: BANGLADESH

1. Inayatullah, 'Internal and External Factors in the Failure of National Integration in

Pakistan', in Stephanie G. Neuman (ed.), *Small States and Segmented Societies* (New York, 1976), p. 91; Tariq Ali, *Can Pakistan Survive? The Death of a State* (Middlesex, 1983), pp. 30–1.

2. The West Pakistanis of course are hardly a nation, but the objective differences (cultural, historical experience, etc.) between Punjabi, Sindhi, Pathan and Baluchi (the four largest ethnic groups) are less pronounced than between these four and the Bengalis.

3. Inayatullah, op. cit., pp. 87–95.

4. Urdu was a prestigious language in the Indian subcontinent, though it was spoken only by a small minority in Pakistan upon independence. See Ali, op. cit., p. 45.

5. Hans J. Morgenthau, *Politics in the Twentieth Century* (Chicago, 1971), p. 163.

6. The Awami League was created by Sahrawardy in 1951. In 1954 the Awami League in alliance with Fazlul Haq's Peasants and Workers Party thoroughly beat the Muslim League in the East.

7. C.W. Choudhury, 'Bangladesh: Why it Happened', *International Affairs* xlviii (April 1972), pp. 242–5; K.P. Misra, 'Intra-State Imperialism: The Case of Pakistan', *Journal of Peace Research* ix (1972), pp. 29–38; Ved P. Nanda, 'Self-Determination in International Law: The Tragic Tale of Two Cities – Islamabad (West Pakistan) and Dacca (East Pakistan)', *American Journal of International Law* lxvi (1972), pp. 328–9; William J. Barnds, 'Pakistan: Old Issues in a New Context', *The World Today* (November 1970), pp. 458–62 and 'Pakistan's Disintegration', *The World Today* (August 1971), pp. 319–21; Pran Chopra, 'East Bengal: A Crisis for India', *The World Today* (September 1971), pp. 272–3; Inayatullah, op. cit., pp. 87–95; T.V. Satyamurthy, 'Indo-Bangladesh Relations: A Structural Perspective', *Asia Quarterly* I (1977), pp. 58–65; M.K. Nawaz, 'Bangladesh and International Law', *Indian Journal of International Law* ii (1971), pp. 252–3; E. Wayne Nafziger and William L. Richter, 'Biafra and Bangladesh: The Political Economy of Secessionist Conflict', *Journal of Peace Research* xiii (1976), pp. 92–106, 108 note 42.

8. See above, note 7. Most elucidating in this regard is an oft-quoted extract from General Ayub Khan's autobiography (the Pakistani leader from 1958 until 1969): the East Bengalis 'have been and still are under considerable Hindu cultural and linguistic influence. As such, they have all the inhibitions of down-trodden races and have not yet found it possible to adjust psychologically to the requirements of the new-born freedom. Their popular complexes, exclusiveness, suspicion, and a sort of defensive aggressiveness probably emerge from this historical background.' Quoted in Crawford Young, *The Politics of Cultural Pluralism* (Madison, 1976), p. 475.

9. Craig Baxter, 'Pakistan and Bangladesh', in Frederick L. Shiel (ed.), *Ethnic Separatism and World Politics* (Lanham, 1984), pp. 211ff.

10. This meant an equal number of seats in parliament for each of the two regions, thereby bypassing the difficulty with the fact that the East was more populous.

11. See above, notes 7 and 9, and the following: Muhamed Ghulan Kabir, *Minority Politics in Bangladesh* (Delhi, 1980), passim; Robert LaPorte Jr., 'Pakistan in 1971: The Disintegration of a Nation', *Asian Survey* xii (February 1972), pp. 98–110; Young, op. cit., pp. 479–82.

12. See above, notes 7, 8 and 11, and the following: Jyoti Sen Gupta, *History of Freedom Movement in Bangladesh* (Calcutta, 1974), p. 306; Moudud Ahmed, *Bangladesh: Constitutional Quest for Autonomy, 1950–71* (Wiesbaden, 1978), pp. 297–9.

13. See above, notes 7 and 11. It has been claimed that General Yahya risked the elections in the firm belief that no party would prevail, in which case he would have emerged as the arbiter. According to another view Rahman had previously agreed to temper his demands, but changed his mind with the election results.

14. Ahmed, op. cit., pp. 292–7; Barnds, 'Pakistan's Disintegration', p. 324; Gupta, op. cit., pp. 305–7; Mohamed Ayoob and K. Subrahmanyam, *The Liberation War* (New Delhi, 1972), p. 152; Lee C. Buchheit, *Secession* (New Haven, 1978), pp. 205–6.

15. Ali, op. cit., pp. 88–94; Satyamurthy, op. cit., p. 66; Ayoob and Subrahmanyam, op. cit., p. 163; M. Rashiduzzaman, 'Leadership, Organization, Strategies and Tactics of the Bangla Desh Movement', *Asian Survey* xii (1972), p. 190.

16. Ibid., pp. 186–8, 190–2; LaPorte, op. cit., p. 107; Ahmed, op. cit., pp. 294, 306–10;

Gupta, op. cit., pp. 334–5, 370; Ayoob and Subrahmanyam, op. cit., pp. 154–5.

17. Justice Choudhury later became the first president of independent Bangladesh. A bitter irony was that at the time of the military crackdown in March 1971 Choudhury was in Geneva, representing Pakistan in the yearly session of the UN Commission on Human Rights.

18. Rashiduzzaman, op. cit., pp. 190, 196–7; Gupta, op. cit., pp. 345–6, 349, 367.

19. The Bangladesh Proclamation of Independence in *Bangladesh – The Birth of a Nation* (Madras, 1972), a documentary sourcebook compiled by Nicholas and Philip Oldenberg (henceforth *Bangladesh*), pp. 77–83; Gupta, op. cit., pp. 306, 339–45, 365; Ahmed, op. cit., pp. 291–2, 295, 297; Rashiduzzaman, op. cit., pp. 185–6; Ali, op. cit., p. 93.

20. Ibid., pp. 194–9; Gupta, op. cit., pp. 338, 361; Satyamurthy, op. cit., pp. 71–3.

21. Tajuddin Ahmed in *Bangladesh*, pp. 79–83; Gupta, op. cit., pp. 345–9, 367; Rashiduzzaman, op. cit., pp. 190, 196–7; Choudhury in Misra, *The Role of the United Nations in the Indo-Pakistani Conflict, 1971* (Delhi, 1973), p. 63.

22. Three million dead was no doubt an overstatement by the Bangladesh propaganda.

23. *Bangladesh*, pp. 77–83.

24. Ibid., p. 82.

25. Ibid., p. 83.

26 Ibid., p. 83.

27. For a cogent presentation of the Pakistani case against India see Mehrunnisa Hatim Iqbal, 'India and the 1971 War with Pakistan', *Pakistan Horizon* xxxv (1972), pp. 21–31.

28. Nanda, op. cit., pp. 328–36; Nawaz, op. cit., pp. 252–63. For an important criticism of such approaches see Buchheit, op. cit., pp. 211–13.

29. LaPorte, op. cit., pp. 102–4; Gupta, op. cit., pp. 305, 360–4; Misra, *The Role of the United Nations*, pp. 53–61; Iqbal, op. cit., pp. 21–31; Chris N. Okeke, *Controversial Subjects of Contemporary International Law* (Rotterdam, 1974), pp. 144–50.

30. See above, note 29.

31. Prime Minister Gandhi, in Okeke, op. cit., p. 146.

32. See above, note 29, and the following: Buchheit, op. cit., p. 213; Young, op. cit., pp. 82, 489; James Crawford, *The Creation of States in International Law* (Oxford, 1979), p. 115.

33. In fact 'double standards' was precisely the cry of Abdullah, the Kashmiri leader, when India began supporting the secessionist Bengalis.

34. Chopra, op. cit., pp. 375, 378; Okeke, op. cit., pp. 147–8; Gupta, op. cit., pp. 360–1; G.W. Choudhury, 'The Emergence of Bangla Desh and the South Asian Triangle', *Year Book of World Affairs* lxii (1973), pp. 72–3; Zubeida Mustafa, 'The USSR and the Indo-Pakistan War, 1971', *Pakistan Horizon* xxv (1972), p. 47; Satyamurthy, op. cit., p. 65. India presented the refugee case not only as a humanitarian one, but also as a form of aggression that entitled it to a right of 'economic' self-defence.

35. See above, note 34.

36. Most of the refugees were Hindu Bengalis. The refugees could strengthen the strong anti-Congress tendency which prevailed then in West Bengal. In Assam, and in the rest of the north, the delicate balance between Muslims, Hindus and Christians (mainly the Nagas) could be upset. Obviously, so long as the East remained in the hands of Islamabad, the refugees would not have been prepared to return, hence the need for swift Indian intervention.

37. Chopra, op. cit., pp. 375–8; Iqbal, op. cit., pp. 21–7; LaPorte, op. cit., pp. 102–7; Satyamurthy, op. cit., pp. 66–7; Barnds, 'Pakistan's Disintegration', pp. 327–8; Gupta, op. cit., pp. 360–1; Vijay Sen Budhray, 'Moscow and the Birth of Bangladesh', *Asian Survey* xiii (May 1973), p. 487.

38. Inayatullah, op. cit., p. 114.

39. Iqbal, op. cit., p. 27.

40. Mustafa, op. cit., pp. 45–52.

41. Budhraj, op. cit., pp. 482–95; Misra, op. cit., passim; Mustafa, op. cit., pp. 45–52;

Notes

Choudhury, 'The Emergence of Bangla Desh and the South Asian Triangle', pp. 70–2; Okeke, op. cit., pp. 150–2.

42. Budhraj, op. cit., pp. 482–3, 491–5; Choudhury, op. cit., pp. 65–71.
43. Ibid., pp. 70–3, 82; Budhraj, op. cit., pp. 483–5; Baxter, op. cit., pp. 242–4; Mustafa, op. cit., pp. 50–1; Khushid Hyder, 'United States and the Indo-Pakistan War of 1971', *Pakistan Horizon* xxv (1972), pp. 66–7.
44. It is well known that India is firmly against extending the principle of self-determination to secession, as illustrated by the position it consistently upholds in the UN on issues of minority rights.
45. Misra, op. cit., passim.
46. Khalida Qureshi, 'Britain and the Indo-Pakistan Conflict over East Pakistan', *Pakistan Horizon* xxv (1972), pp. 32–44; Okeke, op. cit., pp. 153–4.
47. Mustafa, op. cit., pp. 45–52; Qureshi, op. cit., pp. 33–5.
48. See Okeke, op. cit., p. 154.
49. Misra, op. cit., pp. 43–8, 64–124, 162–90.
50. Ibid., passim.
51. Hyder, op. cit., pp. 63–7; Choudhury, op. cit., pp. 78–83; Buchheit, op. cit., pp. 208–9; Baxter, op. cit., pp. 242–5.
52. See above, note 51.
53. Hyder, op. cit., pp. 67–8; Baxter, op. cit., pp. 242–5; Qureshi, op. cit., pp. 33–6.
54. Choudhury, op. cit., pp. 64–9; Misra, op. cit., passim; Iqbal, op. cit., p. 26.
55. Qureshi, op. cit., pp. 33–8; Baxter, op. cit., pp. 242–4; Hyder, op. cit., pp. 68–9.
56. Qureshi, op. cit., p. 36.
57. See Buchheit, op. cit., p. 206.

CHAPTER TEN: THE MORO REGION

1. Linda S. Lichter, 'The Case of the Moros of the Philippines', in W.P. Davison and L. Gordenker (eds.), *Resolving Nationality Conflicts: The Role of Opinion Research* (Princeton, 1980), pp. 132–5; Astri Suhrke and Lela Garner Noble, 'Muslims in the Philippines and Thailand', in Davison and Gordenger, op. cit., pp. 179–80; Lela Garner Noble, 'The Moro National Liberation Movement in the Philippines', *Pacific Affairs* xlix (Fall 1976), pp. 405–8; Alex Turpin, *New Society's Challenge in the Philippines*, Conflict Studies, no. 122 (London, 1980), pp. 8–9.
2. T.J.S. George, *Revolt in Mindanao: The Rise of Islam in Philippine Politics* (London, 1980), p. 226; Martial Dassé, 'Les rébellions des minorités musulmanes en Asie du Sud-Est, *Défence Nationale* (June 1981), p. 116.
3. Noble, op. cit., p. 418.
4. Ibid., pp. 406–7, 411–12, 418; Suhrke and Noble, op. cit., p. 180; George, op. cit., pp. 1–132, 221–2, 243; Lichter, op. cit., pp. 134–5; Turpin, op. cit., pp. 8–9.
5. See above, note 4.
6. Noble, op. cit., pp. 406–9; Lichter, op. cit., pp. 132–5; Suhrke and Noble, op. cit., pp. 180–3; George, op. cit., pp. 195–220; Turpin, op. cit., p. 8.
7. The Philippines, since its independence, has laid a claim on Sabah.
8. Noble, op. cit., pp. 406–12; Lichter, op. cit., pp. 133–4; George, op. cit., pp. 130–5, 194, 219–20; Lela Garner Noble, 'Ethnicity and Philippine–Malaysian Relations', *Asian Survey* xv (May 1985), pp. 456–7; *Far Eastern Economic Review* (henceforth *FEER*) (27 June 1975), p. 21.
9. See above, note 8.
10. Turpin, op. cit., pp. 9–10; Noble, 'The Moro National Liberation Front in the Philippines', p. 409.
11. Ibid., pp. 408–12; Suhrke and Noble, op. cit., p. 183; Turpin, op. cit., p. 11; George, op. cit., pp. 199–201, 207–9.
12. Noble, op. cit., pp. 412–13; Turpin, op. cit., pp. 10–11; *FEER* (8 July 1974), pp. 1–12.
13. See above, note 12, and Geoffrey C. Gunn, 'Radical Islam in Southeast Asia: Rhetoric

and Reality in the Middle East Connection', *Journal of Contemporary Asia* xvi (1986), pp. 47–9.

14. Noble, op. cit., pp. 416–18; George, op. cit., pp. 196–203, 231; *FEER* (27 June 1975), p. 21.
15. Alonto in *FEER* (27 June 1975), pp. 22–3; George, op. cit., pp. 249–56; Lichter, op. cit., pp. 136–8; Suhrke and Noble, op. cit., pp. 186–92; Noble, op. cit., pp. 415–19.
16. See above, note 15.
17. George, op. cit., pp. 224–27, 251–6; Noble, op. cit., pp. 412, 420–1; *FEER* (8 July 1974), pp. 10–12.
18. *FEER* (27 June 1975), p. 21; Noble, op. cit., pp. 416–17; George, op. cit., pp. 202–3.
19. MNLF in Noble, 'Ethnicity and Philippine–Malaysian Relations', p. 459.
20. MNLF in Suhrke and Noble, op. cit., p. 179.
21. The MNLF could not control *datu* territory, nor the guerrilla leaders of Lanao de Sur in the island of Mindanao.
22. Alonto, op. cit.
23. Turpin, op. cit., p. 10; George, op. cit., pp. 241, 253–4.
24. George, op. cit., pp. 233–4; Suhrke and Noble, op. cit., p. 83; Turpin, op. cit., pp. 9–10; Dassé, op. cit., p. 119; Noble, 'The Moro National Liberation Front in the Philippines', pp. 409–10.
25. Ibid., pp. 409, 420; Noble, 'Ethnicity and Philippine–Malaysian Relations', passim; Dassé, op. cit., pp. 9–10.
26. Suhrke and Noble, op. cit., pp. 183–4, 195; George, op. cit., pp. 234–8, 264; Noble, 'The Moro National Liberation Front in the Philippines', pp. 409, 413. See also an official Philippines publication, *The Southwestern Philippines Question*, Ministry of Foreign Affairs, Republic of the Philippines (1980), p. 6.
27. The 'secret weapon' was used once again with the Libyan leader after the Tripoli talks faltered in 1977.
28. For Qaddafi's perspective see among others Edward Mitchell, 'Islam in Colonel Qaddafi's Thought', *The World Today* (July–August 1982), pp. 319–26; Turpin, op. cit., p. 9; Gunn, op. cit., pp. 31–2; Also Qaddafi's interview with Peter Enahoro in *Africa Now* (February 1983), pp. 37–46.
29. Indonesia is one of the countries notorious for disregarding all forms of communal self-assertion in its midst. Note the cases of the Ambonese (Southern Moluccans), the West Papuans and East Timorese (after East Timor was annexed contrary to international law).
30. Noble, 'Ethnicity and Philippine–Malaysian Relations', pp. 456–7, 465; George, op. cit., p. 246; Suhrke and Noble, op. cit., pp. 189–91.
31. George, op. cit., pp. 245–7; Turpin, op. cit., p. 11.
32. Ibid., p. 11; Gunn, op. cit., p. 49.
33. Suhrke and Noble, op. cit., pp. 185–9; George, op. cit., pp. 245–9; Noble, op. cit., pp. 458–9, 466–8; *The Southwestern Philippine Question*, op. cit., pp. 7–10.
34. Noble, op. cit., pp. 462–3, 466, 469; Suhrke and Noble, op. cit., p. 195.
35. Gunn, op. cit., p. 49; *International Herald Tribune* (24 September 1987).
36. According to reports in late 1987, Filipino officers fighting both the leftist New People's Army and the Moros in the south claimed that the Moros were the more formidable guerrilla force of the two. See *International Herald Tribune* (24 September 1987).

CHAPTER ELEVEN: ERITREA

1. The other separatist movements in Ethiopia in the 1980s were the Somalis, the Oromo, the Tigray and more recently the Afars.
2. David Pool, *Eritrea – Africa's Longest War*, Anti-Slavery Society, Report no. 4 (London, 1982), pp. 36–46; David Pool, 'Eritrean Nationalism', in I.M. Lewis (ed.), *Nationalism and Self Determination in the Horn of Africa* (London, 1983), pp. 183–4; Richard Sherman, *Eritrea: The Unfinished Revolution* (New York, 1980), pp. 40–3; Colin Legum, 'Eritrea', in Colin Legum and James Firebrace, *Eritrea and Tigray*, Minority Rights Group, Report no.

Notes

5 (1983), pp. 6–7; Mekahl Harnet, 'Reflections on the Eritrean Revolution', *Horn of Africa* vi, no. 3 (1983–84), pp. 3–4; Tekie Fessehatzion, 'The International Dimension of the Eritrean Question', *Horn of Africa* vi, no. 2 (1983), pp. 7–16; Bereket Habte Selassie, 'The Eritrean Question in International Law', *Horn of Africa* vi, no. 2 (1983), pp. 25–30.

3. The Amhara are the second largest ethnic group in Ethiopia. (The first by far are an underdog ethnic group, the Oromo, formerly known as Galla.) The historical links of the Amhara with Eritrea are a contentious issue among scholars of Ethiopia. Apparently, the ties established by the Kingdom of Axum were severed centuries ago. Prior to the Italian colonization of Eritrea, the region was an apple of discord between the Ethiopian Empire and Egypt.

4. John Franklin Campbell, 'Rumblings along the Red Sea: The Eritrean Question', *Foreign Affairs* (April 1970), pp. 539–43; Fred Halliday, 'The Fighting in Eritrea', *New Left Review* lxvii (May–June 1971), pp. 57–61; Christopher Clapham, 'Ethiopia and Somalia', *Adelphi Papers*, no. 93, IISS (London, 1974), pp. 1–13; Godfrey Morrison, *Eritrea and the Southern Sudan*, Minority Rights Group, Report no. 5 (1976 edition), pp. 3–8; J. Bowyer Bell, 'Endemic Insurgency and International Order: The Eritrean Experience', *Orbis* (Summer 1974), pp. 429–32; Ethiopiawi, 'The Eritrean–Ethiopian Conflict', in Astri Suhrke and Lela Garner Noble (eds.), *Ethnic Conflict in International Relations* (New York, 1977), pp. 127–9; Richard Lobban, 'The Eritrean War: Issues and Implications', *Canadian Journal of African Studies* x (1976), pp. 335–40; Pool, *Eritrea*, pp. 7–20; Pool, 'Eritrean Nationalism', pp. 175–85; Bereket Habte Selassie, *Conflict and Intervention in the Horn of Africa* (New York, 1980), pp. 1–73; Dan Connell, 'The Birth of the Eritrean Nation', *Horn of Africa* iii (January–March 1980), pp. 14–22; Michael and Trish Johnson, 'Eritrea: The National Question and the Logic of Protracted Struggle', *African Affairs* lxxx (April 1981), pp. 181–5; Raman G. Bhardwaj, 'The Growing Externalization of the Eritrean Movement', *Horn of Africa* (January–March 1979), pp. 19–20; Legum, op. cit., pp. 5–6.

5. See above, note 4.

6. See above, note 4.

7. Legum, op. cit., p. 5.

8. Pool, 'Eritrean Nationalism', p. 186; Patrick Gilkes, 'Centralism and the Ethiopian PMAC', in Lewis (ed.), op. cit., p. 203. Note that the Dergue was seriously considering making the Kunama-inhabited area Ethiopia's first autonomous region.

9. See above, note 4.

10. See the Eritrean movement's publication *Eritrean Revolution*, I, no. 3 (January–April 1976), p. 7 and literature in note 4 above.

11. Sherman, op. cit., pp. 40–3; Legum, op. cit., pp. 7–8; Lobban, op. cit., pp. 338–9.

12. Legum, op. cit., p. 4.

13. Mengistu, in ibid., p. 4.

14. See above, note 4, and the following: Dan Connell, 'The Changing Situation in Eritrea', in Basil Davidson et al. (eds.), *Beyond the War in Eritrea* (Nottingham, 1980), p. 56; Colin Legum and Bill Lee, *The Horn of Africa in Continuing Crisis* (New York, 1979), pp. 23, 27–30; Gilkes, op. cit., pp. 201–3; Harnet, op. cit., pp. 7–15.

15. Sherman, op. cit., pp. 41–68; Ethiopiawi, op. cit., pp. 129–32; Halliday, op. cit., pp. 62–8; Lobban, op. cit., pp. 340–2; Pool, op. cit., pp. 184–8.

16. Legum, op. cit., pp. 8–11; Sherman, op. cit., pp. 41–60; Selassie, op. cit., pp. 65–71, 168–9; Harnet, op. cit., pp. 7–10, 13–15.

17. Lobban, op. cit., pp. 341–5; Sherman, op. cit., pp. 42, 46–54; Johnson, op. cit., pp. 184–95; Bhardwaj, op. cit., pp. 21–5; Selassie, op. cit., pp. 66–9, 182–91.

18. Sherman, op. cit., pp. 41–5, 56; Legum, op. cit., p. 8; Lobban, op. cit., pp. 341–2, 346; *Africa* (September 1982), p. 13.

19. See Eritrean publications: *Eritrean Review* (September 1974), p. 9, (December 1974), p. 6, (January 1975), pp. 2–3, (August 1976), p. 10, (February 1980), pp. 4–6, (June 1980), pp. 4–6, (January 1981), p. 5; and *Eritrean Revolution* (January–April 1976), pp. 5–9, (September–November 1978), p. 59. Also see *West Africa* (12 June 1978), pp. 1114–16; *New African* (July 1986), p. 28.

20. See above, note 17.

239

21. See above, note 19, and Ethiopiawi, pp. 128, 133, 138, 140; Bhardwaj, op. cit., pp. 19–20, 27.
22. See above, note 19, and other issues of the Eritrean publications mentioned therein.
23. See above, note 19.
24. 'The Right of the Eritrean People to Self-Determination', EPLF document in Pool, *Eritrea*, Appendix, pp. 68–9.
25. See above, note 19.
26. Campbell, op. cit., pp. 544–5; Halliday, op. cit., p. 64; Clapham, op. cit., p. 11.
27. See above, note 19.
28. See EPLF document, pp. 60–72 and *Eritrean Revolution* (January–April 1976), pp. 5–9.
29. *West Africa* (12 June 1978), pp. 1114–16; *Eritrean Review* (February 1980), p. 6, (June 1980), p. 4 and (December 1980), p. 10.
30. See above, note 19, and the following: Ethiopiawi, op. cit., p. 127; Sherman, op. cit., pp. 48, 153–4; Connell, op. cit., p. 23; Clapham, op. cit., pp. 4, 12; Legum, op. cit., pp. 8, 10, 12.
31. Mordechai Abir, 'Red Sea Politics', *Adelphi Papers*, no. 93, IISS (London, 1972), pp. 32–4; Clapham, op. cit., pp. 11–12; Selassie, op. cit., pp. 156–65; Halliday, op. cit., p. 64; Hakan Wiberg, 'The Horn of Africa', *Journal of Peace Research* xvi (1979), p. 192; Bell, op. cit., pp. 433, 435, 451; Fessehatzion, op. cit., p. 21.
32. Ibid., pp. 434, 437, 441; Abir, op. cit., pp. 32–4; Bhardwaj, op. cit., pp. 19–25; Wiberg, op. cit., p. 192; Sherman, op. cit., pp. 48, 63, 154–5; Selassie, op. cit., pp. 146–50, 160–1; Clapham, op. cit., pp. 4, 12; Legum, op. cit., p. 12; Gerald Cubitt, 'Eritrea: Land without Peace', *Africa Institute Bulletin* xv (1966), pp. 113–16.
33. See above, note 32.
34. See above, note 32.
35. Clapham, op. cit., p. 4; Ethiopiawi, op. cit., pp. 132, 140; Bhardwaj, op. cit., pp. 20, 23; Campbell, op. cit., p. 544.
36. Wiberg, op. cit., p. 192; Legum, op. cit., p. 10–11; *Africa* (September 1982), pp. 13–14.
37. Bell, op. cit., pp. 434, 437, 441, 446; Ethiopiawi, op. cit., pp. 127, 133, 138–41; Selassie, op. cit., pp. 146–65; Campbell, op. cit., pp. 543–4.
38. See among others the seminal work of Michael C. Hudson, *Arab Politics* (New Haven, 1977), pp. 238–44.
39. Ibid., p. 241.
40. Legum, op. cit., p. 10.
41. Adeed Dawisha, 'Saudi Arabia's Search for Security', *Adelphi Papers*, IISS (London, 1979–80), pp. 8, 20; William B. Quandt, 'Riyadh between the Superpowers', *Foreign Policy* xliv (1981), pp. 37–42, 50–2.
42. Bhardwaj, op. cit., pp. 21–3.
43. Legum, op. cit., pp. 11–12.
44. Ibid., p. 12.
45. In 1974 Cuba attempted to place the issue of Eritrean independence on the agenda of the Non-Aligned Conference.
46. Halliday, op. cit., pp. 62–4; Bell, op. cit., pp. 434–6, 441, 447; Clapham, op. cit., pp. 4, 12–13; Sherman, op. cit., pp. 150–1; Abir, op. cit., pp. 29, 33; Lars Bondestam, 'External Involvement in Ethiopia and Eritrea', in Basil Davidson et al. (eds.), op. cit., pp. 68–70; Harry Brind, 'Soviet Policy in the Horn of Africa', *International Affairs* lx (Winter 1983–84), pp. 75–95; Fessehatzion, op. cit., pp. 11–15, 21–22.
47. See above, note 46.
48. Clapham, op. cit., p. 12; Abir, op. cit., pp. 33–4; Bell, op. cit., pp. 431, 441; Bhardwaj, op. cit., pp. 22–3; Wiberg, op. cit., p. 192; Peter Schwab, 'Cold War on the Horn of Africa', *African Affairs* lxxvii (January 1978), pp. 18–19.
49. Clapham, op. cit., p. 12.
50. 'An Interview with TPLF', *Horn of Africa* iv, no. 3 (1982), p. 34; Legum, op. cit., pp. 8, 12; Selassie, op. cit., pp. 86, 96.
51. Legum, op. cit., p. 12.

APPENDICES

1. GLOSSARY OF TERMS

The Centre is a term used as shorthand for the government of a state with centrifugal tendencies.

Secession largo sensu includes two types of secession: secession *stricto sensu* and incremental secession.

Secession stricto sensu is an abrupt unilateral move to independence on the part of a certain region from within the metropolitan territory of a sovereign independent state. It is set forth by an act of declaration of independence which is manifestly opposed by the state in question (the 'Centre').

Incremental secession is political activity which may or may not be violent and which is aimed at independence and short of this at a formula of self-government. Secession is here a process. There is no declaration of independence.

Secessionist front is a militant organization which may or may not have ingroup legitimization and which seeks the independence of a region which is part of the metropolitan territory of a sovereign independent state.

Secessionist movement is a front or fronts that (a) are legitimized by the ingroup concerned not only as to the aim (independence) but also with regard to the means (the use or not of armed violence), and (b) pose a credible threat for the respective Centre.

Indicators of legitimization include results of elections or referenda, manifestations of group mobilization for separatism (e.g., strikes, demonstrations, mass non-cooperation, group petitions, etc.), indications of ingroup active support for the separatist guerrillas (e.g., harbouring of guerrillas and separatist leaders), and most crucially the continued recruitment of fighters and other active members of the cause, thereby swelling the secessionist ranks despite the hardships and violence.

Indicators of credibility of threat include existing ingroup support (legitimization), existence of a sizable and compact secessionist collectivity (a community or a society) in the territory under secession (a good territorial base), a degree of control over a substantial area (at least of a large rural area), an availability of resources for a protracted armed struggle (which can also include the suitability of the terrain

241

for guerrilla warfare) and clear evidence that the Centre is taking the matter seriously, as seen in particular if there is deployment of a considerable proportion of the state's armed forces against the secessionists or if there are appeals to the country's allies for material and other support.

Internationalization of a secession or secessionist movement exists when there is both international activity and partisan international involvement.

International activity exists when, at a minimum, there is a plea for world concern or a plea for involvement on the part of a third-party (state, IGO, NGO or sub-units of these three) by the secessionist front or secessionist government.

Partisan international involvement is activity by a government, IGO, NGO or their sub-units which results in enhancing the position of the secessionists (even if it is not deliberate), or which is aimed at enhancing the secessionist position. Partisan international involvement is of two general types: (a) tangible involvement which is divided into material (or utilitarian) aid, aid by way of access, and assistance by way of services rendered; and (b) political–diplomatic and moral support. Partisan international involvement can be based on instrumental motives and/or on affective motives, there can thus be 'instrumental involvement' and 'affective involvement'.

2. A MODEL OF THE ETIOLOGY OF SEPARATISM/SECESSION

1. The fundamental independent variables:

(a) territorial contiguity;

(b) separate community (nation, ethno-nation, religious group, racial group, sub-ethnic group), or separate society (inter-ethnic alliance, split of a nation);

(c) disadvantage–deprivation (absolute–cumulative, relative–marginal).

2. Secondary independent variables: background facilitating conditions (i.e., colonialism, modernization, etc.)

3. Necessary dependent variables:

(a) a separatist organization or leadership,

(b) precipitants or accelerators from interaction with the Centre,

(c) catalysts (feasibility and viability),
(d) triggering event (opportunity or last resort).

3. PROPOSITIONS

(1) The *sine qua non* elements for the creation of a regionally-based political organization (or leadership) which has an inbuilt potential for separatism are three: the existence of a separate community or society, a degree of actual or perceived disadvantage and territorial contiguity.

(2) If a group in a region of a state constitutes an ethno-nation or nation, a lesser degree of disadvantage is necessary to spur separatism. Conversely, if a self- and other-defined group in a region of a state is not an ethno-nation or nation, a greater degree of disadvantage is needed, amounting to absolute–cumulative inequality, for separatism to develop.

(3) In most instances the Centre has the prerogative, even when to begin with the prospects for integration are bleak (due to the existence of stark inequality between communities and/or the existence of an ethno-nation concentrated in a discernible region of the state–nation). It is basically the Centre through its actions, inactions and reactions that precipitates separatism and its most extreme form, secession.

(4) Once the course for separatism has been set (that is when a separatist organization which possesses overwhelming ingroup support emerges in a state), disintegration (gradual secessionism with violence) is relentless. This process can only be arrested and the conflict at least for a time genuinely resolved if the separatists are provided with a considerable level of self-rule.

(5) All secessionist territories have an international border or outlet to the sea and do not include the capital of the sovereign state in their midst.

(6) The international system is in general disinclined to favour secessionist self-determination and partisan involvement with secessionist movements.

(7) Secessions which have made a declaration of independence tend to be defined as inflexible in their demand for independence and *nolens volens* become inflexible. Thus other forms of separatism, such as extended autonomy, or a federal framework can elude them.

(8) Incremental secessions with their inbuilt greater flexibility (as to the

243

goal, the means and the ability to disappear and fight another battle later) may not have greater chances of creating an independent state than secessions *stricto sensu*, but have greater potential to achieve 'meaningful' home rule.

(9) Secessions *stricto sensu* are faced with total defeat. So long as the Centre does not radically redefine its initial repudiation of secession (something which has not happened in the period following the Second World War) the independence of a secessionist state can only be achieved if two decisive events take place: (1) if there is a large-scale military intervention on the part of a third party (almost by definition a state or states) which results in defeating or somehow neutralizing the Centre and its allies; (2) if there are numerous *de jure* or *de facto* recognitions. Both these events are extremely rare.

(10) There is an international dimension inherent in all secessionist movements, even if only by virtue of the fact that they challenge the territorial integrity of a state.

(11) The longer the war for secessionist independence the greater the potential for splits and permutations within the secessionist movement, despite the unabated external threat, contrary that is to the classical Simmel–Coser postulate.

(12) Whatever the initial basis of leadership and the basis of authority of a secessionist front it ultimately tends to boil down to proficiency in delivering the goods, namely the indispensable goods of secession (arms, sanctuary, access, funds).

(13) Ideology is both a blessing to and a scourge of secessionist movements and has an element of ambivalence, perhaps even lack of credibility. The more precise it is, the greater its potential to consolidate pre-existing internal support and attract external like-minded actors, but at the same time a clear ideology can create devout enemies or alienate potential friends, internally as well as internationally.

(14) Pragmatism prevails in the selection of targets of appeal, and the acceptance of external aid, for the priority is the continuation of the armed struggle and, if need be, negotiating from a position of strength.

(15) The more a secessionist war becomes internationalized the more the inherent weight of the Centre comes to bear, as the Centre is more able to muster external aid and cut down, one by one, the secessionists' allies.

(16) The best persuasion technique is the presentation of a good case for secession. This should be done on the basis that the unity–integrity of the state is impossible due to four main reasons: (1) the

244

outrageous and out of all proportion military onslaught of the Centre against the civilian population of the secessionist; (2) pre-existing and continuing exploitation–discrimination–domination; (3) the existence of a harmonious separate community or society (not necessarily a nation) living compactly in a fairly distinct and integral territory of a state; (4) a realistic image of a more peaceful and advantageous situation after secession for both parties in conflict, the secessionists as well as the Centre; that is a positive sum outcome of the conflict.

(17) As the war drags on, the danger of military escalation is difficult to avoid and sooner or later the secessionist movement is likely to reach a threshold of appeal (or a threshold of greater appeal) for third-party involvement, so long as it is not ready to give up the struggle, negotiate, or be able to somehow disappear or de-escalate the armed conflict and fight another day.

(18) Partisan supporters are more prone to provide 'words' (moral and political support) rather than 'deeds' (tangible support). Although in this sense words appear to be 'cheap', the words that really count, such as extensive politico-diplomatic campaigns and diplomatic recognition (as states or liberation movements), are difficult to come by, even more difficult than extensive tangible support.

(19) Affective and instrumental motives can be equally influential, though there are marked variations from one secessionist movement to another, with instrumental motivation being able to stand on its own, whilst affective motivation is less able to do so.

(20) High-level tangible involvement emanates more from instrumental motives than affective motives. The opposite is only very tenuously the case with regard to diplomatic support and recognition.

(21) The most common single reason for third-state support is instrumental in nature. It is international political gain.

(22) Restraints on involvement by states are almost exclusively instrumental, in particular international political considerations.

(23) Third states that happen to be enemies of the Centre are highly likely to be supporters of the secessionists, mainly in regard to high-level tangible support and to a lesser extent, high-level diplomatic support.

(24) The affective–instrumental motivation dichotomy is not an indicator of the degree of reliability when a third state provides high-level support to secessionists.

(25) States which are enemies of the Centre tend not to be reliable allies, with the exception of rare instances in which the rift between the third state and the Centre appears totally insurmountable.

(26) The motives that make the most reliable supporters are reasons of justice, humanitarian reasons, reasons of personal friendship and non-Marxist ideological affinity, in other words when the persuasion of a state/government is based on identification (empathizing with the secessionists *qua* group) or internalization (believing in the inherent justice of the secessionists' case for self-determination, be it extended autonomy or independence).

(27) Support to secessionist movements has come from a variety of states, from conservative and radical states, from developed and underdeveloped states, from powerful and weak states. Industrial Western states, are, however, more likely to afford tangible aid rather than recognition and overt political support.

(28) The former colonial power is more likely to stand aloof or to assist the Centre rather than to assist the secessionists. If secessionists are assisted there is pressure on the colonial power to stop its aid. Thus on the whole the neocolonialist myth that surrounds secession in general is accurate only in rare instances.

(29) Of the two superpowers, the Soviet Union is far more likely to assist secessionist movements diplomatically and materially. Nevertheless, it is not reliable and may at some stage switch its support to the Centre.

(30) States neighbouring a secessionist region have difficulty in not becoming involved, often on the secessionist side. But their support to the secessionists is reversible and is usually based on a *quid pro quo* arrangement with the state threatened by the secessionist movement.

4. A CATEGORIZATION OF REVOLUTIONARY NATIONALIST MOVEMENTS

Basic categories	*Subcategories*	*Examples*
Revolutionary simpliciter	By the majority group of a state	African National Congress (South Africa)
	By a minority group in a state	Sudan People's Liberation Army (Southern Sudanese)
Against foreign rule	Classical anti-colonial	SWAPO (Namibia), FRELIMO (Portuguese Mocambique)
	Against settler colonization	ZANU, ZAPU (Southern Rhodesia)

	Anti-occupation (anti-annexation)	POLISARIO (Western Sahara), FRETILIN (East Timor), Palestinain Liberation Organization (1974–)
Irredentist	Classical irredentist	World Zionist Organization (1896–1948), PLO (1965–74)
	Pan-irredentist	pan-Ewe, pan-Azande, pan-BaKongo movements
Irredentist-merger	EOKA-B (Cyprus)	
	Settler0 irredentist	OAS (French Algeria), U.D.I. (Southern Rhodesia)
Separatist	Limited separatist	Awami League (East Pakistan), Kurdistan Democratic Party (Iraq), Southern Sudan Liberation Movement, Baluchi People's Liberation Front (Pakistan)
	Secessionist	Biafra (1967–70), Katanga (1960–63), Bangladesh (1971), Eritrean Liberation Front, Liberation Tigers of Tamil Ealan (Sri Lanka)
Secessionist	Western Somali Liberation merger	Front, IRA (Northern Ireland)
Secessionist-	Armenian Secret Army irredentist	for the Liberation of Armenia
Settler	United States (1776) seccessionist	

5. TYPES OF TANGIBLE INVOLVEMENT WITH SECESSIONISTS

Utilitarian/material aid

Arms, ammunition, spare parts, military vehicles, combat aircraft, warships, and other military equipment
Funds, foreign currency
Foodstuffs, medicines
Fuel, electricity and other energy sources
Radio and other communications equipment
Means of transportation.

Access aid

Communication and transportation networks, access to world media, etc.

Assistance by way of services

Sanctuary, asylum, base of operations (military and/ or political-diplomatic), allowing arms trails, arms purchases and transit of arms or men (mercenaries and others), permitting the recruitment of men (mercenaries or individuals from refugee camps), military training, etc.
Personnel as advisers in operational or semi-operational functions, or as technical and political advisers
Artillery cover, military advisers (or trainers) in secessionist territory, combat units fighting with the secessionists, etc.
Full-scale military intervention in support of the secessionists and against the 'Centre'.

6. ESCALATION LADDER OF TANGIBLE INVOLVEMENT

1. Simple transactional involvement: business as usual in regard to transactions (trade, transportation, communications, etc.), in spite of the Centre's ban or blockade.
2. Humanitarian involvement: relief aid to civilians in the secessionist territory.
3. Non-military involvement (aid, access, assistance):
turning a blind eye to arms trails; asylum; finance; advice; access facilities.

4. Military involvement outside the secessionist terrain (indirect military involvement): sanctuary, training camps, base of operations, arms and other military equipment.
5. Involvement of personnel: political and military advisers to the secessionists within secessionist territory.
6. Foreign combat units under secessionist command.
7. Direct military confrontation against the Centre, though of a limited scale: border skirmishes, artillery fire across the border, etc.
8. Full-scale military intervention (invasion, inter-state war).

Note: Steps 4, 5, 6 and 7 constitute 'intervention', that is, 'physical' involvement.

7. ESCALATION LADDER OF VERBAL SUPPORT

1. Humanitarian concern.
2. Call for a negotiated settlement between the two parties, for a settlement which would not put into question the territorial integrity of the state.
3. Call for open-ended peace talks between the two parties.
4. Claim that the secessionists have the right to self-determination.
5. Recognition as a state (*de facto* or *de jure*) or as a liberation movement (in case of 'incremental secessions').

8. THIRD STATE INVOLVEMENT IN THE 7 SECESSIONIST MOVEMENTS

Western States

THIRD STATE	SECESSIONIST MOVEMENT	TANGIBLE SUPPORT	DIPLOMATIC SUPPORT	RECOGNITION LEVEL	MOTIVES	CONSTRAINTS	ASSESSMENT OF ROLE
Belgium	Katanga	high	extensive	self-determination	instrumental	political, economic	crucial
	Biafra	low					
Canada	Biafra	low	minimal		mixed	political (USA,UK, Nigeria)	
Denmark	Biafra	low	minimal		affective	political (USA,UK, Nigeria)	
	Bangladesh		minimal				
France	Katanga	high	occasional	concern	economic	political, economic	significant
	Biafra	high	occasional	self-determination	mixed	political, economic	crucial
	Iraqi Kurdistan	low					
	Bangladesh		occasional		unclear		

THIRD STATE	SECESSIONIST MOVEMENT	TANGIBLE SUPPORT	DIPLOMATIC SUPPORT	RECOGNITION LEVEL	MOTIVES	CONSTRAINTS	ASSESSMENT OF ROLE
Greece	Katanga		minimal		instrumental		
Italy	Katanga		minimal		instrumental		
Malta	Bangladesh		minimal				
Netherlands	Biafra				affective		
New Zealand	Bangladesh		minimal				
Norway	Biafra	low	occasional	considered recognition	affective	U K, West	
Portugal	Katanga	low	minimal		instrumental		useful
	Biafra	medium, high?			instrumental	West	crucial

THIRD STATE	SECESSIONIST MOVEMENT	TANGIBLE SUPPORT	DIPLOMATIC SUPPORT	RECOGNITION LEVEL	MOTIVES	CONSTRAINTS	ASSESSMENT OF ROLE
Sweden	Biafra	low	minimal		affective	U K, West	
Switzerland	Biafra	low	mediatory type		affective	neutrality, West	
UK (Britain)	Katanga	low	occasional		instrumental	internal, USA, Commonwealth, Africa	useful
	Bangladesh	low	occasional		mixed	Pakistan, USA	useful
	Biafra	low			instrumental	vs separatism, international political	
U.S.A.	Iraqi Kurdistan	high, unclear			instrumental	vs separatism, international political	

Eastern States

THIRD STATE	SECESSIONIST MOVEMENT	TANGIBLE SUPPORT	DIPLOMATIC SUPPORT	RECOGNITION LEVEL	MOTIVES	CONSTRAINTS	ASSESSMENT OF ROLE
Bulgaria	Bangladesh		minimal				
	Biafra	low			domestic, affective	USSR	
Czechoslovakia	Iraqi Kurdistan		minimal				
	Bangladesh		minimal				
Hungary	Bangladesh		occasional				
Poland	Bangladesh		minimal				
U.S.S.R.	Iraqi Kurdistan	high, unclear	occasional	self-determination	mostly instrumental	Iraq, geopolitical	useful but unreliable
	Bangladesh	high but indirect	occasional	recognition (after India)	mostly instrumental	political relations with Pakistan	important reliable
	Eritrea	high, unclear	minimal	in early 50's	instrumental		
Yugoslavia	Iraqi Kurdistan		minimal				
	Bangladesh		minimal				

Other States

THIRD STATE	SECESSIONIST MOVEMENT	TANGIBLE SUPPORT	DIPLOMATIC SUPPORT	RECOGNITION LEVEL	MOTIVES	CONSTRAINTS	ASSESSMENT OF ROLE
Israel	Biafra	medium			unclear	international political	worthwhile
	S.Sudan	high			instrumental	international political	crucial reliable
	Iraqi Kurdistan	high			mostly instrumental	international political	worthwhile
	Katanga	medium, high?	extensive	akin to de facto recognition	mixed	UK factor	crucial
Rhodesia	Biafra	unclear					
South Africa	Katanga	medium	occasional	akin to de facto recognition	instrumental		useful
	Biafra	high, unclear	minimal		instrumental		

THIRD STATE	SECESSIONIST MOVEMENT	TANGIBLE SUPPORT	DIPLOMATIC SUPPORT	RECOGNITION LEVEL	MOTIVES	CONSTRAINTS	ASSESSMENT OF ROLE
			African States				
Benin (Dahomey)	Biafra	medium		peace talks		Africa, Nigeria	important
Botswana	Biafra	unclear	minimal		affective		
Burundi	Biafra	low	minimal		affective		
Chad	S.Sudan		mediation?				
Congo-Brazzaville (The People's Rep.of)	Katanga	medium	extensive	akin to de facto recognition	mostly instrumental	Congo-Leopoldville	very useful
	Biafra		mediatory type	concern	affective		
	Biafra		mediatory		unclear	Africa	
	S. Sudan	high	mediatory		instrumental	Sudan, Africa, Arabs	useful but unreliable
Ethiopia	Iraqi Kurdistan		minimal				

THIRD STATE	SECESSIONIST MOVEMENT	TANGIBLE SUPPORT	DIPLOMATIC SUPPORT	RECOGNITION LEVEL	MOTIVES	CONSTRAINTS	ASSESSMENT OF ROLE
Gabon	Biafra	high	extensive	de jure recognition	mixed		useful but unreliable
Ghana	Biafra		mediatory				
	S.Sudan		mediatory				
Ivory Coast	Biafra	high	extensive	de jure recognition	mostly affective	France, French speaking Africa	very important
Kenya	Biafra		mediatory type			Sudan, Africa	
	S.Sudan	low	minimal		affective	Sudan,Africa and domestic	useful
Liberia	Biafra		mediatory	peace talks			
Madagascar (Malagashy Rep.)	Katanga		minimal				
Malawi	S.Sudan		unclear	as liberation movement	unclear		useful
Niger	Biafra		mediatory	concern		domestic: Hausa,Islam	

THIRD STATE	SECESSIONIST MOVEMENT	TANGIBLE SUPPORT	DIPLOMATIC SUPPORT	RECOGNITION LEVEL	MOTIVES	CONSTRAINTS	ASSESSMENT OF ROLE
Rwanda	Biafra	low	minimal		affective		
Senegal	Biafra		mediatory type	peace talks	affective	domestic (Muslim factor), Africa	
	Iraqi Kurdistan		minimal				
	Moro State		mediatory type	concern	affective		
Sierra Leone	Biafra		extensive mediatory type	considered recognition	affective	Nigeria, UK	useful
Somalia	Moro State			concern			
	Eritrea	medium		as liberation movement			

THIRD STATE	SECESSIONIST MOVEMENT	TANGIBLE SUPPORT	DIPLOMATIC SUPPORT	RECOGNITION LEVEL	MOTIVES	CONSTRAINTS	ASSESSMENT OF ROLE
Uganda	Biafra		mediatory	toyed with recognition	affective, idiosyncratic	Buganda, African unity	
Uganda	S.Sudan	high	mediatory	as liberation movement	mostly affective	Sudan	important but unreliable
U.R. of Tanzania	Biafra	high	extensive	de jure recognition	affective	African unity, Nigeria	very important
U.R. of Tanzania	S.Sudan	unclear (humanitarian?)				Sudan and region	
Congo-Leopoldville (Zaïre)	S.Sudan	high			instrumental	Sudan Africa, (OAU) political	important but unreliable
Zambia	Biafra	medium	extensive	de jure recognition		'African solution'	important but unreliable

THIRD STATE	SECESSIONIST MOVEMENT	TANGIBLE SUPPORT	DIPLOMATIC SUPPORT	RECOGNITION LEVEL	MOTIVES	CONSTRAINTS	ASSESSMENT OF ROLE
			Arab States				
Algeria	Iraqi Kurdistan		minimal				
	Eritrea	low					
Dem.Yemen (RDRY)	Eritrea	high			mixed	China	important but unreliable
Egypt (UAR)	Iraqi Kurdistan		minimal	concern		Iraq,region Arabs	
	Moro State	low	minimal	concern			
	Eritrea	low		concern		Ethiopia (Selassie)	
Iraq	Eritrea	high	extensive	as liberation movement	unclear		crucial
Kuwait	Iraqi Kurdistan	low			mixed		
	Moro State			concern	affective		
	Eritrea	medium			mixed		

THIRD STATE	SECESSIONIST MOVEMENT	TANGIBLE SUPPORT	DIPLOMATIC SUPPORT	RECOGNITION LEVEL	MOTIVES	CONSTRAINTS	ASSESSMENT OF ROLE
Lebanon	Iraqi Kurdistan	unclear					
	Eritrea	unclear					
Libyan Arab Jamahiriya	Moro State	high	from extensive to mediatory	right of self-determination	mostly affective and idiosyncratic	Philippines	crucial but unreliable
	Eritrea	high		right of self-determination	mixed and idiosyncratic	USSR	useful
Morocco	Eritrea	low		right of self-determination	affective		
Saudi Arabia	Moro State	medium	mediatory	concern	affective		important
	Eritrea	medium to high (?)	occasional	right of self-determination	mixed	Ethiopia, U S A	very important but unreliable

THIRD STATE	SECESSIONIST MOVEMENT	TANGIBLE SUPPORT	DIPLOMATIC SUPPORT	RECOGNITION LEVEL	MOTIVES	CONSTRAINTS	ASSESSMENT OF ROLE
Sudan	Eritrea	high	extended and mediatory type	right of self-determination	mixed	Ethiopia, Soviet Union, U.S.A.	crucial but unreliable
	Iraqi Kurdistan	high			instrumental	Arabs	important
Syria	Eritrea	high	extensive	recognition as liberation movement	unclear	U S S R	crucial
	Iraqi Kurdistan		minimal				
Tunisia	Eritrea	low		recognition as liberation movement			
United Arab Emirates, Yemen and one more Arab Peninsula State	Eritrea	medium		concern	mixed		useful

THIRD STATE	SECESSIONIST MOVEMENT	TANGIBLE SUPPORT	DIPLOMATIC SUPPORT	RECOGNITION LEVEL	MOTIVES	CONSTRAINTS	ASSESSMENT OF ROLE
			Asian States				
China	Biafra	high	minimal	right of self-determination	mostly instrumental		useful, reliable
	Eritrea	high			unclear		unreliable
India	Bangladesh	high	extensive	de jure recognition	mostly instrumental	China, USA, Pakistan	crucial
Indonesia	Moro State	unclear	mediatory	towards autonomy		regional political	
Iran	Iraqi Kurdistan	high			instrumental	international political	crucial but unreliable
	Eritrea	unclear					
Malaysia /Sabah /	Moro State	high high	mediatory type		mixed affective and idiosyncratic	Philippines Government of Kuala Lumpur	crucial but not so reliable
Mongolia	Iraqi Kurdistan	minimal	approval	minimal			
	Bangladesh		minimal				

THIRD STATE	SECESSIONIST MOVEMENT	TANGIBLE SUPPORT	DIPLOMATIC SUPPORT	RECOGNITION LEVEL	MOTIVES	RECOGNITION	CONSTRAINTS	ASSESSMENT OF ROLE
				Latin American States				
Chile	Biafra		minimal					
Columbia	Biafra		minimal					
Cuba	Bangladesh		minimal					
	Eritrea	high		mediatory type	affective			unreliable
Haiti	Katanga		unclear					
	Biafra		minimal	de jure recognition				
Honduras	Biafra		minimal					
Jamaica	Biafra		minimal					
Peru	Biafra		minimal					

263

SELECT BIBLIOGRAPHY

Abd Al-Rahim, Muddathir, 'Arabism, Africanism, and Self-Identification in the Sudan', *Journal of Modern African Studies* viii, no. 2 (1970), pp. 233–49.

Abelson, Robert P., 'Modes of Resolution of Belief Dilemmas', *Journal of Conflict Resolution* iii, no. 4 (1959), pp. 342–52.

Abir, Mordechai, 'Red Sea Politics', *Adelphi Papers*, no. 93, IISS (London, December 1972), pp. 25–41.

Adamson, David, *The Kurdish War* (London, 1964).

Aguda, Oluwadere, 'Arabism and Pan-Arabism in Sudanese Politics', *Journal of Modern African Studies* xi, no. 2 (1972), pp. 177–200.

Ahmed, Moudud, *Bangladesh: Constitutional Quest for Autonomy, 1950–1971* (Wiesbaden, 1978).

Akpan, Ntiyong U., *The Struggle for Secession, 1966–1970* (London, Cass, 1971).

Akuchu, Gemuh E., 'The Organization of African Unity Peacemaking Machinery and the Nigerian–Biafran Conflict' (University of Denver, Ph.D. thesis, 1974).

Alcock, A.E., B.K. Taylor, and J.W. Welton (eds.), *The Future of Cultural Minorities* (London, 1979).

Ali, Tariq, *Can Pakistan Survive? The Death of a State* (Middlesex, 1983).

Alport, Lord, *The Sudden Assignment* (London, 1965).

Aluko, Olajide, 'Ghana and the Nigerian Civil War', *The Nigerian Journal of Economic and Social Studies* xii, no. 3 (November 1970), pp. 342–60.

——, 'The Civil War and Nigerian Foreign Policy', *The Political Quarterly* xl (April 1971), pp. 177–90.

Amin, Samir, *The Arab Nation* (London, 1978).

Anafulu, Joseph C., 'An African Experience: The Role of Specialized Libraries in War Situations', *Special Libraries* lxii (January 1971), pp. 32–40.

Anber, Paul, 'Modernization and Political Disintegration: Nigeria and the Ibos', *Journal of Modern African Studies* v, no. 2 (1967), pp. 163–79.

Anglin, Douglas G., 'Zambia and the Recognition of Biafra', *The African Review* i, no. 1 (September 1972), pp. 102–36.

Argyle, W.J., 'European Nationalism and African Tribalism', in P.H. Gulliver (ed.), *Tradition and Transition in East Africa* (London, 1969), pp. 41–55.

Axelrod, Robert (ed.), *Structure of Decision: The Cognitive Maps of Political Elites* (Princeton, 1976).

Ayoub, Mohammed and K. Subrahmanyam, *The Liberation War* (New Delhi, 1972).

Bach, Daniel, 'Le Général de Gaulle et la guerre civile au Nigeria', *Canadian Journal of African Studies* xiv, no. 2 (1980), pp. 259–72.

Badal, R.K., 'The Rise and Fall of Separatism in Southern Sudan', *African Affairs* lxxv, no. 301 (October 1976), pp. 463–73.

Baker, Ross K., 'The Emergence of Biafra: Balkanization or Nation-Building', *Orbis* xii, no. 2 (Summer 1968), pp. 518–33.

Baldwin, David A., 'The Power of Positive Sanctions', *World Politics* xxiv, no. 1 (1971), pp. 19–38.

Banks, Michael and C.R. Mitchell, 'Conflict Theory, Peace Research and the Analysis of Communal Conflicts', *Millennium: Journal of International Studies* iii, no. 3 (Winter 1974–75), pp. 252–67.

Banton, Michael, *Racial and Ethnic Competition* (Cambridge, 1983).

Barnds, William J., 'Pakistan's Disintegration', *The World Today* (August 1971), pp. 319–70.

Barrows, Walter L., 'Ethnic Diversity and Political Instability in Black Africa', *Comparative Political Studies* ix (July 1976) pp. 139–70.

Barth, Fredrik, 'Introduction', in Barth (ed.), *Ethnic Groups and Boundaries* (Boston, 1969), pp. 9–38.

Batmanian, 'La politique africaine de la Côte d'Ivoire de son accession à l'indépendance à la fin de la guerre civile au Nigéria' (University of Paris I, doctorat d'état, 1973).

Baxter, Craig, 'Pakistan and Bangladesh', in Frederick L. Shiel (ed.), *Ethnic Separatism and World Politics* (Lanham, 1984), pp. 209–62.

Beitz, Charles R., *Political Theory and International Relations* (Princeton, 1979).

Bell, J. Bowyer, 'Endemic Insurgency and International Order: The Eritrean Experience', *Orbis* (Summer 1974), pp. 472–50.

——, 'The Conciliation of Insurgency: The Sudanese Experience', *Military Affairs* xxxix, no. 3 (October 1975), pp. 105–13.

Bell, Wendell and Walter E. Freeman (eds.), *Ethnicity and Nation-Building* (Beverly Hills, 1974).

Benjamin, Charles, 'The Kurdish Nonstate Nation', in Judy S. Bertelsen (ed.), *Nonstate Nations in International Politics* (New York, 1977), pp. 69–97.

Bertelsen, Judy S. (ed.), *Nonstate Nations in International Politics* (New York, 1977).

Beshir, Mohamed Omer, *The Southern Sudan: Background to Conflict* (London, 1968).

——, *Diversity, Regionalism and National Unity*, Scandinavian Institute of African Studies, Report no. 54 (Uppsala, 1979).

Bhardwaj, Raman G., 'The Growing Externalization of the Eritrean Movement', *Horn of Africa* ii, no. 1 (January–March 1979), pp. 19–27.

Birch, Anthony, 'Minority Nationalist Movements and Theories of Political Integration', *World Politics* xxx, no. 3 (April 1978), pp. 325–44.

Blau, Peter M., *Exchange and Power in Social Life* (New York, 1964).

Blaut, J.M., 'Nationalism as an Autonomous Force', *Science and Society* i (Spring 1982), pp. 1–23.

Boulding, Kenneth E., 'National Images and International Systems', *Journal of Conflict Resolution* iii, no. 2 (1959), pp. 120–31.

Brownlie, Ian, *Principles of Public International Law* (Oxford, 1973).

Buchheit, Lee C., *Secession: The Legitimacy of Self-Determination* (New Haven, 1978).

Budhraj, Vijay Sen, 'Moscow and the Birth of Bangladesh', *Asian Survey* xiii, no. 5 (May 1973), pp. 482–95.

Burgess, M. Elaine, 'The Resurgence of Ethnicity: Myth or Reality?', *Ethnic and Racial Studies* i, no. 3 (July 1978), pp. 265–85.

Burns, James MacGregor, 'Wellsprings of Political Leadership', *American Political Science Review* lxxv, no. 1 (March 1977), pp. 266–75.

Burton, John W., *Conflict and Communication* (London, 1969).

——, 'Resolution of Conflict', *International Studies Quarterly* xivi, no. 1 (March 1972), pp. 5–30.

——, 'The Relevance of Behavioral Theories of the International System', in John Norton Moore (ed.), *Law and Civil War in the Modern World* (Baltimore, 1974), pp. 92–110.

——, *Deviance, Terrorism and War: The Process of Solving Unsolved Social and Political Problems* (Oxford, 1979).

Burton, John W., A.J.R. Groom, C.R. Mitchell and A.V.S. de Reuck, *The Study of World Society: A London Perspective*, Occasional Paper no. 1 (International Studies Association, University of Pittsburg, 1974).

Campbell, John Franklin, 'Rumblings along the Red Sea: The Eritrean Question', *Foreign Affairs* (April 1970), pp. 537–48.

Capatorti, Francesco, *Study on the Rights of Persons Belonging to Ethnic,*

Bibliography

Religious and Linguistic Minorities (United Nations, E/CN.4/Sub.2/ 384/Rev.I, New York, 1979).

Cervenka, Zdanek, *A History of the Nigerian War, 1967–1970* (Ibadan, 1972).

Chopra, Pran, 'East Bengal: A Crisis for India', *The World Today* (September 1971), pp. 372–79.

Choudhury, G.H., 'Bangladesh: Why it Happened?', *International Affairs* xlviii, no. 2 (April 1972).

——, 'The Emergence of Bangla Desh and the South Asian Triangle', *Year Book of World Affairs* lxii (1973), pp. 62–89.

Clapham, Christopher, 'Ethiopia and Somalia', *Adelphi Papers*, no. 93, IISS (London, December 1972), pp. 1–23.

Cohen, Abner (ed.), *Urban Ethnicity* (London, 1974).

Collins, Robert O., *The Southern Sudan in Historical Perspective* (Tel Aviv, 1975).

——, *Shadows in the Grass: Britain in the Southern Sudan, 1918–1956* (New Haven, 1983).

Connell, Dan, 'The Birth of the Eritrean Nation', *Horn of Africa* iii, no. 1 (January–March 1980), pp. 14–24.

Connor, Walker, 'Nation-Building or Nation-Destroying?', *World Politics* xxiv, no. 3 (April 1972), pp. 319–55.

——, 'Ethnonationalism in the First World', in Milton J. Esman (ed.), *Ethnic Conflict in the Western World* (Ithaca, 1977), pp. 19–45.

——, 'A Nation is a Nation, is a State, is an Ethnic Group, is a. . .', *Ethnic and Racial Studies* i, no. 4 (October 1978), pp. 377–400.

Coser, Lewis A., *The Functions of Social Conflict* (New York, 1954).

Crawford, James, *The Creation of States in International Law* (Oxford, 1979).

Cronje, Susan, *The World and Nigeria* (London, 1972).

Curle, Adam, *Making Peace* (London, 1971).

Dann, Uriel, 'The Kurdish National Movement in Iraq', *Jerusalem Quarterly* ix (Fall 1978), pp. 131–44.

Dassé, Martial, 'Les rébellions des minorités musulmanes en Asie du Sud-Est', *Défense Nationale* (June 1981), pp. 111–23.

Davidson, Basil, Lionel Cliff and Bereket Habte Selassie (eds.), *Beyond the War in Eritrea* (Nottingham, 1980).

Davis, Morris, 'Negotiating about Biafran Oil', *Issue* iii, no. 2 (Summer 1973), pp. 23–32.

——, *Interpreters for Nigeria: The Third World and International Public Opinion* (Urbana, 1977).

Davister, Pierre, *Katanga – enjeu du monde* (Brussels, 1960).

Dayal, Rajeshwar, *Mission for Hammarskjöld: The Congo Crisis* (London, 1976).

De St Jorre, John, *The Nigerian Civil War* (London, 1972).

Deutsch, Karl W., *Nationalism and Social Communication* (Cambridge, Mass. 1966 edn.).

Deutsch, Morton, *The Resolution of Conflict: Constructive and Destructive Processes* (New Haven, 1973).

Duchasek, Ivo D., *Comparative Federalism: The Territorial Dimension of Politics* (New York, 1970).

——, 'Antagonistic Cooperation: Territorial and Ethnic Communities', *Publius* vii, no. 4 (Fall 1977), pp. 3–29.

Dudley, Billy J., 'Nigeria's Civil War: The Tragedy of the Ibo People', *The Round Table* lviii, no. 229 (January 1968), pp. 28–34.

Duner, Bertil, 'The Many-Pronged Spear: External Military Intervention in Civil Wars in the 1970s', *Journal of Peace Research* xx, no. 1 (1983), pp. 59–72.

Edmonds, C.J., 'The Kurdish National Struggle in Iraq', *Asian Affairs* (June 1971), pp. 147–58.

——, 'Kurdish Nationalism', *Journal of Contemporary History* vi, no. 1 (1971), pp. 87–107.

Emerson, Rupert, *From Empire to Nation: The Rise to Self-Assertion of Asian and African Peoples* (Cambridge, Mass., 1960).

——, 'Self-Determination', *American Journal of International Law* lxv (1971), pp. 459–75.

Enloe, Cynthia H., *Ethnic Conflict and Political Development* (Boston, 1973).

——, 'Internal Colonialism, Federalism, and Alternative State Development Strategies', *Publius* vii, no. 4 (Fall 1877), pp. 145–60.

Eprile, Cecil, *Sudan: The Long War*, Conflict Studies, no. 21 (March 1972).

Esman, Milton J., 'The Management of Communal Conflict', *Public Policy* xxi, no. 1 (Winter 1973), pp. 49–78.

——, 'Perspectives on Ethnic Conflict in Industrialized Societies', in Esman (ed.), *Ethnic Conflict in the Western World* (Ithaca, 1977), pp. 371–90.

Espiell, Hector Gross, *The Right to Self-Determination: Implementation of United Nations Resolutions* (United Nations, E/CN.4/Sub.2/-405/Rev.I, New York, 1980).

Ethiopiawi, 'The Eritrean–Ethiopian Conflict', in Astri Suhrke and Lela Garner Noble (eds.), *Ethnic Conflict in International Relations* (New York, 1977), pp. 127–45.

Bibliography

Eze, Onyeabo, 'Nigeria–Biafra Conflict: Social and Economic Background' (University of Basle, Ph.D. thesis, 1971).

Falk, Richard A., 'Janus Tormented: the International Law of Internal War', in James N. Rosenau (ed.), *International Aspects of Civil Strife* (Princeton, 1964), pp. 194–248.

Farer, Tom J., 'The Regulation of Foreign Intervention in Civil Armed Conflict', *Receuil des Cours*, Hague Academy of International Law, cxlii (1974), vol. ii, pp. 297–406.

Fessehatzion, Tekie, 'The International Dimension of the Eritrean Question', *Horn of Africa* vi, no. 2 (1983), pp. 7–24.

Festinger, Leon, *A Theory of Cognitive Dissonance* (Stanford, 1957).

Fromm, Erich, *The Anatomy of Human Destructiveness* (Greenwich, Conn., 1973).

Galtung, Johan, 'Violence, Peace and Peace Research', *Journal of Peace Research* vi (1969), pp. 167–91.

——, *Peace: Research, Education, Action. Essays in Peace Research*, vol. I (Copenhagen, 1975).

——, *The True Worlds: A Transnational Perspective* (New York, 1980).

Geertz, Clifford, 'The Integrative Revolution: Primordial Sentiments and Civic Politics in the New States', in C.E. Welch (ed.), *Political Modernization* (Belmont, 1967), pp. 167–88.

Gellner, Ernest, *Nations and Nationalism* (Oxford, 1983).

George, T.S., *Revolt in Mindanao: The Rise of Islam in Philippine Politics* (London, 1980).

Gérard-Libois, Jules, *Katanga Secession* (Madison, 1966).

Gilkes, Patrick, 'Centralism and the Ethiopian PMAC', in I.M. Lewis (ed.), *Nationalism and Self Determination in the Horn of Africa* (London, 1983), pp. 195–211.

Glazer, Nathan and Daniel P. Moynihan (eds), *Ethnicity: Theory and Experience* (Cambridge, Mass., 1975).

Goldstone, Jack A., 'Theories of Revolution: The Third Generation', *World Politics* xxxii, no. 3 (April 1980), pp. 425–53.

Gray, Richard, 'The Southern Sudan', *Journal of Contemporary History* vi, no. 1 (1971), pp. 108–20.

Greenstein, Fred, *Personality and Politics* (Chicago, 1970).

Groom, A.J.R., *Peacekeeping*, Research Monograph no. 4 (Lehigh University, Bethlehem, 1973).

Groom, A.J.R. and Alexis Heraclides, 'Integration and Disintegration', in Margot Light and A.J.R. Groom (eds). *International Relations: A Handbook of Current Theory* (London, 1985), pp. 174–93.

Guelke, Adrian, 'International Legitimacy, Self-Determination, and

Northern Ireland', *Review of International Studies* ii, no. 1 (January 1985), pp. 37–52.

Gupta, Jyotti Sen, *History of Freedom Movement in Bangladesh* (Calcutta, 1974).

Gurr, Ted Robert, *Why Men Rebel* (Princeton, 1971).

Haas, Ernest B., 'What is Nationalism and Why Should We Study it?', *International Organization* xl, no. 3 (Summer 1986), pp. 707–44.

Halliday, Fred, 'The Fighting in Eritrea', *New Left Review* lxvii (May–June 1971), pp. 57–67.

Harris, George S., 'The Kurdish Conflict in Iraq', in Astri Suhrke and Lela Garner Noble (eds.), *Ethnic Conflict and International Relations* (New York, 1977), pp. 68–92.

Healy, Sally, 'The Changing Idiom of Self-Determination in the Horn', in I.M. Lewis (ed.), *Nationalism and Self Determination in the Horn of Africa* (London, 1983), pp. 93–109.

Hechter, Michael, *Internal Colonialism: The Celtic Fringe in the British National Development* (London, 1975).

Hechter, Micahel, and Margaret Levi, 'The Comparative Analysis of Ethnoregional Movements', *Ethnic and Racial Studies* ii, no. 3 (July 1979), pp. 260–74.

Heikal, Mohamed, *The Return of the Ayatollah* (London, 1981).

Hentsch, Thierry, *Face au blocus: la Croix-Rouge Internationale dans le Nigéria en guerre* (Geneva, 1973).

Heraclides, Alexis, 'The International Dimension of Secessionist Movements' (University of Kent, Ph.D. thesis, 1985).

——, 'Janus or Sisyphus? The Southern Problem of the Sudan', *Journal of Modern African Studies* xxv, no. 2 (June 1987), pp. 213–31.

——, 'From Autonomy to Secession: Building Down', in A.J.R. Groom and Paul Taylor (eds.), *Frameworks for International Cooperation* (London, forthcoming).

Higgins, Rosalyn, 'Internal War and International Law', in C.E. Black and Richard A. Falk (eds.), *The Future of the International Legal Order*, vol. III (Princeton, 1972), pp. 81–121.

——, 'The United Nations Operation in the Congo' in Higgins, *United Nations Peacekeeping 1946–1967: Documents and Commentary* (London, 1980).

Himmelstrand, Ulf, 'Tribalism, Nationalism, Rank-Equilibration and Social Structure: A Theoretical Interpretation of Some Socio-Political Processes in Nigeria', *Journal of Peace Research* vi (1969), pp. 81–103.

——, 'Tribalism, Regionalism, Nationalism and Secession in Nigeria', in

Bibliography

S.N. Eisenstadt and Stein Rokkan (eds.), *Building States and Nations*, vol. II (Beverly Hills, 1973), pp. 427–67.

Hoffman, Stanley, 'In Search of a Thread: the UN in the Congo Labyrinth', *International Organization* (Spring 1962), pp. 331–61.

Holsti, Ole R., 'Foreign Policy Formation Viewed Cognitively', in Robert Axelrod (ed.), *Structure of Decision* (Princeton, 1976), pp. 18–54.

Horowitz, Donald L., 'Multicultural Politics in the New States: Toward a Theory of Conflict', in Robert J. Jackson and Michael B. Stein (eds.), *Issues in Comparative Politics* (New York, 1971), pp. 232–44.

——, *Ethnic Groups in Conflict* (Berkeley, 1985).

Hoskyns, Catherine, *The Congo since Independence, January 1960–December 1961* (London, 1965).

Howell, John F., 'Political Leadership and Organization in the Southern Sudan' (University of Reading, Ph.D. thesis, 1977).

——, 'Horn of Africa: Lessons from the Sudan Conflict' *International Affairs* liv, no. 3 (July 1978), pp. 421–36.

Howell, John F. and M. Beshir Hamid, 'Sudan and the Outside World, 1964–1968', *African Affairs* lxviii, no. 273 (October 1969), pp. 299–315.

Hudson, Michael C., *Arab Politics: The Search for Legitimacy* (New Haven, 1977).

Hunt, Sir David, *On the Spot: An Ambassador Remembers* (London, 1975).

Huntington, Samuel P., 'Civil Violence and the Process of Development', *Adelphi Papers*, no. 83, IISS (London, December 1971), pp. 1–15.

Ifejika, S.U., 'Mobilizing Support for the Biafran Regime: The Politics of War and Propaganda', (York University, Canada, Ph.D. thesis, 1979).

Ijalaye, David A., 'Was "Biafra" at any Time a State in International Law?', *American Journal of International Law* lxv (1971), pp. 551–59.

Iklé, Fred Charles, *How Nations Negotiate* (New York, 1964).

Inayatullah, 'Internal and External Factors in the Failure of National Integration in Pakistan', in Stephanie G. Neuman (ed.), *Small States and Segmented Societies* (New York 1976), pp. 84–120.

Iqbal, Mehrunnisa Hatim, 'India and the 1971 War with Pakistan', *Pakistan Horizon* xxv, no. 2 (1972), pp. 21–31.

Isaacs, Harold R., *Idols of the Tribe: Group Identity and Political Change* (New York, 1976).

Jawad, Sa'ad, *Iraq and the Kurdish Question* (London, 1981).

Jervis, Robert, *Perception and Misperception in International Politics* (Princeton, 1976).

Johnson, Michael and Trisha Johnson, 'Eritrea: The National Question and the Logic of Protracted Struggle', *African Affairs* lxxx, no. 313 (April 1981), pp. 181–95.

Jorgensen-Dahl, Arnfinn, 'Forces of Fragmentation in the International System: The Case of Ethno-Nationalism', *Orbis* ii (Summer 1975), pp. 652–74.

Kamanu, Onyenoro S., 'Secession and the Right of Self-Determination: An O.A.U. Dilemma', *Journal of Modern African Studies* xii (1974), pp. 355–76.

Kanza, Thomas, *Conflict in the Congo* (Middlesex, 1972).

Kasfir, Nelson, 'Explaining Ethnic Political Participation', *World Politics* xxxi, no. 3 (April 1979), pp. 365–88.

Kedourie, Elie, *Nationalism* (London, 1966).

Kelman, Herbert, 'Compliance, Identification, and Internalization: Three Processes of Attitude Change', *Journal of Conflict Resolution* ii (1958), pp. 51–60.

——, (ed.), *International Behavior* (New York, 1965).

Kende, Itvan, 'Twenty-five Years of Local Wars', *Journal of Peace Research* viii (1971), pp. 5–22.

——, *Local Wars in Asia, Africa and Latin America, 1945–1969*, Centre of Afro–Asian Research of the Hungarian Academy of Sciences, Report no. 60 (Budapest, 1972).

Keyes, Charles F., 'Towards a new Formulation of the Concept of Ethnic Group', *Ethnicity* iii (September 1976), pp. 203–13.

Kilner, Peter, 'Better Outlook for the Sudan', *The World Today* (April 1972), pp. 181–88.

Kirk-Greene, A.H.M, 'The Cultural Background to the Nigerian Crisis', *African Affairs* lxvi, no. 262 (1967), pp. 3–11.

——, *Crisis and Conflict in Nigeria: A Documentary Sourcebook, 1966–1970* (London, 1971).

——, *Genesis of the Nigerian Civil War and the Theory of Fear*, Scandinavian Institute of African Studies, Report no. 27 (Uppsala, 1975).

Krippendorff, Ekkehart, 'Minorities, Violence, and Peace Research', *Journal of Peace Research* xvi, no. 1 (1979), pp. 27–40.

Kuhn, Thomas S., *The Structure of Scientific Revolutions* (Chicago, 1970 edn).

Kuper, Leo, *Race, Class and Power* (London, 1974).

Kuper, Leo, and M.G. Smith (eds.), *Pluralism in Africa* (Berkeley, 1969).

Kyle, Kyth, 'The Southern Problem in the Sudan', *The World Today* (December 1966), pp. 512–20.

Ladouceur, Paul, 'The Southern Sudan: A Forgotten War and a

Forgotten Peace', *International Journal* xxx (Summer 1975), pp. 406–27.

LaPorte Jr, Robert, 'Pakistan in 1971: The Disintegration of a Nation', *Asian Survey* xii, no. 2 (February 1972), pp. 97–108.

Lasswell, Harold D. and Abraham Kaplan, *Power and Society* (New Haven, 1950).

Lauterpacht, Hersch, *Recognition and International Law* (Cambridge, 1947).

Lefever, Ernest, *Crisis in the Congo: A United Nations Force in Action* (Washington DC, 1965).

——, *Uncertain Mandate: Politics in the UN Congo Operation* (Baltimore, 1967).

Legum, Colin and James Firebrace, *Eritrea and Tigray*, Minority Rights Group, Report no. 5 (1983).

Legum, Colin and Bill Lee, *The Horn of Africa in Continuing Crisis* (New York, 1979).

Lemarchand, René, 'The Limits of Self-Determination: The Case of the Katanga Secession', *American Political Science Review*, lvi, no. 2 (June 1962), pp. 404–16.

——, 'The C.I.A. in Africa: How Central? How Intelligent?', *Journal of Modern African Studies*, 14, no. 3 (1976), pp. 401–26.

Lesch, Ann Mosely, 'Confrontation in the Southern Sudan', *The Middle East Journal*, xl, no. 3 (Summer 1986).

LeVine, Robert A. and Donald T. Campbell, *Ethnocentrism: Theories of Conflict, Ethnic Attitudes and Group Behavior* (New York, 1972).

Lichter, Linda S., 'The Case of the Moros in the Philippines', in W.P. Davison and L. Gordenker (ed.), *Resolving Nationality Conflicts: The Role of Public Opinion Research* (Princeton, 1980), pp. 132–39.

Lieberson, Stanley, 'Stratification and Ethnic Groups', in Anthony Richmond (ed.), *Readings in Race and Ethnic Relations* (Oxford, 1972), pp. 199–209.

Lijphardt, Arend, 'Consociational Democracy', *World Politics* xxi (January 1969), pp. 207–25.

——, 'Political Theories and Explanation of Ethnic Conflict in the Western World: Falsified Predictions and Plausible Postdictions', in Milton J. Esman (ed.), *Ethnic Conflict in the Western World* (Ithaca, 1977), pp. 46–64.

Little, Richard, *Intervention: External Involvement in Civil Wars* (London, 1975).

Lloyd, P.C., 'The Ethnic Background of the Nigerian Crisis', in S.K. Panter-Brick (ed.), *Nigerian Politics and Military Rule: Prelude to Civil War* (London, 1970), pp. 1–13.

Lobban, Richard, 'The Eritrean War: Issues and Implications', *Canadian Journal of African Studies* x, no. 2 (1976), pp. 335–46.

Lodge, Juliet, 'Loyalty and the EEC: The Limits of the Functional Approach', *Political Studies* xxvi, no. 2 (1978), pp. 232–48.

Lustick, Ian, 'Stability in Deeply Divided Societies: Consociationalism versus Control', *World Politics* xxxi, no. 3 (April 1979), pp. 325–44.

McDowall, David, *The Kurds*, Minority Rights Group, Report no. 23 (London, 1985).

MacFarlane, S.N., 'Intervention and Security in Africa', *International Affairs* lx, no. 1 (Winter 1983/1984), pp. 53–73.

Mack, Raymond and Richard C. Snyder, 'The Analysis of Social Conflict: Towards an Overview and Synthesis', *Journal of Conflict Resolution* i, no. 2 (1957), pp. 212–48.

McKay, James and Frank Lewins, 'Ethnicity and the Ethnic Group: A Conceptual Analysis and Reformulation', *Ethnic and Racial Studies* i, no. 4 (October 1978), pp. 412–27.

Mahoney, Richard Doyle, 'The Kennedy Policy in the Congo, 1916–1963' (Johns Hopkins University, Ph.D. thesis, 1980).

Matthews, Robert O., 'Domestic and Inter-State Conflict in Africa', *International Journal* xxv (1970), pp. 459–85.

Mazrui, Ali A., 'The Multiple Marginality of the Sudan', in Yusuf Fadl Hasan (ed.), *Sudan in Africa* (Khartoum, 1971), pp. 240–55.

Melson, Robert and Howard Wolpe, 'Modernization and the Politics of Communalism: A Theoretical Perspective', in Melson and Wolpe (eds.), *Nigeria: Modernization and the Politics of Communalism* (East Lansing, 1971), pp. 1–42.

Mercier, Paul, 'On the Meaning of "Tribalism" in Black Africa', in Pierre L. van den Berghe (ed.), *Africa: Social Problems of Change and Conflict* (San Francisco, 1965), pp. 483–501.

Misra, K.P., 'Intra-State Imperialism: The Case of Pakistan', *Journal of Peace Research* ix (1972), pp. 27–39.

——, *The Role of the United Nations in the Indo-Pakistani Conflict, 1971* (Delhi, 1973).

Mitchell, C.R., 'Civil Strife and the Involvement of External Parties', *International Studies Quarterly* xiv, no. 2 (June 1970), pp. 166–94.

——, *Peacemaking and the Consultant's Role* (London, 1981).

Modelski, George, 'The International Relations of Internal War', in James N. Rosenau (ed.), *International Aspects of Civil Strife* (Princeton, 1964), pp. 122–53.

——, 'International Settlement of Internal War', in James N. Rosenau (ed.), *International Aspects of Civil Strife* (Princeton, 1964), pp. 122–53.

Montagu, Ashley (ed.), *Man and Aggression* (London, 1973).

Morrison, Godfrey, *Eritrea and the Southern Sudan*, Minority Rights Group, Report no. 5 (London, 1976 edn.)

Mughan, Anthony, 'Modernization, Deprivation, and the Distribution of Power Resources: Toward a Theory of Ethnic Conflict', *New Community* v, no. 4 (Spring–Summer 1977), pp. 360–70.

Naamani, Israel T., 'The Kurdish Drive for Self-Determination', *The Middle East Journal* xx, no. 3 (Summer 1966), pp. 279–95.

Nafziger, E. Wayne and William L. Richter, 'Biafra and Bangladesh: The Political Economy of Secessionist Conflict', *Journal of Peace Research* xiii (1976), pp. 91–109.

Nanda, Ved P., 'Self-Determination in International Law: The Tragic Tale of Two Cities – Islamabad (West Pakistan) and Dacca (East Pakistan)', *American Journal of International Law* lxvi (1972), p. 321–38.

Nawaz, M.K., 'Bangladesh and International Law', *Indian Journal of International Law* xi (1971), pp. 321–38.

Neuberger, Benyamin, 'The African Concept of Balkanization', *Journal of Modern African Studies* xiv, no. 3 (1976), pp. 523–29.

Nixon, Charles R., 'Self-Determination: The Nigeria/Biafra Case', *World Politics* xxiv (July 1972), pp. 473–97.

Noble, Lela Garner, 'Ethnicity and Philippine–Malaysian Relations', *Asian Survey* xv, no. 5 (May 1975), pp. 453–72.

——, 'The Moro National Liberation Front in the Philippines', *Pacific Affairs* xlix, no. 3 (Fall 1976), pp. 405–24.

Nordlinger, Eric A., *Conflict Regulation in Divided Societies* (Harvard, Mass., 1972).

O' Ballance, Edgar, *The Kurdish Revolt 1961–1970* (London, 1973).

——, *The Secret War in the Sudan (1955–1972)* (London, 1977).

O'Brien, Conor Cruise, *To Katanga and Back* (London, 1962).

O'Connell, James, 'Political Integration: The Nigerian Case', in Arthur Hazlewood (ed.), *African Integration and Disintegration* (London, 1967), pp. 129–84.

——, 'Authority and Community in Nigeria', in Robert Melson and Howard Wolpe (eds.), *Nigeria: Modernization and the Politics of Communalism* (East Lansing, 1971).

Okeke, Chris N., *Controversial Subjects in Contemporary International Law* (Rotterdam, 1974).

Okpaku, Joseph (ed.), *Nigeria: Dilemmas of Nationhood* (Westport, 1972).

Onwubu, Chuchuemeka, 'Ethnic Identity, Political Integration and

National Development: The Igbo Diaspora in Nigeria', *Journal of Modern African Studies* xiii, no. 3 (1975), pp. 399–413.

Palley, Claire, 'The Role of Law in Relation to Minority Groups', in A.E. Alcock, B.K. Taylor, and J.W. Welton (eds.), *The Future of Cultural Minorities* (London, 1979), pp. 127–60.

Panter–Brick, S.K., 'The Right of Self-Determination: Its Application to Nigeria', *International Affairs* xliv, no. 2 (April 1968), pp. 254–66.

Patterson, Orlando, 'Context and Choice in Ethnic Allegiance: A Theoretical Framework and a Caribbean Case Study', in Glazer, Nathan and Daniel P. Moynihan (eds.), *Ethnicity: Theory and Experience* (Cambridge, Mass., 1975), pp. 305–49.

Perham, Margery, 'Reflections on the Nigerian Civil War', *International Affairs* lxvi, no. 2 (April 1970), pp. 231–46.

Petersen, William, 'Ethnicity in the World Today', *International Journal of Comparative Sociology* xx, nos 1–2 (1979), pp. 3–13.

Phillips, Claude S., 'Nigeria and Biafra', in Frederick L. Shiel (ed.), *Ethnic Separatism and World Politics* (Lanham, 1984), pp. 151–207.

Pirouet, M. Louise, 'The Achievement of Peace in Sudan', *Journal of Eastern African Research and Development* vi, no. 1 (1976), pp. 115–45.

Pool, David, *Eritrea: Africa's Longest War*, Anti-Slavery Society, Report no. 3 (London, 1982).

——, 'Eritrean Nationalism', in I.M. Lewis (ed.), *Nationalism and Self Determination in the Horn of Africa* (London, 1983), pp. 175–93.

Post, K.W.J., 'Is there a Case for Biafra?' *International Affairs* (January 1968), pp. 26–39.

Poulantzas, Nicos, *L'état, le pouvoir, le socialisme* (Paris, 1978).

Qureshi, Khalifa, 'Britain and the Indo-Pakistan Conflict over East Pakistan', *Pakistan Horizon* xxv, no. 2 (1972), pp. 23–44.

Rabushka, Alvin and Kenneth E. Shepsle, *Politics in Plural Societies* (Columbus, Ohio, 1972).

Rashiduzzaman, M., 'Leadership, Organization, Strategies and Tactics of the Bangla Desh Movement', *Asian Survey* xii, no. 3 (1972), pp. 185–200.

Redslob, Robert, 'Le principe des nationalités', *Recueil des Cours*, Hague Academy of International Law, xxxvii (1931), vol. III, pp. 5–82.

Richmond, Anthony, 'Ethnic Nationalism and Postindustrialism', *Ethnic and Racial Studies* vii, no. 1 (January 1984), pp. 4–18.

Ronen, Dov, *The Quest for Self-Determination* (New Haven, 1979).

Rosenau, James N., 'The Concept of Intervention', *Journal of International Affairs* xx, no. 2 (Summer 1968), pp. 165–76.

——, (ed.), *International Aspects of Civil Strife* (Princeton, 1964).

Bibliography

Rothchild, Donald, 'Ethnicity and Conflict Resolution', *World Politics* xx, no. 1 (October 1969), pp. 597–616.

Rothschild, Joseph, *Ethnopolitics: A Conceptual Framework* (New York, 1981).

Russell, Peter and Storrs McCall, 'Can Secession be Justified? The Case of the Southern Sudan', in Dunstan M. Wai (ed.), *The Southern Sudan: The Problem of National Integration* (London, 1973), pp. 93–121.

Ryan, Selwyn D., 'Civil Conflict and External Involvement in Eastern Africa', *International Journal* xxviii (1972–73), pp. 465–510.

Satyamurthy, T.V., 'Indo-Bangladesh Relations: A Structural Perspective', *Asia Quarterly* i (1977), pp. 52–75.

Schelling, Thomas, *Strategy and Conflict* (London, 1963).

Schermerhorn, Richard A., 'Ethnicity in the Perspective of the Sociology of Knowledge', *Ethnicity* i (April 1974), pp. 1–14.

Schmidt, Dana Adams, 'The Kurdish Insurgency', *Strategic Review* ii, no. 3 (Summer 1974), pp. 51–8.

Schwarz, Walter, 'Foreign Powers and the Nigerian War', *Africa Report* (February 1970), pp. 12–14.

Selassie, Bereket Habte, *Conflict and Intervention in the Horn of Africa* (New York, 1980).

Shepherd George W., Jr, 'National Integration and the Southern Sudan', *Journal of Modern African Studies* vi, no. 2 (1966), pp. 193–212.

Sherif, Mujafer, *Group Conflict and Co-operation* (London, 1966).

Sherman, Richard, *Eritrea: The Unfinished Revolution* (New York, 1980).

Short, Martin and Anthony McDermot, *The Kurds*, Minority Rights Group, Report no. 23 (London, March 1977 edn.).

Sim, Richard, *Kurdistan: In Search of Recognition*, Conflict Studies, no. 124 (London, November 1980).

Sircar, Perbati, 'The Crisis of Nationhood in Nigeria', *International Studies* (New Delhi) x (July 1968–April 1969), pp. 245–69.

Sklar, Richard L., 'Contradictions in the Nigerian Political System', *Journal of Modern African Studies*, iii, no. 2 (1965), pp. 201–3.

Smith, Anthony D., *The Ethnic Revival* (Cambridge, 1981).

——, 'Conflict and Collective Identity: Class, *Ethnie* and Nation', in Edward E. Azar and John W. Burton (eds.), *International Conflict Resolution* (Brighton, 1986), pp. 63–84.

Smith, Arnold (with Clyde Sanger), *Stitches in Time* (London, 1981).

Smith, M.G., *Corporations and Society* (London, 1974).

Stremlau, John J., *The International Politics of the Nigerian Civil War (1967–1970)* (Princeton, 1977).

277

Suhrke, Astri and Lela Garner Noble (eds.), *Ethnic Conflict in International Relations* (New York, 1977).

——, 'Muslims in the Philippines and Thailand', in Suhrke and Noble (eds.), *Ethnic Conflict in International Relations* (New York, 1977), pp. 178–212.

Sureda, A. Rigo, *The Evolution of the Right of Self-Determination* (Leiden, 1973).

Tajfel Henri, *The Social Psychology of Minorities*, Minority Rights Group, Report no. 38 (London, December 1978).

Tamuno, Tekena N., 'Separatist Agitations in Nigeria since 1914', *Journal of Modern African Studies* viii, no. 4 (1970), pp. 563–84.

Taylor, Paul, *The Limits of European Integration* (London, 1983).

Thompson, Joseph E., 'American Foreign Policy Toward Nigeria, 1967–1970' (The Catholic University of America, Ph.D. thesis, 1977).

Tilly, Charles, *From Mobilization to Revolution* (Reading, Mass., 1978).

Trent, John, 'The Politics of Nationalist Movements – A Reconsideration', *Canadian Review of Studies on Nationalism* ii, no. 1 (Fall 1974), pp. 157–71.

Turpin, Alex, *New Society's Challenge in the Philippines*, Conflict Studies, no. 122 (London, September 1980).

Uwechue, Raph, *Reflections on the Nigerian Civil War* (New York, 1971).

Van Bilsen, A.A.J., 'Some Aspects of the Congo Problem', *International Affairs* xxxviii (January 1962), pp. 41–51.

Van den Berghe, 'Ethnic Pluralism in Industrial Societies: A Special Case?', *Ethnicity* iii, no. 3 (1976), pp. 242–55.

Van Dyke, Vernon, 'Self-Determination and Minority Rights', *International Studies Quarterly* xiii, no. 3 (September 1969), pp. 226–33.

Vanly, Ismet Chériff, *Le Kurdistan irakien: entité nationale* (Neuchatel, 1970).

——, 'Kurdistan in Iraq', in Gérard Chaliand (ed.), *People without a Country: The Kurds and Kurdistan* (London, 1980), pp. 153–210.

Vickers, Michael, 'Competition and Control in Modern Nigeria', *International Journal* xxv (Summer 1970), pp. 603–33.

Vincent, R.J., *Nonintervention and International Order* (Princeton, 1974).

Wai, Dunstan M. (ed.), *The Southern Sudan: The Problem of National Integration* (London, F. Cass, 1973), pp. 93–121.

——, 'Revolution, Rhetoric and Reality in the Sudan', *Journal of Modern African Studies* xvii, no. 1 (1979), pp. 71–93.

——, *The African–Arab Conflict in the Sudan* (New York, 1981).

Wallerstein, Immanuel, 'Ethnicity and National Integration in West Africa', in Pierre L. van den Berghe (ed.), *Africa: Social*

Problems of Change and Conflict (San Francisco, 1965), pp. 472–82.

——, 'Two Modes of Ethnic Consciousness: Soviet Central Asia in Transition?', Soviet Central Asia (New York, 1973), pp. 168–75.

Welensky, Sir Roy, *Welensky's 4000 Days* (London, 1964).

Whiteman, Kaye, 'Enugu: The Psychology of Secession, 20 July 1966 to 30 May 1967', in S.K. Panter-Brick (ed.), *Nigerian Politics and Military Rule: Prelude to Civil War* (London, 1970).

Wiberg, Hakan, 'The Horn of Africa', *Journal of Peace Research* xvi, no. 3 (1979), pp. 189–96.

——, 'Self-Determination as an International Issue', in I.M. Lewis (ed.), *Nationalism and Self Determination in the Horn of Africa* (London, 1983), pp. 43–65.

Wiseberg, Laurie S., 'The International Politics of Relief: A Case Study of the Relief Operations Mounted During the Nigerian Civil War' (University of California at Los Angeles, Ph.D. thesis, 1973).

——, 'Humanitarian Intervention: Lessons from the Nigerian Civil War', *Human Rights Journal* vii, no. 1 (1974), pp. 61–98.

Wol Wol, Lawrence, 'Réflexions sur la conscience nationale au Sud-Soudan' (University of Bordeaux III, thèse pour le doctorat de 3ème cycle, 1971).

Young, Crawford, 'The Politics of Separatism: Katanga 1960–63', in Gwendolen M. Carter (ed.) *Politics in Africa: 7 Cases* (New York, 1966), pp. 166–75.

——, 'Nationalism and Separatism in Africa', in Martin Kilson (ed.), *New States in the Modern World* (Cambridge, Mass., 1975), pp. 57–74.

——, *The Politics of Cultural Pluralism* (Madison, 1976).

——, 'The Temple of Ethnicity', *World Politics* xxxv, no. 4 (July 1983), pp. 652–62.

Young, Oran R., *The Intermediaries: Third Parties in International Crises* (Princeton, 1967).

INDEX

285